AF478570

CONTEMPORARY ARTS MUSEUM HOUSTON
presents

AN EXHIBITION

The OLD, Weird AMERICA
Folk Themes in Contemporary Art

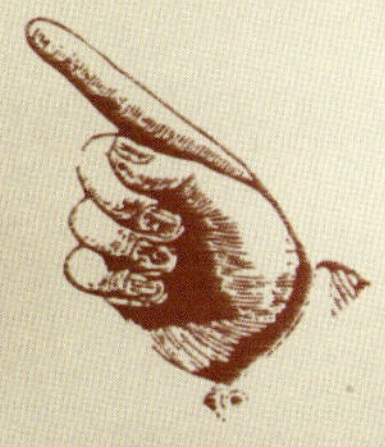

Eric Beltz	Aaron Morse
Jeremy Blake	Cynthia Norton
Sam Durant	Greta Pratt
Barnaby Furnas	David Rathman
Deborah Grant	Dario Robleto
Matthew Day Jackson	Allison Smith
Brad Kahlhamer	Kara Walker
Margaret Kilgallen	Charlie White

McDermott & McGough

May 10 - July 20, 2008

Traveling to
Frederick R. Weisman Art Museum, University of Minnesota, Minneapolis
August 23, 2008 - January 4, 2009

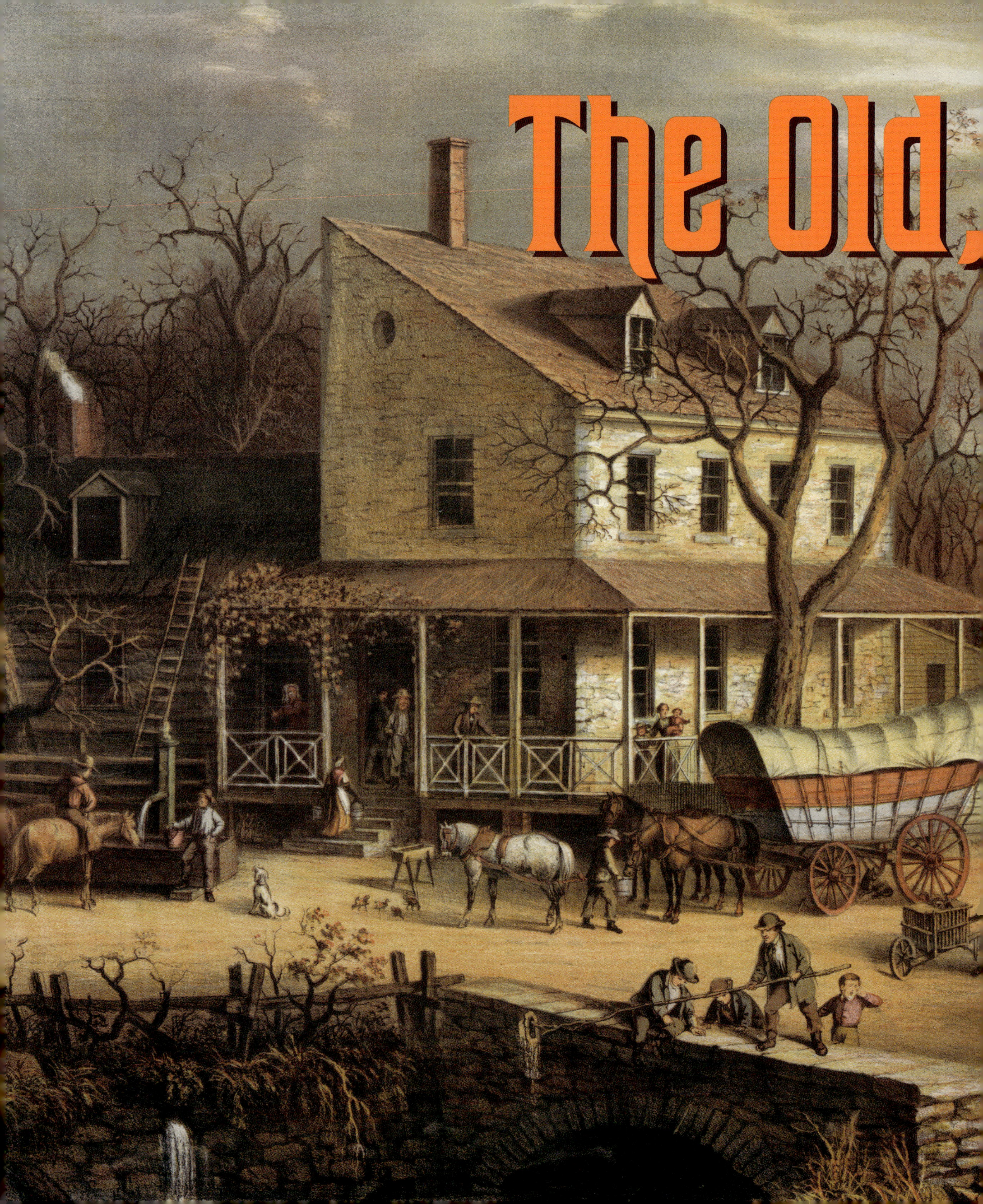
The Old,

Weird America

Folk Themes in Contemporary Art

TOBY KAMPS

with essays by

MICHAEL DUNCAN

COLLEEN SHEEHY

CONTEMPORARY ARTS MUSEUM HOUSTON

The Old, Weird America has been made possible by generous support from the Union Pacific Foundation and Nina and Michael Zilkha.

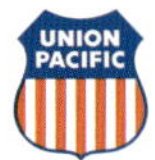

This exhibition has been supported by the patrons, benefactors, and donors to the Museum's Major Exhibition Fund:

MAJOR PATRON
Fayez Sarofim

PATRONS
Chinhui Juhn and Eddie Allen
Mr. and Mrs. A. L. Ballard
Mr. and Mrs. I. H. Kempner III
Ms. Louisa Stude Sarofim
Leigh and Reggie Smith
Michael Zilkha

BENEFACTORS
Marita and J.B. Fairbanks
George and Mary Josephine Hamman Foundation
Jackson Hicks / Jackson and Company
Elizabeth Howard
King & Spalding L.L.P.
Elisa J. Stude
The Susan Vaughan Foundation, Inc.

DONORS
Anonymous
Anonymous
Baker Botts, LLP
Bergner and Johnson Design
Jana and Richard Fant
Julia and Russell Frankel
Mr. and Mrs. William Goldberg /
    Bernstein Global Wealth Management
Karol Kreymer and Robert J. Card, M.D.
Judy and Scott Nyquist
David I. Saperstein
Karen and Harry Susman
Mark Wawro and Melanie Gray
Mr. and Mrs. Wallace Wilson

The catalogue accompanying the exhibition is made possible by a grant from The Brown Foundation, Inc.

The Museum's operations and programs are made possible through the generosity of the Museum's trustees, patrons, members, and donors. The Contemporary Arts Museum Houston receives partial operating support from the Houston Endowment, Inc., the City of Houston through the Houston Museum District Association, the National Endowment for the Arts, and the Texas Commission on the Arts.

Continental Airlines Official airline of the Contemporary Arts Museum Houston.

The Artphone is supported in part by Will Golden.

This catalogue has been published to accompany the exhibition *The Old, Weird America* organized by Toby Kamps, Senior Curator, for the Contemporary Arts Museum Houston.

Exhibition tour itinerary:

Contemporary Arts Museum Houston
May 10–July 20, 2008

Frederick R. Weisman Art Museum,
University of Minnesota, Minneapolis
August 23, 2008–January 4, 2009

Library of Congress Control Number: 2007942793
ISBN 978-1-933619-12-5

Contemporary Arts Museum Houston
5216 Montrose Boulevard
Houston, Texas 77006-6598
Phone: (713) 284-8250
Fax: (713) 284-8275
www.camh.org

Available through D.A.P./ Distributed Art Publishers, Inc.
155 Sixth Avenue, 2nd Floor
New York, New York 10013
Tel: (212) 627-1999, Fax: (212) 627-9484
www.artbook.com

cover: Digital illustration by Sonny Windstrup, with Don Quaintance, based on nineteenth-century wood type

frontispiece: *American Scenery—The Inn on the Roadside*, 1872, chromolithograph published by E. Sacshe & Co., Baltimore. Courtesy the Prints and Photographs Collections, Library of Congress, Washington, D.C.

pages 12–13: *Great House Plantation, Saint Augustine, Maryland*, 1933. Courtesy Historic American Buildings Survey, Library of Congress, Washington, D.C., photograph by E. H. Pickering

pages 52–53: *The wood-burning locomotive General Haupt in front of the railyard roundhouse*, Alexandria, Virginia, 1863. Courtesy Library of Congress, Washington, D.C., photograph by Andrew J. Rusell

pages 142–143: *Immigrants in Conestoga wagon*, Central Oregon, 1910. Courtesy Library of Congress, Washington, D.C.. photograph by B. B. Bokowski

CONTENTS

7   Lenders to the Exhibition

LINDA SHEARER   9   Foreword

TOBY KAMPS   10   Acknowledgments

ESSAYS

TOBY KAMPS   14   The Old, Weird America

MICHAEL DUNCAN   26   American Soul Underground

COLLEEN SHEEHY   38   Waking the Dead:
Music, Art, and the Basement Noise of History

Catalogue entries by
TOBY KAMPS   PLATES

54   Eric Beltz
58   Jeremy Blake
64   Sam Durant
68   Barnaby Furnas
74   Deborah Grant
80   Matthew Day Jackson
84   Brad Kahlhamer
90   Margaret Kilgallen
94   McDermott & McGough
100   Aaron Morse
106   Cynthia Norton
110   Greta Pratt
114   David Rathman
120   Dario Robleto
128   Allison Smith
134   Kara Walker
138   Charlie White

140   Catalogue of the Exhibition

Compiled by
NATALIA FERREYRA-BEASLEY   145   ARTISTS' BIOGRAPHIES AND BIBLIOGRAPHIES

ACME., Los Angeles

Carlos Bacino, Houston

Blum & Poe, Los Angeles

Laura Lee Brown and Steve Wilson,
Louisville, Kentucky

Cheim & Read, New York

Chris DeBolt, Los Angeles

D'Amelio Terras, New York

Dunn and Brown Contemporary, Dallas

Sam Durant

Greg S. Feldman, New York

Suzanne and Howard Feldman

Barnaby Furnas

Pam and Bob Goergen

Deborah Grant

Sherri Grace

Guild and Greyshkul, New York

Matthew Day Jackson

Neils Kantor

The Estate of Margaret Kilgallen

Kinz, Tillou + Feigen, New York

Lio Malca, New York

McDermott & McGough

Aaron Morse

Nerman Museum of Contemporary Art,
Johnson County Community College,
Overland Park, Kansas

Cynthia Norton

Greta Pratt

Private Collection

Private Collection, New York

David Rathman

Paul Rickert, San Francisco

Nicholas Robinson Collection

Dario Robleto

Jeffrey and Elana Rose, Los Angeles

San Antonio Museum of Art

Sikkema Jenkins & Co., New York

Stefan Simchowitz

Allison Smith

Fern and Lenard Tessler, New York

Jennifer Tytel

Kara Walker

Jennifer and Lance Volland, Long Beach, California

Wohnmaschine, Berlin

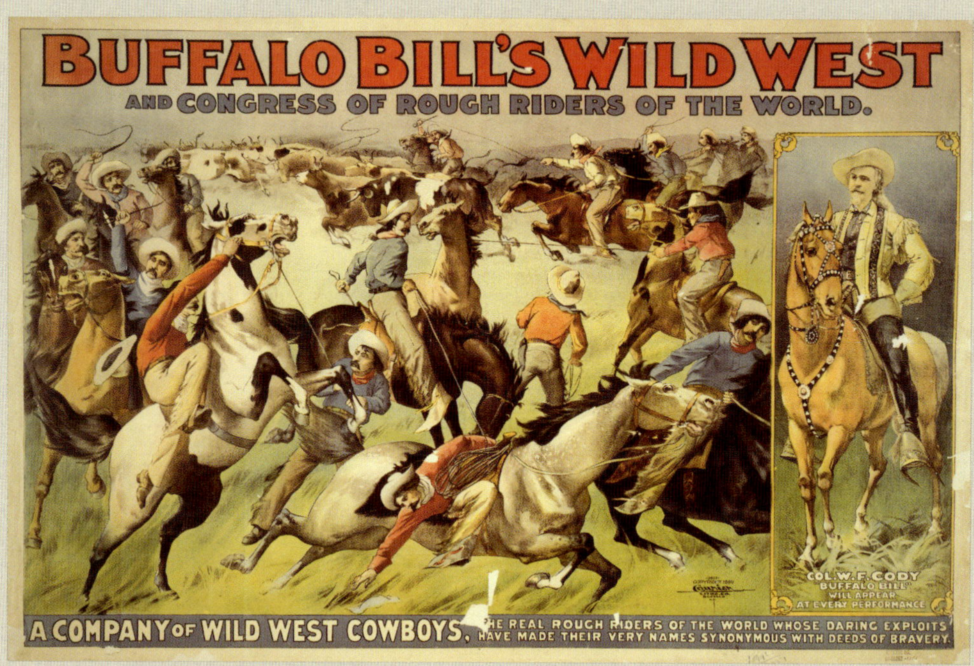
BUFFALO BILL'S WILD WEST
AND CONGRESS OF ROUGH RIDERS OF THE WORLD.
COL. W. F. CODY
BUFFALO BILL
WILL APPEAR
AT EVERY PERFORMANCE
A COMPANY OF WILD WEST COWBOYS, THE REAL ROUGH RIDERS OF THE WORLD WHOSE DARING EXPLOITS HAVE MADE THEIR VERY NAMES SYNONYMOUS WITH DEEDS OF BRAVERY.

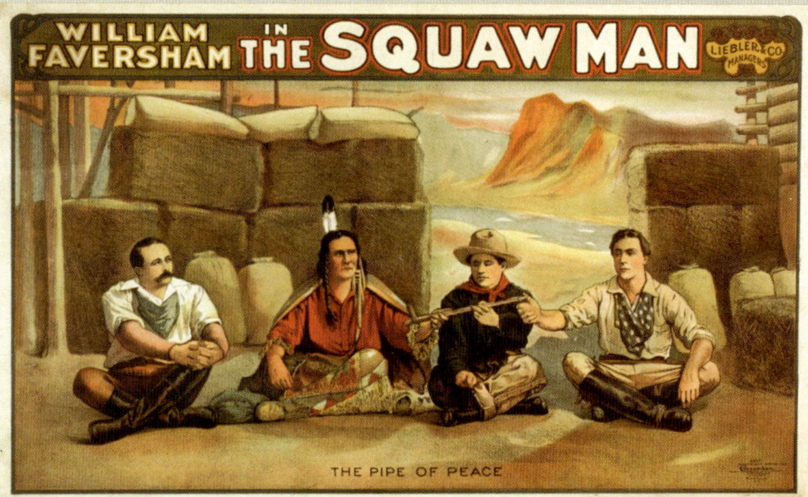
WILLIAM FAVERSHAM IN THE SQUAW MAN
LIEBLER & CO. MANAGERS
THE PIPE OF PEACE

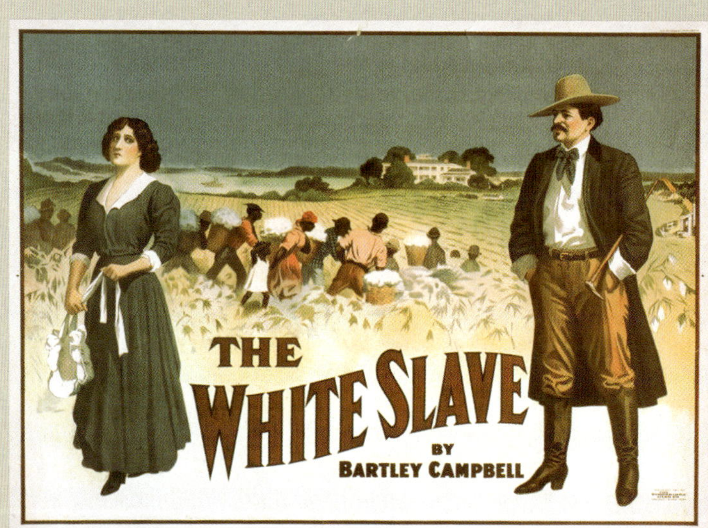
THE WHITE SLAVE
BY
BARTLEY CAMPBELL

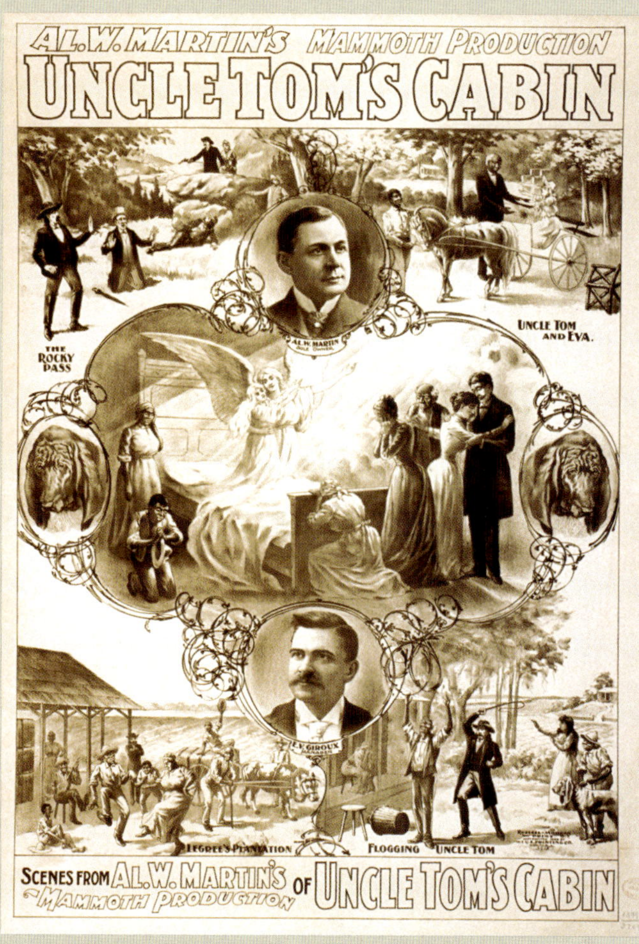
AL. W. MARTIN'S MAMMOTH PRODUCTION
UNCLE TOM'S CABIN
THE ROCKY PASS
UNCLE TOM AND EVA.
LEGREE'S PLANTATION
FLOGGING UNCLE TOM
SCENES FROM AL. W. MARTIN'S MAMMOTH PRODUCTION OF UNCLE TOM'S CABIN

FOREWORD

*A*n unusual title for an exhibition and its accompanying publication, *The Old, Weird America* immediately suggests the question, "What does that mean?" Before knowing the story behind the title, archetypal images are already cropping up in one's mind—cowboys and Indians, Paul Revere's midnight ride, the Headless Horseman, and on and on. And as the realm of the art museum is ultimately visual, that reaction is entirely appropriate.

This exhibition, which looks at a resurgence of folk themes in contemporary art, has been in the planning stages for a number of years and marks Senior Curator Toby Kamps's first large-scale effort since his arrival at the Contemporary Arts Museum Houston early in 2007. Its range, depth, thoughtfulness, and originality are characteristic of Kamps's imaginative scholarship. Both the title and the inspiration come from a layered and complex amalgam of writing, music, history, and culture: in 1997 cultural critic Greil Marcus wrote *The Old, Weird America: The World of Bob Dylan's Basement Tapes*[1] which examines Dylan's album, *The Basement Tapes* (recorded 1967, released 1975), which in turn was inspired by ethnomusicologist Harry Smith's 1952 *Anthology of American Folk Music*. We are enormously grateful to Greil Marcus for granting permission to apply his haunting and apt title to our exhibition.

Kamps's study of an unsettling folk history in current American art comes in the wake of 9/11, a time in our collective histories that changed our world forever. Both the Patriot Act and Homeland Security—seemingly folksy titles for dubious government programs, put in place as a result of the World Trade Center tragedy—eerily hark back to a simpler and safer time in our nation's past.

And, just as our present image in the international world has been tarnished by recent events, some of the themes explored in this study have a resonance beyond our national borders. But this is not necessarily a new phenomenon. For example, the fascination for a strangely "exotic" Americana can be traced back to the German writer, Karl May, whose late nineteenth-century popular novels romanticized the American Old West and created lasting stereotypes of the uniquely American identity that exist to this day in the global imagination.

Like so many of today's artists, the eighteen included in this exhibition look to the world around them, to their personal pasts and collective histories, especially as they themselves have been defined by a so-called American eye. Other areas, such as music, folklore, history, social criticism, and identity politics, have helped to inform and shape the art of our time. This exhibition and catalogue can provide us with the opportunity to examine and try to understand why these artists, like so many Americans in the United States at this moment, are looking back at their own mythology and history.

It has been a genuine pleasure to follow Kamps's thought process as he has narrowed and focused his ideas on this subject. I would like to acknowledge his contribution, along with the members of the Museum staff who have characteristically demonstrated ingenuity and diligence at every step of the way. Of course, no exhibition is possible without the generosity of the lenders to the exhibition and the participation of the artists. I am particularly appreciative of the support we have received from the exhibition's sponsors the Union Pacific Foundation and Nina and Michael Zilkha and from our donors to the Museum's Major Exhibition Fund. The Museum is most fortunate to receive funding from The Brown Foundation, Inc., for its publications and I would like to single out their important support.

I am delighted that the exhibition will travel to the Frederick R. Weisman Art Museum at the University of Minnesota in Minneapolis where it will be on view at the time of one of our country's most fascinating rituals, the Republican Party Convention. It is my hope that the audiences visiting this exhibition, both in Houston and Minneapolis, will gain insights into the myth-making processes of American culture, and come to appreciate the critical role that artists play in helping us to understand the world around us.

—Linda Shearer
Interim Director

Americana posters: *Buffalo Bill's Wild West and Congress of Rough Riders of the World with Col. W. F. Cody* (1899), *The Squaw Man* (1905), *Uncle Tom's Cabin* by Harriet Beecher Stowe (A. W. Martin's production, 1899), and *The White Slave* by Bartley Campbell (1911)

1. Re-titled for the 2001 edition, the book's original title was *Invisible Republic: Bob Dylan's Basement Tapes*.

ACKNOWLEDGMENTS

A project of this size and ambition is realized only because of the labor, generosity, and commitment of many. First, we are extremely grateful to the artists, collectors, and institutions who have lent their works and whose names appear on page 7. The artists' willingness to share works from their studios and personal collections for the exhibition as well as their ideas and inspirations for the catalogue essays is a wonderful vote of confidence for the project and its premise. Similarly, the collectors, galleries, and museums who have so generously loaned works to the exhibition redouble their support for the artists by allowing their works to be shown in this new, illuminating context, and to be seen by broad audiences.

An equal debt of gratitude is owed to the project's patrons, who provided the funding to realize this ambitious exhibition and publication. *The Old, Weird America* is made possible by generous support from the Union Pacific Foundation and Nina and Michael Zilkha. In addition, The Brown Foundation, Inc., provided crucial support for this publication. The Contemporary Arts Museum Houston's Major Exhibition Fund group has made major contributions as well. A list of these funders appears on page 4.

I also am grateful to our colleagues at the Frederick R. Weisman Art Museum at the University of Minnesota, Minneapolis, who have worked to bring the exhibition to the Twin Cities in fall 2008. Lyndel King, director and chief curator; Diane A. Mullin, associate curator; and Colleen Sheehy, director of education, have been strong and steady partners.

Sheehy and art historian, critic, and curator Michael Duncan each contributed insightful, revelatory catalogue essays on the exhibition artists and themes. Their illuminating texts are testament to the accomplishments of the exhibition artists and to the power of visual artists throughout history to illuminate a nation's culture.

Don Quaintance of Public Address Design, aided by design/production assistant Elizabeth Frizzell, did a wonderful job developing the exhibition catalogue, and his sensitive feel for the simultaneously old and new spirit of the project shows through in all aspects of its graphic identity. I also wish to thank editors Polly Koch and Heather Brand for their thoughtful edits of the curator's texts, and intern Natalia Ferreyra-Beasley who ably compiled the artists' biographies and bibliographies.

Each member of the Contemporary Arts Museum Houston's talented staff contributed in one way or another to realizing the project. Former Director Marti Mayo gave the project the initial green light, and Interim Director Linda Shearer has provided her full support. Special recognition must also go to Mike Reed, assistant director; Karen Cornelius, development director; Justine Waitkus, curatorial manager; Tim Barkley, registrar; Jeff Shore, head preparator; Paula Newton, director of education and public programs; Jim Mulvihill, former public relations director; Alison Griffith, grants and gifts manager; Kelly Hamman, special events manager; Cheryl Blissitte, administrative assistant, director's office; Andy Balajadia, IT manager/webmaster; and Valerie Cassel Oliver, curator, for their help in developing the exhibition, catalogue, and related programs. The names of all staff members are listed on page 158, and I wish to extend my gratitude to each of them, as well as to the installation crew for their diligence and respect for the artists and their work.

A number of other individuals deserve special recognition for their contributions to the project. Former colleagues Scott Boberg, education curator, and Maiza Hixson, curatorial assistant at the Contemporary Arts Center in Cincinnati were important brainstormers at an early stage. Professor Karl Lindahl, Martha Gano Houston Research Professor of English at the University of Houston, also assisted with research for the exhibition by allowing me to audit his amazing class on the history of folklore. The following individuals also should receive acknowledgment for their assistance: Jeffrey Uslip, McDermott & McGough Studio, New York; Christina Vassallo and Lance Kinz, Kinz, Tillou + Feigen, New York; Suzanne Geiss and Jasmine Levett, Deitch Projects, New York; John Steele, Blum & Poe, Los Angeles; Lis Ivers, Marianne Boesky Gallery, New York; Chris Acuna-Hansen, Acuna-Hansen Gallery, Los Angeles; Christopher D'Amelio, D'Amelio Terras, New York; Brent Sikkema, Sikkema Jenkins & Co., New York; William Morrow, 21C Foundation Museum, Louisville,

Kentucky; Bruce Hartman and Whitney Gameson, Nerman Museum of Contemporary Art, Johnson County Community College, Overland Park, Kansas; David Rubin and Marion Oettinger Jr., San Antonio Museum of Art; Alejandra Navarro, Lio Malca Fine Art, New York; and Sarah Stork, Dunn and Brown Contemporary, Dallas. Of course, a project of this scale evolves through countless conversations with artists, colleagues, and friends. To all those who helped me by weighing in with their ideas about things, old, weird, and American, I am grateful.

Certainly, all of us at the Contemporary Arts Museum Houston are indebted to the Board of Trustees for their support, leadership, and passionate advocacy for the Museum and for contemporary art. Their names appear on page 158, and we appreciate their labors of love.

Finally, special debts of gratitude are owed to two individuals instrumental to the exhibition's realization. Jeremy Blake, who tragically took his own life in the summer of 2007, was an enthusiastic supporter of the project at its inception and helped give it shape through many illuminating and enjoyable conversations. You should be with us, Jeremy! And Greil Marcus very graciously gave us his permission to again use his wonderful title phrase "The Old, Weird America," which provided the inspirational spark for the project and so brilliantly sums up the fascinating complexity of this nation's mythic past.

—Toby Kamps
Senior Curator

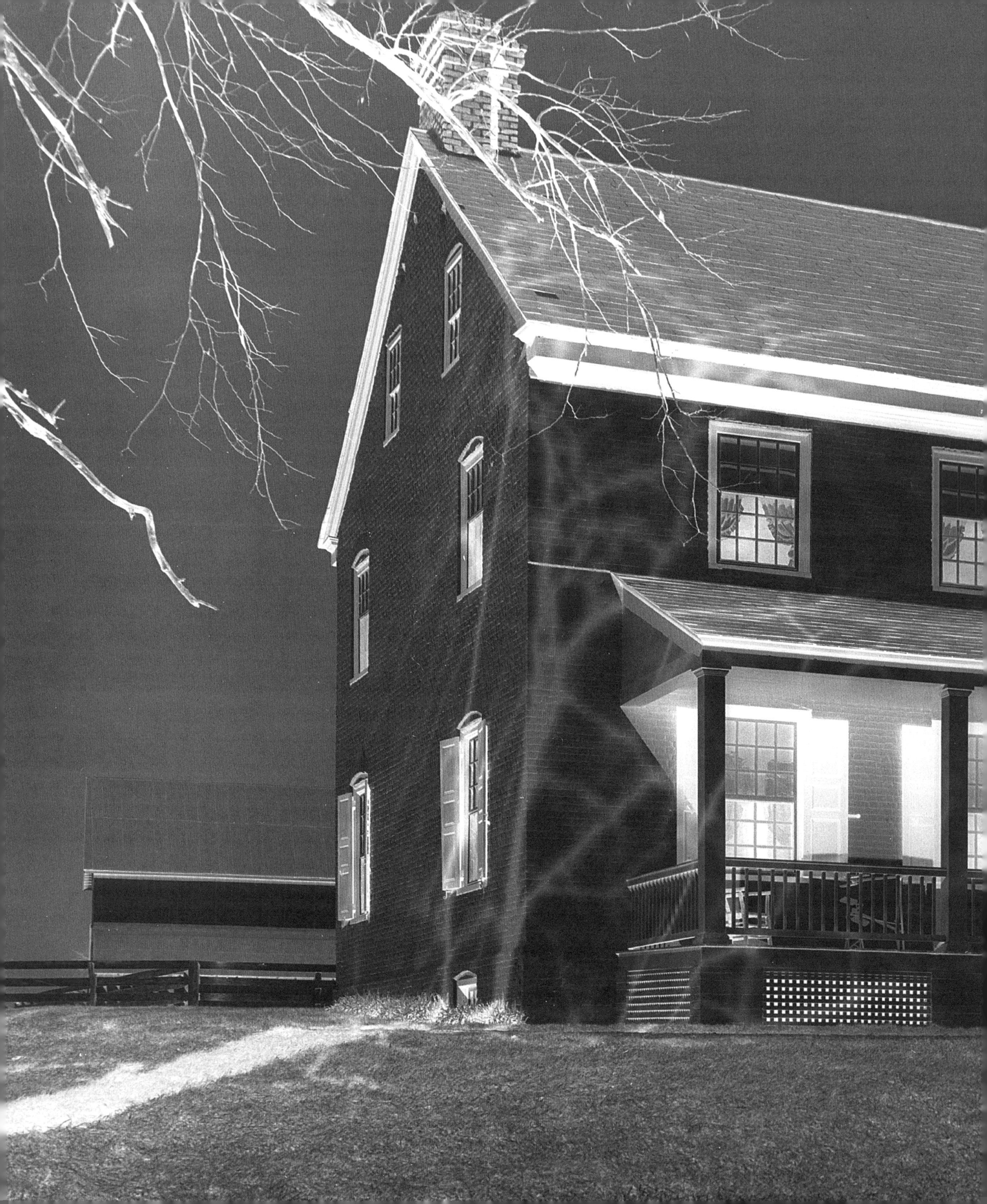

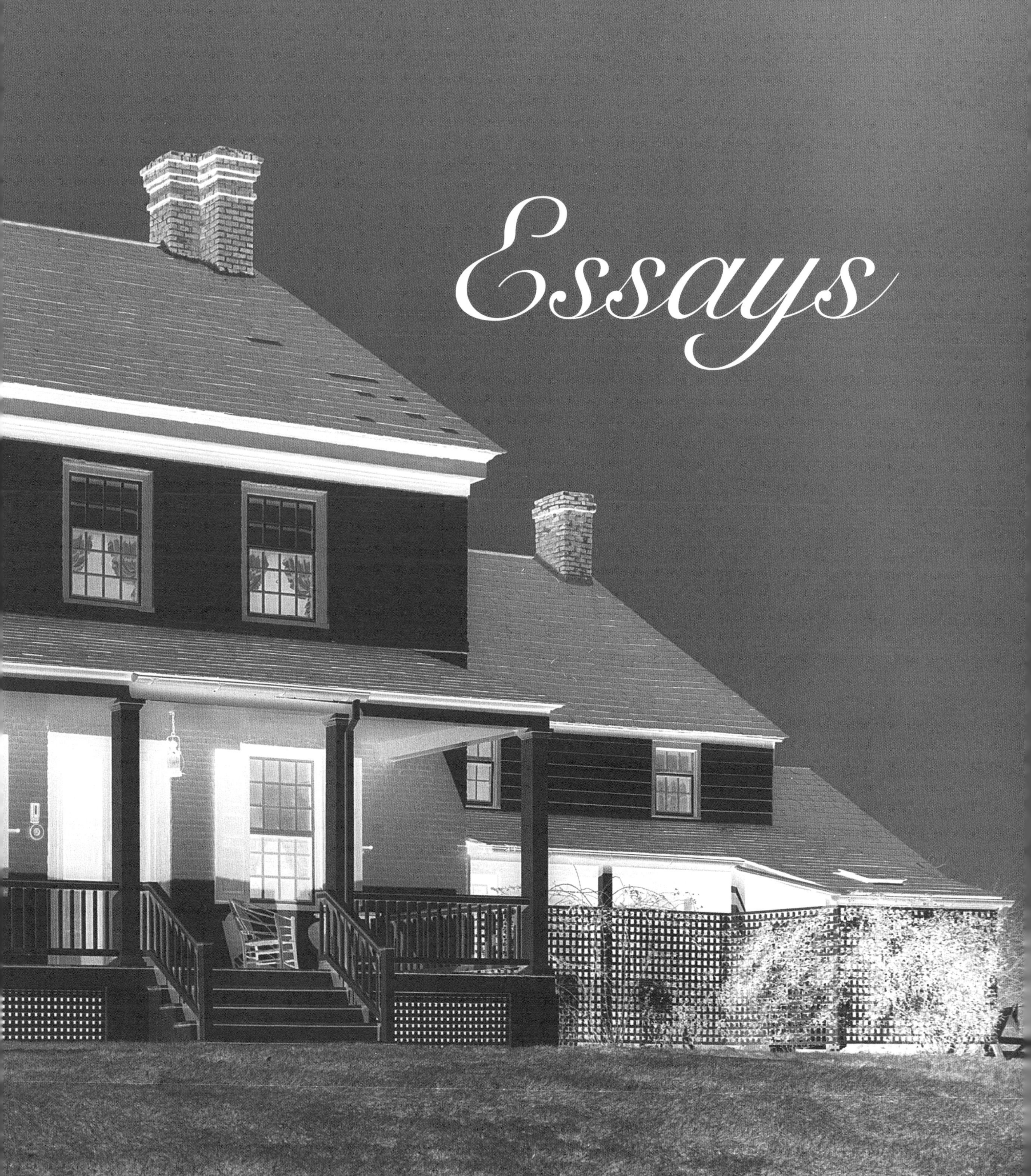
Essays

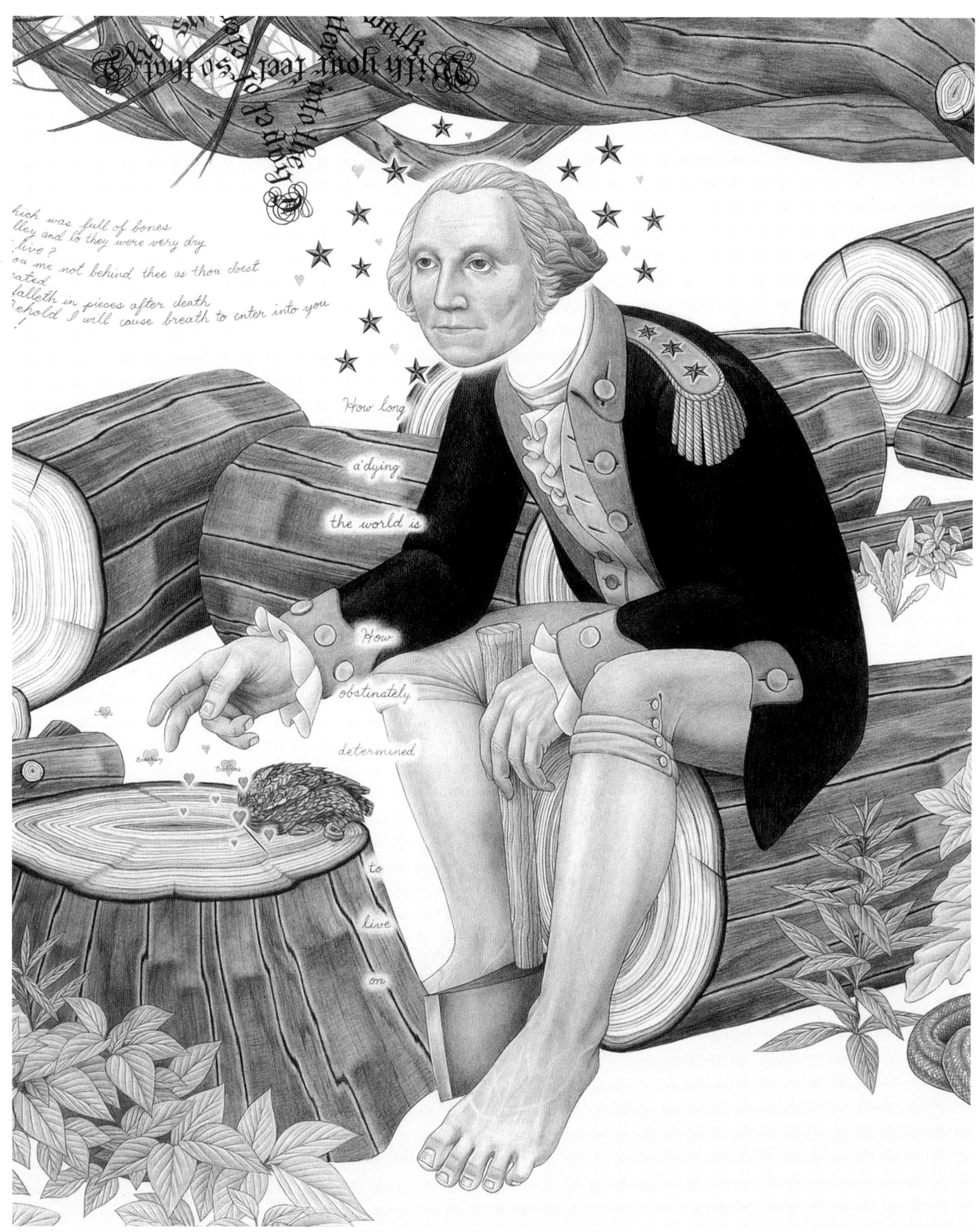

With your feet so that I ... deep into the ... dying
hich was full of bones
lley and lo they were very dry
live?
ou me not behind thee as thou doest
ated
falleth in pieces after death
ehold I will cause breath to enter into you
!
How long
a'dying
the world is
How
obstinately
determined
to
live
on

The Old, Weird America

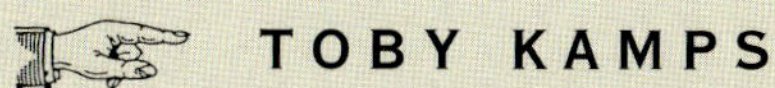

*The pure products of America
go crazy—
mountain folk from Kentucky*

*or the ribbed north end of
Jersey
with its isolate lakes and*

*valleys, its deaf-mutes, thieves
old names
and promiscuity between*

*devil-may-care men who have taken
to railroading
out of sheer lust of adventure—*

*and young slatterns, bathed
in filth
from Monday to Saturday*

*to be tricked out that night
with gauds
from imaginations which have no*

*peasant traditions to give them
character…*

—William Carlos Williams,
from "Spring and All," 1923[1]

Since that fateful late summer day in the inaugural year of the new millennium, life in the United States has gotten especially strange. Balance and serenity have never been hallmarks of our culture, but the nation's mood at the moment is exceptionally jangled and fractious. We see this in our pervasive fear of terrorism, in our hornet's nest of international entanglements, and in our internal sniping over identity and values. In this new, weird America of high emotion and sweeping change, it is natural to look for inspiration in the similarly volatile and mercurial old, weird America of folk history. To a degree not seen since the heyday of the Regionalist movement in the 1930s, visual artists are examining America's social history—the stories and characters we share to remind ourselves of who we are.

The exhibition and catalogue *The Old, Weird America* examines the widespread resurgence of folk themes in contemporary art in the United States. The project features eighteen artists who explore native, idiomatic, and communal subjects from America's past: Eric Beltz, Jeremy Blake, Sam Durant, Barnaby Furnas, Deborah Grant, Matthew Day Jackson, Brad Kahlhamer, Margaret Kilgallen, Aaron Morse, the collaborative team of McDermott & McGough, Cynthia Norton, Greta Pratt, David Rathman, Dario Robleto, Allison Smith, Kara Walker, and Charlie White. Covering the period from the first Thanksgiving in 1621 to the beginning of the Space Age in 1957, their representational paintings, sculptures, drawings, photographs, installations, and videos reconsider important legends and figures in United States history. Indians, Pilgrims, Founding Fathers, cowboys, Civil War widows, bobby soxers, and Depression-style drifters are among the Ur-American characters populating storytelling works that—like all good folklore—recklessly combine myth and fact to suggest an alternative national history.

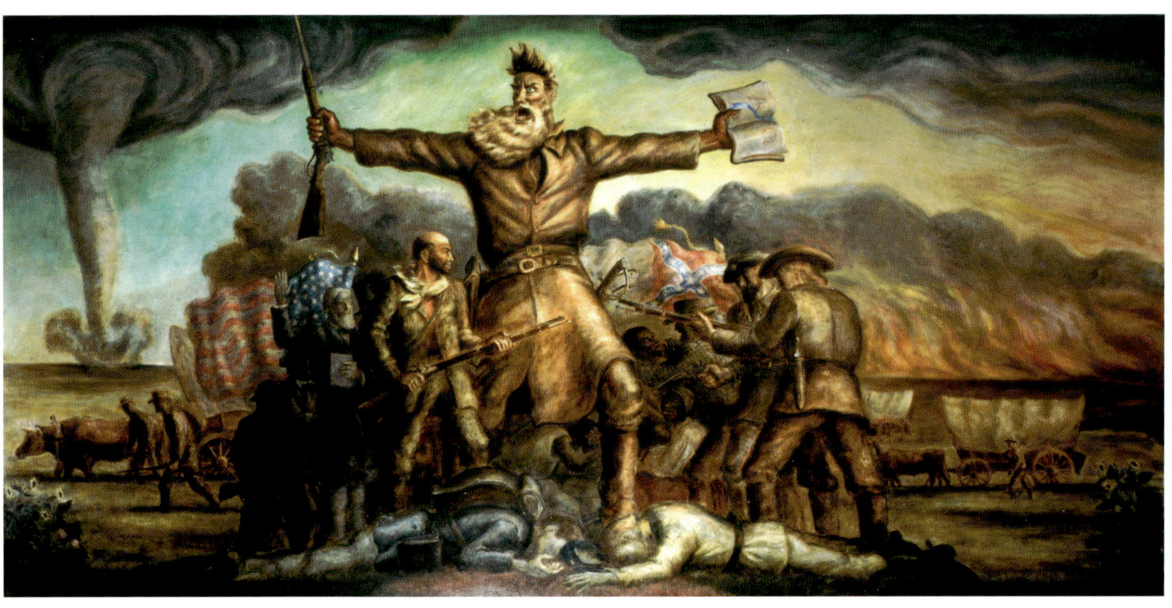

The Old, Weird America borrows its title and inspirational spark from a 1997 book of the same name by cultural critic Greil Marcus, which looks at Bob Dylan's legendary 1975 studio album *The Basement Tapes*, re-corded with The Band in 1967, as a window onto the nation's social history.[2] Dylan was so influential, Marcus argues, because he found—using artist and ethnomusicologist Harry Smith's 1952 six-record *Anthology of American Folk Music* as his road map—songs and stories in an older, half-forgotten world of legend that seemed at once stranger and more genuine than anything in the postwar mainstream. Marcus has given permission to use his title, which so succinctly conjures up lost times and spirits, because the exhibition has the same goal as his wide-ranging study of Dylan and folk music: to tell a deeper, weirder story of America. This exhibition and catalogue consider the ways contemporary artists reconsider the country's legendary past to illuminate its cultural life—a unique mixture of civilization and barbarism, enlightenment and madness.

THE FOLKLORIC IMPULSE

In academic terms, folklore is commonly defined as artistic communication in small groups.[3] It consists of the stories, music, jokes, proverbs, and superstitions that communities sustain in order to pass on information, mark group identity, and reinforce social control. The study of folklore originated in Germany during the late eighteenth century. The philosopher Johann Gottfried von Herder (1744–1803) encouraged documenting popular stories and traditions reflecting the spirit of the German peoples because he regarded them as ideolog-ical tools that could support his concept of romantic nationalism and fuel the nascent movement for German unification. A reaction against top-down imperial rule, romantic nationalism espoused a bottom-up political unity based on culture—race, language, religion, and customs. As shown in the famous story of Snow White in *Kinder- und Hausmärchen* (*Children's and Household Tales*), the first Herder-inspired collection of German folktales published by the brothers Wilhelm and Jakob Grimm in 1812, folklore is not bound to established history or religion and can reflect a culture's creativity and accomplishments as well as its prejudices and brutality.[4]

As an everyday term and the framing concept of this exhibition, folklore is the id to the ego of official culture. It is a mysterious world of slippery symbols and characters, Jungian unconscious patterns, superstitions, and outright nonsense. In the twenty-first century, folklore is alive and well and spreading its revelatory half-truths through all conventional channels, as well as through the exceptionally fact-flexible space of the internet. The artists in this exhibition focus on stories and characters from a premodern world where rough edges have not been smoothed away by centralized news and entertainment. However, although their subjects might be folkish, the artists are not. Without exception, they are academically trained and live in large cities. They have researched their subjects deeply, and they are anything but self-taught isolates unself-conscious about their craftsmanship. In this respect, they resemble painter Marc Chagall (1887–1985), a Paris cosmopolite dreaming of tiny, magical villages in the Pale of Tsarist Russia. And it may be that folklore itself is a product of the citified classes' nostalgia for simpler times. After all, it was Harvard Square beatniks and not Appalachian farmers who were the primary audience for the field recordings and rare commercial releases featured in Harry Smith's *Anthology*. This project testifies to the fact that, even though urbanization and conglomerization have decimated the local and indigenous, the haunting skeleton of culture represented by America's folklore still thrills the imagination. The meta-Americana in this exhibition may contain layers of irony not usually found in folk art, yet these visions of the nation's mythological history still pack a potent punch. So deeply ingrained and closely held are this country's foundational legends that anyone reared or educated in the United States must resonate—sympathetically or not—with their retellings in *The Old, Weird America*.

MASTER (AND SLAVE) NARRATIVES

During times of change and social stress, cultures look to their master narratives. The Regionalist movement of the 1930s and 1940s, when American artists rejected European Modernism's emphasis on formal innovation and turned their attention to depicting rural and domestic life in realist styles, was a high point of this aesthetic introspection. Partially in reaction to the upheavals of the First World War, a time of unprecedented horror but also of rising American geopolitical power, Regionalists like Grant Wood, Thomas Hart Benton, and John Steuart Curry created, variously, pastoral, moralizing, and gen-

tly satirizing visions of America (fig. 2). They invoked eternal forces in American culture both to seek reassurance and to assert a culture coming into its own. In the 1960s, Pop Art cast a cool eye on American culture, highlighting its commercialization and plasticization. The current, arguably overdue revival of American folk imagery, however, has as much in common with German art of the 1970s and 1980s as it does with that of the Regionalists. Motivated by the Cold War-*realpolitik* suppression of Germany's Nazi past, as well as by the apparent disconnect between American Minimal and Conceptual art and the country's simultaneous involvement in Vietnam, German artists like Georg Baselitz, Anselm Kiefer, and Jörg Immendorff made paintings roiling with repressed history and biting political criticism as a means of exorcizing the demons of a society gripped by legacies of violence and denial. Similarly, the artists in *The Old, Weird America* rummage in the attic of American culture to search for the forgotten, the unresolved, and the tragic—the gunpowder trails leading to the early twenty-first century's unsettling foreign and domestic predicaments.

In the late 1990s, Kara Walker gained international fame for transforming the cut-paper silhouette, previously the domain of genteel, parlor-room portraitists, into a medium for hard-hitting, room-scale tableaux depicting the obscenity of slavery in America. Pushing every possible racial, sexual, and gender-role hot button, Walker created outrageous, Breughelian spectacles of stereotyping, miscegenation, and debasement. This exhibition's animated, Balinese-style shadow-puppet video, *8 Possible Beginnings or: The Creation of African-America, a Moving Picture by Kara E. Walker* (2005, fig. 3 and pls. 94–98), fearlessly satirizes black origin myths and white racism in outrageous vignettes featuring slave ships, gay master-and-slave sex, and dancing cotton-boll babies. In his sculptural installation *Pilgrims and Indians, Planting and Reaping, Learning and Teaching* (2006, fig. 4 and pls. 11–15), Sam Durant also reframes American history by juxtaposing two stories of the Thanksgiving holiday. He restages two amateurish dioramas from the defunct Plymouth National Wax Museum in Massachusetts on top of a rotating circular platform, so that the work alternately displays radically different versions of how the Jamestown Colony came to celebrate the first Thanksgiving in 1621. One side of the platform shows the famous, feel-good legend: Native Americans teaching Pilgrims how to use fish to fertilize corn and ensuring a bountiful harvest. The other shows the true catalyst: Captain Myles Standish killing the defiant Pequot

Fig. 3
Kara Walker
Video still from *8 Possible Beginnings or: The Creation of African-America, a Moving Picture by Kara E. Walker*, 2005
DVD video, running time: 15:57 minutes (with sound)
Courtesy Sikkema Jenkins & Co., New York

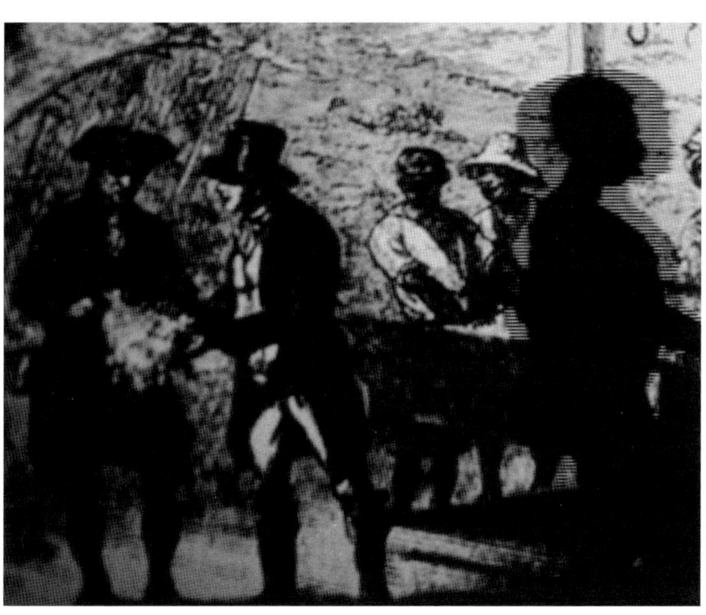

Fig. 4
Sam Durant
*Pilgrims and Indians, Plant-
ing and Reaping, Learning
and Teaching* (detail), 2006
Mixed media, motorized
platform
Courtesy the artist and
Blum & Poe, Los Angeles

Fig. 5
Greta Pratt
*Lincoln and Log Cabin RV,
Hodgenville, Kentucky,* 2000
Lambda print
30 x 30 inches
Courtesy the artist

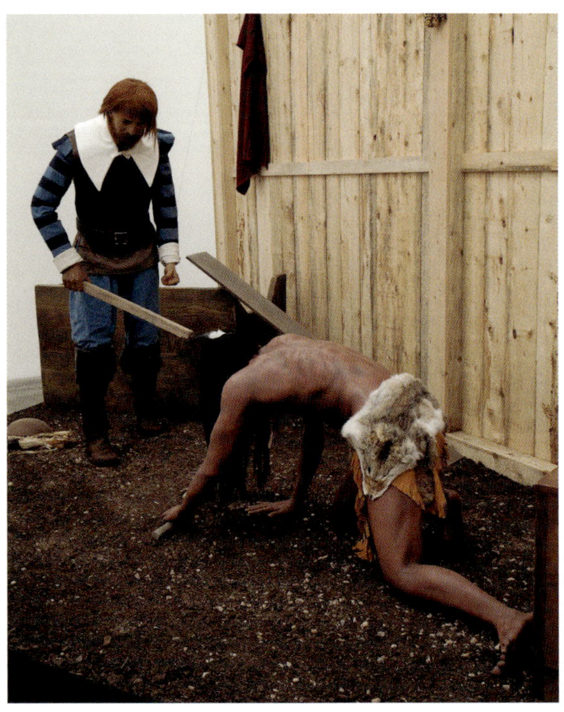

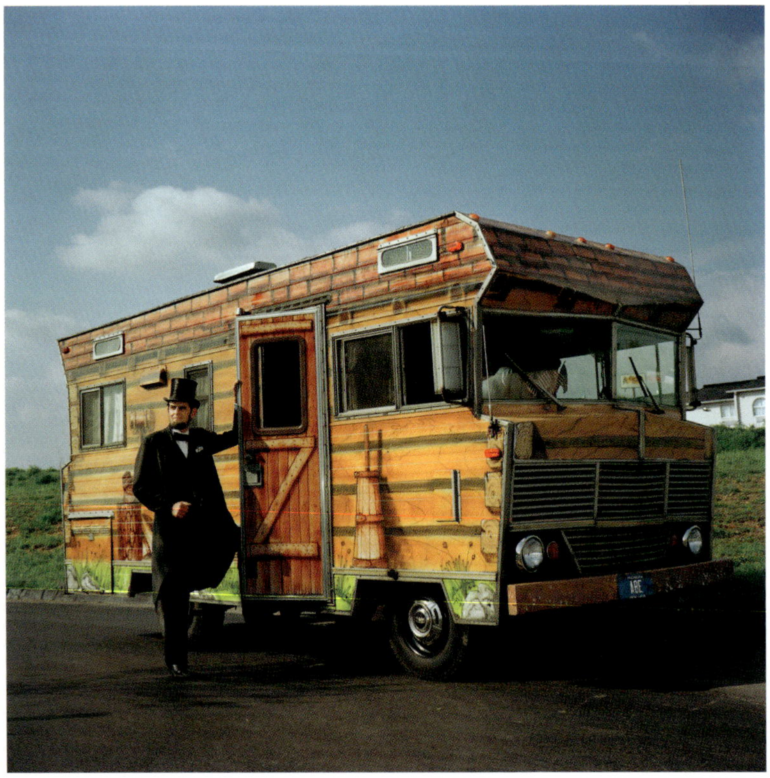

Indian Pecksuot in a fit of rage. Pecksuot's insults to Standish, Durant reminds us in an accompanying text panel,
sparked a bloody raid on the Pequots, the success of which
the colonists celebrated with a feast of thanksgiving.

Americans' complex relationship with the past, real
and imaginary, is also the subject of Greta Pratt's documentary photographs. Traveling to historical sites, com-
memorative festivals, and living-history museums, Pratt
creates candid and posed images of Americans attempt-
ing—with comically variable success—to relive their
country's intrepid past. Her *19 Lincolns* (2005, pl. 70),
a grid of portraits of bearded and top-hatted Abraham
Lincoln impersonators made at a meeting of the Society of Lincoln Presenters in Hodgenville, Kentucky,
highlights the abiding power of a martyred president to
inspire ordinary citizens to travel the country —one in
a log-cabin camper (fig. 5)—taking on his high moral
code and distinctively craggy appearance. Similarly,
Charlie White creates a quintessentially American historic scene in his fictional, painstakingly constructed
tableau photograph *1957* (2006, pl. 99). Working with
Hollywood prop houses and movie extras, and carefully
quoting well-known images of racial tension by illustrator Norman Rockwell and youth-culture hijinks by photographer Joseph Sterling, he staged, photographed,
and then digitally constructed an image of *Rebel Without
a Cause*-era teenagers lounging in and around a tail-
finned Buick. An eerily too-perfect period piece that
reads like a Parthenon frieze of national obsessions (sex,
race, and cars), *1957* crackles with menace and what
White calls the "American mythological, the American
artificial, and the American uncanny."

BOB DYLAN, HARRY SMITH,
AND THE CALL OF ANOTHER LIFE

Folklore is both a thing and a process. It is a body of
stories, and it is an ongoing process of invention and
adaptation by which cultural shibboleths, or signs of
identity, are perpetually remolded by successive generations. When Dylan raided the American folk songbook
to make *The Basement Tapes*, he tapped into a rich, copy-
right-free reservoir of shared tradition. In the process
of reinterpreting traditional songs and creating new,
timeless-seeming classics, Marcus says, the musician
from Minnesota mined the disarmingly familiar yet
mysterious heart of a nation of "imbecile complexity"
perpetually moving between "the confessional and the
bawdy house."[5] The folk revival Dylan led had tremen-
dous traction during a period of transition marked by the

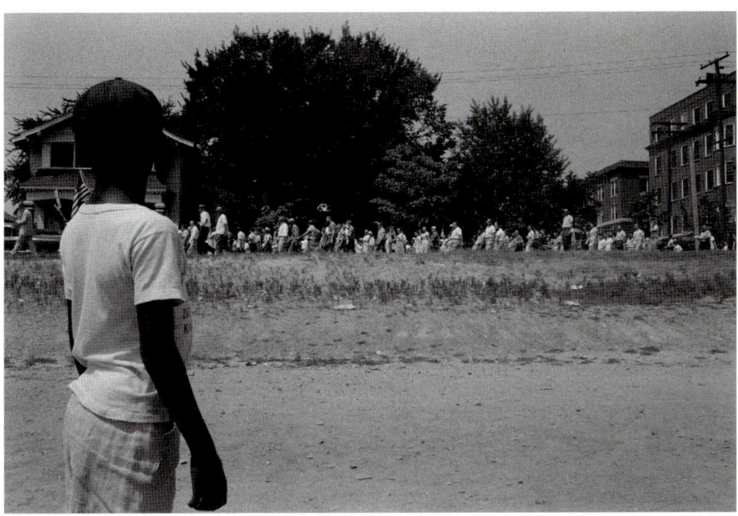

Fig. 6
John T. Bledsoe
Little Rock, Mob Marching from Capitol to Central High,
1959
Gelatin silver print
8 x 10 inches
Courtesy Library of
Congress, Washington, D.C.

Fig. 7
Dario Robleto
Your Lullaby Will Find a Home in My Head (detail), 2005
Hair braids made of stretched
and curled audio tape . . .
(see pl. 78)
26 x 3½ x 30 inches
Collection of Carlos Bacino,
Houston

Vietnam War and the Civil Rights Movement (fig. 6). As historian Robert Cantwell noted, it "made the romantic claim of folk culture—oral, immediate, traditional, idiomatic, communal, a culture of characters, of rights, obligations, and beliefs, against a centrist, specialist, impersonal, technocratic culture, a culture of types, functions, jobs and goals."[6] Greil Marcus's imaginative description of Harry Smith's research might also apply to these artists' attempts to uncover a primordial America:

> As Smith searched for the hillbilly classics and primitive blues made in the commercial half-light of the Jazz Age, he found himself in the first years of his own childhood. He might have heard what people have always heard in strange music: the call of another life. He might have imagined that, going back to his first years with his oldest records, he was reliving and rewriting his life from the start. It would have been only a first step; the history of the republic, the story of the country told itself, was just as vulnerable. As Smith learned the contours of old styles, as he tracked melodies and phrases through the Chinese boxes of folk etymology, he found himself in the 1800s and then back further still, decades tumbling into centuries, ghost lovers and backwoods crimes replacing the great personages and events of national life.[7]

The artists in *The Old, Weird America* live and work in a time quite different from Smith's. But like previous generations of musicians, they recognize the eternal power of their folkloric subjects. In the Homeric tradition (the *Odyssey* was based on oral history), they delve into the cycles and lessons of America's unofficial history, and retell its epics anew.

TIME OUT OF MIND

Many of the artists in *The Old, Weird America* practice forms of time travel. In works of art and performance-based projects, they project themselves or their points of view into America's emotional history. From 1985 to 1995, lovers and artistic collaborators David McDermott and Peter McGough lived as early twentieth-century dandies in New York. Wearing paper collars, driving a Model T Ford, and lighting their vintage town house in New York's East Village solely with candles, the artists performed "an experiment in time," making paintings, sculptures, and photographs, each with an ostensible as well as an actual date, that revived queer and other hidden histories of America. Saturated with submerged narratives and eroticism, works like *San Francisco Earthquake Box, 1906* (1988, pl. 59), a vitrine containing a shattered floral vase commemorating the Great San Francisco Earthquake, evoke vanished atmospheres and desires. In another attempt to collapse past and present, Dario Robleto often inserts into his sculptures real historical artifacts (fig. 7), including Civil War bullets, widows' mourning dresses, human bones, and shavings from

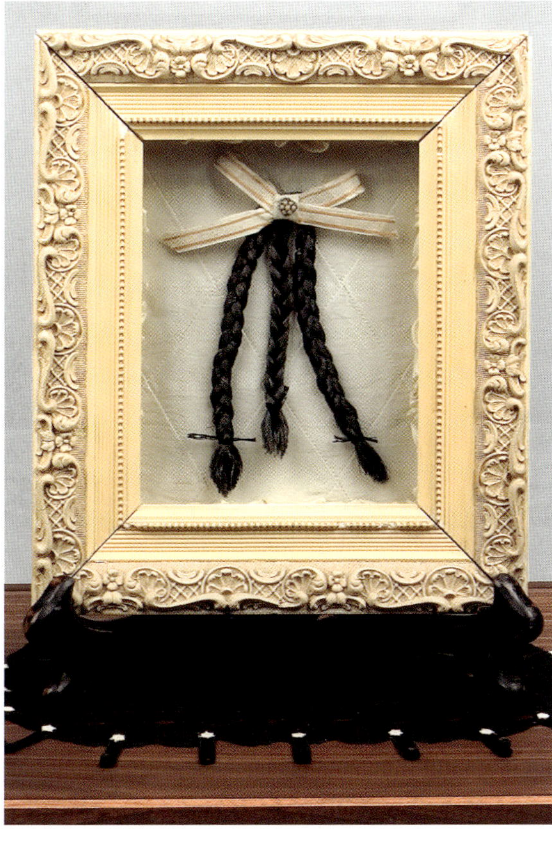

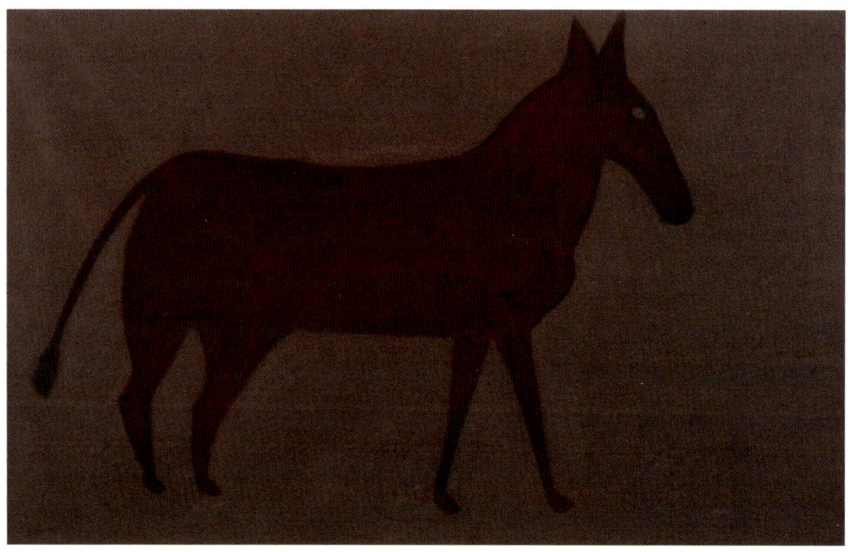

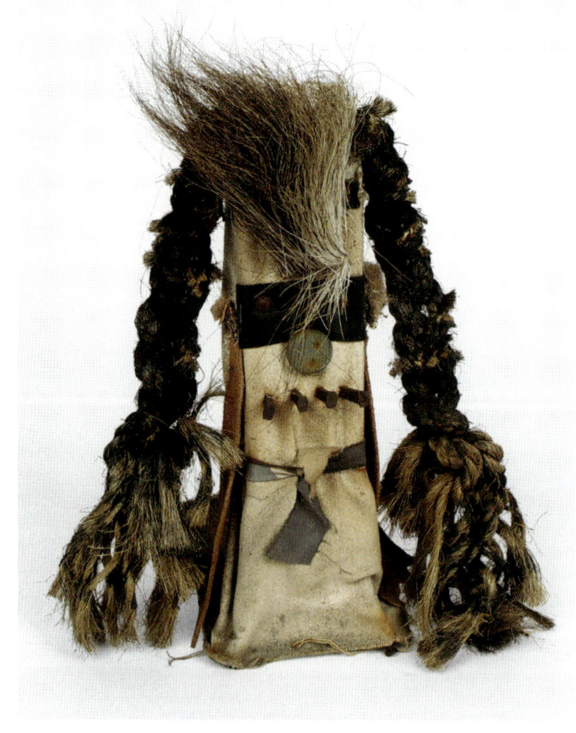

early rock 'n' roll albums. Like slivers of the True Cross or the tiny quantities of disease-carrying microorganisms in homeopathic remedies, these charged fragments give Robleto's historical investigations shiver-inducing mojo. A memorial to the last three widows of Civil War veterans, including scraps of antique mourning dresses (pl. 80); a Shaker apothecary cabinet, containing medicinal plants (pls. 83–84); and a history of American science, spirituality, and music, told through imaginary album covers (pl. 79), are among Robleto's narrative-rich contributions to the exhibition.

By overlapping sensibilities of an early American novel and contemporary action films, Aaron Morse reimagines the country's frontier in paintings and watercolors based on the five mid-nineteenth-century books of James Fenimore Cooper's The Leatherstocking Tales. He draws ideas from cinematic and illustrated children's versions of Cooper's stories, showing just how strong the romance of the frontier, the wilderness, and Native America remain in the contemporary imagination— even though they were already threatened well before Cooper's time. Filled with mountains of game or storyboarded like movie scripts, Morse's images suggest the roots of contemporary America's excesses and self-dramatization (pls. 62–65). Using Conceptual Art strategies as well as a DJ's turntable sampling techniques,

Deborah Grant investigates alternative histories of American art by analyzing the iconography of folk artist Bill Traylor (ca. 1856–1949, fig. 8 & see fig. 45). Her grid of images in black and blue acrylic on birch panels, *Where Good Darkies Go* (pls. 23–28), dissects the self-taught Traylor's playful figures and scenes from rural, African-American life into spare, nearly hieroglyphic images for the purpose of analysis. The work updates Traylor's early twentieth-century imagery for the rapid-fire visual communication of the information age, studying them like punchy song hooks or portentous symbols from another world. In intricate, large-scale drawings filled with an explosive and humorous range of Native American and pop-culture imagery, Brad Kahlhamer investigates and imagines his own origins—in particular something he calls a "third place" between his upbringing with white, adoptive parents in Wisconsin and his birth to an unknown Native American mother in Arizona. Gathering inspiration from road trips through reservation lands and meetings with Native communities, Kahlhamer creates idiosyncratic Kachina dolls (fig. 9 and pls. 38–50) and swirling compositions of skulls, Indian warriors, eagles, and poetic texts—rendered in a dazzling array of styles— that suggest grand processionals of ancestors, actual and imaginary (pls. 37, 51, & 52).

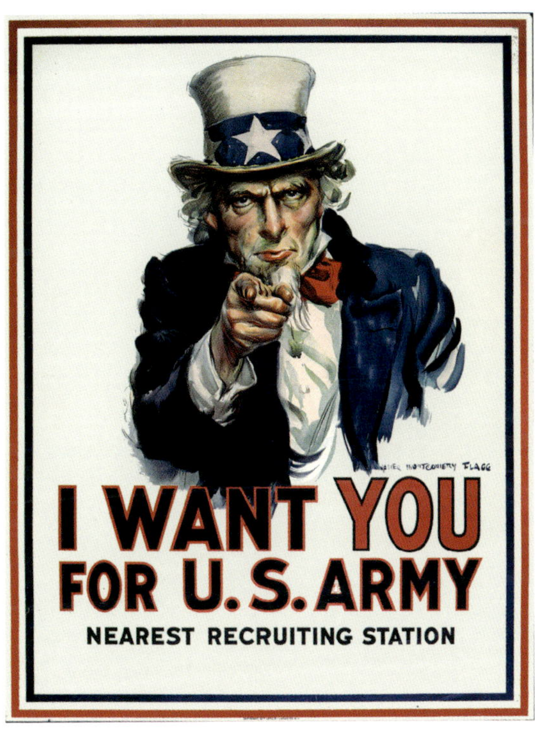

BARBARIAN NATION

In the United States, literary and folk culture arose simultaneously with nationhood.[6] Rapidly expanding immigrant populations and declining indigenous populations contributed their own stories and traditions, and westward-migrating settlers disseminated them. (Another, extreme example of this accelerated form of mythmaking is Israel, where a folklore, including a style of folk dancing, had to be invented to give its embattled population a legitimizing "native" cultural export.) Whether the independent, entrepreneurial spirit America so prides itself on is a result or cause of the country's comparatively laissez-faire governance and survival-of-the-fittest social structure is an ongoing chicken-and-egg debate. But what is clear is that there is a complex feedback process at work, whereby myths and attitudes both reflect and promote national concerns. Every civilization has its pantheon of quasi-sacred founders, and the United States has Christopher Columbus, George Washington, and Abraham Lincoln, as well as a constellation of mythical characters, places, and creatures including Uncle Sam (fig. 10), Graceland, and Bigfoot.

Anthropologists study the proverbial "savage"—practitioners of primitive societies and beliefs. Folklorists consider "the barbarian" an all-purpose ancestor from a just-out-of-reach time endowed with modern intellect but unfettered by the constraints of civilization. Holding itself to its primary mirror, Europe, the United States is a barbarian nation, and a shoot-from-the-hip emphasis on direct expression and action has been extolled as the national personality. As folklorist Simon Bronner rhapsodizes, the American character is "generous, easy-going, well-met, obtuse, and naïve, friendly first and suspicious only later—it is quite unlike the hard, integrated peasant simplicity of the folk of Europe."[8] Recurrent themes in American folklore include struggles with authority, labor, and land, and humor is omnipresent, piercing all facades and pretensions.[9]

O BROTHER, WHERE ART THOU?

For many citizens, a nostalgic image of America's "Good Old Days" lingers in the imagination. Tinged no doubt by Hollywood and Madison Avenue, this is a pre-highway, pre-mass media place of direct and significant communication and experience. Both picturesque and picaresque, it is peopled by preachers, prospectors, blues singers, and a panoply of snake-oil salesmen and visionaries. For those who suffered in the Depression in the 1930s (fig. 11), the period was perhaps not as lighthearted as that described so vividly in Joel and Ethan Coen's 2000 comedy-odyssey film about a band of musical escaped convicts journeying across the South,

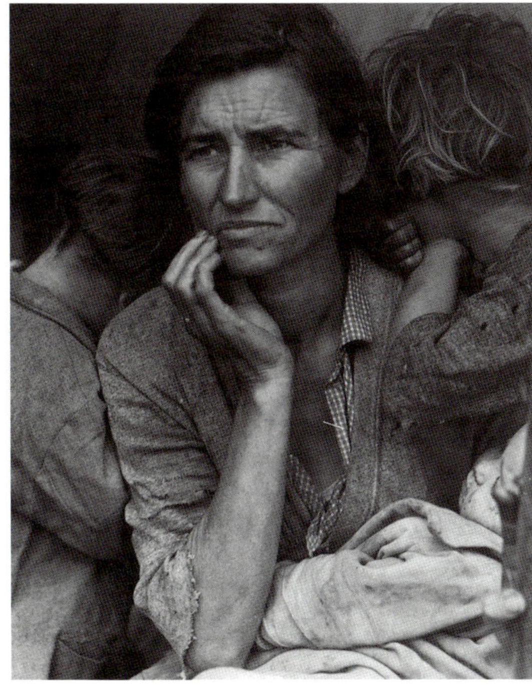

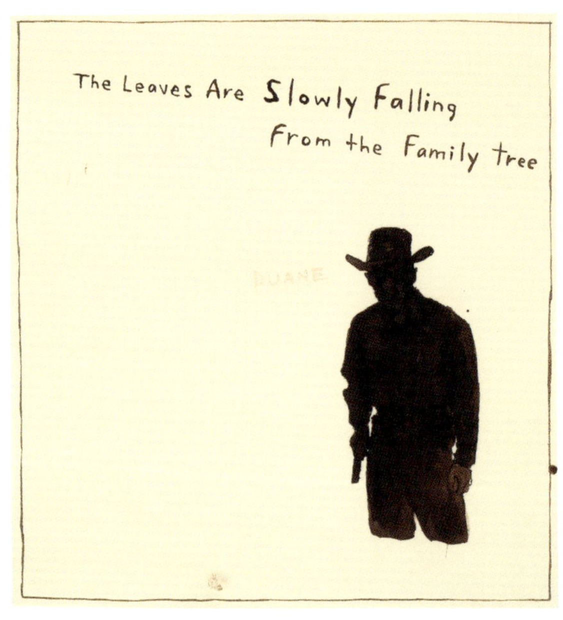

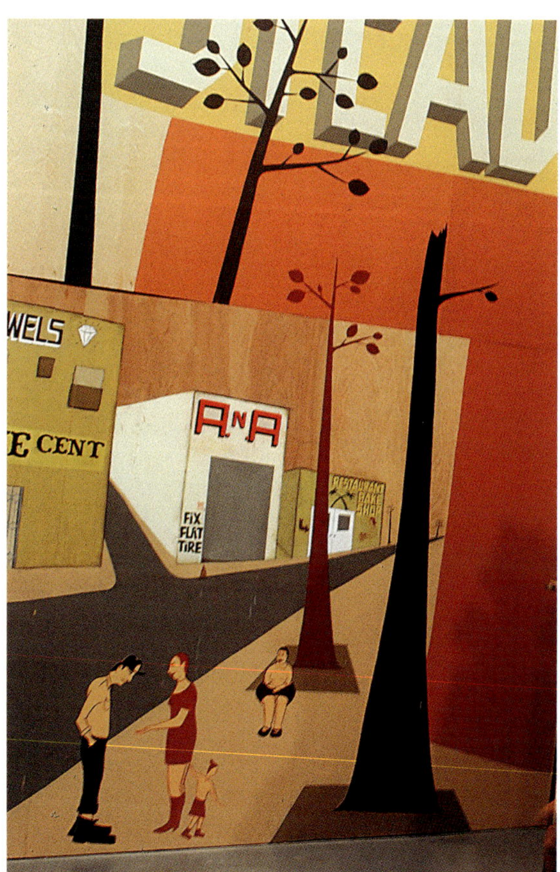

O Brother, Where Art Thou? Still, that time, as well as the Red Scare of the 1950s and the Civil Rights Movement of the 1960s, represents a world where character, conviction, and a "get up and go" spirit seemed more decisive than it does today. David Rathman's small ink-on-paper drawings, giving traditional Old West characters an existential twist, express both the nearness and inaccessibility of that American dream (fig. 12 and pls. 71–77). Freeze-framing Westerns to find striking compositions of cowboys and riflemen at rest and in action, he sketches vignettes hand-captioned with phrases like "Hell You Ain't Dead. Just Shut Up a Little" and "It's Funny to Start Thinking About Women." The works comically and tellingly mix Ben Stiller neuroses with John Wayne tough-guyisms. Margaret Kilgallen also depicts a bygone, forlornly beautiful America in her installation *Main Drag* of 2001 (fig. 13 and pls. 53–57). Painted in a playful, cartoonish style on panels of scrap wood, the work consists of hand-painted signs in decorative, antique fonts broadcasting all-American words like "kook" and "sloe" alongside images of a main street in a low-rent town of the imagination inhabited by a charmingly deadbeat cast of indigenous characters: surfers, hobos, juvenile delinquents, and dames in beehive hairdos. To revive the emotions of vanished times, Cynthia Norton invents machines that perform their ecstatic rituals. Her kinetic sculptures *Dancing Squared* (2004, pls. 66, 68), a motorized square-dance machine that whirls crinolined dresses, and *Fountain (emotion)* (2002, pl. 67), a working distillery jury-rigged from a magazine stand and other household detritus, represent, Norton says, the soul- and mind-expanding contributions of outsiders—Shaker and Quaker dancers and moonshiners—to the culture. Allison Smith also animates early American social forces in her installations and performances, which put a conceptual spin on traditional crafts. Fascinated with the Civil War and the thousands of Americans who reenact its battles, Smith has made life-size dolls in her own image that are dressed as Zoaves, volunteer soldiers—many of them former firefighters from New York City—whose flamboyant, self-styled uniforms and fighting techniques appeal to her interests in historical reenactment and gender theory (pls. 85–93).

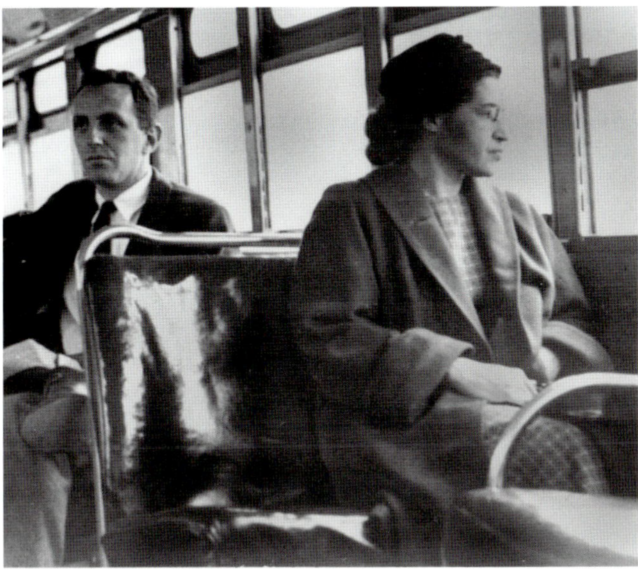

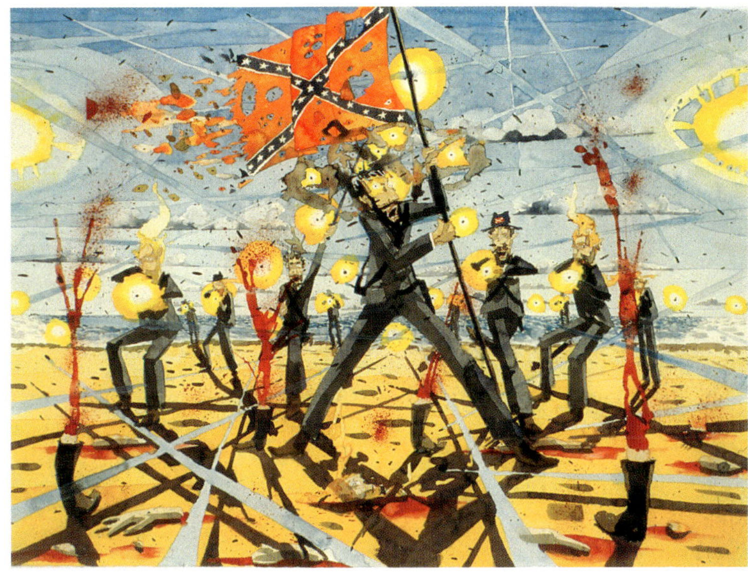

REPRESENTATIONAL MEN (AND WOMEN)

At heart, the very idea of the United States—that power resides with the people—is folkloric. The nation's earliest visionaries regarded the country as a "new Adam," where order would flow naturally from its citizenry, a place innocent of the original sin of Europe's monarchies. Writers like Ralph Waldo Emerson and Walt Whitman promoted the idea of the country as a utopia redeemed by its own optimism and naïveté, espousing a culture of insight over tradition and upstart energy over civilized refinement.[10] Many of the nation's heroes embody these values. Rosa Parks (fig. 14), Martin Luther King Jr., and Bob Dylan are all, in different ways, the "representational" citizens we see celebrated in folklore studies. Cultural lightning rods, they stand for the freedoms and responsibilities of the individual in the face of oppression. Because of their intrinsically anti-authoritarian leanings and their ability to embody the sense of loss inherent in a rapidly modernizing society, folk revivalists, too, have often been suspect in America. As folklorist R. Serge Denisoff notes, "In 1963 the Fire and Police Research Association of Los Angeles stated: 'folk music was being used as an unidentified tool of Communist psychological and cybernetic warfare to ensnare and capture youthful minds.'"[11] This situation is not unique to the United States. The modern concept of folklore has been exploited by both the Right and the Left since its inception. However, as Greil Marcus points out in his 2006 post-9/11 cultural study *The Shape of Things to Come: Prophecy and the American Voice*, American's extreme idealism makes its social fabric especially fragile.[12] Better than any other form of cultural expression, folk stories and history highlight the country's contradictory social dynamics. At best, the nation's ongoing dialectic between stasis and change, liberty and control, is energizing and progressive. At worst, it builds a tower of Babel based on economic, religious, racial, and political difference, where citizens are pitted against each other in endless power struggles.

THE PURE PRODUCTS OF AMERICA GO CRAZY

In his 1923 poem "Spring and All," William Carlos Williams described with epic bleakness the wild and desolate undercurrents running through United States history:

The pure products of America go crazy— [13]

Explosive violence, righteous anger, and madness run through American lore. Inspired by the realistic descriptions of Civil War combat in Stephen Crane's 1895 novel *The Red Badge of Courage*, Barnaby Furnas makes paintings and watercolors expressing the chaos and confusion of battle (figs. 15 & 48 and pls. 16–22). Updating the Cubist concept of simultaneity of time and space for the information age, Furnas fills his images of combat and abolitionist John Brown with glowing blood, explosions, and tracer bullets as well as representations of time-lapse movement reminiscent of film and video-game special effects. Depicting this terrible national legacy of violence is cathartic, Furnas says, because it empowers him against his fears. Matthew Day Jackson also illustrates decisive moments in American history but rejects any attempt at synthesis for a more fragmentary, open-ended constellation of images and objects. In the exhibition's new wall-work, *The Garden of Earthly Delights (Spiritual America)* (2008, fig. 16 and pls. 29–36), Jackson combines a wide range of found and recycled materials and mass-media images—including reproductions of unspoiled American landscapes by painter Albert Bierstadt, photographs of astronauts and a black-power protest at the 1968 Olympics, and a vitrine filled with religious and automotive flotsam and jetsam—to create a "webwork" of cultural totems, portentous signs, and symbols the viewer must decipher. Eric Beltz foregrounds his own interests in shamanism, medicinal herbs, and the occult in slyly surreal and subversive drawings of George Washington, Thomas Jefferson, and Benjamin Franklin. Works like *Fuck You Tree* (fig. 1 & pl. 1), a humorous reprise of Grant Wood's sentimental *Parson Weems' Fable* (1939, see fig. 47) showing a stoned Washington sitting on a dismembered cherry tree surrounded by mystical plants and animals, skewer the hagiographies surrounding the nation's Founding Fathers. Jeremy Blake's digitally composed video *Winchester* gives sumptuous form to haunted aspects of America's past (fig. 17 and pls. 4–8). Inspired by the San Jose, California,

house of rifle heiress Sarah Winchester, a labyrinth of sealed rooms and dead-end staircases designed to stave off the spirits of those killed by Winchester guns, Blake's lush, colorful imagery continually morphs. It blends vintage photographs of the house, mysterious cowboy shadows, and Blake's own abstract "digital paintings" to create an engulfing image of a uniquely American form of madness. Tragically, Blake's own life may have come to resemble Sarah Winchester's. Believing themselves to be persecuted by the CIA and Scientologists, Blake committed suicide shortly after his longtime partner Theresa Duncan took her own life in the summer of 2007.

HOME ON THE RANGE

If the alternative history of the country proposed in *The Old, Weird America* teaches us anything, it is that you have merely to scratch the surface of the culture to discover layers of maddening, magical complexity and contradiction. Business, politics, and media may attempt to tamp down or homogenize America's folklife, but the artists in this exhibition bring its anarchic energy—and potential for social change, adventure, and revelation—vividly to life. Perhaps the painters, sculptors, photographers, and draftspeople in this exhibition are such successful translators of the old, weird America because they have so much in common with

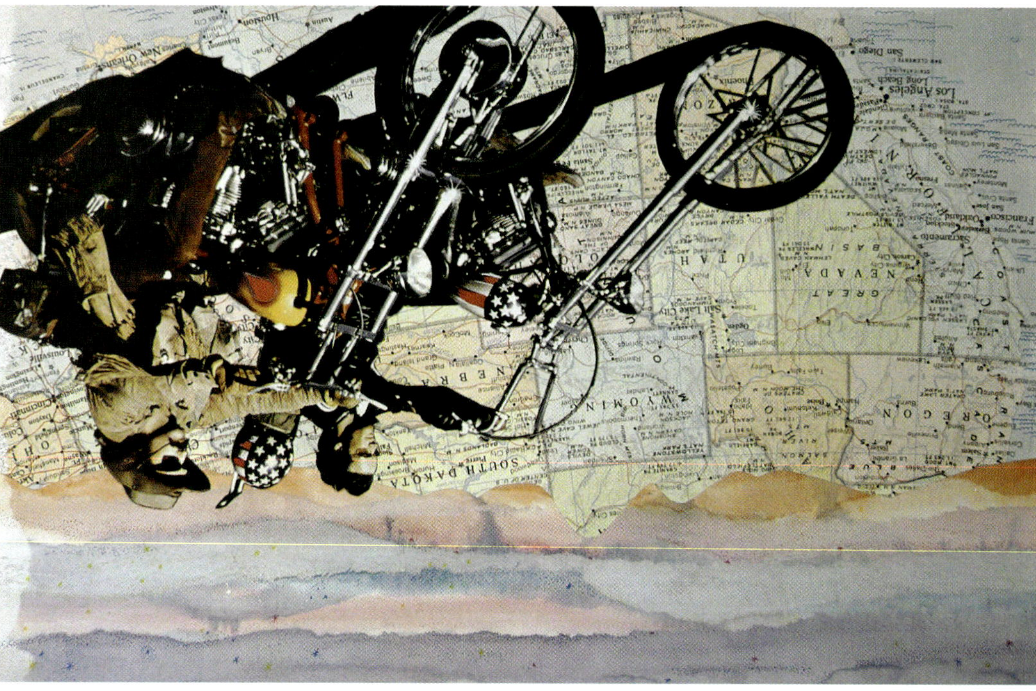

Fig. 16
Matthew Day Jackson
Garden of Earthly Delights (Spiritual America) (detail), 2008
Posters, needlepoint, glass and steel vitrine, wool, paint, C-print, fake taxidermy, wood, blower scoop
180 x 180 x 60 inches (approximately)
Courtesy the artist

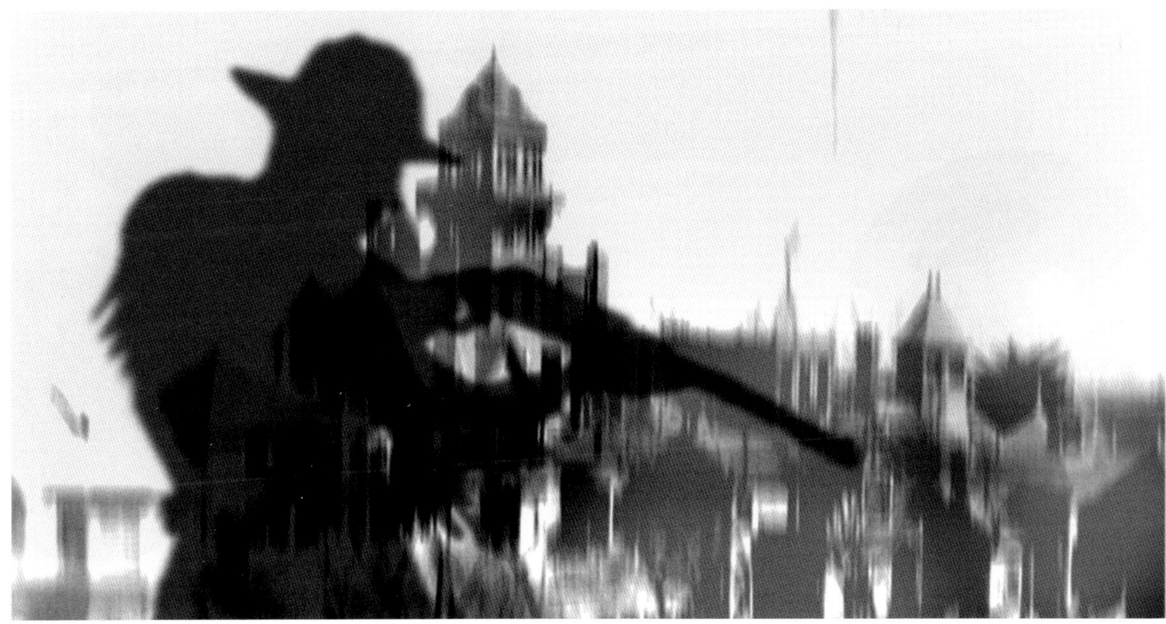

Fig. 17
Jeremy Blake
Video still from *Winchester*,
2002
DVD: color, sound,
18 minutes (continuous loop)
Courtesy Kinz, Tillou +
Feigen, New York

the characters they depict. Each of our earliest ancestors had to put a stake in the ground. They have to feed, clothe, and shelter themselves from scratch, and they also had to stand for something, good or bad. Leading lives of both creation and destruction, they shaped the country's physical and social landscape according to their base drives and high principles. In today's overpopulated, hyperspecialized world, where activism and self-reliance have taken a back seat to production and consumption, it seems as if there is little room for individuals to change the world. In this sense, artists may be the last of the Mohicans. Like pioneers, they must develop a vision and commit themselves to it wholeheartedly. Staking their livelihoods on ideas and images, artists fight for the freedom for alternative visions to be heard and to make a difference. In this exhibition, they stoke the ever-flickering fires of folk culture to shed light on a dim moment in American history. Their visions of the country's mythology may be stranger and less reassuring than what we have grown accustomed to, yet they represent the endless evolution of folklore as its stories are played forward by succeeding generations. This exhibition's inspired, troubling images of an old, weird America remind us that both the salvation and damnation of the nation lies in the hands of its folk.

NOTES

1. William Carlos Williams, "Spring and All," *William Carlos Williams: Selected Poems* (New York: New Directions, 1963), 36.

2. Greil Marcus, *The Old, Weird America: The World of Bob Dylan's Basement Tapes* (New York: Picador, 1997).

3. This definition was developed by Dan Ben-Amos, professor of folklore and Asian and Middle Eastern studies, University of Pennsylvania.

4. Transforming Herder's interest in *das Volk* into a racist obsession, the Nazis celebrated Snow White as an object lesson for Germans seeking Aryan marriage partners, as noted in A. S. Byatt, "Introduction," in *The Annotated Brothers Grimm*, ed. Maria Tatar (New York: W. W. Norton, 2004), xxxviii–xxxix.

5. Marcus, *The Old, Weird America*, 91 and xix, respectively.

6. Gene Bluestein, *The Voice of the Folk* (Amherst: University of Massachusetts Press, 1972), 1.

7. Marcus, *The Old, Weird America*, 20.

8. Simon J. Bronner, *Folk Nation: Folklore in the Creation of American Tradition* (Wilmington, Delaware: Scholarly Resources, 2002), 148.

9. Bluestein, *The Voice of the Folk*, 75.

10. Ibid., 18, 41.

11. R. Serge Denisoff, "The Proletarian Renaissance: The Folkness of Ideological Folk," *The Journal of American Folklore*, vol. 82, no. 323 (January–March, 1969), 63.

12. Greil Marcus, *The Shape of Things to Come: Prophecy and the American Voice* (New York: Farrar, Straus and Giroux, 2006).

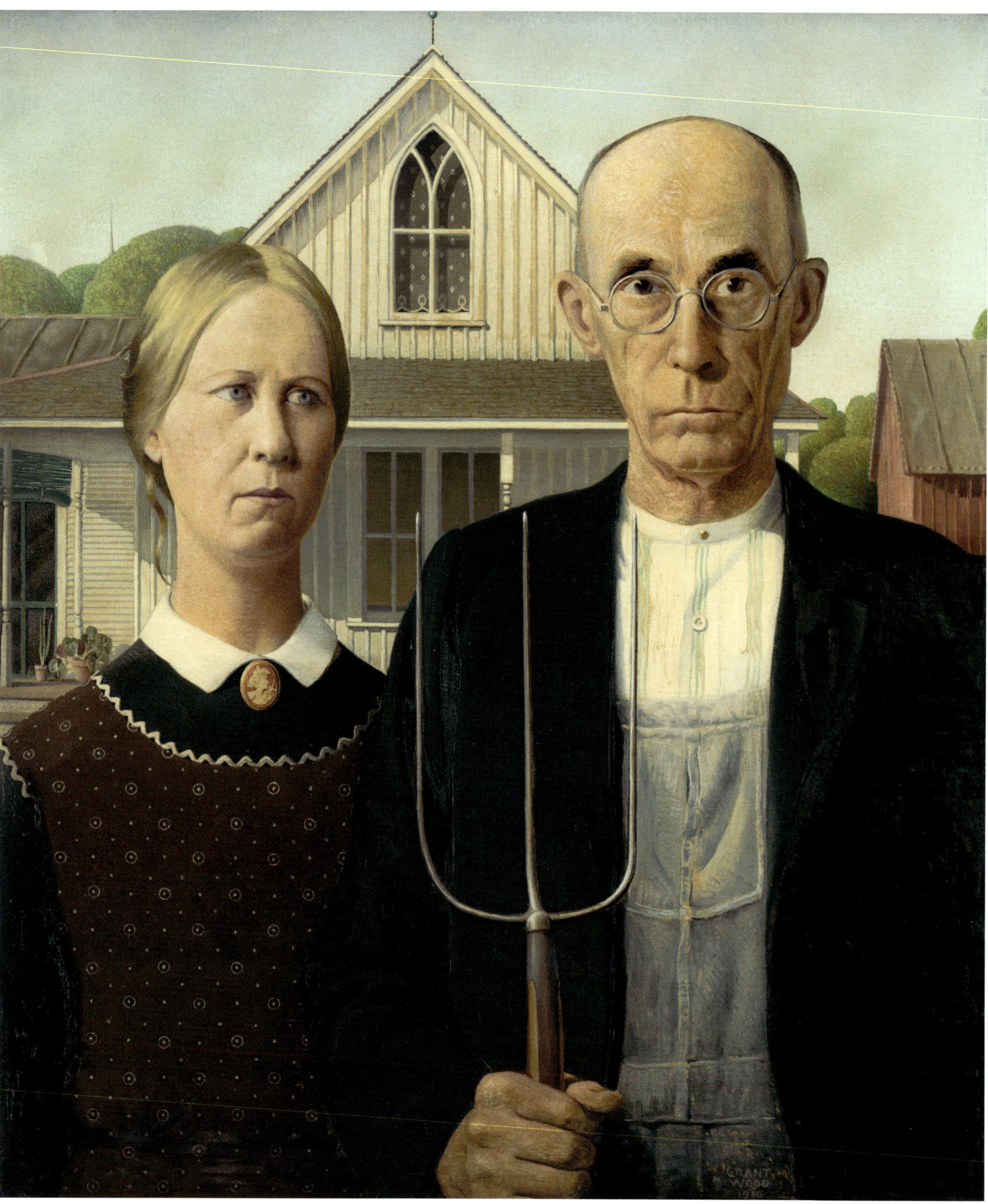

American Soul Underground

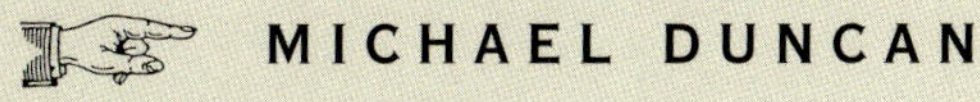

There are two ways of being American: and the chief, says Mr. Williams, is by recoiling into individual smallness and insentience, and gutting the great continent in frenzies of mean fear. It is the Puritan way. The other is by touch; touch America as she is; dare to touch her! And this is the heroic way. And this, this sensitive touch upon the unseen America, is to be the really great adventure in the New World.

—D. H. Lawrence,
review of William Carlos Williams's
In the American Grain,
The Nation, April 14, 1926[1]

Fig. 18
Grant Wood
American Gothic, 1930
Oil on beaverboard
30⅞ x 25⅝ inches
The Art Institute of Chicago,
Friends of American Art Collection, 1930.934
Art © Estate of Grant Wood/
Licensed by VAGA, New York,
NY. *American Gothic*, 1930, by
Grant Wood. All rights reserved by
the Estate of Nan Wood Graham

In the Bush era, discussion of distinctly American art has become a cringe-worthy endeavor.

The nation's reputation and identity have been sullied by a suspect war and an administration indifferent to many of the ideas and values inherent in the establishment of the American democracy. The erosion of individual rights, skewing of the balance of power, and subtle disintegration of the separation of church and state have caused the country to lose much of the rest of the world's respect.

At the same time, stoked by the rhetoric of globalism, curators and historians have begun to question the effects on artists of national identity. The curators of the 2006 Biennial at the Whitney Museum of American Art justified their show's inclusion of artists who live outside the U.S. by arguing for the "geographical fluidity" of today's artists and curators, pointing as precedent to the Euro-American activities of Marcel Duchamp.[2]

But globalism too has begun to lose its luster. Post-9/11 security measures have made international travel neither as easy nor as glamorous as it used to be. Violent sectarianism continually questions the very notion of one-world idealism—even in the production and exhibition of art. Critics have objected to the uniform rosters of international biennials that choose their participants from a market-sanctioned A-list of artists—most of whom have studios both in far-flung homelands and London, Berlin, or New York. The recent market explosion of derivative contemporary Chinese art has confirmed suspicions that the new global inclusiveness only seeks to confirm western tastes.

Never accessible to more than an elite, the sanctioned global art world seems to be fracturing. At first hailed as a unifying factor in the viewing of new art, the internet is increasingly becoming the promoter of niche audiences and cult specificity. Reacting against the predominant Euro-American esthetic, many emerging Third-World artists are now making works that refer or apply to their own specific communities.[3] As a reaction to and commentary upon this state of affairs, it seems only logical that artists might again investigate the notion of national identity.

Throughout the last century—up to the present—the attempt by artists to investigate "Americanism" has been praised and scorned, variously caught up in stylistic wars, political rhetoric, and the global art market. In his 1935 manifesto "Revolt Against the City," American Scene painter Grant Wood cited writer and photographer Carl Van Vechten's statement that America rediscovers itself every thirty years or so:

> About once in each generation, directed by political or economic or artistic impulses, we have reevaluated or reinterpreted ourselves. It happened in 1776, of course, and again a generation later with the Louisiana Purchase and subsequent explorations and the beginnings of a national literature. It came again with the expansion of the Jacksonian era in the eighteen-thirties, accompanied by a literary flowering not only in New England but in various frontier regions. It was marked in the period immediately after our Civil War, when Emerson observed that a new map of America had been unrolled before us. In the expansionist period at the turn of the century, shortly after the Spanish War when the United States found herself a full-fledged world power, we had a new discovery of resources and values. And now, with another thirty-year cycle, it comes again. It is always slightly different, always complex in its causes and phenomena; but happily it is always enlightening.[4]

Wood was promoting his era's burst of interest in self-conscious Americana—evident, as we can see now, in WPA depictions of historical incidents and folk legends; the home-spun scenes of Wood, Thomas Hart Benton (fig. 19), and John Steuart Curry; the first exhibitions of folk art at the Whitney Museum and Museum of Modern Art; the folk music documentation of John and Alan Lomax; and James Agee and Walker Evans's *Let Us Now Praise Famous Men*.[5]

Following Wood and Van Vechten's cyclical line of thinking, World War II displaced this introspection, encouraging an international consciousness and discouraging any sense of American folk identity in light of the nationalistic bluster of Nazi Germany and Imperial Japan. The young H. W. Janson, in fact, issued a critical attack on American Scene painters Wood and Benton in 1946, claiming their mythologizing treatment of the heartland provided a stepping-stone for fascism.[6] The American Scene movement was soon forgotten in favor of abstract expressionism which became an international style.

In the next cycle, the beat and hippie movements of the 1950s and 1960s rekindled interest in folk traditions as a reaction to the postwar conformity and industrial expansion of the Eisenhower era. Artists and writers like Jack Kerouac, Allen Ginsberg (fig. 20), Wallace Berman, Bruce Conner, and Bob Dylan vehemently reexamined the values and mythos of the American experience. Nearly three decades have followed, marked by political disillusion, yuppie consumerism, Enron corruption, the corporate global economy, and pointless Bush-era wars. And now the time again seems right for another wave of interest in Americanism—evident in the works of this exhibition by contemporary artists.

Fig. 19
Thomas Hart Benton
Achelous and Hercules, 1947
Tempera and oil on canvas, mounted on plywood
62 7/8 x 264 1/8 inches
Smithsonian American Art Museum, Washington, D.C. Photograph: Smithsonian American Art Museum/ Art Resource, New York
Art © T. H. Benton and R. P. Benton Testamentary Trusts/UMB Bank Trustee/Licensed by VAGA, New York, N.Y.

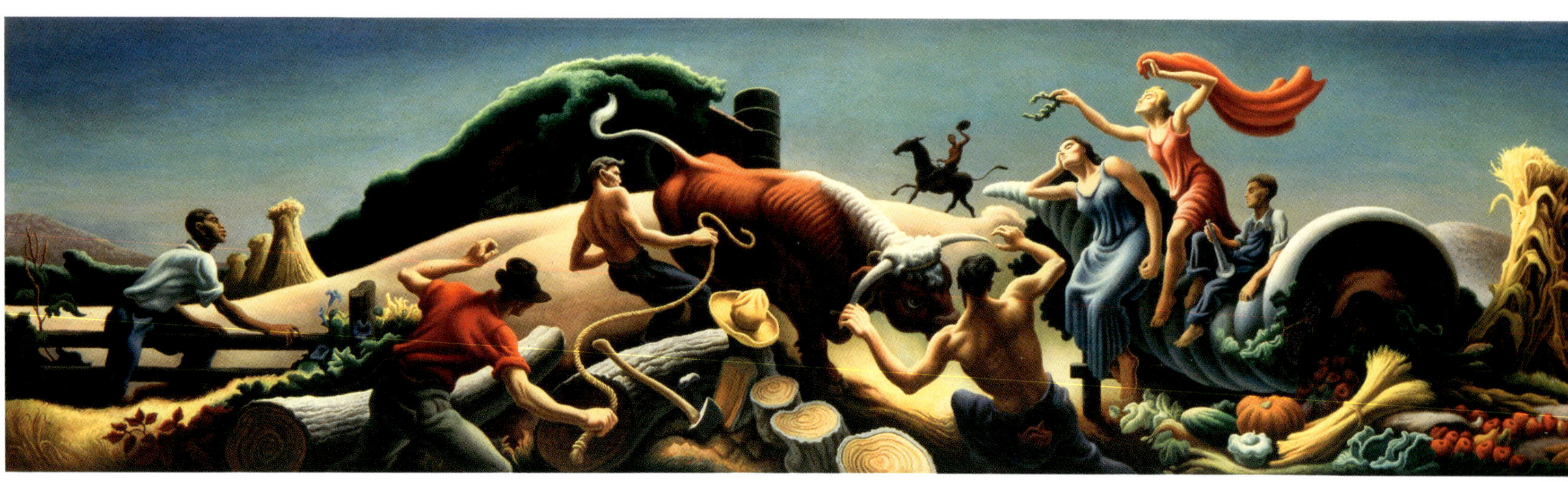

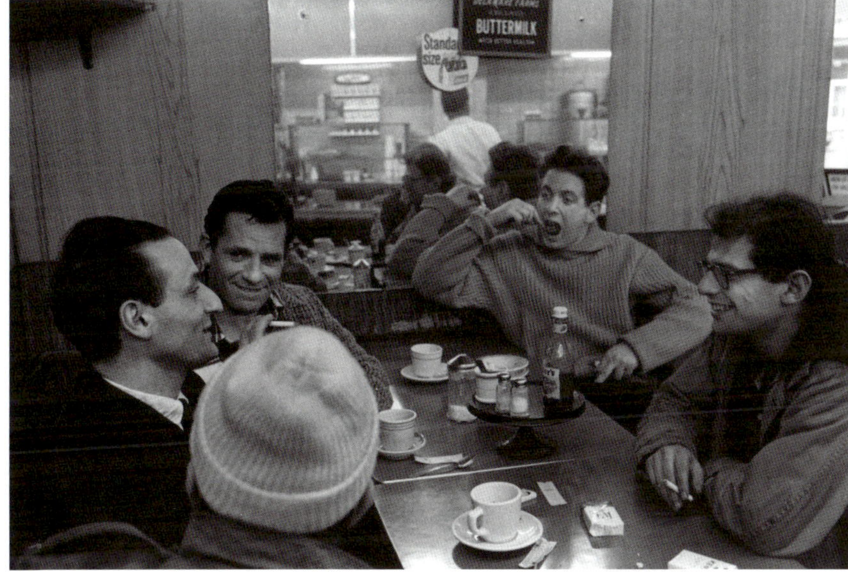

Fig. 20
John Cohen
Larry Rivers, Jack Kerouac,
Gregory Corso (back to camera),
David Amram, and Allen
Ginsburg, New York, 1957
Gelatin silver print
11 x 14 inches
© John Cohen/Getty Images

today, given the country's moral, civic, and ethical de-
cline. Yet for a variety of reasons the culture seems
largely blocked from deep self-analysis. The profound
contradictions inherent in American identity require a
kind of poetic understanding and sympathy that seem to
be no longer sanctioned in the age of political correctness
and the sound bite. Decades of emphasis on formal
analysis in art and the psychoanalytic deconstruction of
the author's voice have distanced readers and viewers
from the content and subject matter of art and literature. The complexities of the American spirit have tra-
ditionally been mirrored in the great works of American
fiction, exposed in the tortured psyches of characters
like Melville's Ahab, Hawthorne's Dimmesdale, Fitz-
gerald's Gatsby, and Faulkner's Sutpen. Although wildly
varied and infinitely complex, their tragic fates all might
be said to result from faith in the freedoms espoused by
a republic oblivious of its roots in land-grabbing, genocide, slavery, and sexual repression.

Furthermore, the slippery and troublesome nature
of Americanism seems rooted in the impossible notion
of a democracy dedicated at the same time to both individual rights and the common good. As Greil Marcus
states in *The Shape of Things to Come: Prophecy and the
American Voice* (2006),

> The promises made in the Declaration of Independ-
> ence and the Constitution—the promise that all would
> find themselves free to say what they had to say, the guar-
> antee of equal justice under law, that governments were

formed to respect and protect those rights, that citizens
owed governments no respect if they did not—were so
great that their betrayal has become part of the promise.[7]

Marcus tracks the way that the nation's "great sense
of experiment, of preordained defeat" has sparked certain maverick contemporary artists to try to find a public
voice—no matter how individualistic. In analyzing the
recent dark novels of Philip Roth, Marcus asserts that

> . . . the secrets that lie at the root of American identity tell
> the story of how the burden of creating a new nation, a
> new society, has shifted into the thrilling, terrifying obli-
> gation to create a new self. That obligation in turn shifts
> back to the social: it shifts into the obligation to connect
> the personal drama to the nation's drama, so that the story
> becomes at once specific and shared, perverse and com-
> mon, the outcast the insider.[8]

Marcus's analysis of the way Americans have inter-
nalized the contradictions of their culture follows in the
vein of D. H. Lawrence's *Studies in Classic American Literature* (1923) and William Carlos Williams's *In the American Grain* (1925), perhaps the last century's two most
trenchant, poetic, and tough-minded assessments of the
American character. In Lawrence's mystical-psycholog-
ical vision, indigenous New World "demons" must exact
a deadly—or deadening—poetic justice from any American cultural effort that seeks to combine the "spiritual"
with the "white." The very concept of the American
spirit exacts an impossibly heavy toll, one that must
contend with the inestimable psychic losses of the slave

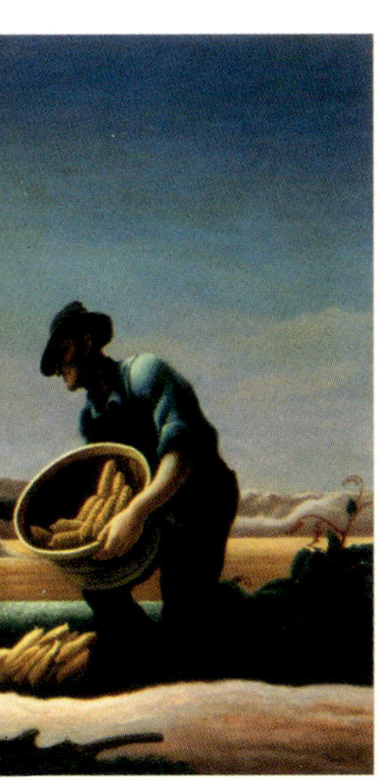

ship, auction yard, buffalo field, and tribal reservation. Taken particularly with the psychic fallout of the great novels of Hawthorne and Melville, Lawrence saw the tendency of the Puritan-bred soul to become "hard, isolate, stoic, and a killer."[9]

Williams similarly groped for a way to break the deeply rooted stranglehold of Puritanical repression, seeking to rekindle the spirit lost in the annihilation of Native American cultures such as that of Montezuma's Tenochtitlan. Williams attempted to circumvent that kind of spiritual roadblock by resurrecting the development of an authentic American culture. As Williams stated, "All that will be new in America will be anti-Puritan."[10]

Culling through personal accounts of the continent's early explorers, politicians, and writers, Williams called for a new structure of historical myth—one including the quirky Aaron Burr rather than the stodgy George Washington; the humane Jesuit priest Père Rasles rather than the paranoid Cotton Mather. The descent into authenticity that Williams sought represents a darker American Romanticism than that of Emerson and Whitman, one that, he readily would admit, could as yet only be dimly envisioned: "However hopeless it may seem, we have no other choice: we must go back to the beginning; it must all be done over; everything that is must be destroyed."[11]

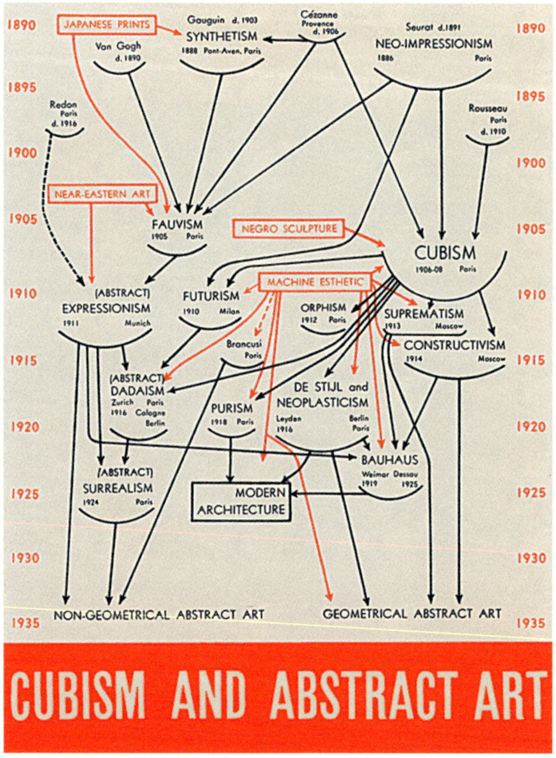

A return-to-beginnings is perhaps the key impetus of Modernism, manifested in the stylistic and thematic breakdown of the conventions of nineteenth-century French salon painting and the espousal of tribal and primitive art by artists like Picasso and Brancusi. It might be argued that the most truly "American" artists of the past century are formal iconoclasts like Pollock, de Kooning, Warhol, and Rauschenberg who expanded the stylistic parameters of art.

According to Alfred Barr Jr.'s now infamous flowchart of "isms" featured in the catalogue for the 1936 Museum of Modern Art show *Cubism & Abstract Art* (fig. 21), the last century began under the sway of Neo-Impressionism and Syntheticism with Fauvism, Analytical Cubism, and Futurism just on the horizon. Art history textbooks have followed Barr's lead, chronicling the "triumph" of postwar American abstract expressionism followed by a succession of formal movements largely starring American artists: Pop, Minimalism, Earth Art, performance, Conceptual art. Works that haven't fit or foretold those categories have been swept under the carpet, duly confined to museum backrooms and basements.

In his 1951 autobiography, Williams recalled his objections to T. S. Eliot's wholehearted embrace of European myth and culture in *The Waste Land* (1923), "Critically Eliot returned us to the classroom just at the moment when I felt we were on the point of an escape to matters much closer to the essence of a new art form itself—rooted in the locality which should give it fruit. I knew at once that in certain ways I was most defeated."[12]

Williams encouraged the development of American themes in the work of his peers. He praised, for example, artist Charles Sheeler's collection of Shaker furniture, appreciating its appearance in Sheeler's paintings as a way "to transfer values into a new context, to make a poem again (see fig. 38)."[13] Williams's desire for an indigenous American art was manifested in his own works, most notably in the epic poem *Paterson* (1946–1958), which used the fragmented history and immediate local color of a New Jersey small town to get at the essence of American place. However, for American artists like Williams who were interested in art "rooted in locality," it has been an uphill battle.

Party-line art history gives no berth to something as evasive and contradictory as investigations of the American soul. An alternate way to approach the art of the past century is to examine the undercurrent of artists who have directly addressed American themes. These

Fig. 21
Cover of exhibition catalogue, *Cubism and Abstract Art*, 1936, diagram by Alfred J. Barr Jr. © Museum of Modern Art, New York

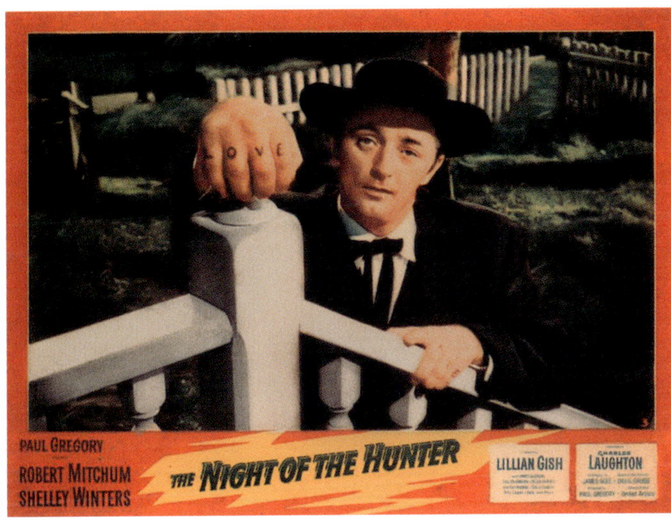

Fig. 22
Lobby card for *The Night of the Hunter*, 1955, featuring Robert Mitchum.
© United Artists

figures have delved into the country's psyche, tweaking and critiquing false values in order to assert more palatable mythologies. Reaching beyond the platitudes and easy fixes of social realism and political correctness, these maverick visions have yet to be closely examined or celebrated.

A QUIRKY YET DEFINING TOUCHSTONE FOR THIS

art lies in American folk music, perhaps best surveyed in Harry Smith's *Anthology of American Folk Music*, a 1952 three-volume compilation of twenties and thirties recordings.[14] The "Anthology" was culled from Smith's massive 78 RPM record collection of traditional songs originally recorded between 1927 and 1932, including a wide variety of mostly rural music, juxtaposing country blues, Cajun instrumentals, English-derived ballads, hillbilly yodels, topical novelty songs, and Southern gospel hymns and shouts.[15]

With an ear for off-kilter, unique performances, Smith brought together songs featuring gratuitous murders, deep-seated jealousies, self-destructive passions, sexual boasts, and oddball confessions. The extensive discography and bibliography in the booklet Smith wrote for the Anthology traces the folk origins of each of the songs; its "Alphabetical Index" also catalogues the songs' common themes and references, such as "Dreams mentioned on record" (4 entries), "Law mentioned on record" (13 entries), and "Death mentioned on record" (26 entries). Like a field anthropologist, Smith provides data and case studies ripe for cultural theory.

Fraught with haunted visions, seemingly ancient warblings, and stories of primal violence, the Anthology lives up to the mythic schema Smith provided for it—one reflecting the values and nature of what Greil Marcus has dubbed "The Old, Weird America." Smith's thematic sequencing downplayed differences among genres and ethnic groups. The booklet's commentary in fact completely avoided mention of the performers' race. Smith mischievously reported in a 1968 interview, "It took years before anybody discovered that Mississippi John Hurt wasn't a hillbilly."[16]

Mixing grim goings-on and unflappable silliness, the Anthology as a whole conjures an American past of stubborn individuality, quirky humor and unpredictable violence, insisting at the height of the bland Eisenhower era that, as Marcus put it, "against every assurance to the contrary, America was itself a mystery."[17] Weaving its themes of betrayal, economic obsolescence, and sexual longing into a kind of *Überlied*, Smith's work stands as an impassioned, darkly lyrical portrait of the national psyche.

The rough-hewn spirit of the Anthology's songs has been manifested in a variety of works from the past century—to name only a few particularly trenchant postwar examples from literature, film, and music: the short stories of Flannery O'Connor and Eudora Welty, Charles Laughton & James Agee's *Night of the Hunter* (1955, fig. 22), Arthur Penn's *Bonnie & Clyde* (1964), Ishmael Reed's *Mumbo Jumbo* (1972), Terrence Malick's *Gates of Heaven* (1980), Marilynne Robinson's *Housekeeping* (1981), Bob Dylan & The Band's *The Basement Tapes* (1967, released 1975), and Dylan's *Love & Theft* (2006).

In the visual arts—given the critical emphasis on form over content—work of this ilk has emerged less frequently, seemingly almost underground. The artists who have pursued a spiritual reading of the nation have done so in wildly independent fashion, without guideposts or immediate mentors. Marcus refers to the artists he writes about in *The Shape of Things* as "solitaries" which seems an apt way to refer to these maverick American sensibilities.[18]

It is obviously beyond the scope of this essay to provide a history of this kind of American art. Yet, as a complement to this exhibition, it seems pertinent to point to a few select works from the past century that tap this spirit. Burrowing into a deeper sense of place, these works all were made against the grain of the larger culture. Their approaches to American myths vary wildly, from the oblique to the direct, from a sense of reverence to scathing satire. What is shared, however, is a desire to go beyond the platitudes of mass media to touch the workings of the American soul.

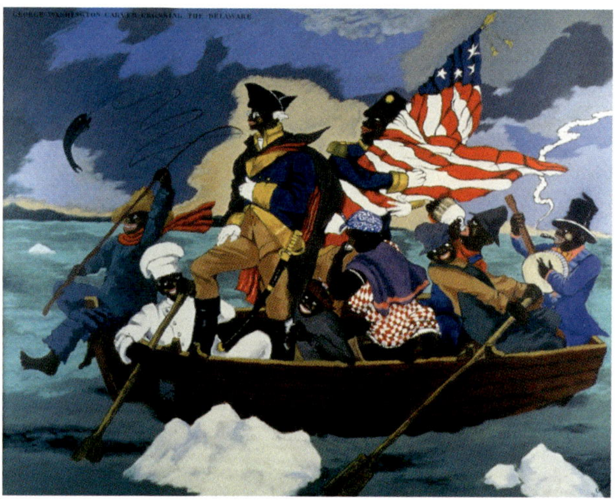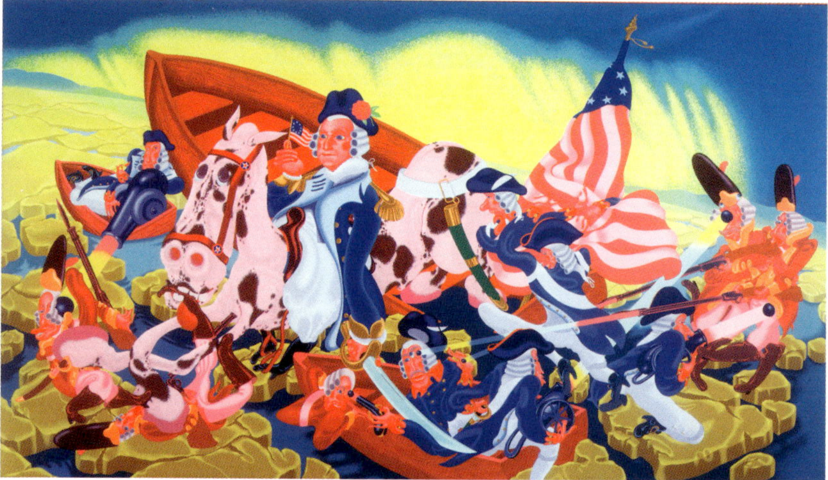

Fig. 23
Robert Colescott
George Washington Carver Crossing the Delaware: Page from an American History Textbook, 1975
Acrylic on canvas
84 x 108 inches
Collection Robert H. Orchard, St. Louis, Missouri.
Photograph courtesy Phyllis Kind Gallery, New York

Fig. 24
Peter Saul
Washington Crossing the Delaware, 1975
Acrylic on canvas
89 × 151 inches
Private collection
Photograph courtesy George Adams Gallery, New York

THE AMERICAN SCENE PAINTERS GAINED ATTENTION for their self-conscious, homespun renditions of the heartland, achieving widespread recognition with *Time* magazine's 1934 cover story on Thomas Hart Benton. But by the late thirties, the movement had taken severe critical hits, first from the Right, then the Left, and Benton nailed the coffin with a series of loud homophobic diatribes against the museum establishment. The group has been largely ignored by art historians until only recently.[19]

Ironically, a fair share of the renewed interest in the American Scene painters has stemmed from revelations of *American Gothic* painter Grant Wood's hidden homosexuality. Since the death of Wood's litigious, overly protective sister Nan in 1990, it has been revealed that allegations about his sexual preference played a major factor in the loss of his teaching job at the University of Iowa in 1941—only a year before his premature death from cancer at age 50.[20] Wood's homosexuality changes the understanding and implications of his work. As cultural commentator John Seery has brilliantly stated, looking at *American Gothic* (1930) as a painting by a deeply closeted sexual outsider invites a host of new readings:

> What was once a cartoonlike painting about work, family, and religion now becomes a scandal possibly involving hypocrisy, repression, and denial, and even abuse, incest, violence, devilishness, gender terror, and at the least, threatening body language. The woman's averted eyes now tell an untold story, and the man's defiant stance no longer looks like straightforward American self-reliance in the face of dashed dreams. On second view, the pitchfork becomes menacing, not just an emblem of rural living and a work ethos clinging to a premechanized era. The black Sunday jacket starts to disturb. Play the painting backward, scratch the surface, and the "Gothic" elements start to look quite devilish, now suggesting yet another pun: these are "Goth" people—coarse, uncivilized, and maybe even barbarous. Exceeding its representational limits, the painting reproduces the experience of, and the difficulties in talking about one's family secrets in public. I would prefer, however, to see and talk about those shortcomings, those unspoken and virtually unspeakable sexual and gender conflicts, as a *national* issue, an American Gothic story, and not simply as a local Iowa concern.[21]

Despite his folksy, overalls-wearing persona, Wood lived at odds with the mainstream values of his Iowa community. His public life and his art were about myth-making, and he consciously came to see himself as a kind of fabulist showman. Set in an idyllic folk-art-like Colonial backyard, one of Wood's last great paintings, *Parson Weems' Fable* (1939, see fig. 47), is an iconic depiction of the young George Washington confessing his tree-chopping sin to his father. In a proto-postmodern touch, the scene is framed by curtains, in front of which stands the writer Parson Weems, the man who invented the mythical cherry tree incident for his wildly popular, fanciful biography of Washington in 1800. Standing bolt upright, Weems betrays the hint of a mischievous smile, pointing with his finger to the boy, whose face Wood has surreally rendered with a mask of the adult Washington, appropriated from the well-known Gilbert Stuart portrait. Weems seems Wood's stand-in, aware of his role as a theatrical manipulator and myth-maker. Furthering the picture's ironies, Wood depicts an idealized black man and woman in the background who blithely harvest cherries without damaging a tree, oblivious of both the myth-making and debunking of the future First President. As possessions of the slave-holding Washington family, they are merely background players—prey to the bigger lies and myths of America.

Wood's subtly caustic allusion to race in regard to Washington presages the more in-your-face satire of Robert Colescott's *George Washington Carver Crossing the Delaware: Page from an American History Textbook* (1975, fig. 23), a bicentennial-ready parody of the 1851 history painting of the first President by Dusseldorf-trained artist Emanuel Leutze. Mixing characters who are the pride and shame of the African-American history book, Colescott presents the bespectacled scientist/role-model as the captain of a crew of black stereotypes that includes a banjo-picking minstrel, a shoe-shine boy, and Aunt Jemina—who is giving head to Carver's flag-hugging lieutenant. Colescott ridicules both avatars and stigmas on this ship of clichéd black identity. Throughout his career he has chucked the whole notion of role-models and stereotypes, reshaping art history to suit his wholly individualistic viewpoint. Colescott milks the old stories and myths of America for their emotional juice, using them to turn racial myths inside out and to promote a more cosmopolitan notion of identity.

In perverse narratives founded on historical events, art history, and mythology, fellow satirical artist Peter Saul has revealed the lust, greed, envy, gluttony, pride, sloth, and wrath that have made America the disgraced superpower it is today.[22] Aiming for the jugular, he renders his subjects as caricatures, with a special emphasis on race and gender. Mocking left-wing platitudes at the same time as attacking racism, sexism, and capitalist exploitation, his works depict politics as a melodrama of victimization and exploitation. The persecution of blacks, electrocution of serial killers, annihilation of Vietnam, oppression of women, and abuse of artists by critics are all struggles within a sadomasochistic system that thrives on the oblivious dominance of power and the hapless martyrdom of the oppressed.

In his whipped-up retelling of *George Washington Crossing the Delaware* (1975, fig. 24), the First President's rowboat has capsized while he rides horseback across the ice floes, his men scattered in a frenzied battle against attacking British soldiers. Waving a tiny flag, he scampers across the river, oblivious to the chaotic stew of gunfire and mangled bodies around him. In Saul's three versions of *Custer's Last Stand* (1972, 1974, and 1989) the artist seems to relish the Indian massacre of the U.S. cavalry led by the bumbling Custer, tapping into the defeat's significance as an enduring symbol of white guilt and expatiation over the decimation of the Native American people.[23] This perverse "feel good" depiction of slaughter is the kind of subject matter that Saul particularly loves. He intends to provoke P.C. squeamishness in regards to race and gender, in narratives rendered in the most lurid manner imaginable.

Saul can transform certain American current events into soul-crushing exposés. *Bush at Abu Ghraib* (2006, fig. 25) presents the President in a snapshot pose like those of the infamous prison guards, mugging for Laura and the twins á la Alfred E. Neuman while humiliating a prisoner whose face is a tortured scramble of misplaced features, open wounds, and bullet holes. "What me worry?" George W. seems to ask as he sticks his finger up the nose of his prey. Portrayed as Bush sees him, the monstrous disfigured prisoner reflects the extremity of Bush's deep-seated racism and family grudge. Saul shows us the enemy as our warmongers see them and asks which of these two is really the monstrous other.

The painting can be seen as an update of Grant Wood's *American Gothic* in which the self-conscious dignity of the rural couple has been replaced by sadistic obliviousness and exploitation. Wood's commentary on American values is morphed into Saul's bitter exposé of moral bankruptcy. The farmer's pitchfork has become Bush's finger up the nose. In his darkly satiric treatment of the twisted values of America, Saul seems a contemporary heir to the

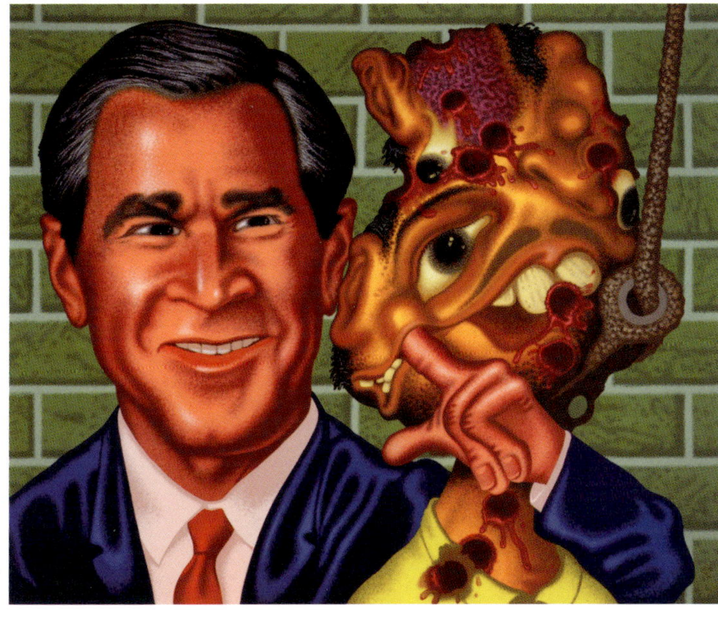

Fig. 25
Peter Saul
Bush at Abu Ghraib, 2006
Acrylic on canvas
78 × 90 inches
Private collection, Connecticut, courtesy David Nolan Gallery. Photograph: Kevin Noble, New York, courtesy David Nolan Gallery

nationalistic concerns of the American Scene painters. Like them, he has self-consciously attempted to grapple with particularized American subject matter and to shape outsider recognition of American themes.

Another rare voice of rectitude in today's art world, Los Angeles artist Llyn Foulkes confronts the demons of American culture head-on and comes out kicking. Earnest and theatrical, he conveys a dark vision of American culture in trouble. Walt Disney has been Foulkes's bête noire, targeted as a symbol of conformity and aesthetic mediocrity. Assuming a kind of personal responsibility for the skewed values of American culture, Foulkes has cast himself in a variety of mythic pop-culture roles as the defeated hero. In the loopy but frightening allegory *The Last Outpost* (1983), for example, Foulkes's stand-in, the fifties TV character, the Lone Ranger, has been gunned down, lying prostrate before a homesteader woman with the head of Mickey Mouse.

The astonishing *The Lost Frontier* (1997–2005, fig. 26), is Foulkes's masterpiece, an 8-foot-tall, mixed medium painted relief on plywood panel that depicts a bleak Los Angeles skyline and the city's ruinous basin as viewed from the outlying hills. Old tires, garbage, animal corpses and the charred remains of fires litter the vista, which is expertly rendered in thick trompe-l'oeil relief. The trashed landscape, skillfully constructed from bits of smashed or carved plywood and found materials, powerfully conveys the consequences of an urban society run totally amok.

Presiding on a distant hilltop is the figure of a shotgun-toting frontier woman with the head of Mickey Mouse—Foulkes's symbol of corporate brainwashing. In the lower left corner, a forlorn Indian crouching next to an empty basket references the indigenous people of the region, now forgotten. The attention of a rear-viewed male figure in the foreground has been diverted from the rubble stretching out before him by a small, blank television screen. *The Lost Frontier* takes us out of the suburban living room to depict the monstrous city as a whole. With its shimmering light and sense of sublime vastness, this commanding work invokes a new kind of *terribilità*, born of waste, hubris and human indifference.

With a contrasting tone to the direct punches of Colescott, Saul, and Foulkes, the finely rendered, out-of-kilter tableaux common to the style known as magic realism offer a more subtle way to get at the complexities of the American spirit.[24] Structured like a Renaissance altarpiece, the five-part epic painting *Tribute to the American*

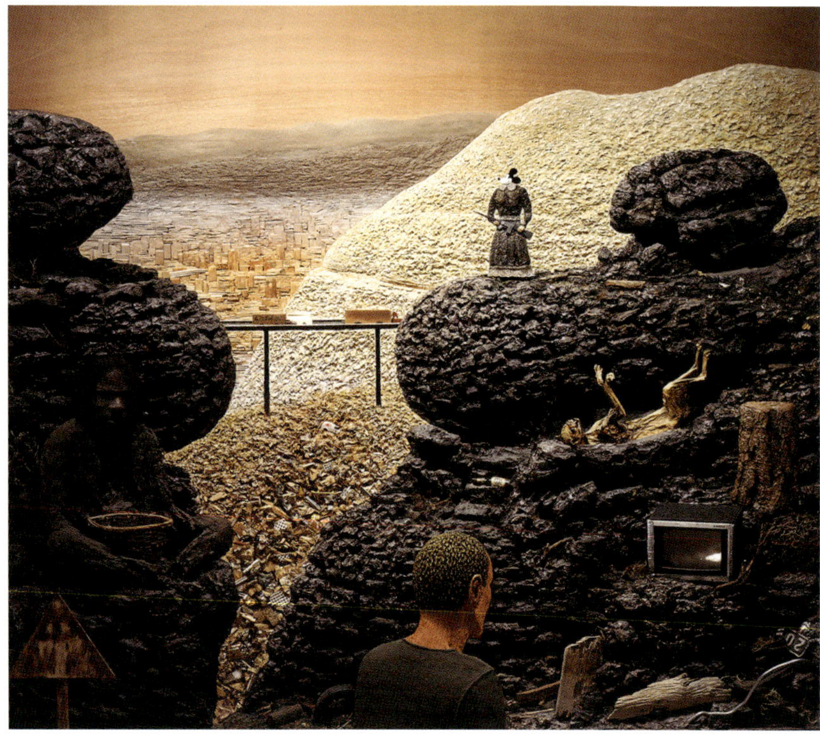

Fig. 26
Llyn Foulkes
The Lost Frontier, 1997–2005
Mixed media on wood panel
87 x 96 x 8 inches
Photograph courtesy the artist
and Kent Gallery, New York

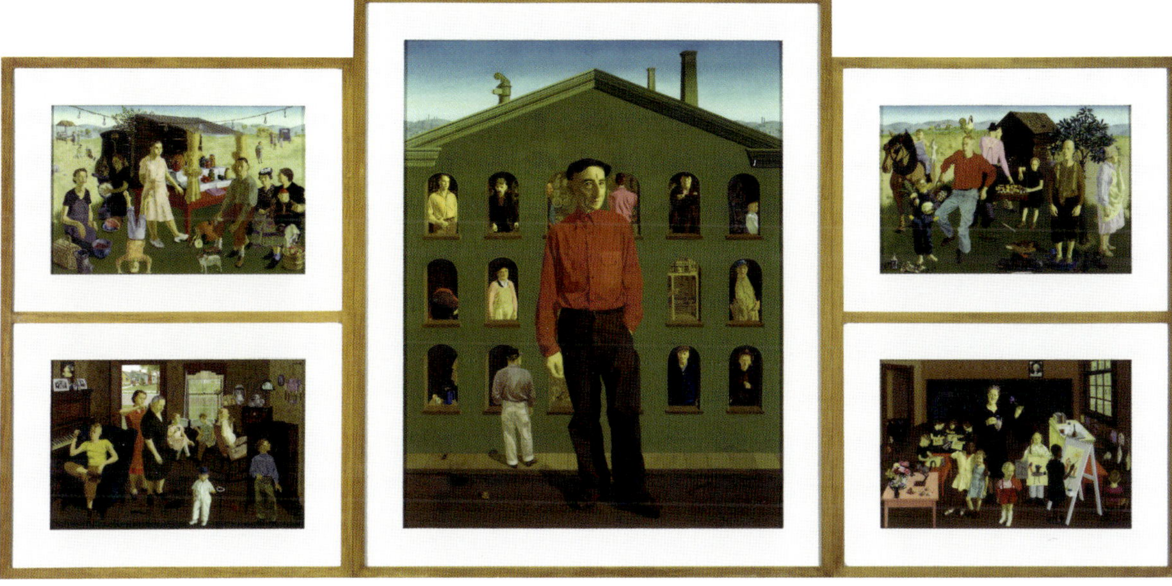

Working People (1946–1951, fig. 27) by the vastly underrated painter Honoré Sharrer presents precisely articulated scenes of everyday life and play, featuring a crowd of isolated American workers and farmers, each consumed by his or her own worries or desires. Odd groupings and surreal details—a goofy-looking young boy with corn coming out of his pockets, a farmer dancing with a rooster on his head—skew any notion here of the homespun or sentimental. Art historian Erika Doss has shown how the off-the-cuff poses of FSA photographs of working people inspired *Tribute*'s overall sense of anomie as well as its unsettling details. Emanating what Doss calls "a sense of dehumanization and ennui,"[25] Sharrer's *Tribute* was also able to transcend the pedestrian social realism of the time in its emphasis on women's work and the nurturing role of women in the workplace.

For the past five decades, Sharrer has continued to astound and confound viewers with elliptical, loosely allegorical paintings that are both comic and deeply disturbing. Taking its title from the lyrics of "The Banks of the Ohio," an early American ballad best known from a 1936 recording by the Blue Sky Boys included in Harry Smith's Anthology, Sharrer's painting *Don't Murder Me, I'm Not Ready for Eternity* (1985, fig. 28) depicts a plain country woman standing on a bleak small town sidewalk executed in perspective that leads into the last glow of a burning sunset.

In the song, the Blue Sky Boys frighteningly chronicle—in tight harmony and a twang free of emotion—the brutal murder of a girl who dares to turn down the marriage proposal of the coolly psychotic Willie.[26] Rather than illustrating the song's grim story, Sharrer opts for more oblique allegory. Holding a black apron to her lips, Sharrer's woman winces, clenching tight her eyes, bracing herself for disaster. Bad omens abound on the otherwise deserted Hopper-esque street: a simple dining chair flies topsy-turvy as if tossed in a brawl, a drawer discarded on the sidewalk holds a bottle of medicine or poison, a cup and spoon lie nearby. Perched on the drawer, a bold-eyed giant owl with fierce talons presides, not quite ready to make his move.

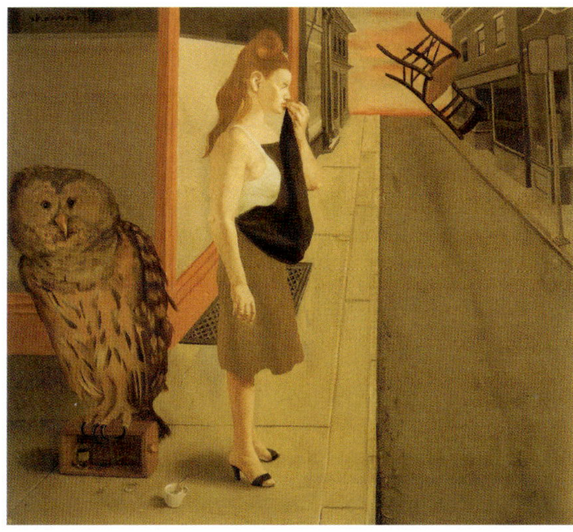

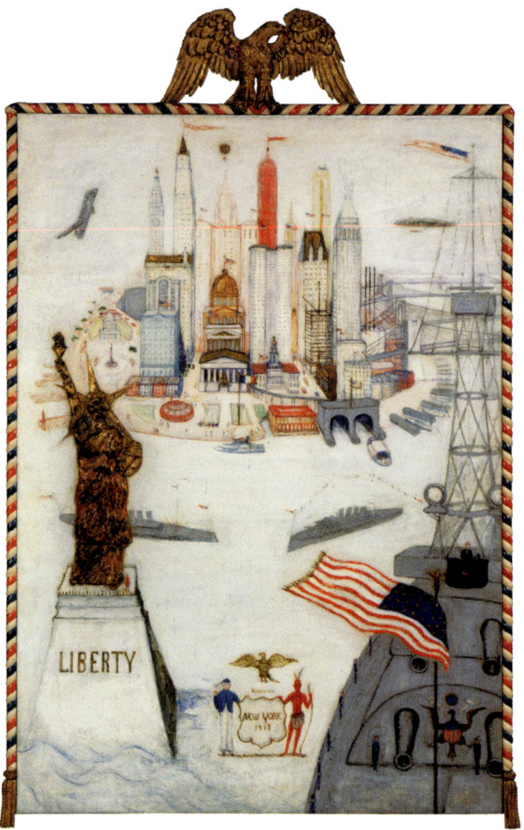

Fig. 29
Florine Stettheimer
New York/Liberty, 1918
Oil on canvas
60 x 42 inches
Collection William Kelly
Simpson, New York.
Photograph: Jerry L.
Thompson

Fig. 30
Florine Stettheimer
The Cathedrals of Broadway,
1929
Oil on canvas
60⅛ x 50⅛ inches
The Metropolitan Museum
of Art, New York, Gift of
Ettie Stettheimer, 1953

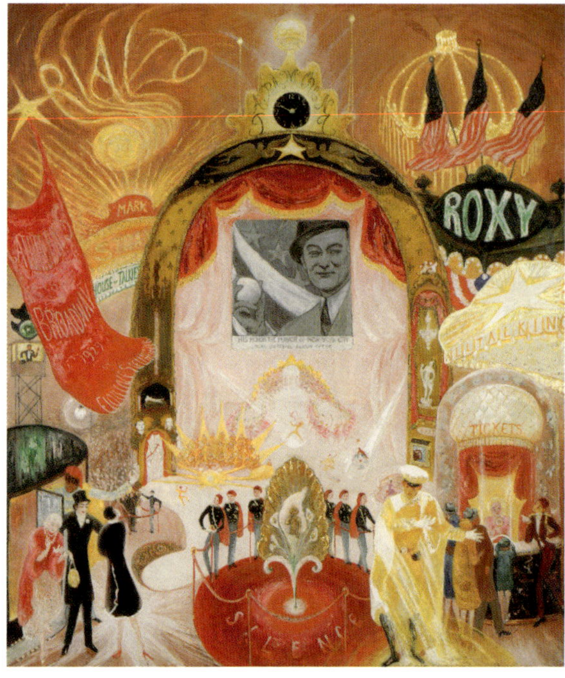

SOCIAL CRITIQUE AND BLEAK VISIONS ARE NOT THE only routes to the American spirit. The *Anthology of Folk Music* included not just ballads about murder and revenge but also songs of perverse celebration, hope, and ecstatic desire.[27] Standing as an alternate voice amongst all the alternate American voices of the last century is Florine Stettheimer whose candy-colored visions describe a hyper-decorated idealized nation of fireworks, department store sales, lounging swimmers, and Broadway openings. Although her uptown fantasies might seem a long way from the downbeat world of folk music, her sensibility taps a kind of quintessential American innocence and idealism.

A sophisticated modernist and virtuosic painter who transgressed expectations about color, composition, gender, portraiture, content, and tone, Stettheimer created a hyper-decorated world, populated by family and friends and set in a bustling Manhattan. Coming into her own after World War I, she and her sisters cultivated the cream of New York's bohemian set, entertaining in their uptown salon the likes of Duchamp, Nadelman, Picabia, Demuth, and Tchelitchew.

Besides her strange, fanciful portraits of family and friends, Stettheimer made giddy paeans to the nation. She collected George Washington memorabilia, kept a marble bust of the first president in her studio's "patriotic" niche,[28] and asserted a glittering version of Manhattan that served as her ideal America. Inspired by Woodrow Wilson's visit to the postwar Peace Conference, *New York/Liberty* (1918, fig. 29) depicts Manhattan Island presided over by a giant American Eagle and Statue of Liberty modeled in relief impasto and covered in gold leaf.[29]

In the glittering light display of *The Fourth of July No. 1* (1927), Stettheimer takes her decorative impulse skyward with fireworks that outshine a huge full moon. Her last and most ambitious paintings, the *Cathedrals* series (1929–1944), depict four arenas of contemporary life; Broadway (fig. 30), Fifth Avenue, Wall Street, and the art world. Teeming with advertising slogans, marquees, and celebrities, the works describe an upbeat fantasy world, a dreamland America of wedding days, opening nights, and marching bands. Although "The Old, Weird America" as Marcus defined it seems to revolve around guilt, retribution, and sexual angst, the national psyche has an upbeat side too, one encapsulated by Stettheimer's buoyant energy. The title of a dazzling 1930 painting *Love Flight of a Pink Candy Heart* indicates how far her sensibility lies from the repression and gloom of the Puritans.

Artist "solitaries" have explored the idea of America in a variety of tones and attitudes. Other telling clues to the American psyche lurk in works by twentieth-century artists like Isabel Bishop, Joan Brown, Joseph Cornell, Aaron Douglas, Philip Evergood, Jared French, Grace Hartigan, Alexandre Hogue, Yasuo Kuniyoshi, Dorothea Lange, Ralph Eugene Meatyard, and Larry Rivers. In the past few years, polls conducted by the Pew Research Center have shown continually plummeting international opinion ratings for the policy and behavior of the United States.[30] In a time when the rest of the world seems to understand America better than we do, it is a matter of urgency to pay attention to what our art reveals about the twists and turns of the American soul.

NOTES

1. D. H. Lawrence, "*In the American Grain* by William Carlos Williams," in *Phoenix, The Posthumous Papers of D. H. Lawrence* (New York: Viking Press, 1968), 335.

2. Chrissie Iles and Philippe Vergne, "Preface and Acknowledgements," *Whitney Biennial 2006: Day for Night* (New York: Whitney Museum of American Art, 2006), 19.

3. See Pamela Lee, "Boundary Issues: The Art World Under the Sign of Globalism," *Artforum* 42, no. 3 (November 2003), 164–167.

4. Grant Wood, *Revolt Against the City* (Iowa City: Clio Press, 1935), 10–11.

5. In 1924 the Whitney Studio Club held an exhibition of American folk art, including works borrowed from Charles Demuth and Charles Sheeler. In 1931, Edith Halpert opened an offshoot of her prestigious Downtown Gallery that focused on folk art and the next year the Museum of Modern Art displayed an exhibition titled, "American Folk Art: The Art of the Common Man in America 1750–1900." See Dickran Tashjian, *William Carlos Williams and the American Scene: 1920–1940* (New York: Whitney Museum of American Art, 1978), 105.

6. "The movement is essentially anti-artistic in its aims and character…. Since the regionalists profess to be so suspicious of any alien influence, it is unfortunate that their own views should bear an embarrassing resemblance to certain European ideologies. These, to be sure, are not the product of the much hated French: their home is on the other side of the Rhine. . . [Regionalism is] nourished by some of the fundamental ills of our society—the same ills that, in minor virulent form, produced National Socialism in Germany." "Benton and Wood: Champions of Regionalism," *The Magazine of Art* 39, no. 5 (May 1946), 184–186, 198–200.

7. Greil Marcus, *The Shape of Things to Come: Prophecy and the American Voice* (New York: Farrar, Straus and Giroux, 2006), 11.

8. Ibid., 100.

9. D.H. Lawrence, *Studies in Classic American Literature* (Cambridge: Cambridge University Press, 2003), 65.

10. William Carlos Williams, *In the American Grain* (New York: Albert & Charles Boni, 1925), 120.

11. Williams, ibid., 215.

12. William Carlos Williams, *The Autobiography of William Carlos Williams* (New York: New Directions, 1967), 174.

13. Tashjian, ibid., 109.

14. See Greil Marcus, "The Old, Weird America," *Invisible Republic: Bob Dylan's Basement Tapes* (Henry Holt: New York, 1997) (later published as *The Old, Weird America*), 87–126; and Michael Duncan, "Report from Los Angeles: An American Original [Harry Smith]," *Art in America* (November 2001), 69–73. Based on Smith's sequencing and notes, a posthumous Volume Four of the Anthology was released in 2000 by Revenant Records.

15. Record collecting in the 1940s turned out to be of significant archival importance since so many early recordings with limited pressings were destroyed during World War II to clear warehouses for military supply. Smith and his collector cohorts were able to buy scores of then rare 1920s 78s from vast warehouse sales at bulk prices.

16. Marcus, ibid., 104.

17. Ibid., 96.

18. Ibid., 38.

19. See James M. Dennis, *Renegade Regionalists: The Modern Independence of Grant Wood, Thomas Hart Benton, and John Steuart Curry* (Madison: University of Wisconsin Press, 1998); Erika Doss, *Benton, Pollock, and the Politics of Modernism: From Regionalism to Abstract Expressionism* (Chicago: University of Chicago Press, 1991); Henry Adams, *Thomas Hart Benton: An American Original* (New York: Knopf, 1989).

20. Sue Taylor "Grant Wood's Self Fashioning," lecture, Spokane, Washington, November 14, 2006. Thanks to Taylor for providing me with the transcript of a lecture based on a section of her forthcoming critical biography of Wood. See also, Joni L. Kinsey, "Cultivating Iowa: An Introduction to Grant Wood," in *Grant Wood's Studio: Birthplace of American Gothic* (New York: Prestel, 2005), 29–32; John Seery, "Grant Wood's Political Gothic," in *America Goes to College: Political Theory for the Liberal Arts* (Albany: State University of New York Press, 2002), 117–231.

21. Seery, ibid., 130.

22. This discussion of Saul is excerpted from my forthcoming catalogue essay, "The Spectacular Wrath of Saul: Peter Saul's History Paintings," in Dan Cameron, ed., *Peter Saul: A Retrospective* (Newport Harbor, California: Orange County Museum of Art, 2008).

23. Custer's demise has been the subject of several Hollywood movies and The Battle of Little Bighorn continues to be reenacted each summer in Hardin, Montana.

24. The style is best known from the 1943 Museum of Modern Art exhibition, *American Realists and Magic Realists*, curated by Alfred Barr, which included works by Sharrer, Jared French, John Wilde, Paul Cadmus, and others subsequently labelled as "magic realists."

25. Erika Doss, "Sharrer's *Tribute to the American Working People*: Issues of Labor and Leisure in Post-World War II American Art," *American Art* (Fall 2002), 55–81.

26. For a brilliant analysis of the song, see Marcus, *The Shape of Things to Come*, ibid., 155–158.

27. A few examples: "King Kong Kitchie Kitchie Ki-Me-O" by Chubby Parker and his Old Time Banjo (1928), "Indian War Whoop" by Floyd Ming and his Pep-Steppers (1928), "John the Revelator" by Blind Willie Johnson (1930), "No Depression in Heaven" by The Carter Family (1936), "Way Down the Old Plank Road" by Uncle Dave Macon (1926), and "Fishing Blues" by Henry Thomas (1929).

28. Barbara Bloemink, *The Life and Art of Florine Stettheimer* (New Haven: Yale University Press, 1995), 216.

29. Linda Nochlin, "Florine Stettheimer: Rococo Subversive (1980)" in *Florine Stettheimer: Manhattan Fantastica* (New York: Whitney Museum of American Art, 2000), 105.

30. See online reports from the Pew Global Attitudes Project, 2007: http://pewglobal.org/reports/display.php?ReportID=256 (accessed February 2008).

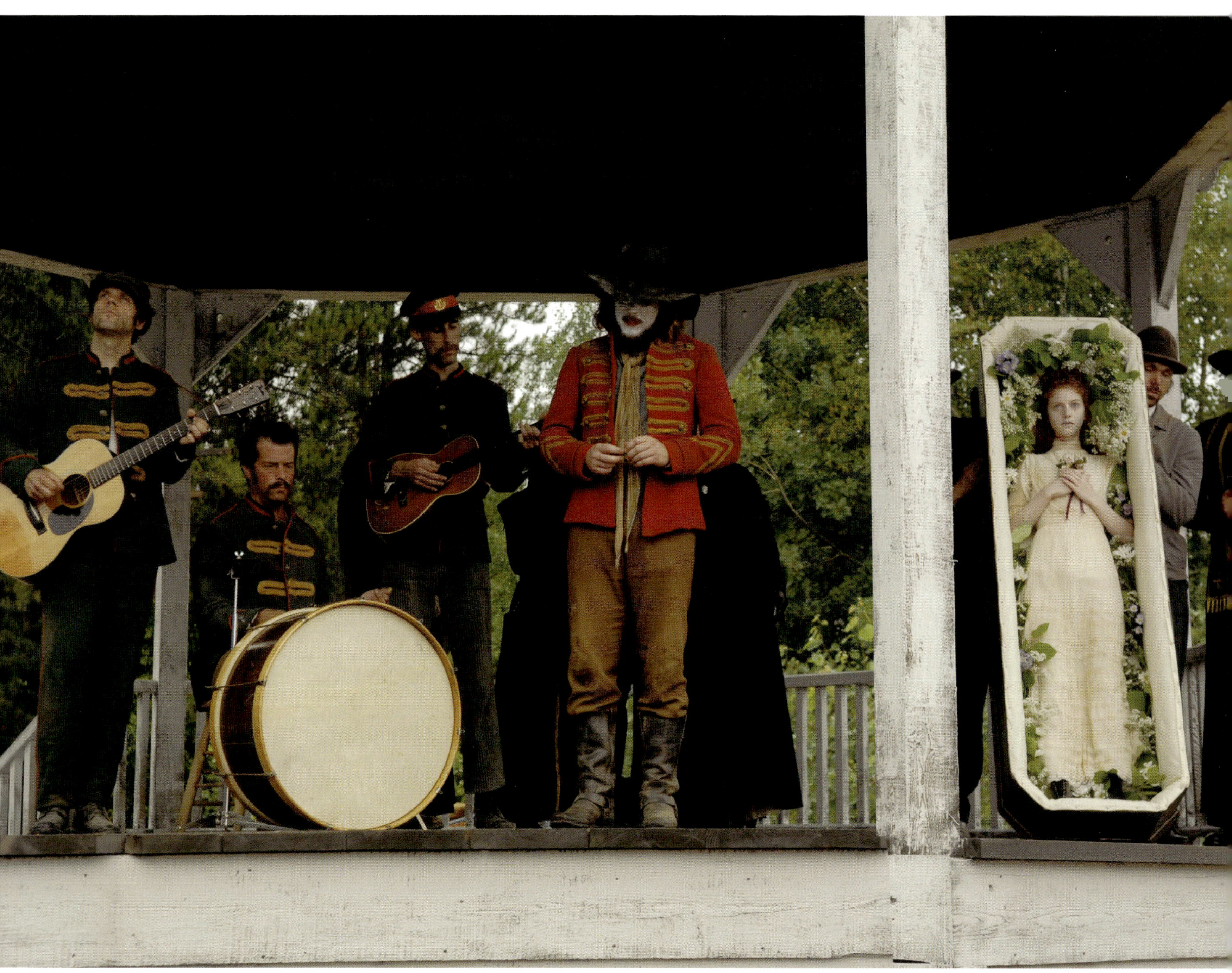

Waking the Dead:
Music, Art, and the Basement Noise of History

COLLEEN SHEEHY

Fellow-citizens, we cannot escape history.
—Abraham Lincoln, 1862

She says, "You can't repeat the past." I say, "You can't?
What do you mean, you can't? Of course you can."
—Bob Dylan,
"Summer Days," 2001

Old spirits of the American past rise up in Riddle, Missouri, in Todd Haynes's 2007 film "I'm Not There."

Far from making a standard biopic on Bob Dylan, Haynes meets his creative subject with equal artistic inventiveness. He locates Dylan's ancestors in this little Missouri town. In one scene, a gang of ghoulish children languishes, sick or half-dead, outside a Halloween store oddly situated on its nineteenth-century main street. A man steals something—a child?—from a homestead while a woman screams, running after him. An Ophelia-like beauty, dead by her own hand, is displayed on stage, upright in her coffin, eyes wide open. Dwarfs, carnival workers, hardy pioneer types, a black man with an American flag painted on his face (after a famous poster from the Civil Rights Movement) converge for the young woman's funeral to hear a ragtag Salvation Army band play a mournful dirge (fig. 31). Jim James from the indie band My Morning Jacket sings in an otherworldly voice Dylan's "Goin' to Acapulco" from *The Basement Tapes*.[1]

Billy the Kid, played by Richard Gere, and Woody Guthrie, played by young black actor Marcus Carl Franklin, walk through Riddle. Supposedly this is one of Woody's birthplaces, as he told two drifters met hopping a freight train. The lawman Pat Garrett appears on stage in a wheelchair, waist-length hair and beard making him look like an American Moses, John Brown, or other strange prophet (fig. 32). He's too ancient and decrepit to pursue Billy the Kid, though he suspects that his old nemesis lurks behind a hokey Halloween mask.

Just as Haynes's film doesn't stay within its own boundaries—it migrates into the territories of Sam Peckinpah's *Pat Garrett and Billy the Kid* (in which Dylan appeared); Fellini's *8½*; the films of Godard; Robert Altman's *McCabe and Mrs. Miller*—Riddle, Missouri, isn't confined to the nineteenth-century past. Its era is conflated with more modern times. The scene's backstory involves the imminent threat of a six-lane freeway being built right through town. Riddle's folks are evacuating, carrying their belongings as though escaping

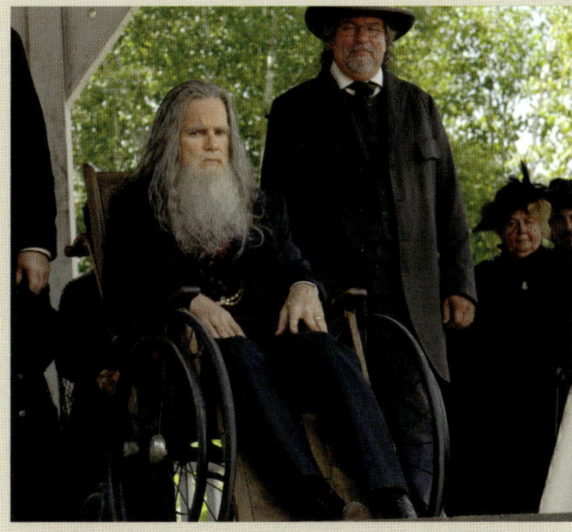

Figs. 31 & 32
Film stills from *I'm Not There*, written and directed by Todd Haynes, 2007, Jonathan Wenk, The Weinstein Company

"

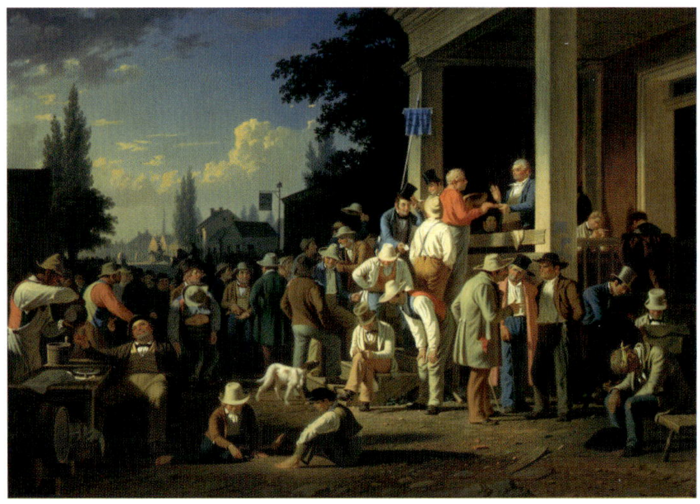
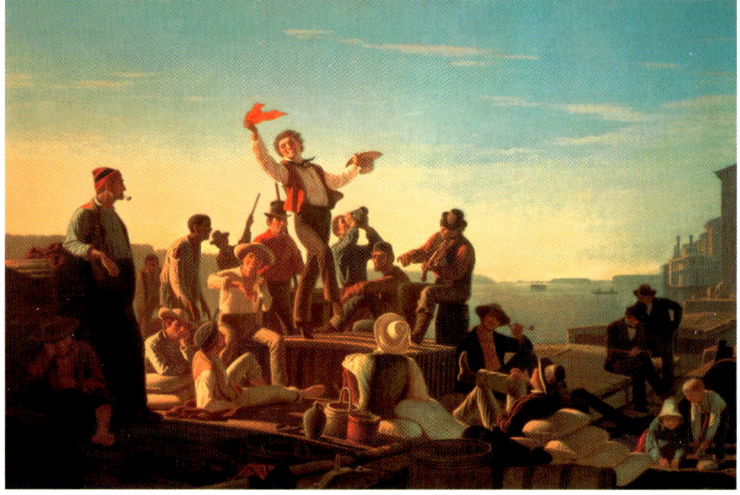

Fig. 33
George Caleb Bingham
The County Election, 1852
Oil on canvas
38 x 52 inches
St. Louis Art Museum, St.
Louis, Gift of Bank of
America

Fig. 34
George Caleb Bingham
Jolly Flatboatmen in Port
1857
Oil on canvas
47 1/8 x 69 5/8 inches
St. Louis Art Museum, St.
Louis, Museum Purchase

catastrophe. A man escorts an ostrich out of town. Another leads a giraffe. Earlier in the film, Billy the Kid
searches the horizon for a far-off Riddle in a lush, hilly
landscape, hearing the sounds of a carnival, when a
bomb from the Vietnam War seems to explode in its
vicinity. The mix of visual styles, overlapping narratives, and temporal epochs of *I'm Not There* make for a
surreal rendering of the relationship between past and
present. As Billy the Kid states, "It's like you got yester-
day, today, and tomorrow all in the same room. There's
no telling what can happen."

Todd Haynes's Riddle, Missouri, is the capital of
The Old, Weird America, the visionary apparition of the
American past that Greil Marcus hears in Dylan's *The
Basement Tapes*, his 1967 sessions with The Band (then
called The Hawks). Unlike the wholesome democratic
images of free American citizens depicted by Missouri
painter George Caleb Bingham in his paeans to nineteenth-century frontier life (figs. 33 & 34), Riddle is
more murder ballad than ballot box. Its name alone un-
derscores the puzzling dimensions of American history
and culture found at the center of the country's spiritual
geography as much as it describes Dylan.

Marcus's study *The Old, Weird America: The World of
Bob Dylan's Basement Tapes* (1997) is one of his most elo-
quent and haunting achievements in a career marked
by sharp insights into the relationship between American history and music.[2] He creates a travel guide to
"Smithville," an imagined historic town, brought back
to life by Dylan and The Hawks' playful meanderings
in sessions in Woodstock and West Saugerties, New
York, when they channeled the sounds of Harry Smith's

evocative musical landscape from the *Anthology of American Folk Music*. He writes

> "the basement tapes can begin to sound like a map; but
> if a map, what country, what lost mine, is it that they cen-
> ter and fix? They begin to sound like an instinctive exper-
> iment, a laboratory: a laboratory where, for a few months,
> certain bedrock strains of American cultural language were
> retrieved and reinvented."[3]

Marcus performs acts of archaeology, uncovering some
of the forgotten contours and social types of the American
past that link Dylan to Harry Smith and earlier folk
music. He finds both the commonplace and the utterly
strange underpinnings of American history expressed in
the blues and ballads anthologized by Smith in 1952.

Like Marcus's feats of rediscovery, the visual artists
gathered together in the exhibition *The Old, Weird America* revive the American past in their imagery, subjects,
forms, materials, and performances. Like their counter-
parts in music—Dylan most prominently but many other
contemporary songwriters as well—they mobilize American history and folklore but give them contemporary
spins that make their work powerful commentary on our
current state of affairs. Their artwork vacillates between
the official histories of heroes like Abraham Lincoln
and John Brown and unofficial lore from the world of
folk legend. Some embrace the forms and materials of
folk objects to rebuild connections to a past that can be
both inspirational and diabolical.

Like Dylan, who in his 2005 memoir, *Chronicles:
Volume One*, revealed an obsession in the 1960s with a war
from a hundred years earlier, the artists in *The Old, Weird*

Fig. 35
John Cohen
Bob Dylan on My Roof, 1962
Gelatin silver print
14 x 11 inches
© John Cohen. Used by
permission of the artist

America revisit the Civil War era. Some engage with the preoccupations of other Americans who re-enact Civil War battle scenes or impersonate Abraham Lincoln for public audiences (pls. 69–70). Dario Robleto revives the memory of the war's widows (pls. 80–81). Barnaby Furnas uses contemporary visual styles from extreme video games and Hollywood films to impart the intense carnage of Civil War battlefields (pls. 16–22), their grim facts recounted in great detail, along with discussion of their larger cultural impact, by historian Drew Gilpin Faust in *This Republic of Suffering: Death and the American Civil War*. Faust has noted that more than 60,000 books have been published on the Civil War, a staggering number that reveals its continuing grip on Americans.[4]

Like Dylan's excavation of blues and folk music going back to nineteenth-century songs with even earlier origins, and like Haynes in *I'm Not There*, the artists here open a portal in time through their work that fosters fluidity between past and present, waking the ghosts that still haunt America today. In doing so, they raise questions about American memory and American mythologies, asking, how did we get here? What have we forgotten and what do we need to remember? What ideas and values from the past continue to shape today's politics, discourse, social behavior, racial conundrums, and persistent divisions? What is valuable to retain or necessary to abandon? They invoke legendary figures, both real and imagined, to prompt critical questions. Many seek the vitality, originality, and resourcefulness of earlier ways of life prior to the regimentation of a modern, industrialized nation. Questioning the founding mythologies of American culture, they ponder how we might move ahead, either carrying the weight of the past or being buoyed by it.

That so many contemporary artists are mining American history is notable. History often has been problematic for American visual artists since the early twentieth century. The past was something to throw off, rebel against, in pursuit of the avant-garde. Artists were not supposed to look back but invent things anew. In turning to historic imagery and forms, the artists in *The Old, Weird America* have adopted strategies used by American musicians, who, for at least fifty years, have rediscovered the treasure troves of earlier folk musics and their cultures, not to restage them in nostalgic tributes, but to move ahead into new territories that carry the resonance of history. Tellingly, several artists in the exhibition are also musicians, DJs, or deeply informed by both folk and popular music. Their work reveals an engagement with American myths, history, and folk

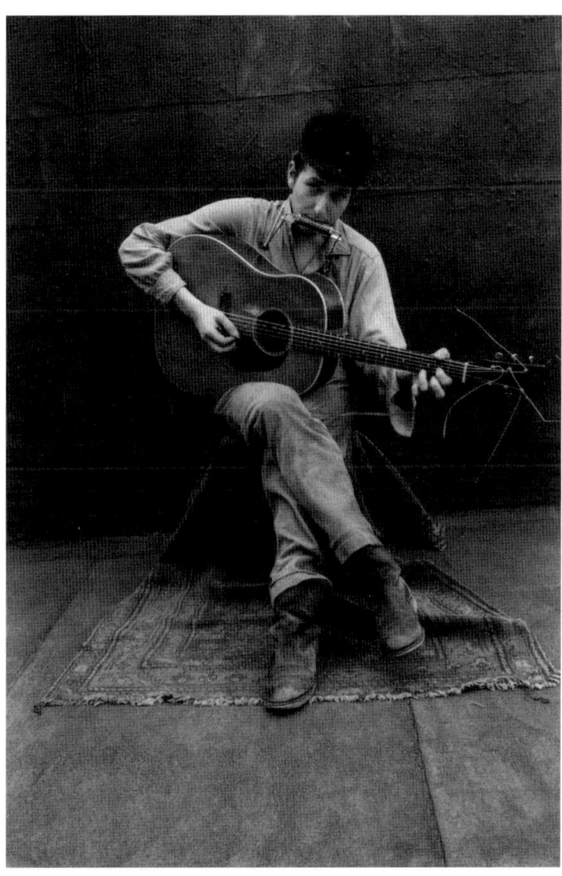

culture that resembles the way musicians have sought creative sources.

It is this deep exploration of the past that Greil Marcus recognized in Bob Dylan's basement experiments, and Dylan serves as a pivotal figure in moving historical music into the mainstream. From the time of his youth in Hibbing, Minnesota, in the 1950s, Dylan felt transported by old music, "It made me feel like I was someone else," he relates in Martin Scorsese's documentary, *No Direction Home*. In 1959, the young musician discovered Woody Guthrie's music in coffeehouses and house parties in Minneapolis's Dinkytown neighborhood, which launched his devotion to American folk music. Hearing Guthrie, Dylan relates, "For me, it was like an epiphany, like some heavy anchor had just plunged into the waters of the harbor."[5] His Minneapolis friends and subculture of folk aficionados—Tony Glover, John Koerner, Paul Nelson, Dave Whitaker, Bonnie Beecher, Jon Pankake—provided Dylan's education in folk and blues music, introducing him to Harry Smith's Anthology and other records, most of which were not readily available but passed around and collected as precious talismans. Dylan plunged into the folk repertoire, trading in his electric guitar for a Martin acoustic. By the time Dylan got to New York City in early 1961, he had mastered Guthrie's entire songbook and a wide catalog of other traditional music (fig. 35).

Over the next several years, as the singer ventured from his first recording, comprised mostly of traditional songs, into increasing sonic, vocal, and lyrical innovations and international stardom, Dylan remained anchored by folk music, particularly the blues. The music described an ancient landscape and old cultures grounded in a mysterious, resilient past. Describing traditional music in a 1966 interview, Dylan said:

> It could be called arsenic music, or perhaps Phaedra music…. Traditional music is based on hexagrams. It comes about from legends, Bibles, plagues, and it revolves around vegetables and death. There's nobody that's going to kill traditional music. All those songs about roses growing out of people's brains and lovers who are really geese and swans that turn into angels—they're not going to die.[6]

Folklore conveyed what he called "just plain simple mystery" as "a fact—a traditional fact."[7] Historian George Lipsitz has argued that popular musicians engage in a dialogic process with the past that draws on collective memory but also moves contemporary work past nostalgia or cliché.[8] Working in this vein, Dylan recognized how old songs with stories and characters "full of myth" could make new songs ring with the echoes of history.[9]

The vivid image of roses growing out of people's bodies comes straight from the folk song, "Barbara Allen," a story of unrequited love, and a persistent part of traditional repertoire for centuries.[10] While not included on Smith's Anthology, the song shares similar sensibilities to many others in his compendium: its ill-fated lovers, mysterious deaths, and portentous signs from the natural world. One of twentieth-century America's most original eccentrics, Smith was an amateur anthropologist, a wanderer, experimental filmmaker, archivist, and legendary mooch, who compiled a work, greater than its individual parts, that remains a cultural pivot point (fig. 36). An ingenious, opportunist collector, Smith selected from his vast archive eighty-four songs that had been recorded between 1929 to 1932 by singers like Dock Boggs, the Carter Family, Blind Lemon Jefferson, and Charley Patton. The original singers hailed from rural and small town America, mostly in the South. Their original recordings had taken regional music and sensibilities to nationwide audiences but had fallen into

obscurity since their first releases. Smith's six-album set inspired musicians in the folk revival as well as Beat poets of the 1950s. Writer Luc Sante called the *Anthology* "… a philosopher's stone or a Rosetta Stone, a treasure map of an ancient, now hidden America … it is an essential element of American culture, deserving of a place on the narrow shelf between *Huckleberry Finn* and Walker Evans's *American Photographs*."[11] Realizing the impact his *Anthology* had on generations of musicians and on American society, Smith said, when accepting a special Grammy Award in 1991 shortly before his death, "My dreams came true. I saw America changed through music."[12] Its songs of inexplicable tragedies, brutal murders, heroic exploits, undying or unrequited love gave Dylan access to a cabinet of curiosities filled with treasures and oddities from the American past.

After the basement noise in upstate New York, Dylan used old song styles to find a way forward. In 1968, he released *John Wesley Harding*, an album of austere music and sentiments, with figures from the past telling allegorical stories, a dramatic departure from the driving electric *Blonde on Blonde* from 1966.[13] Sensibilities like these taught U2's Bono that "the best way to serve

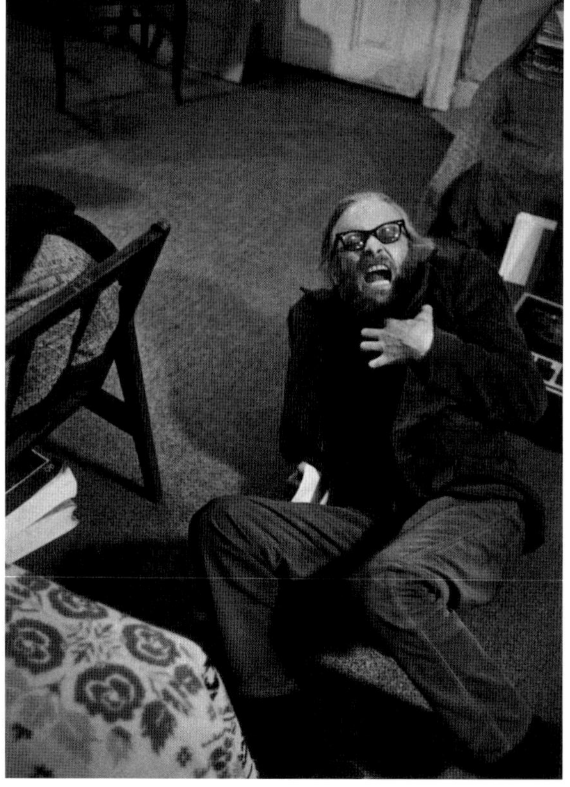

Fig. 36
John Cohen
Harry Smith at the Chelsea Hotel, 1969
Gelatin silver print
14 x 11 inches
© John Cohen. Used by permission of the artist

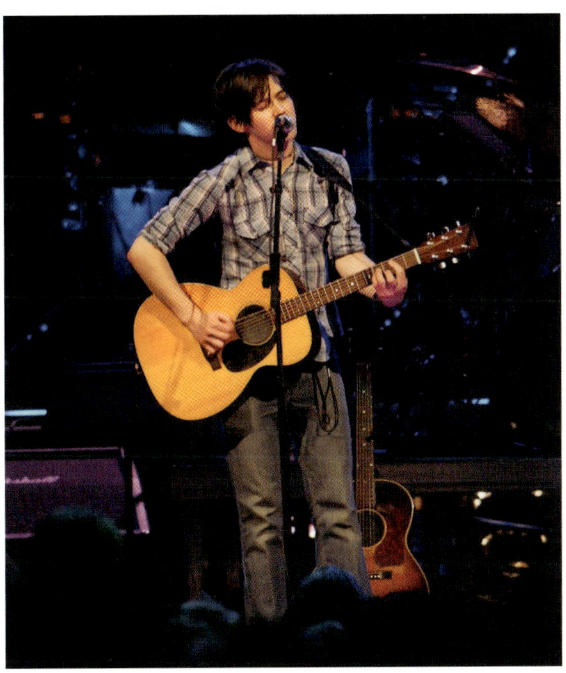

the age is to betray it," as he observed in one commentary, noting how Dylan brilliantly combined the epitome of modernity with a connection to the ancient.[14] In the 1990s, Dylan reinvented himself after a decade of musical doldrums with the release of two albums of traditional songs, *Good As I Been To You* (1992) and *World Gone Wrong* (1993). He followed with some of the strongest music of his forty-five-year career in *Time Out of Mind* (1997), *"Love and Theft"* (2001), and, most recently, *Modern Times* (2006), his first chart-topping album since 1975. In his new CD, Dylan alludes to the past in thinly altered lines from Confederate poet Henry Timrod as well as in lyrics that draw on a certified ancient, the Roman poet, Ovid.[15]

Other musicians followed Dylan's lead from early on. With Dylan very much as inspiration—Dylan had made folk music cool—American musicians of the sixties embraced the folk sound, moving beyond its earlier subculture status. Others joined with British musicians in forging a blues revival, then ramped up folk into "folk-rock" (a term Dylan disdained), which also merged with a countrified rock 'n' roll in the 1970s. In recent decades, Dylan has been regarded as an important precursor to the development of alt-country and the resurgence of all kinds of roots music by young musicians. A series of "new Dylans," anointed by critics and eager fans, recognized his ongoing influence on generations of musicians' style, sound, and use of old musical genres. Bruce Springsteen, one of the more prominent to bear the weight of this title, didn't really connect sonically to folk music until his stark 1982 *Nebraska*. Since then, Springsteen has returned regularly to simple folk arrangements as well as full-blown, rollicking cover versions, as in his 2006 *We Shall Overcome: The Seeger Sessions*. The latest "new Dylan," Conor Oberst of Omaha—a musical prodigy from age twelve—is known for his phenomenal output under his band name of Bright Eyes. He has been linked to the older musician for his lyrical imagery, alternating between simple folk songs and complex surrealistic poetry, and for a singing style that, like the early Dylan, combines innocence with intense delivery. Oberst also inhabits the strange territories that folk music lays claim to, exploring the inexplicable and the paranormal in his latest CD, *Cassadaga*, named for a real town in Florida filled with psychics.

"The past never quits," Conor Oberst sang from the stage at the 400 Bar, cornerstone of Minneapolis's West Bank, in a new song he tried out in this intimate venue to close out 2007. It was a good place to test drive songs with a roadhouse feel. This was the same West Bank where the folk and blues revivals of the late 1950s and 1960s took root in Minneapolis, the same West Bank where Dylan performed and hung out when he was eighteen and nineteen. Months earlier in his hometown, Oberst railed against the slick, modern design of the Omaha concert venue, the new Peter Kiewit Concert Hall. Stamping his foot on the stage, the singer snarled, "This is a nice place … but there's not enough history here." No spirits of other musicians had seasoned the place; no audiences had anointed it with their cheers and applause. Instead, the town's favorite son initiated the hall with its first rock 'n' roll show (fig. 37).

Oberst's work reflects the dialogic relationships musicians continue to forge with history and tradition, putting them to contemporary ends. In 1999, Chicago indie band Wilco and British folk singer Billy Bragg teamed up to write music for a dozen Woody Guthrie lyrics that had gone unscored in his lifetime. The resulting homage, *Mermaid Avenue*, beautifully linked past and present. Colin Meloy, lead singer for The Decemberists, writes songs with the sensibility of Anglo-Irish ballads, sung with the chiming, clear voice of old folk songs. Portland, Oregon, roots artist M. Ward sings in a hollow, haunting voice that recalls the sounds of old singers on the *Anthology of American Folk Music*, as does his friend and collaborator, Jim James of My Morning Jacket. In an artistic convergence, Ward, James, and Oberst toured together in 2005 performing at the Newport Folk Festival

Fig. 38
Charles Sheeler
American Interior, 1934
Oil on canvas
32 1/2 x 30 inches
Yale University Art Gallery,
New Haven, Gift of Mrs.
Paul Moore

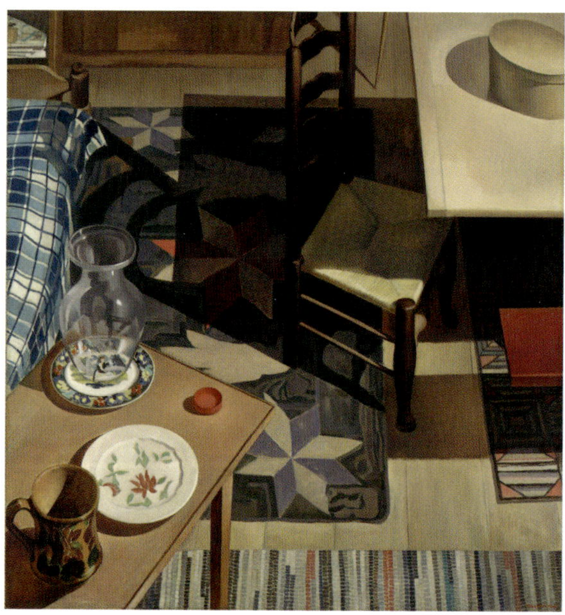

(sadly, now called the "Dunkin' Donuts Newport Folk Festival"), where Dylan made history in 1963 and 1964 as a folk singer and in 1965 as a rock 'n' roller. The three young singers closed their set with Dylan's "Girl of The North Country," each singing a verse, joining together on the chorus, and reviving its Dylan-Johnny Cash rendition.

Younger musicians look to Dylan for secrets of creative longevity, from Bono and Jack White of The White Stripes to Ryan Adams. Historian Benjamin Filene recounts the advice the older singer gave to Bono when, in 1987, the biggest band in the world was feeling a creative impasse about future directions. "Well you have to reach back into the music. You have to reach back," Dylan told him, urging the band to explore American blues, gospel, and folk music. Filene comments that more than any individual song Dylan's "... most enduring product is the example he offered of how to negotiate the relationship between the past and present. He demonstrated that dramatic, innovative, even angry change could at the same time be evolutionary and firmly rooted."[16] Tradition could provide a means to reinvention and also to connecting with issues of cultural identity in contemporary times.

Folklore, or traditional culture, has frequently helped to forge and to recreate national identity. Folklore is not synonymous with history. If history is official accounts of past events, usually written and promulgated by a professional class, folklore is the common people's popular gloss on those events, told through oral narratives circulated in conversations and stories. Ordinary people interpret events in such a way as to provide meaning within their specific groups or folk cultures. People make meaning of the past, knitting it into their present lives, through a multitude of traditional creative forms that shape content and ways of passing on. Folklore includes stories, sayings, jokes, songs, material objects, customs, dance, and celebrations, to name some common forms.

While all cultures create folklore as a means to transmit earlier forms of knowledge, artistic expressions, beliefs, and ways of doing things—prominent interest in traditional cultures often arises at times of crisis in cultural identity. Folklore was first "discovered" in nineteenth-century Europe in tandem with a growing emphasis on nation formation and national identity. The customs and culture of peasants and working classes, many believed, uniquely expressed the essence of a national culture. With industrialization changing rural and village ways of life, intellectuals, collectors, and antiquarians embarked on efforts to document and save what they thought were vanishing cultures, and eventually, to systematize their findings. Germans Jakob and Wilhelm Grimm (The Brothers Grimm) were early collectors of the folk tales of German peasants. Antii Aarne collected folk tales in Finland, comparing them to stories from other countries. Intrigued by their commonalities, he developed an influential motif index to international folk tales, published in 1910. In the British Isles scholars also went out into the countryside to collect folk songs, legends, and other stories, and to learn folk beliefs and customs. In the mid-nineteenth century, an American scholar from Harvard, Francis James Child, studied archived folk songs from Britain. He developed a numbering system to identify them, publishing *British and Scottish Popular Ballads* in 1857, a key volume that generated what became called the "Child Ballads," a strong basis for later study of American folk songs. In the United States, the American Folklore Society formed in 1888, followed by many state folklore societies. Their members of historians and collectors reflected the growing interest in American tales, songs, and customs at a time when the United States was becoming an industrialized nation after the Civil War and the growth of cities challenged ideas about national identity based in the American frontier.[17]

American artists have shown interest in folklore and folk art at times of crisis. In the 1920s, it was the rapid speed of modernization and the mass media transforming lives in cities along with the challenges of forging a new art in response to European advances in abstraction and cubism. Artists as far ranging as Marsden Hartley, Yasuo Kuniyoshi, and Charles Sheeler looked to folk art for precedence and inspiration for their pictorial innovations. Sheeler was absorbed with the austere beauty of crafts made by the Shakers (fig. 38). Hartley was fascinated with the folk cultures of Nova Scotia, Maine, and New Mexico, places where he spent significant time painting, trying to achieve "a sturdier kind of realism" to create a truly American art.[18] His archaic portraits rely on the flat areas of color, simplified modeling of the figure, and outlining of form common to American folk painting, as seen in his work *Adelard, The Drowned, Master of the "Phantom"* (fig. 39).

In the 1930s, the crises brought on by the Great Depression generated a widespread interest in American folklore and folk art among artists as well as the general populace. From 1930 to 1932, Holger Cahill mounted the first exhibitions surveying American folk art at the Newark Museum and the Museum of Modern Art. Edith Halpert, owner of the progressive Downtown Gallery in New York City, and Abby Aldrich Rockefeller, who helped to found the Museum of Modern Art, were pioneers in recognizing American folk art as a valuable heritage for modern artists. In 1935, Abby Aldrich Rockefeller put her huge collection of American quilts, sculpture, crafts, paintings, and other Americana on display at Colonial Williamsburg, an historic site that was being renovated to the styles and décor of its colonial past, through the efforts of Reverend W. A. R. Goodwin and John D. Rockefeller Jr.[19]

Interest in the American past was supported to a great extent through the New Deal projects of the Roosevelt administration. (Holger Cahill was appointed national director of the Federal Art Project.) The Federal Writer's Project hired people to collect oral traditions in every state, amassing the expressions, stories, and songs of regional subcultures, including, importantly, the narratives, spirituals, and blues songs of former slaves. The Works Progress Administration (WPA) paid artists to create easel painting, prints, and sculpture, most of which documented "the American Scene," and to teach art workshops to the public. Under the Federal Art Project, the Index of American Design catalogued over 18,000 handmade artifacts from around the nation, everything from weathervanes and toys to stoneware and quilts. Artists documented these objects through exquisite photorealist watercolor renderings (fig. 40).[20] The Treasury Section of Painting and Sculpture hired

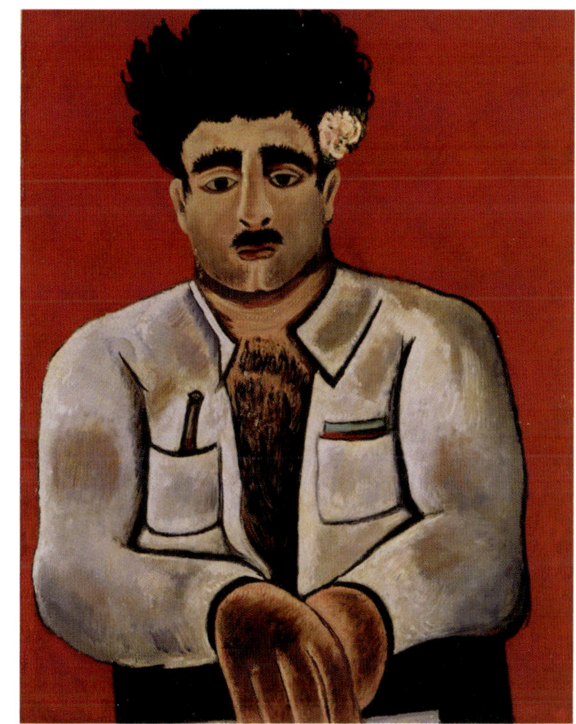

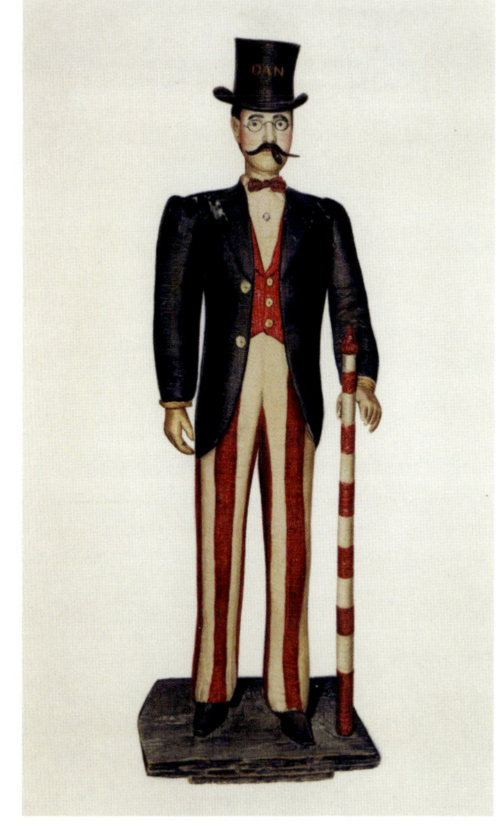

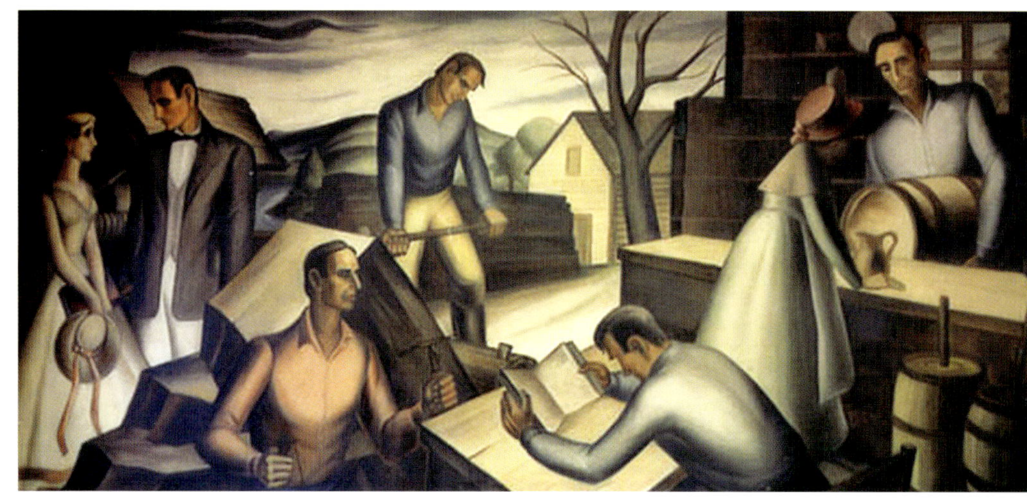

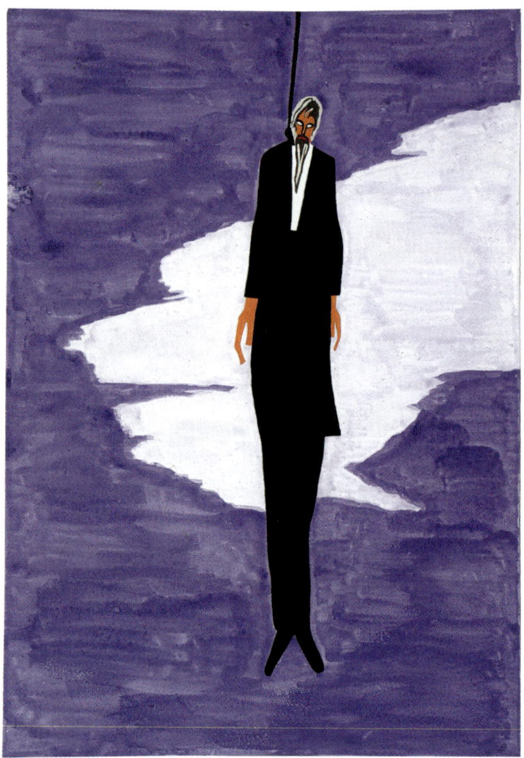

artists to paint murals in public buildings. Art historian Karal Ann Marling argues that the post-office murals of the Federal Art Project served as a means to use images of the American past, filled with cowboys, settlers, workers, and farm wives in reassuring narratives that helped people weather the very uncertain present and questionable future of 1930s America.[21] Taken together, the New Deal's documentations constitute the fullest reflection of American cultures before or since. That crescendo of image, story, performance, and artifact helped Americans survive the severe challenges of the Great Depression.

American Regionalists painted historical figures along with images of the common folk of the past. Abraham Lincoln was an important touchstone, as seen in a montage of scenes from his early, virtuous life on the Illinois prairie in a 1938 mural in the Petersburg Illinois Post Office, painted by John Winters (fig. 41). Kansas painter John Steuart Curry revisited other Civil War leaders by chronicling abolitionist John Brown's fiery exploits in murals for the Kansas Statehouse, painted between 1937 and 1941 (see fig. 2). In 1941, working in New York City, a young Jacob Lawrence created a twenty-two piece series devoted to the life of John Brown (fig. 42). When the John Brown series was exhibited at Edith Halpert's Downtown Gallery, one reviewer noted:

> The artist has made of this saga a powerful and compelling series…this review hopes that the new owner [collector Milton Lowenthal] can be prevailed upon by an alert publisher to issue the series in book form. It would be an authentic contribution to the aesthetic folklore of America.[22]

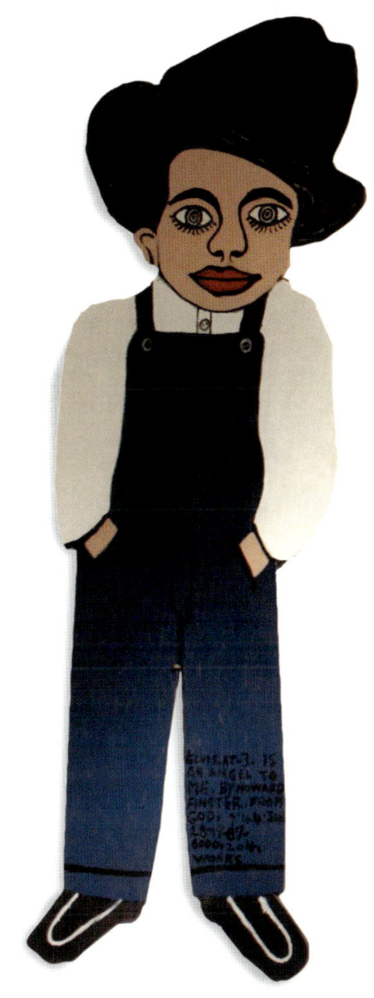

Lawrence had completed John Brown shortly after his historical series on two other heroes of nineteenth-century American history: Frederick Douglass and Harriet Tubman. In the work of these artists and others, history told important lessons for contemporary times.

From early in American history to the present, folk artists have been drawn to legendary figures, too, people who strike them as exemplary, extraordinary, worth remembering. Political leaders like George Washington, Lincoln, and John Brown have been frequent subjects for folk and self-taught artists since the nineteenth century, followed in more recent times by John F. Kennedy, Martin Luther King Jr., and Elvis. Folk artists Howard Finster, Lillian Colton, James Harold Jennings, Anderson Johnson, and Sam Doyle created heroic depictions of the famous, imbuing their images with elegiac qualities and sometimes achieving an iconic status to honor figures they considered saints and martyrs. Their lives — as depicted for example in Finster's *Elvis at Three* (fig. 43) and Colton's *Abraham Lincoln* (1973, fig. 44)— represent important models and cautionary tales about the rigors of war, politics, and fame.[23] "I liked people who made a good impression," Colton reported about her portrait subjects, ranging from Christ to American presidents and musicians.[24]

Folk artists also render ordinary people with a similar sense of dignity and strength as the famous, in part due to their choice of materials and techniques. Wood sculpture made without joints lends an upright, stiff pose to the figure, a technique used by artists inspired by folk art, such as Elie Nadelman in the 1930s.[25] In *The Old, Weird America*, McDermott & McGough adopt a folk sculpture style in *Sacred Love and Pain, 1960* (2006, pl. 61) to weave back into the past the history of gay life, normalizing its presence through a style connected to homespun values. In contrast to its honorific impulses, folk art can display playfulness and humor, veering at times into the ribald, erotic, and scatological, just as folklore's oral traditions of jokes, jests, slang, and boasting games like "playing the dozens" upset ideas of propriety. Eric Beltz's cuss words in his drawings of historical figures and scenes seem at odds with the folksy imagery but also give his works a humorous bite, making revered historical figures seem more human and vital (pls. 1–3).

Folk arts, craft, vernacular artifacts, and the work of self-taught artists serve as important sources for ideas, values, techniques, and materials for many artists in *The Old, Weird America*. Drawings by African-American folk artist Bill Traylor, with his simplified, silhouetted

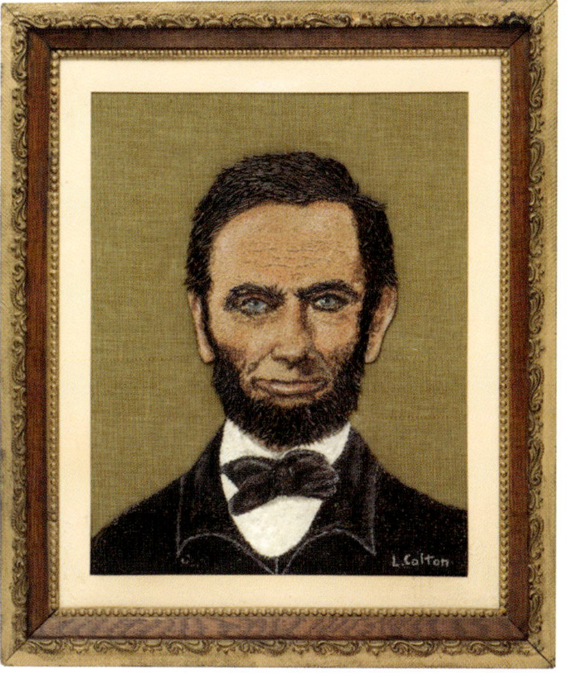

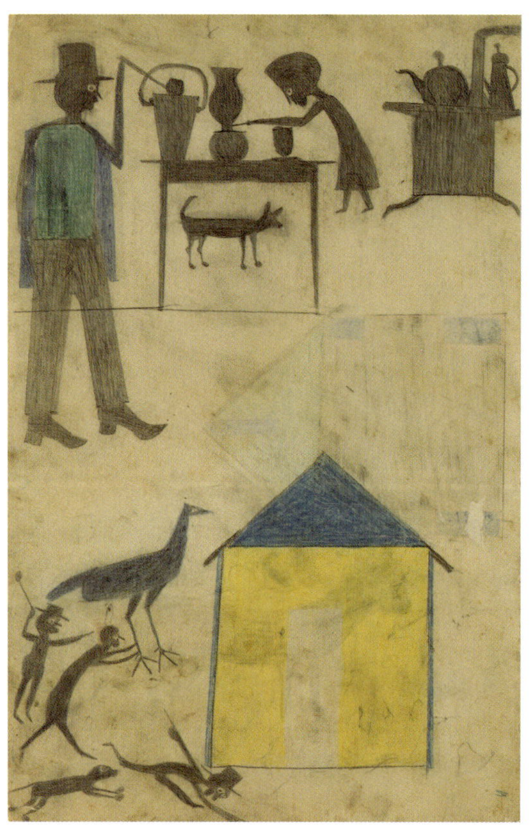

figures (fig. 45), inspire Deborah Grant's imagery in *Where Good Darkies Go* (pls. 23–28). Another reference in her work is to cut silhouettes, a vernacular form of portraiture before the advent of photography for those who could not afford to commission a painter. Silhouette cutting was also a form of popular entertainment in the early republic, as practiced at Charles Willson Peale's Philadelphia museum in the early nineteenth-century, where his former slave, Moses Williams, cut visitors' silhouettes for one cent (fig. 46). Using a device called a "phisiognotrace," Williams created a faithful likeness by tracing the sitter's shadow onto paper, which was then cut out. People displayed these portraits in home parlors and bound them into albums.[26] Though not using the same device to create her silhouetted scenarios, Kara Walker also references this vernacular art form. In her hands, the recording of figural shadows is fraught with a sense of buried undercurrents and repressed dreams that morph into monstrous couplings and violence, exposing the tangled legacies of racist oppression and racial desire.

Artists in the exhibition participate in a broad resur-

gence of craft in contemporary art.[27] The handmade object can be laden with deeply embedded values of love, care, simplicity, time investment, and authenticity, ideas connected to handmade objects since William Morris helped to spur the Arts and Crafts movement in late nineteenth-century England and the U.S. In her word-and-cartoon-based installation work, Margaret Kilgallen employs historic woodblock typefaces from vernacular styles of old broadsides, posters, and signage common in earlier American landscapes (pls. 53–57). The disjunction between her Americana style and modern messages fuels a productive dissonance about contemporary American life. Dario Robleto crafts meticulous objects with the antique patina of historical artifacts in mourning wreaths, hair jewelry, mourning mementos, and handmade boxes (pls. 78 & 80–84). His work combines craft with material science. For many pieces, he first creates magical concoctions drawn from a naturalist's botanical cabinet, mixed with carefully selected tracks of pop music vinyl, melted to liquid or ground into powder. He then carves or molds the solid substances made from these mixtures. In other gestures, he braids audiotape bearing highly symbolic old music, radio shows, or poetry into forms that mimic human hair. The weight of history adheres in materials recycled into his sculptures: lace from a widow's mourning dress; hair flowers braided by widows from American wars; and soldiers' letters dissolved to make handmade paper in *The Pause that Became Permanence*. His historic and contemporary materials express the inextricable, alchemical mixing of past and present. Informed by DJ culture as much as artistic assemblage or material science, Robleto has commented, "There is no such thing as a good DJ who is historically ignorant," endowing hip-hop sampling with a poet's sense of allusion.[28]

A modern attraction to folk art and craft arises from their ability to convey startlingly direct understanding of people's physical experiences in times past. Objects provide essential means by which we can experience an embodied history that moves beyond words, an idea conveyed by other artists in the exhibition. Allison Smith crafts new artifacts used in her performances and installations that re-enact historic events, working with people who practice traditional crafts or re-stage historic battles (pls. 85–93). Greta Pratt's Lincoln re-enactors physically adopt the President's style of clothes, beard, stance, gait, and language, prompting psychic transformations that have remarkable effects on their thoughts and behavior (pls. 69–70).[29] Similar to other contemporary art that features clothing in symbolic ways, Cynthia Norton's

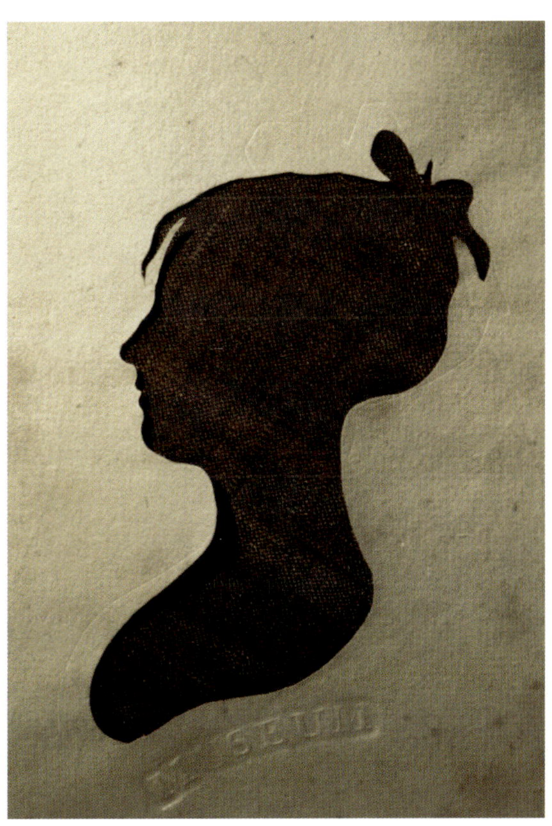

Fig. 46
Peale Museum, Philadelphia
Silhouette of Victorine du Pont Buduy,
c. 1810–1820
White wove paper backed with brown weave wool
5 x 4 inches
Winterthur Museum, bequest of Henry Francis du Pont

long trail drives to get cattle to railheads for shipping to urban slaughterhouses. Rather than being rugged individualists, cowboys were part of a capitalist system that involved railroads and markets. Yet from this reality, the folklore of the cowboy grew, fueled by Eastern artists and writers as well as Buffalo Bill's popular Wild West Show. The mythic cowboy became laden with the desires of Americans who looked backward as the frontier closed. In their formulations, the cowboy stood as an arbiter of justice, ready to use violence to uphold principles and overcome adversaries—hostile Indians, wild Nature, or dangerous criminals. The folklore of the cowboy has been continually renewed and revised, most prominently in American film and, frequently, in American politics.[31]

In the exhibition, Jeremy Blake's silhouetted cowboy images emerge spookily from lush, saturated color fields, alternating with scenes of the Winchester House (pls. 4–8). Sarah Winchester, heir to the fortune made selling rifles that subdued and settled the West, was haunted by spirits of the dead and compelled to add to her house to appease them. Through the cowboy, Blake calls up a national subconscious with Sarah Winchester's house and mind as emblems of a collective psyche, haunted by violence.[32] David Rathman uses silhouetted cowboy figures in a lighter vein, exposing the psychological fault lines of the tough guy persona in their absurd, trite, or oddly poetic pronouncements (pls. 71–77). The disparity between the real lives and the legends of the American cowboy underscore the ways in which a group or nation's folklore is shaped and enlisted to meet the needs of the present.

Though looking backward, the artists in *The Old, Weird America* aim to regenerate the present. In this, they echo Marcus's vision of an older country as a territory of mind and spirit, where the strange and uncanny sit side-by-side with openness and possibility. In some ways, the original title for Marcus's book, *Invisible Republic*, more accurately conveys the notion that the American nation remains to be made and remade by those—the unknown as much as the well-known—who can move forward, informed but not trapped by history. Recognizing a past that "never quits," in Oberst's words, the artists here attempt to wake the dead, past and present, including those among us who may be breathing, talking, and walking the streets today.

country square dance dresses wittily invoke American folk dances and our personal and collective memories of bodies in synchronized movements (pls. 66 & 68). Her piece celebrates the vitality of rootsy American creativity and an imagined time of closer community bonds.[30]

In other works in the exhibition, the lean, tough figure of the cowboy recurs as a silhouetted type rather than a full-fledged person or character. The settling of the West serves as an enduring creation story for the United States, and the cowboy became one of the most persistent folkloric elements of our national myth ever since nineteenth-century dime novels fascinated Eastern audiences, and Frederic Remington popularized images of rugged cowboys in paintings and drawings. The historic cowboy did not roam freely over the plains, mountains, or deserts, as often depicted in Hollywood westerns and television shows, but was a worker in a short-lived period from 1865 to 1885. The limited rail system at that time required cowboys to embark on

NOTES

1. Many thanks to my colleagues and friends, sources of conversation and inspiration, whose spirits lie behind this essay, including George Lipsitz, Greil Marcus, Dave Marsh, Karal Ann Marling, Devin McKinney, Ellen Stekert, Robert Polito, Dario Robleto, Patty Dean, Kat Lenaberg, Kat Day-Coen, and Thom Swiss.

2. Greil Marcus, *The Old, Weird America: The World of Bob Dylan's Basement Tapes* (New York: Picador, 1997); see also his *Mystery Train: Images of America in Rock 'n' Roll Music* (New York: Penguin, 1975); and *The Shape of Things to Come: Prophecy and The American Voice* (New York: Farrar, Strous, and Giroux, 2006).

3. Ibid, xix.

4. Drew Gilpin Faust, *This Republic of Suffering: Death and the American Civil War* (New York: Knopf, 2008); and Eric Foner, "Battle Pieces," *The Nation* (January 28, 2008), 20–32.

5. Bob Dylan, *Chronicles: Volume One* (New York: Simon & Shuster, 2004), 244.

6. Interview with Nat Hentoff for *Playboy*, March 1966 in Jonathan Cott, ed., *Bob Dylan: The Essential Interviews* (New York: Werner Books, 2006), 98.

7. Ibid.

8. George Lipsitz, "Against the Wind: Dialogic Aspects of Rock and Roll" in *Time Passages: Collective Memory and Popular Culture* (Minneapolis: University of Minnesota Press, 1990), 99–132.

9. "full of myth" is from Bob Dylan interview with Nora Ephron and Susan Edmiston, "Positively Tie Dream," August 1965, in Jonathan Cott, ed., *Bob Dylan: The Essential Interviews* (New York: Werner Books, 2006), 50.

10. Dave Marsh, "Barbara Allen" in Sean Wilentz and Greil Marcus, eds., *The Rose and the Briar: Death, Love and Liberty in the American Ballad* (New York: W.W. Norton, 2005), 9–17.

11. Luc Sante, liner notes for *Anthology of American Folk Music*, CD box set, Smithsonian Folkways Recordings, Washington, DC, 1997, 30–31.

12. See liner notes booklet for the box set of covers of Anthology songs by contemporary musicians (ranging from Beck to Lou Reed, David Johansen, Wilco to Kate and Anna McGarrigle), released as *The Harry Smith Project: Anthology of American Folk Music Revisited* by the Harry Smith Archives at the Getty Research Institute and Sony, 2006. The music was performed in concerts held in London, New York, and Los Angeles from 1999 to 2001. Smith's Anthology was re-released as a box set of CDs in 1997 by Smithsonian Folkways. Both of these releases have kept these songs pertinent to contemporary music.

13. On Dylan's reliance on allegory and its ties to Andy Warhol, see Thomas E. Crow, "Lives of Allegory: Bob Dylan and Andy Warhol," in Colleen Sheehy and Thom Swiss, eds. *Highway 61 Revisited: Dylan's Road from Minnesota to the World* (Minneapolis: University of Minnesota Press, forthcoming).

14. Bono, Foreword, in Mark Blake, ed., *Dylan: Visions, Portraits & Back Pages* (London: DK Publishing with Mojo Music Magazine, 2005), 8.

15. Robert Polito, "Bob Dylan's Memory Palace" in Colleen Sheehy and Thom Swiss, eds., *Highway 61 Revisited: Bob Dylan's Road from Minnesota to the World* (Minneapolis: University of Minnesota Press, forthcoming).

16. Benjamin Filene, *Romancing the Folk: Public Memory and American Roots Music* (Chapel Hill: University of North Carolina, 2000), 232; Jay Cocks, "U2 Explores America," *Time* (November 21, 1988), 146.

17. On the early history of folklore studies and collecting, see Richard Dorson, ed., *Folklore and Folklife* (Chicago: University of Chicago Press, 1972), 1–50; Filene's discussion of folk song collectors is valuable, too, Filene, 9–46. On uses of tradition, see Simon Bronner, *Following Tradition: Folklore in the Discourse of American Culture* (Logan: Utah State University Press, 1998; and Michael Kammen, *Mystic Chords of Memory: The Transformation of Tradition in American Culture* (New York: Knopf, 1991).

18. On interest in folk art by modern artists, see Beatrix Rumford, "Uncommon Art of the Common People: A Review of Trends in the Collecting and Exhibiting of American Folk Art" in Ian Quimby and Scott Swank, *Perspectives on American Folk Art* (New York: W. W. Norton, 1980), 13–25; Virginia Tuttle Clayton, "Picturing a 'Usable Past,'" in *Drawing on America's Past: Folk Art, Modernism, and the Index of American Design* (Washington, D.C.: National Gallery of Art, 2002), 23–27; Michael Kammen, 327–329. On Marsden Hartley, see Patricia McDonnell, *Marsden Hartley: American Modern* (Minneapolis: Weisman Art Museum, 1997), 50–67.

19. Holger Cahill, *American Folk Art: The Art of the Common Man in America, 1750–1900* (New York: Museum of Modern Art, 1932); Kammen, 268.

20. See Virginia Tuttle Clayton, "Picturing a 'Usable Past,'" 1–43, and Erika Doss, "American Folk Art's 'Distinctive Character': The Index of American Design and New Deal Notions of Cultural Nationalism," 61–73, in *Drawing on America's Past: Folk Art, Modernism, and the Index of American Design* (Washington, DC: National Gallery of Art, 2002).

21. Karal Ann Marling, *Wall-to-Wall America: A Cultural History of Post-Office Murals in the Great Depression* (Minneapolis: University of Minnesota Press, 1982).

22. Ellen Harkins Wheat, *Jacob Lawrence: American Painter* (Seattle: University of Washington with the Seattle Art Museum, 1986), 66.

23. See examples of their work, see Alice Rae Yelen, *Passionate Visions of the American South: Self-Taught Artists from 1940 to the Present* (New Orleans: New Orleans Museum of Art with University of Mississippi Press, 1993); *Baking in the Sun: Visionary Images from the South* (Lafayette: University Art Museum, University of Southwestern Louisiana, 1987); Jean Lipman and Alice Winchester, *The Flowering of American Folk Art 1876–1976* (New York: Penguin with the Whitney Museum of American Art, 1976); Colleen Sheehy, *Seed Queen: The Story of Crop Art and the Amazing Lillian Colton* (St. Paul: Minnesota Historical Society Press, 2007).

24. Colleen Sheehy interview with Lillian Colton, March 17, 2006, Owatonna, Minnesota.

25. Doss, 68.

26. David Brigham, *Public Culture in the Early Republic: Peale's Museum and Its Audiences* (Washington, D.C.: Smithsonian Press), 68–82.

27. Shu Hung and Joseph Magliaro, eds., *By Hand: The Use of Craft in Contemporary Art* (New York: Princeton Architectural Press, 2007); and recent exhibitions at the Museum of Arts and Design (formerly the American Craft Museum) in New York City, particularly, *Radical Lace and Subversive Knitting* (2007) and *Extreme Embroidery* (2007–08).

28. Dario Robleto, "I Love Everything Rock and Roll (Except the Music)," www.presentspace.com/presenttwo/presents/robleto/robletoessay.htm (accessed February 3, 2008).

29. Nato Thompson, ed., *Ahistoric Occasion: Artists Making History* (North Adams: Massachusetts Museum of Contemporary Art, 2006), 78–83.

30. On clothing in contemporary art, see Judith Hoos Fox and Amy Ingrid Schlegel, eds., *Pattern Language: Clothing as Communicator* (Medford, Massachusetts: Tufts University Gallery, 2007); on the important relation of dress and textiles to memory, see Judith Attfield, *Wild Things: The Material Culture of Everyday Life* (Oxford, England: Berg Publishers, 2000), 121–148.

31. On history of the cowboy and his mythic dimensions, see Lonn Taylor, *The American Cowboy* (New York: Harper and Row for the American Folklife Center, 1983); Edward G. White, *The Eastern Establishment and the Western Experience* (New Haven, Connecticut: Yale University Press, 1968; on Remington, see Peter Hassrick, *Frederic Remington* (New York: Abrams, and the Amon Carter Museum, Fort Worth, 1973); and Harold McCracken, *Frederic Remington: Artist of the Old West* (New York: J.B. Lippincott Co., 1947), and Ben Merchant Vorpahl, *Frederic Remington and the West* (Austin: University of Texas Press, 1978). On Wild West shows, see Don Russell, *The Wild West or A History of the Wild West Shows* (Fort Worth: Amon Carter Museum, 1970).

32. *Jeremy Blake Winchester* (San Francisco: San Francisco Museum of Modern Art, 2005); and *The Gospel of Lead: Dario Robleto and Jeremy Blake* (Austin, Texas: Arthouse, 2006).

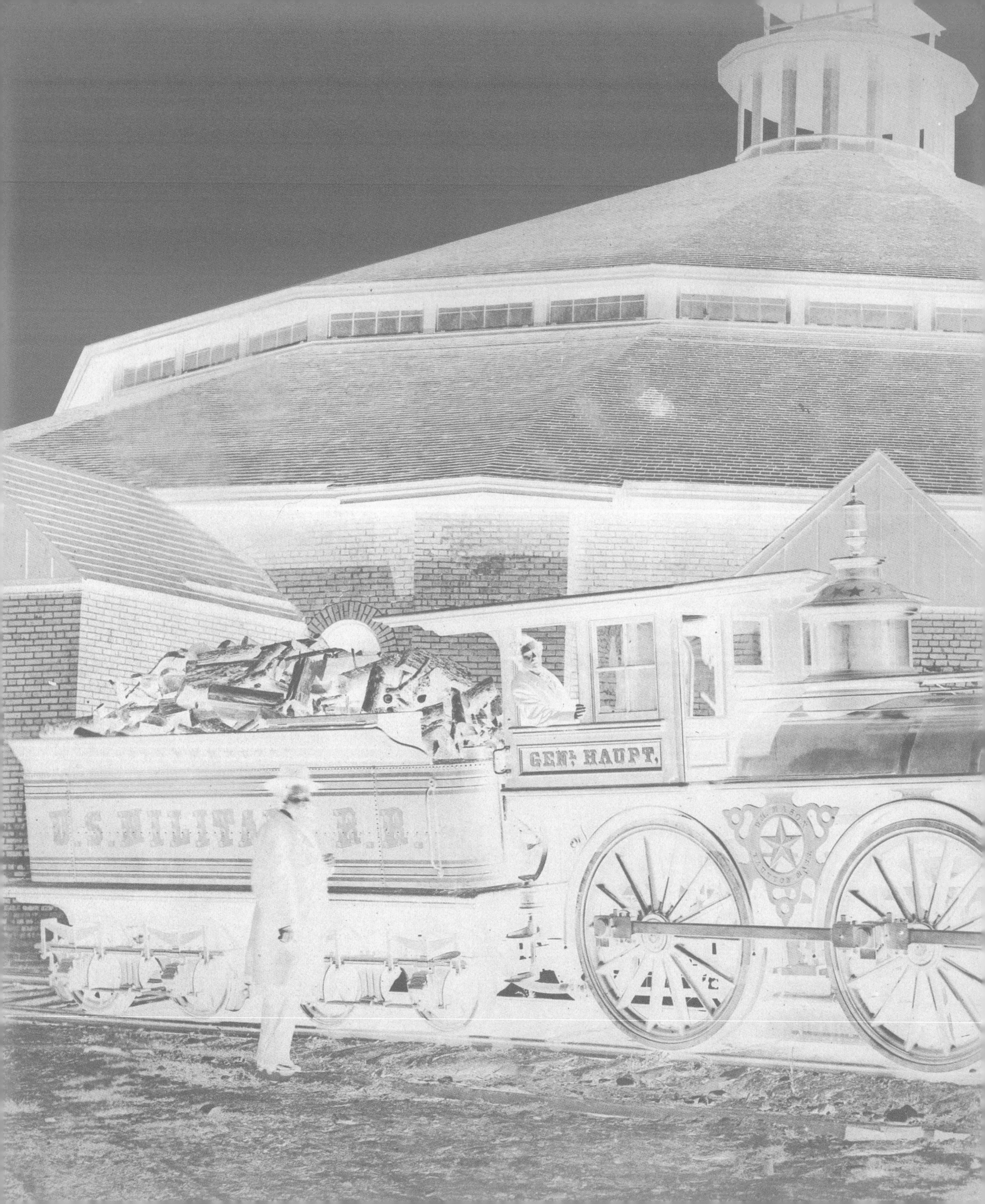
GENL HAUPT,
U.S. MILITARY R.R.

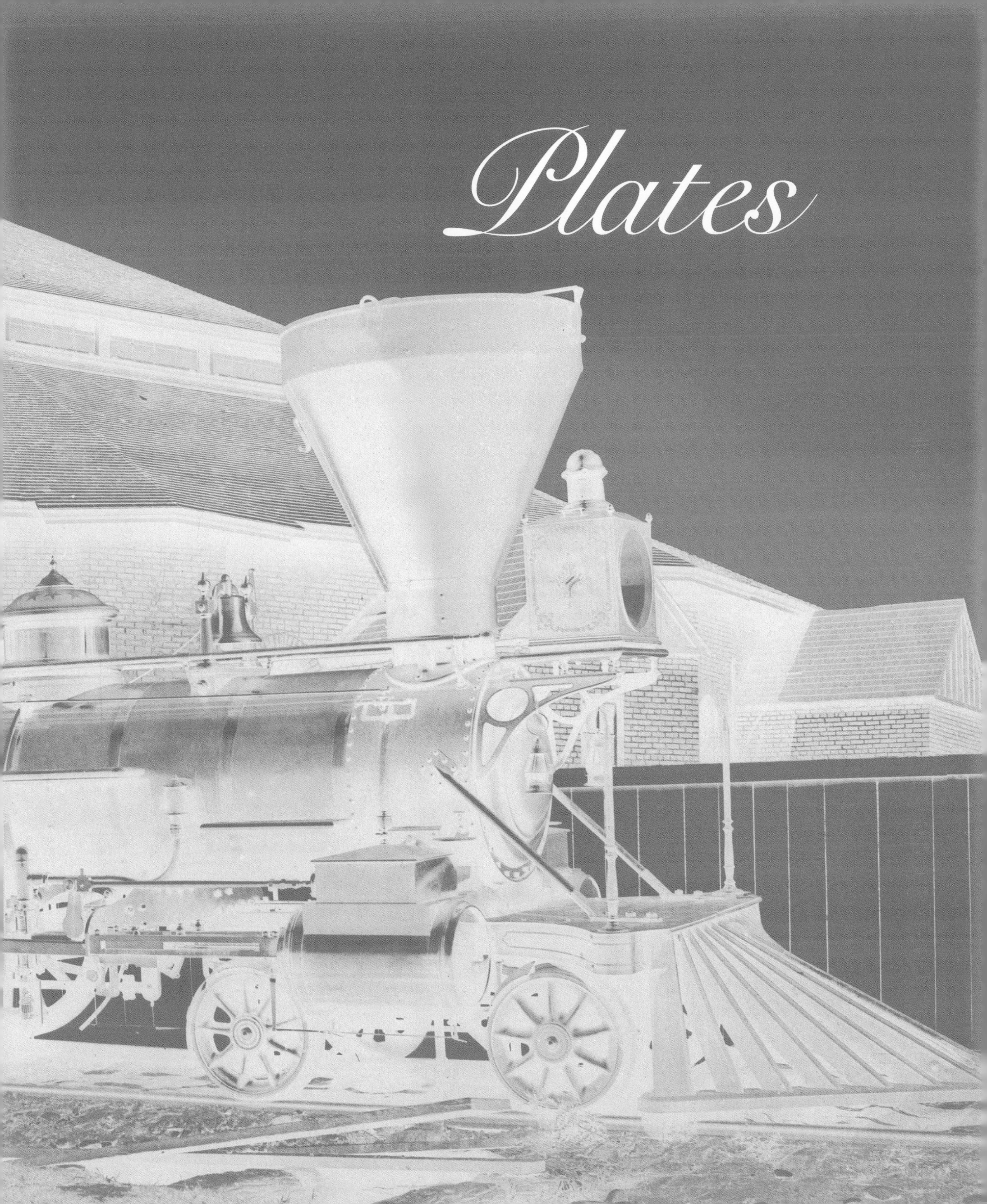
Plates

Eric Beltz

1 *(page 55)*
ERIC BELTZ
Fuck You Tree, 2007
Graphite on Bristol board
40 x 30 inches
Collection Chris DeBolt, Los
Angeles

Fig. 47
Grant Wood
Parson Weems' Fable, 1939
Oil on canvas
38⅜ x 50⅛ inches
Amon Carter Museum,
Fort Worth

Generally, America's founding fathers are idealized figures, but we've all heard stories that take them down a notch: Thomas Jefferson fathered illegitmate children with one of his slaves, Benjamin Franklin slept around, George Washington grew hemp. In his fantastical, fanatically detailed, and downright freaky graphite portraits of these heroes of American history, Eric Beltz uses rumor, legend, and outright fabrication as starting points for an irreverent and surreal meditation on the nation's beginnings. Drawing on sources as diverse as the subjects' own writings, Americana clip art, the Bible, the Tibetan Book of Dying, the Egyptian Book of the Dead, and tomes on witchcraft and herbal medicine, Beltz creates his own addled versions of America's creation story. In *Fuck You Tree* (2007), Washington sits on a dismembered cherry tree, humorously reprising *Parson Weems' Fable* (1939, fig. 47), Grant Wood's famous representation of the wholly fictional object lesson of the young president-to-be's honesty. But where Wood showed Washington as an upstanding man-boy, Beltz shows him as a beset adult, surrounded by ominous symbols: medicinal plants that grow when old growth forest is cut, a coiled rattlesnake labeled "Never Surrender," and a decapitated owl, signifying the demon Stola, a prince of hell.[1] A woozy halo of thirteen stars encircles Washington's head, which is detached from his body, echoing the

brain-like crown of the tree, while floating fragments of text describe curses and impending death. *Breath of Satan* (2007), the artist writes, "…shows Benjamin Franklin on a vision quest, sitting on a hilltop, surrounded by herbs, orchids, bats, and his spirit animal the wild turkey."[2] Its composition inspired by Francisco de Goya's famous etching *The Sleep of Reason Produces Monsters* (1797–1798), the work is laced with text implying that the world and its problems might have been created by Satan and not God. *Good Luck Assholes* (2007) is inspired by Beltz's fantasy of what a curmudgeonly Thomas Jefferson might have said at his retirement party. Depicting Jefferson smoking a pipe by a wood-pile outside his retreat home at Poplar Forest, the image includes a group of wild turkeys flying through a line of text representing, the artist says, "…the track of his soul to the 'Happy Place' described in the Egyptian Book of the Dead as well as AA programs."[3]

Fascinated by shamanism and the oftentimes related field of ethnobotany, Beltz wanted to depict these political visionaries in moments of psychic transformation, where dualities like life and death, idealism and nihilism, hang in the balance. "Looking at Washington, Jefferson, and Franklin in 2007, it's impossible not to see their idealistic desire to create a utopian state against the unraveling of that dream over time," he says. "Lately I've been reading histories of America by David McCullough and Joseph Ellis, and feeling nostalgic for a time when we could look at our founders and origin myths in heroic terms, but since this is no longer possible, I'm trying to find a position that blends historical fact, rational thought, and mysticism, which I believe is closer to the truth."[4] Beltz's psychedelic statesmen may be American versions of Frankenstein's monster made from spiritual and cultural detritus, but they also are illuminating emblems of how meaning accrues to figures over time. Just as the artist feels free to pick and choose from any number of cross-cultural sources to create his portraits, so too do politicians shape the images and intentions of their predecessors according to their own agendas. One cannot help but wonder if Washington, Jefferson, and Franklin would long for some mind-altering substances if they could see their country today.

1–3. Eric Beltz, unpublished notes emailed to the author, October 16, 2007.

4. Eric Beltz, telephone interview with the author, December 3, 2007.

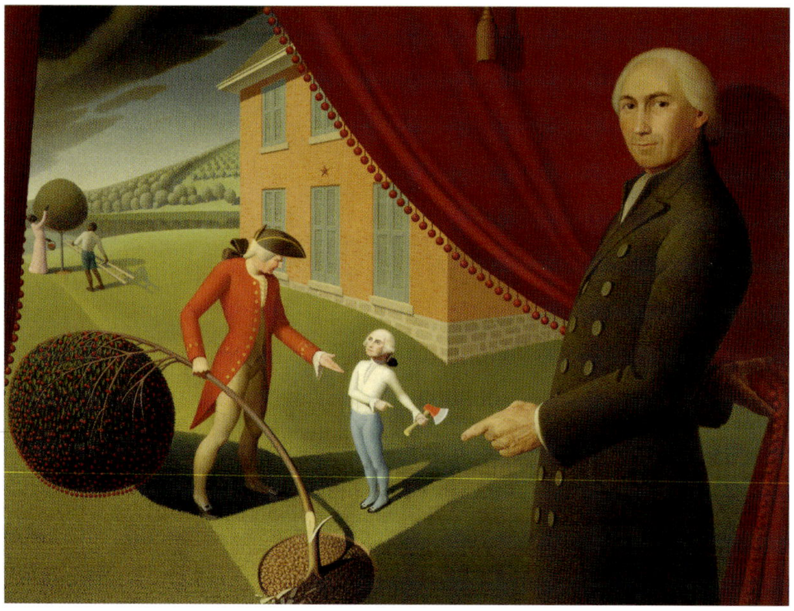

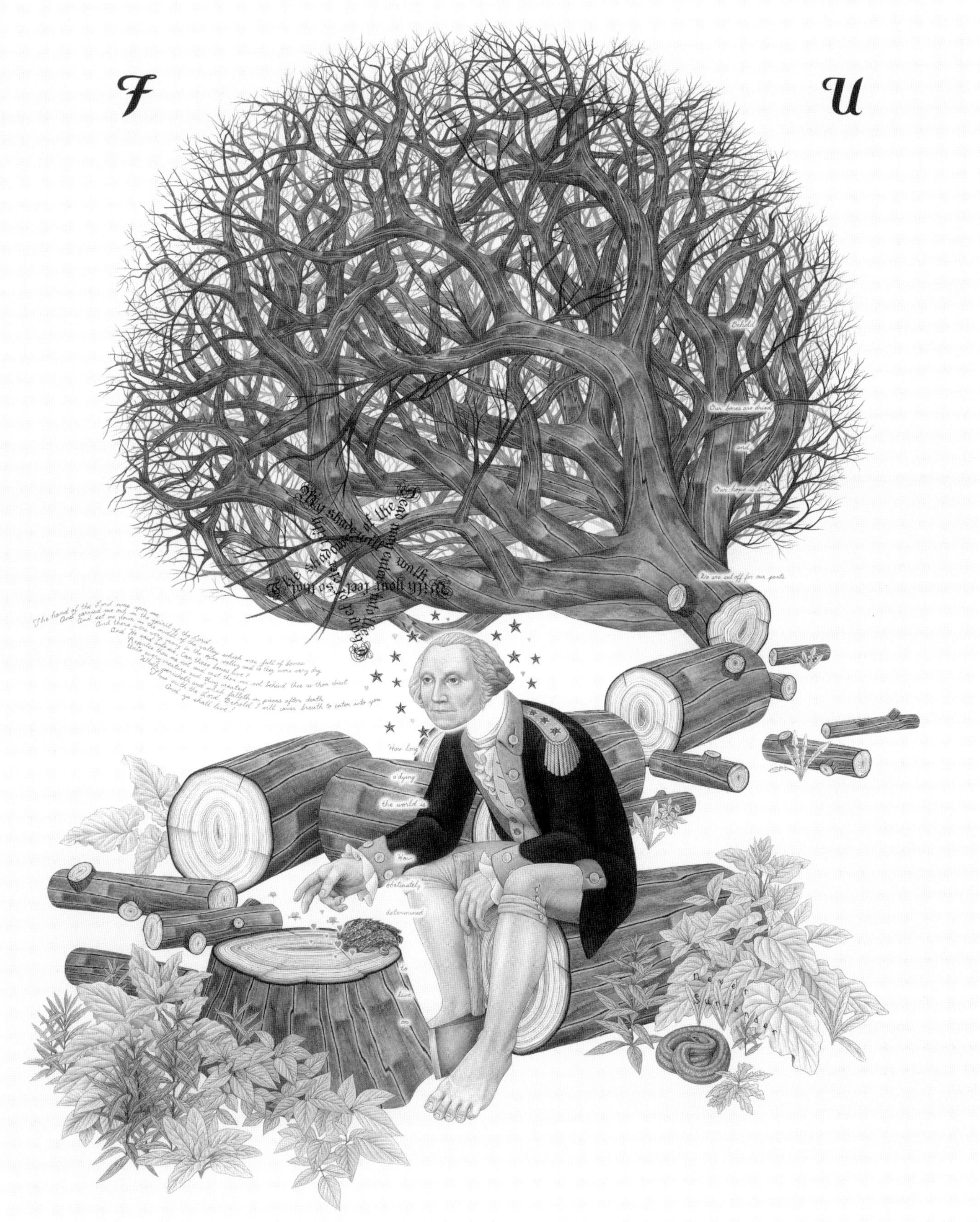

F
U
The hand of the Lord was upon me
And carried me out in the spirit of the Lord
And set me down in the midst of the valley which was full of bones
And there were very many in the open valley and lo they were very dry
And He said unto me, Can these bones live?
Refuse thou me not and cast thou me not behind thee as thou doest
Unto every creature and thing created
Which perisheth and which falleth in pieces after death
Thus saith the Lord, Behold I will cause breath to enter into you
And ye shall live!

55

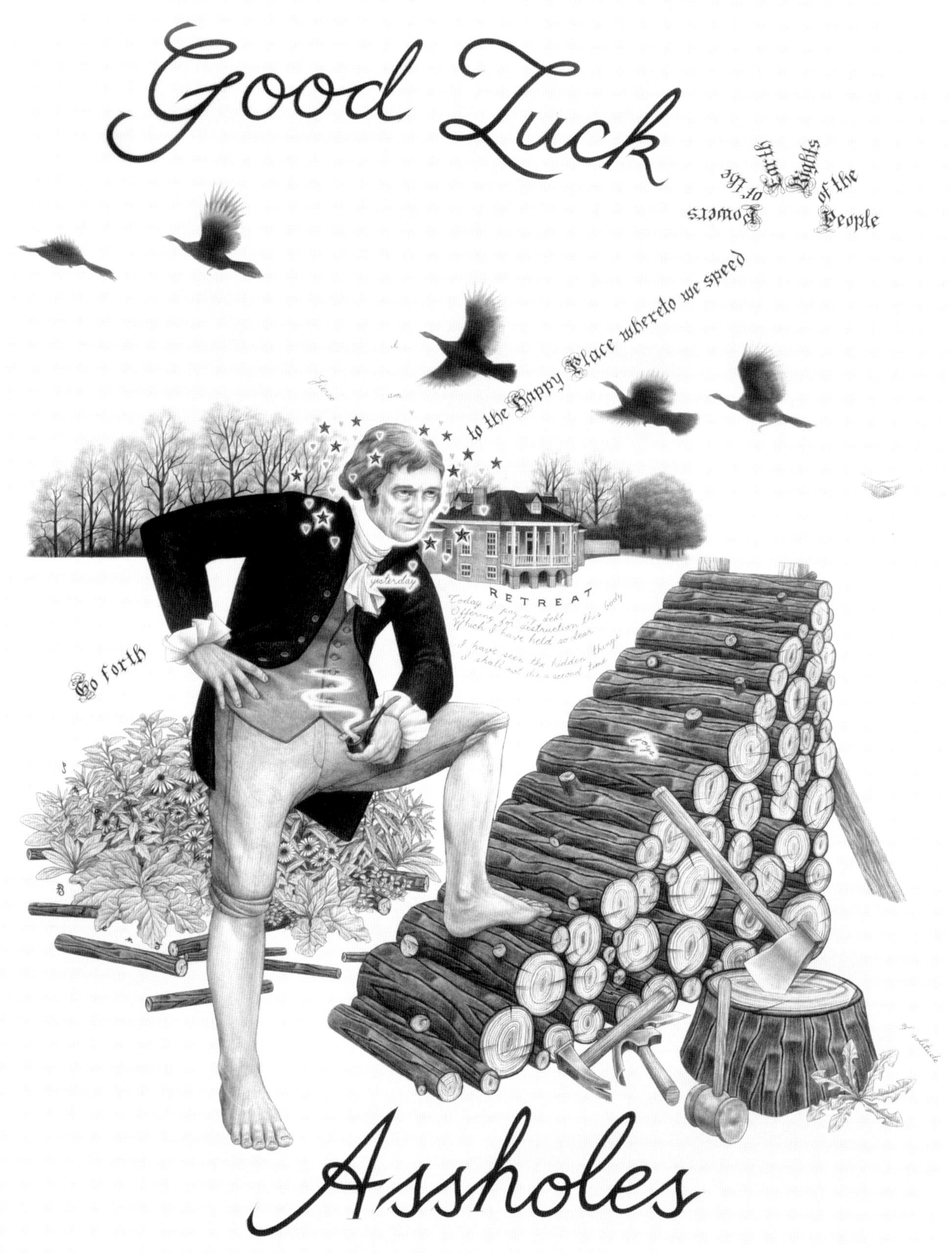

Good Luck
Rights of the People
Earth
Powers of Life
to the Happy Place whereto we speed
RETREAT
Go forth
Assholes

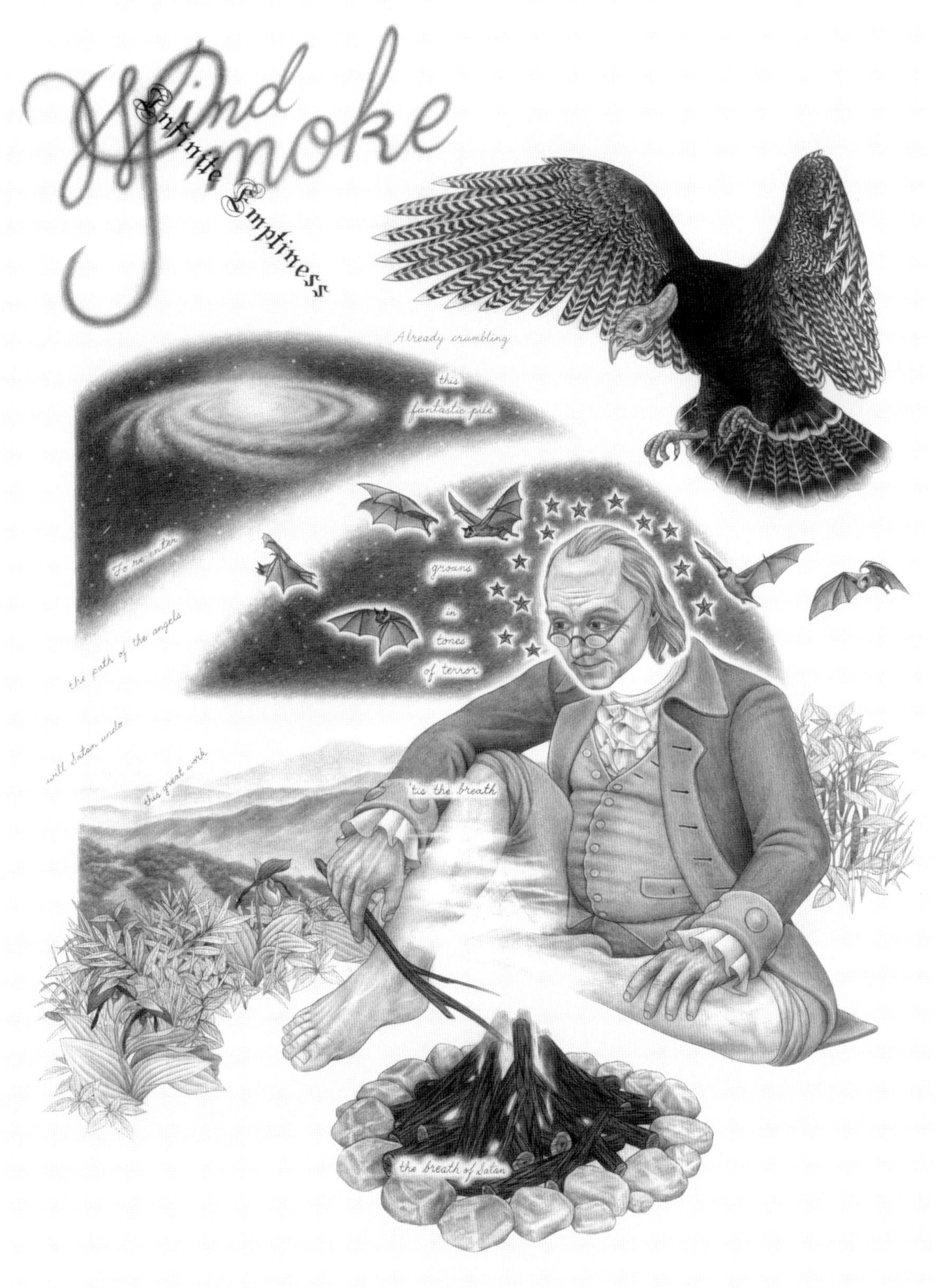

2 *(page 56)*
ERIC BELTZ
Good Luck Assholes, 2007
Graphite on Bristol board
28 x 22 inches
Collection Jeffrey and Elana Rose, Los Angeles

3
ERIC BELTZ
Breath of Satan, 2007
Graphite on Bristol board
23 x 17 inches
Collection Chris DeBolt, Los Angeles

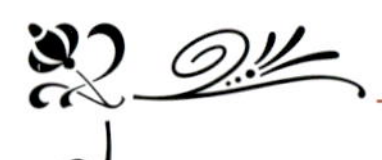

Jeremy Blake

Jeremy Blake was a connoisseur of film, music, fashion, and American mythopoetics. He made what he called "time-based paintings"—lush, color-saturated videos that fluidly shift between realism and abstraction—that present a subversive, psychedelic take on the histories of art and popular culture. Blake was trained as a painter and throughout his career made abstract as well as representational works such as *The All-American Boy* (2000) and *Big Pink* (2000), a portrait of a young Dylan and a depiction of the house in West Saugerties, New York, where Dylan and The Band recorded the folk-art classsic *The Basement Tapes* in 1967—both included in *The Old, Weird America* as emblems of the exhibition's inspiration and Blake's contributions to it.[1] Blake began using video, which he produced on computers using a wide array of editing techniques, because he envied the dynamism of filmmaking: "I wanted to get the emotion of abstract painting some other way, give it some juice by making it move, make it unstable, and then do something like add sound to disorient people and say to the viewer: 'Keep watching, keep watching. Something's going to happen.'"[2] Among Blake's video projects are *Reading Ossie Clark* (2003), an homage to the swinging-sixties style of the British clothing designer, and a "peep show for poets" entitled *Sodium Fox* (2005), made in collaboration with poet and musician Dave Berman. He also created a video and the album art for Beck's CD *Sea Change* (2002) and contributed interstitial abstract scenes for the film *Punch Drunk Love* (2002) that feature his signature combination of diaphanous areas of translucent color and digitally collaged photographic images.

The fourteen-minute video *Winchester* (2002) is part of a trilogy of works inspired by the Winchester Mystery House in San Jose, California. Sarah Winchester (1839–1922), heir to the Winchester rifle fortune, fell under the influence of a psychic who told her that in order to escape the angry spirits of those killed by her family's guns, she needed to move from Connecticut to California and build a labyrinthine mansion, which must remain under constant construction. Now a popular tourist attraction, the Winchester House has nearly 160 rooms and is riddled with doors and stairways leading nowhere. The work incorporates photographs of the Victorian-Baroque house, sounds of whirring film projectors, and ghostly silhouettes of rifle-toting cowboys, which dissolve and morph into abstract butterflies, flowers, and aurorae borealis of color. Like the other parts of the trilogy—*1906*, which focuses on the interior of the house and those parts damaged by the San Francisco earthquake, which Winchester interpreted as an omen and so built around them, and *Century 21*, which features three adjacent domelike, space-age-modernist movie theaters and snippets from Hollywood pulp films—*Winchester* is a poetic meditation on madness and excess. In light of Blake's suicide in the summer of 2007, which followed that of his longtime partner, screenwriter and blogger Theresa Duncan, and which seems to have been precipitated by the couple's belief that they were being persecuted by Scientologists and the CIA, *Winchester* seems doubly, tragically symbolic.

1. Blake was involved in the earliest conversations about this project and was instrumental in helping shape *The Old, Weird America*'s premise.

2. Jeremy Blake, quoted in Steven Madoff, "Guns and Ghosts: The Winchester Witch Project," *New York Times*, February 28, 2005, p. A38.

4
JEREMY BLAKE
Video still from *Winchester*, 2002
DVD: color, sound, 18 minutes (continuous loop)
Courtesy Kinz, Tillou + Feigen, New York

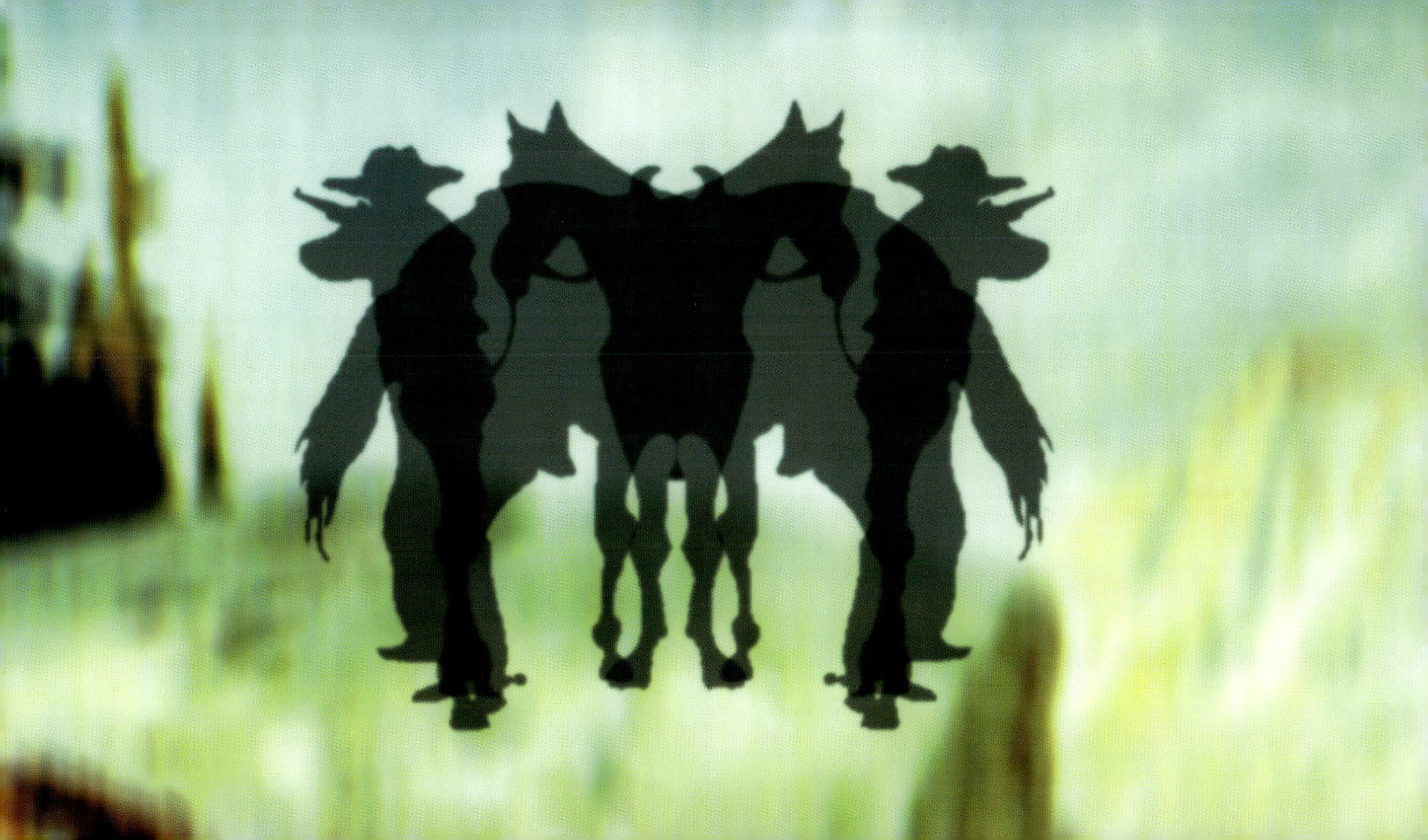

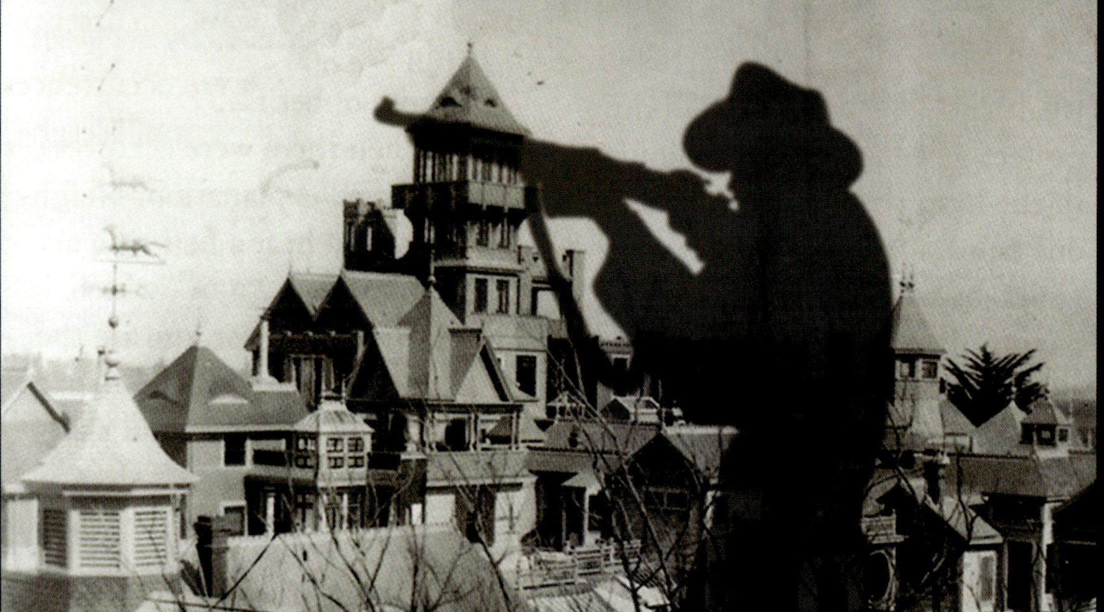

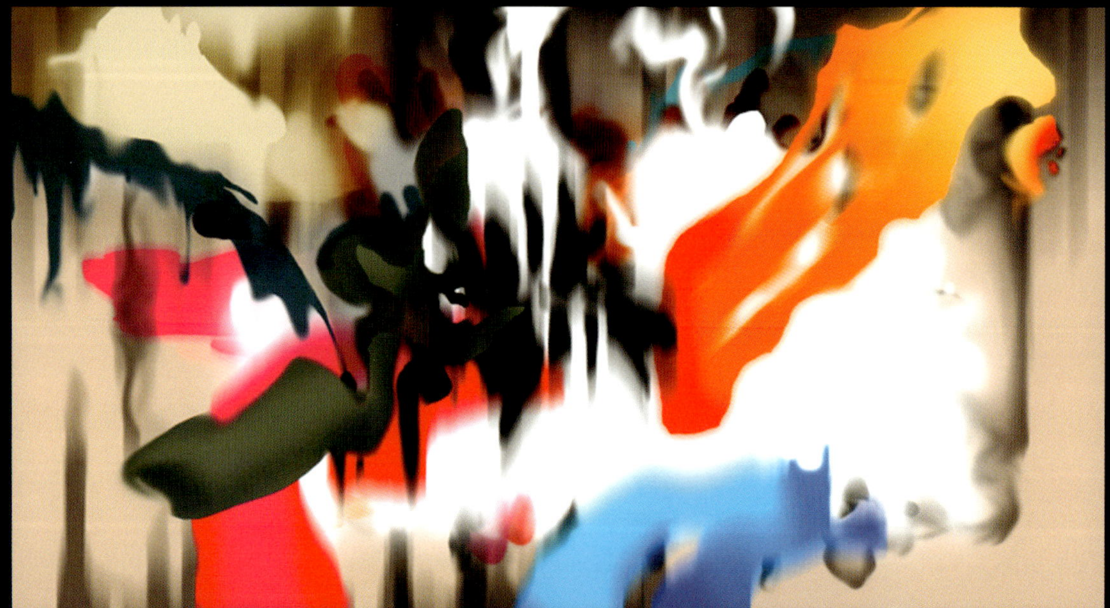

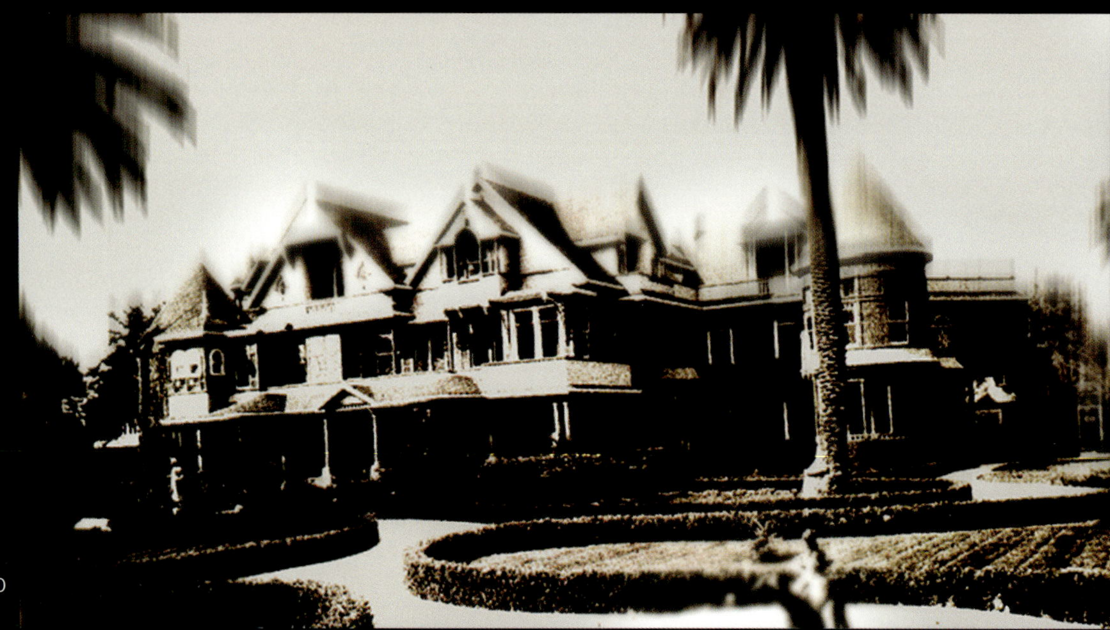

5–8
JEREMY BLAKE
Video stills from *Winchester*, 2002
DVD: color, sound, 18 minutes
(continuous loop)
Courtesy Kinz, Tillou + Feigen,
New York

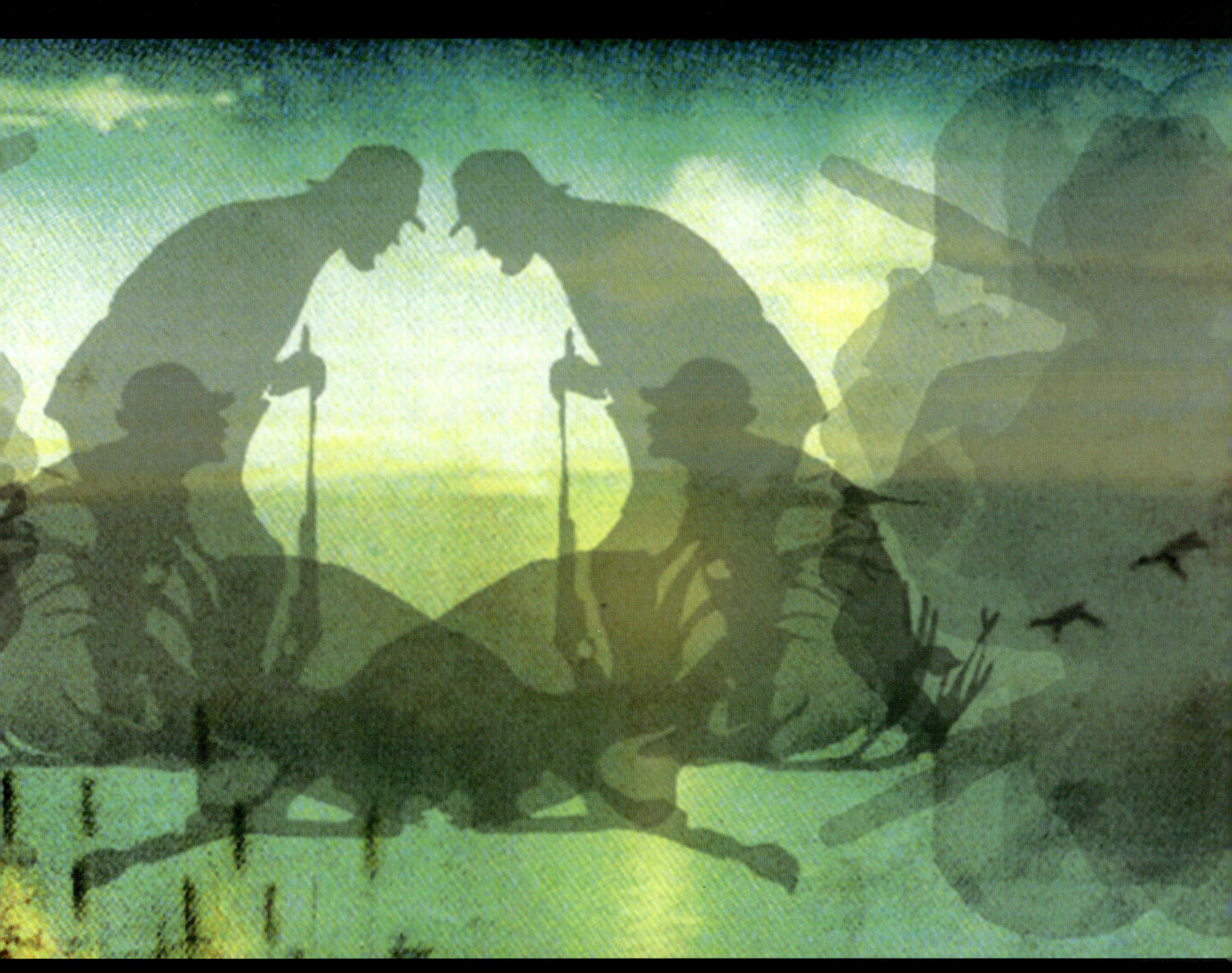

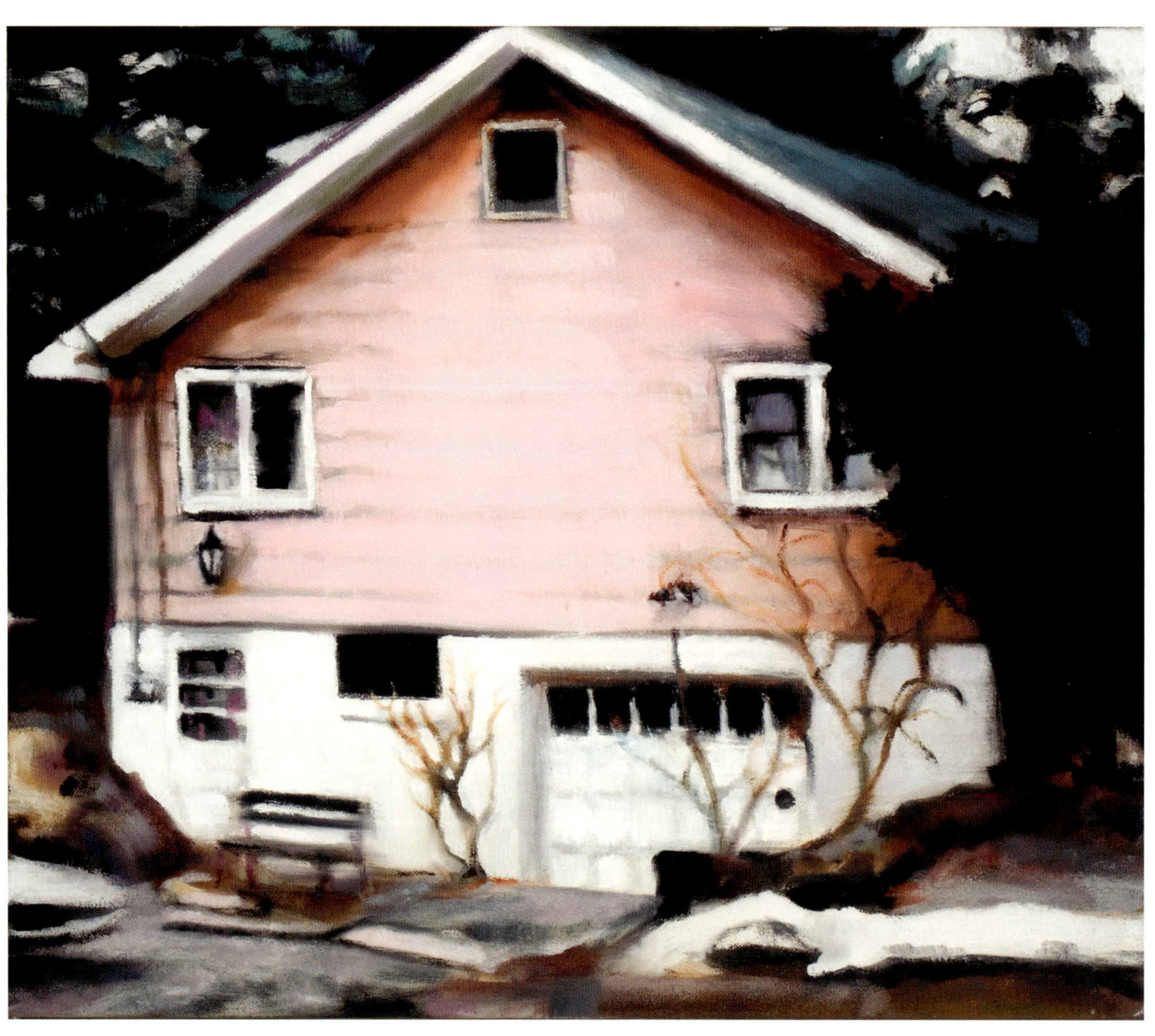

9
JEREMY BLAKE
Big Pink, 2004
Oil on canvas
12 x 14 inches
Private Collection

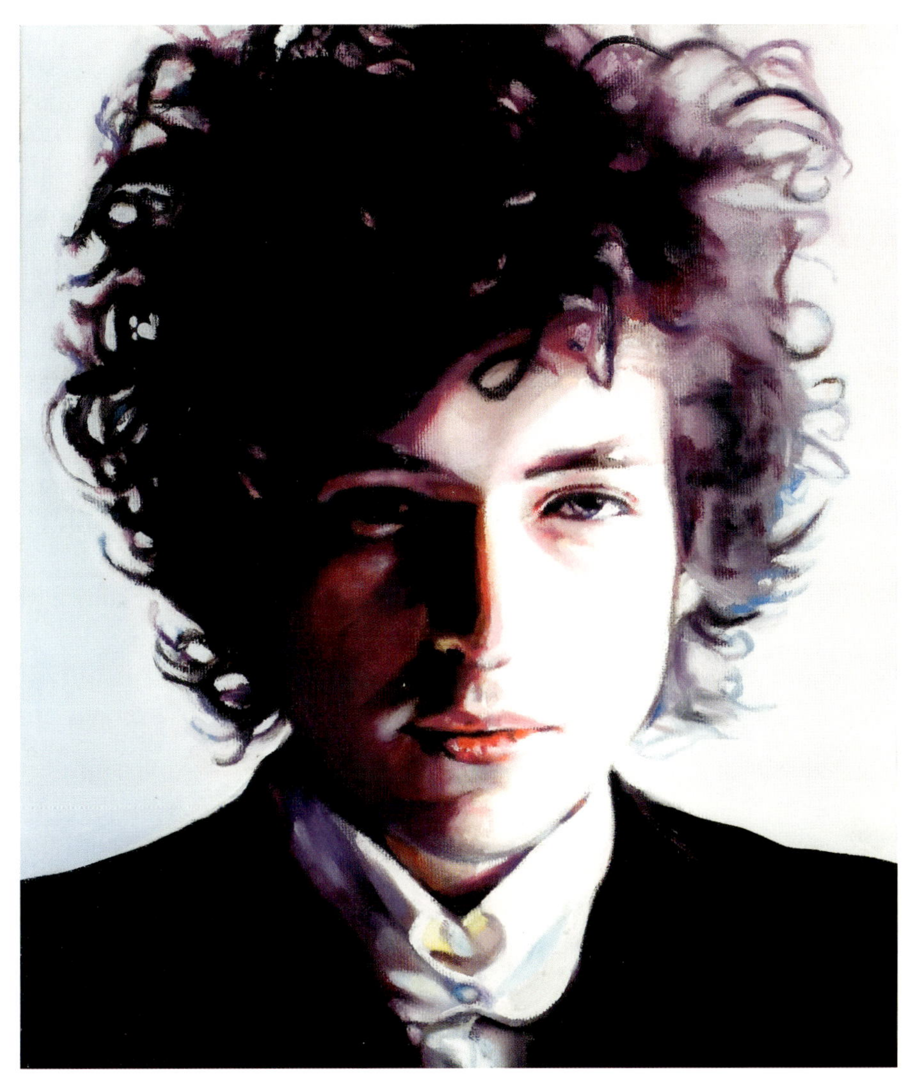

10
Jeremy Blake
The All-American Boy, 2004
Oil on canvas
12 x 10 inches
Private Collection

Sam Durant

Sam Durant is interested in the evolution of American culture. His drawings, photographs, sculptures, and installations draw on history, art, and popular culture to excavate complex histories of race and politics, art and protest, and fact and fable. Particularly interested in clashes between ideals and reality, Durant often juxtaposes images and objects from charged historical events to expose rifts in the social fabric of the United States. Durant's many projects include collages that combine shots of rampaging bikers from seedy motorcycle magazines into images of elegant modernist architecture; a collection of drawings, sculptures, and period music conflating two groundbreaking events that took place at Ohio's Kent State University in 1970: the completion of Robert Smithson's famous Land Art project *Partially Buried Woodshed* and the killing of four students protesting the Vietnam War; and a re-creation of a poor farmer's shack whose front porch holds a turntable and collection of albums tracing the transformation of African-American blues into white rock 'n' roll. Preferring dispassionate rearrangement and recombination to impassioned distortion or commentary, Durant coolly spotlights the dark recesses of American exceptionalism.

In *The Old, Weird America*, Durant presents a life-size, rotating diorama in two parts, each consisting of a wax-figure tableau set against a painted backdrop entitled *Pilgrims and Indians, Planting and Reaping, Learning and Teaching* (2006). The work turns on a motorized circular platform and is made from two displays the artist purchased from the defunct Plymouth National Wax Museum in Massachusetts. One side illustrates the story Americans commonly accept as the origin of the communal spirit that inspired the first Thanksgiving: a Native American teaching a Pilgrim settler how to grow corn by fertilizing the seed with herring, ensuring a good harvest in the fall. The other side tells the lesser-known, true story of the holiday: Captain Myles Standish killing the Pequot Indian Pecksuot. According to Edward Winslow's 1624 report from the Plymouth Colony, *Good News from New England*, when the much taller Pecksuot questioned his strength and courage, Standish flew into a fit of rage and stabbed him. Standish then organized a raiding party to wipe out the Pequots, declaring a day of thanksgiving after their successful return.

Durant, who grew up near Plymouth, remembers seeing the Wax Museum but not the Standish/Pecksuot diorama, which was removed in the 1970s because of visitor complaints. He also remembers a 1970 protest declaring Thanksgiving a "National Day of Mourning" after activist Frank B. Wamsutta James was disinvited from a state dinner celebrating the 350th anniversary of the Pilgrims' arrival at Plymouth when he refused to rewrite a speech that called the holiday "the beginning of the end" for Native peoples. "I wanted to set up a comparison," Durant says. "Each of these dioramas tells different sides of the Thanksgiving story. But the Native side of the story, like Pecksuot and the Pequots, has been suppressed."[1] Because it perpetually presents two radically different sides of the Thanksgiving story, *Pilgrims and Indians…* is an ambivalent—literally two-sided—memorial to both the fantasy image of the holiday and the terrible legacy of violence and genocide associated with it.

1. Sam Durant, telephone interview with the author, November 18, 2007.

11
SAM DURANT
Pilgrims and Indians, Planting and Reaping, Learning and Teaching (installation view, Massachusetts College of Art and Design, Boston), 2006
Mixed media, motorized platform
Courtesy the artist and Blum & Poe, Los Angeles
Photo: John Paul Doguin

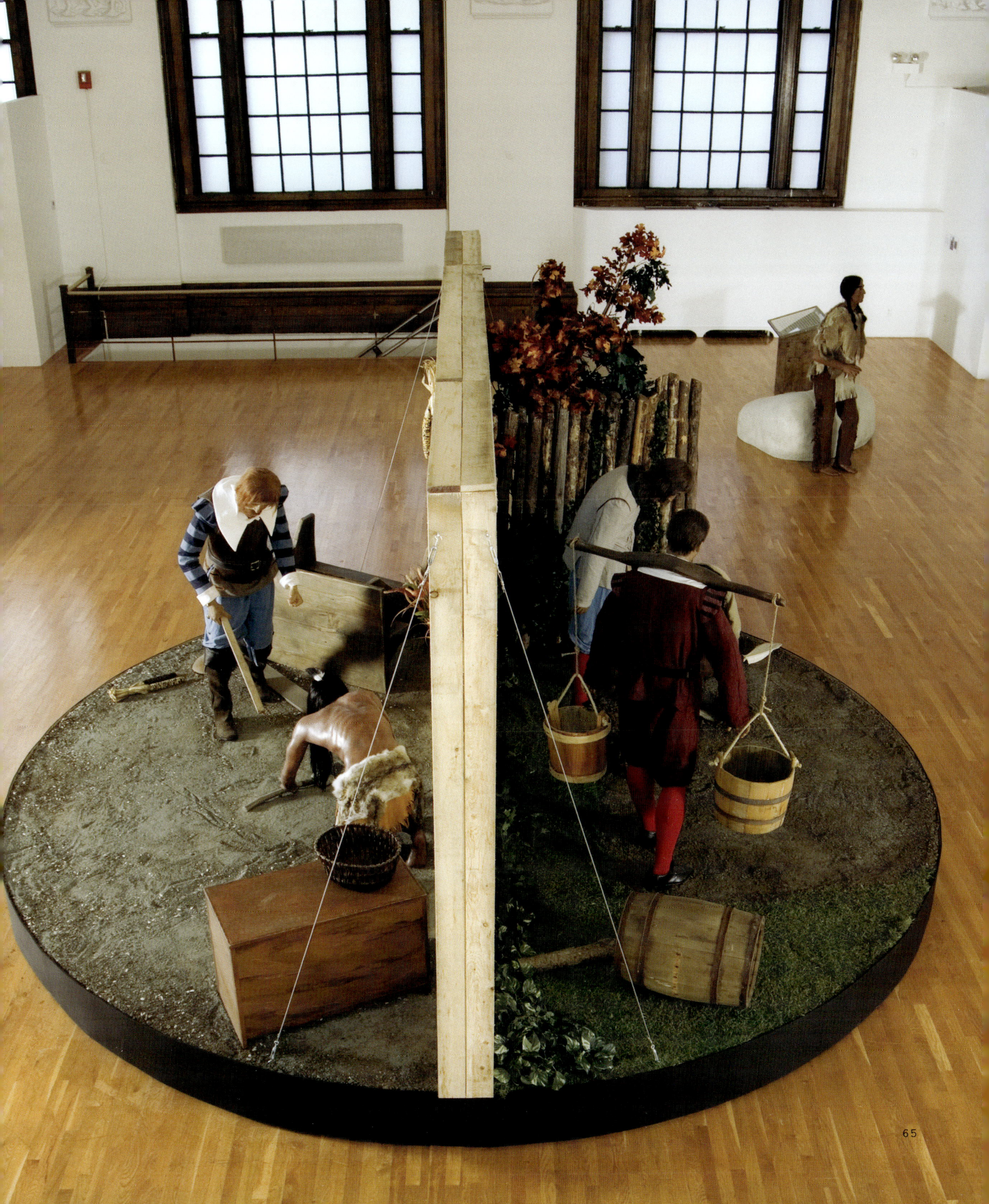

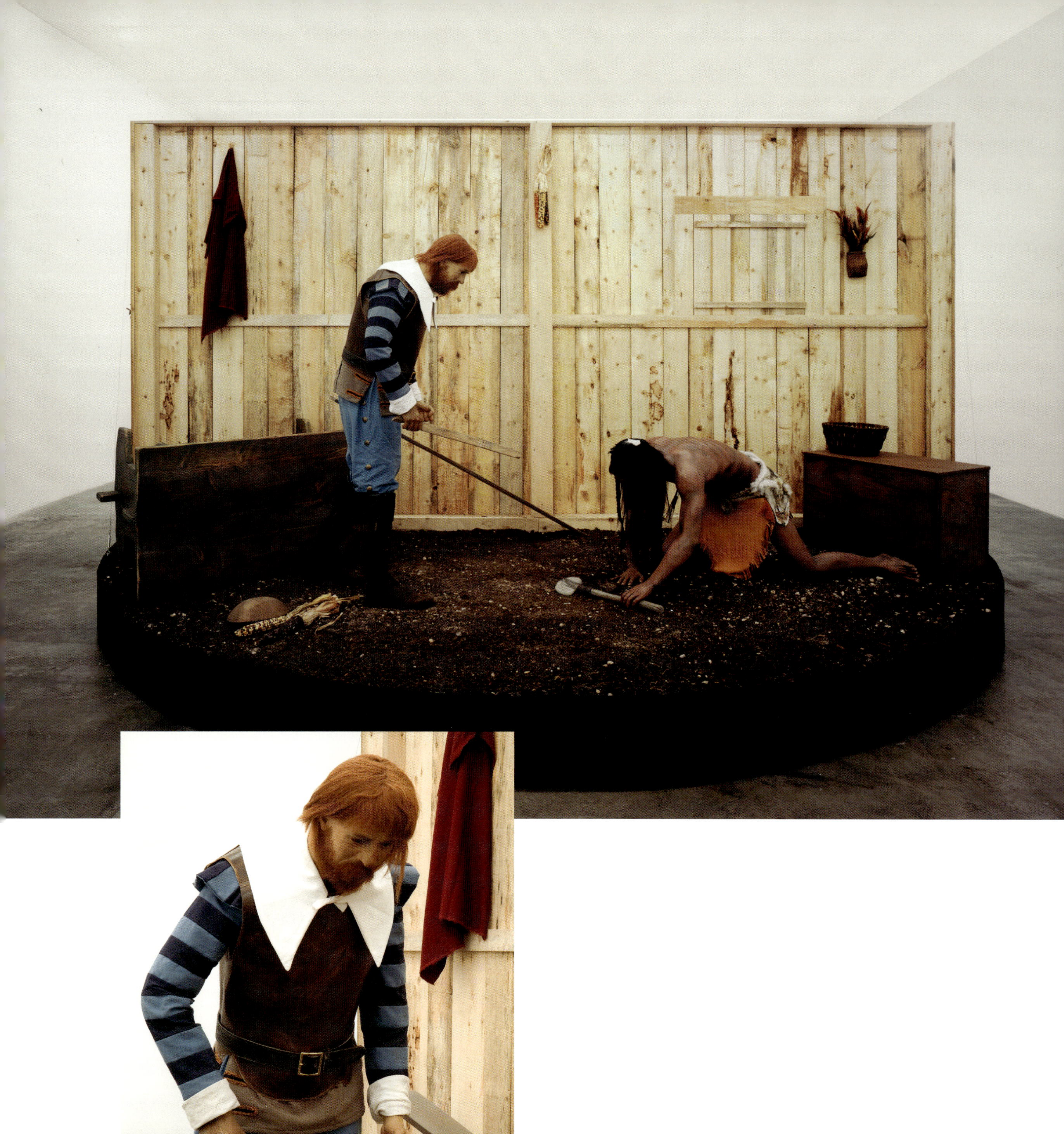

12–15
SAM DURANT
Pilgrims and Indians, Planting and Reaping, Learning and Teaching (details), 2006
Mixed media, motorized platform
Courtesy the artist and Blum & Poe, Los Angeles

66

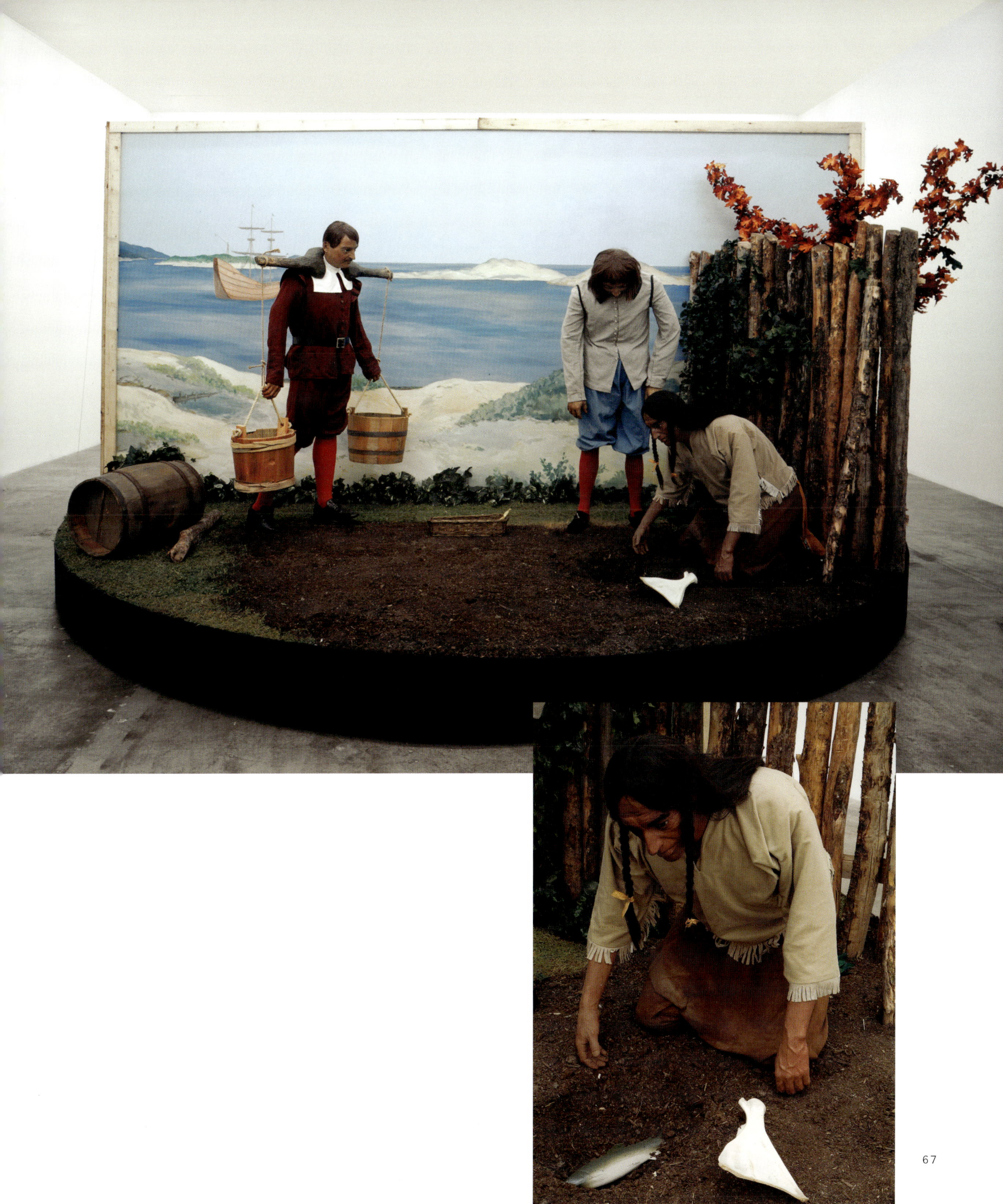

Barnaby Furnas

Barnaby Furnas makes history paintings for the digital age. His images of American presidents, Civil War battles, and abolitionist John Brown vibrate with the luminous colors and explosive special effects of video games and Hollywood movies. Blood spatters, bullets trace glowing trajectories, and movement fractures into dazzling post-modern, Cubist shimmers (fig. 48). An interest in sensationalism drives Furnas' work. In fact, he conceived of his action- and violence-packed paintings and watercolors as attempts to create "blockbuster American paintings."[1] According to Furnas, "Art can be seen as a series of changes in visual appetites, and there's a continuum from Renaissance realism, to nineteenth-century panoramas and dioramas, to action films. For example, Théodore Géricault's *Raft of the Medusa* (1818–1819, fig. 49) and its gory story of a shipwreck was too controversial for the Paris salons and was originally exhibited at Barnum and Bailey's circus—sort of like the precursor to IMAX films." The work of Kara Walker, another exhibition artist, also provided an inspirational spark. "When I saw her personal, imaginary takes on the history of slavery, I thought, 'I want a complicated fantasy life, too!'," Furnas says. Thinking of French psychoanalyst Jacques Lacan's belief that "releasing fantasies" would provide clues to his character, Furnas returned to his childhood practice of drawing battle scenes as a kind of play, in which he would trace bullets and cannon shells and their impacts—something that did not harmonize with his pacifist Quaker upbringing. His harrowing and hyperkinetic representations of aggression, madness, and fierce principles in American history are, Furnas says, "attempts at painting my fears—with the hope the process will empower me against them in some way."

Furnas' works often focus on familiar moments of American tragedy but give them an uncanny, visceral twist, heightened by his radiant paints, made from mixing pigment with urethane. In *John Brown* (2005), set in a field of flowerlike muzzle-flashing pistols, he depicts the hellbrand anti-slavery campaigner standing with a noose around his neck as a messiah-like figure who defiantly stares down the viewer. In *Assassination (Abraham Lincoln)* (2007), the blast from a shadowy John Wilkes Booth's gun haloes the doomed president's head. And in *Second Inaugural* (2003), an image of Lincoln's Biblical condemnation of slavery at the end of the Civil War itself morphs into a chaotic firefight. Similar cathartic action pervades his watercolor battle-scenes, which lend his Matrix-style, time-lapse imagery a precise, cartoonlike immediacy. Furnas' grownup translations of his childhood action-drawings are rooted in wanting to understand and experience an event. Just as he relives the awe and dread of his stories in their telling, he hopes his images will drive home the legacy of the searing struggles undergirding contemporary American life.

1. This and all subsequent quotes by the artist are from an interview with the author, November 13, 2006.

Fig. 48
Barnaby Furnas
Cemetery Ridge, April 24, 2001, 2001
Watercolor on paper
25 x 37 inches
Collection Greg S. Feldman, New York

Fig. 49
Théodore Géricualt
The Raft of the Medusa, 1819
Oil on canvas
193 ½ x 282 inches
Musée de Louvre, Paris

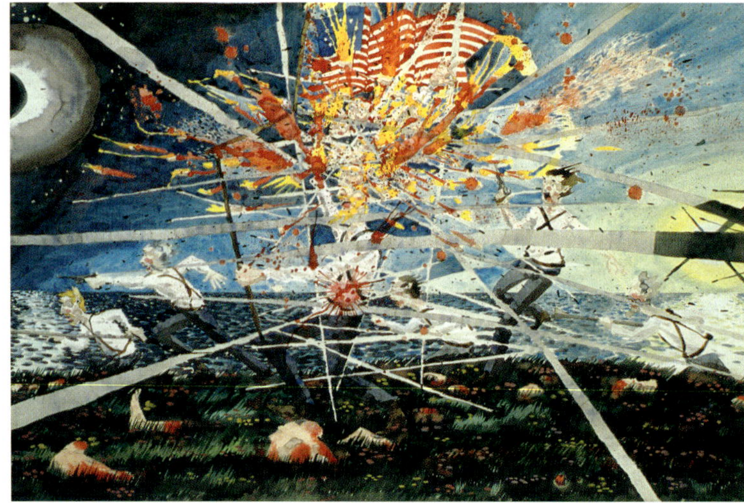

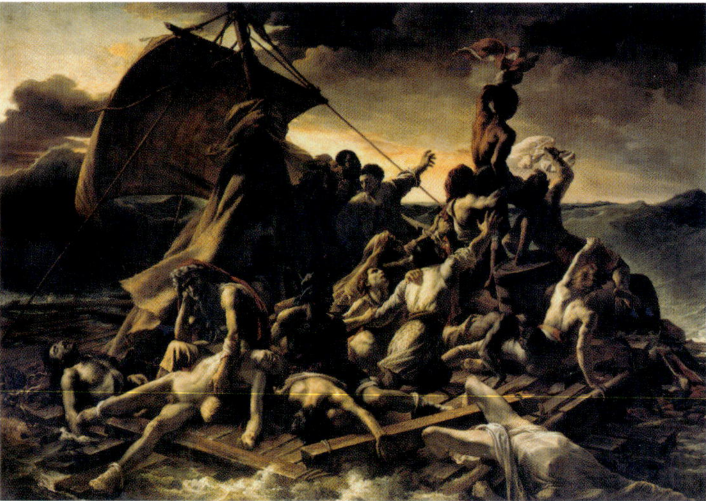

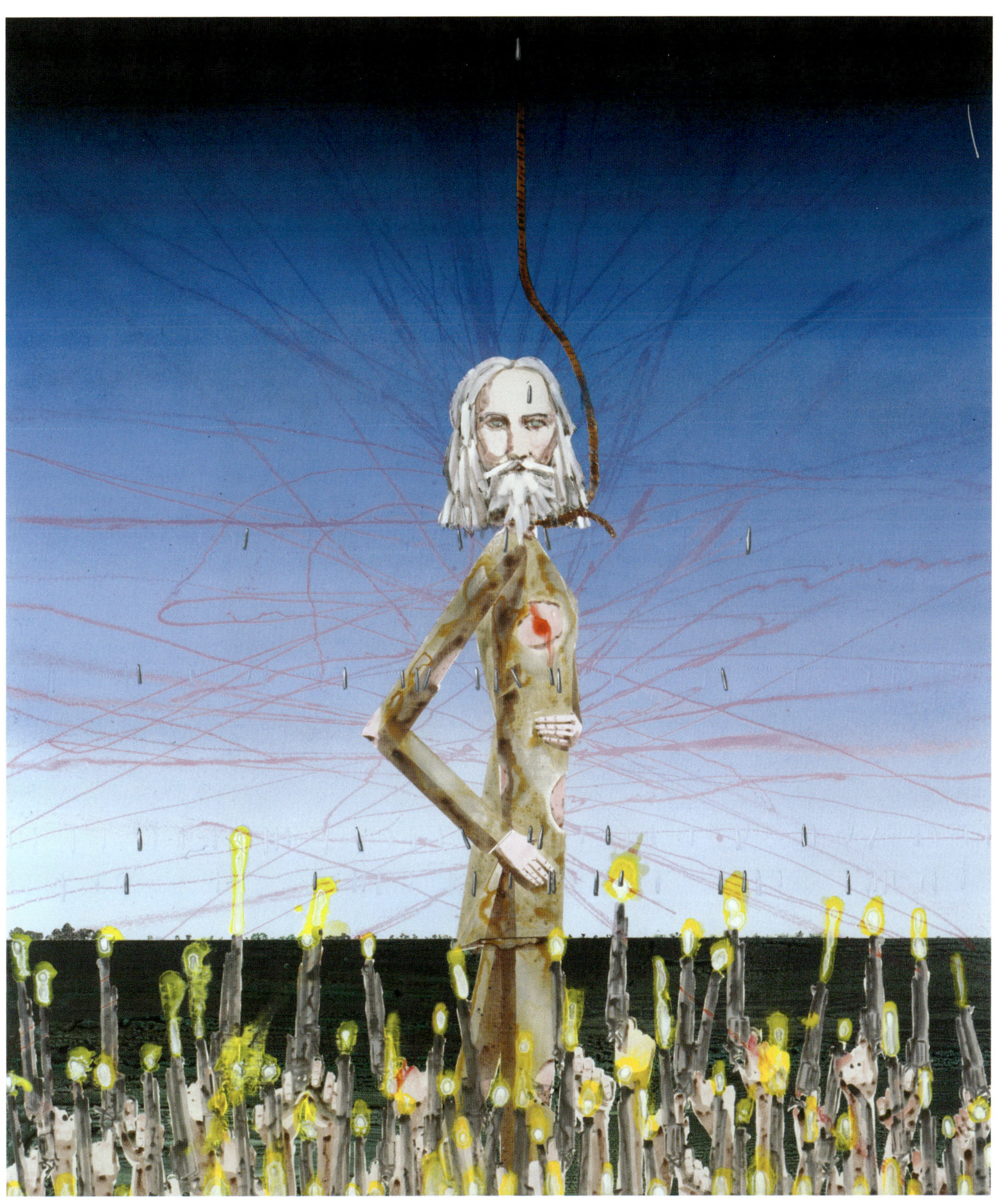

16
BARNABY FURNAS
John Brown, 2005
Urethane and dye on linen
72 x 60 inches
Private Collection, New York

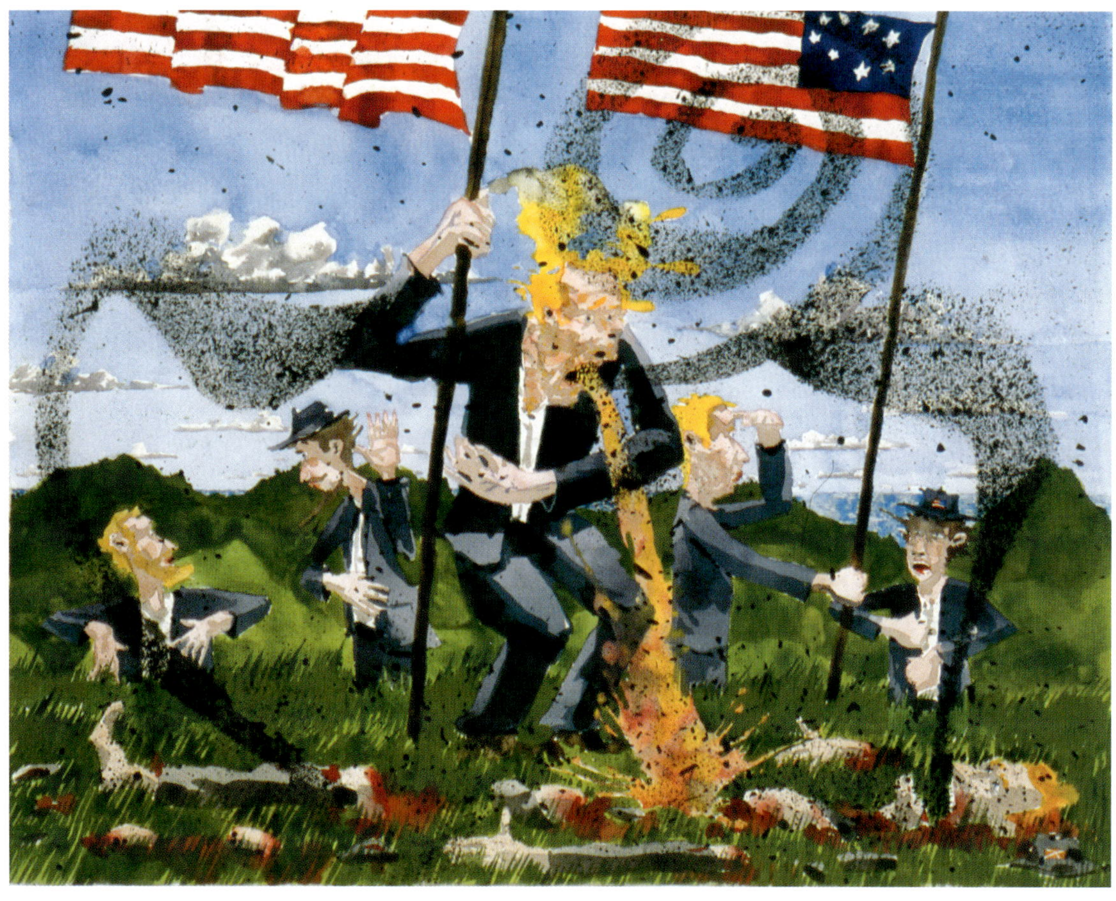

17
BARNABY FURNAS
Flys on Shit, May 18, 2001, 2001
Watercolor on paper
13 1/2 x 17 1/4 inches
Suzanne Feldman

18
BARNABY FURNAS
Untitled, July 16, 2001, 2001
Watercolor on paper
12 x 18 inches
Collection Jennifer Tytel

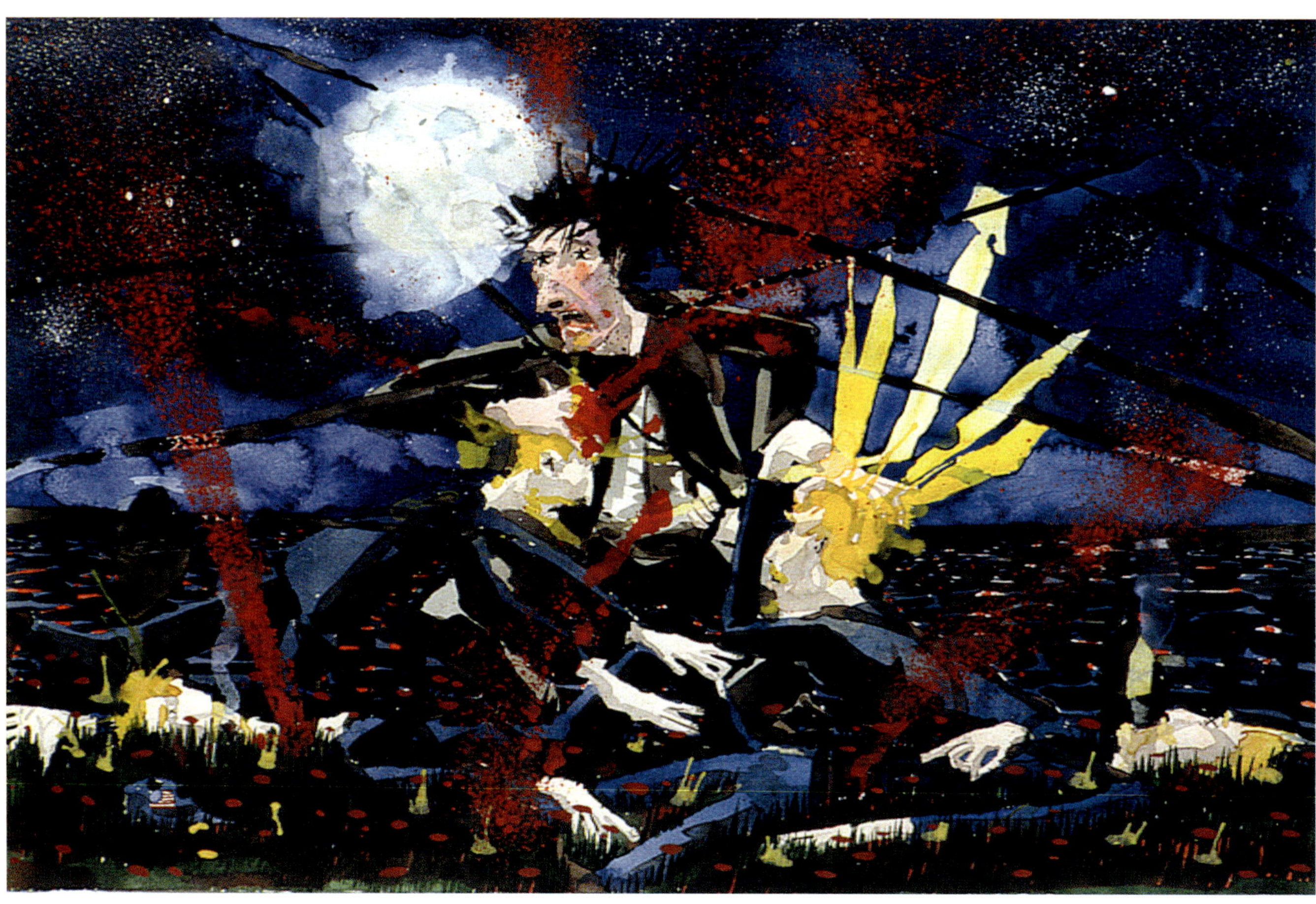

19
BARNABY FURNAS
Untitled Battlescene, 1999
Watercolor on paper
6¼ x 8½ inches
Collection Fern and Lenard
Tessler, New York

20
BARNABY FURNAS
Untitled Battlescene,
October 17, 2001, 2001
Watercolor on paper
12⅝ x 19 inches
Collection of the artist

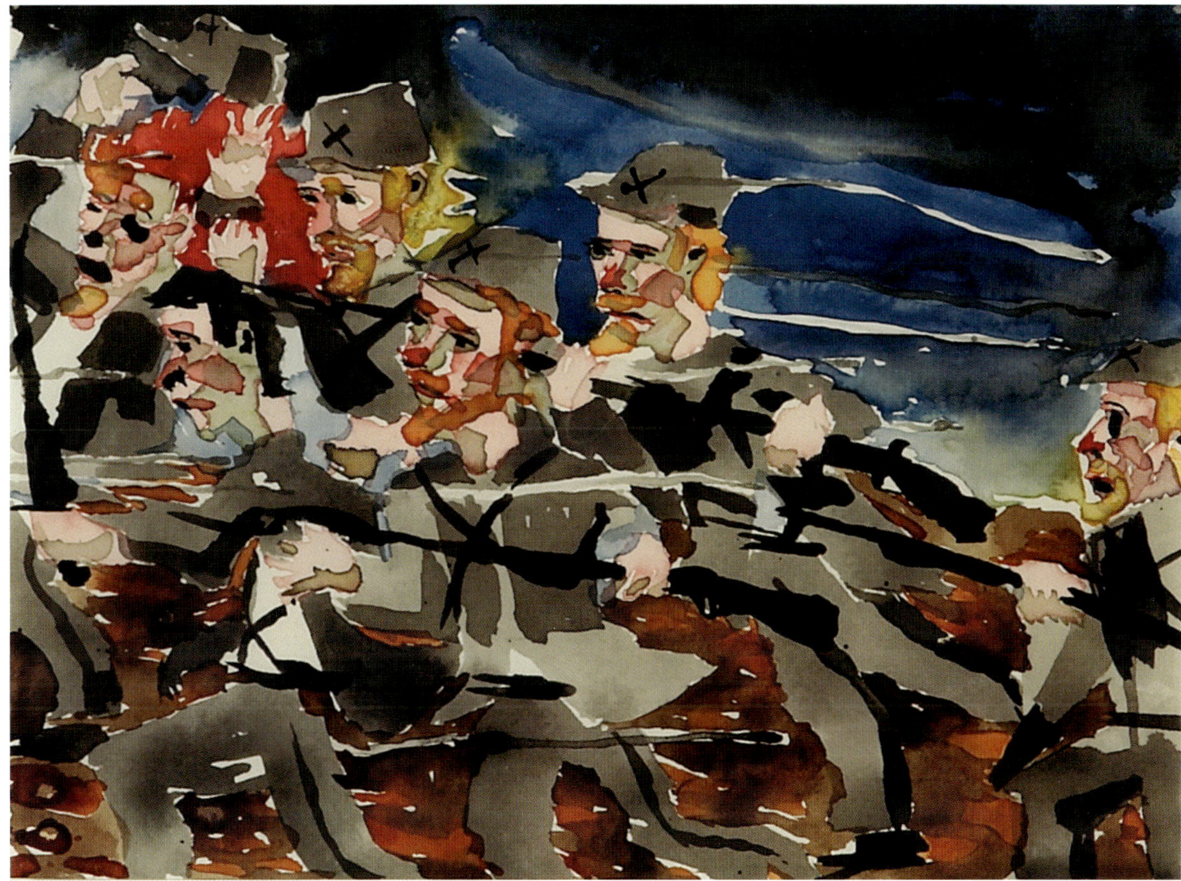

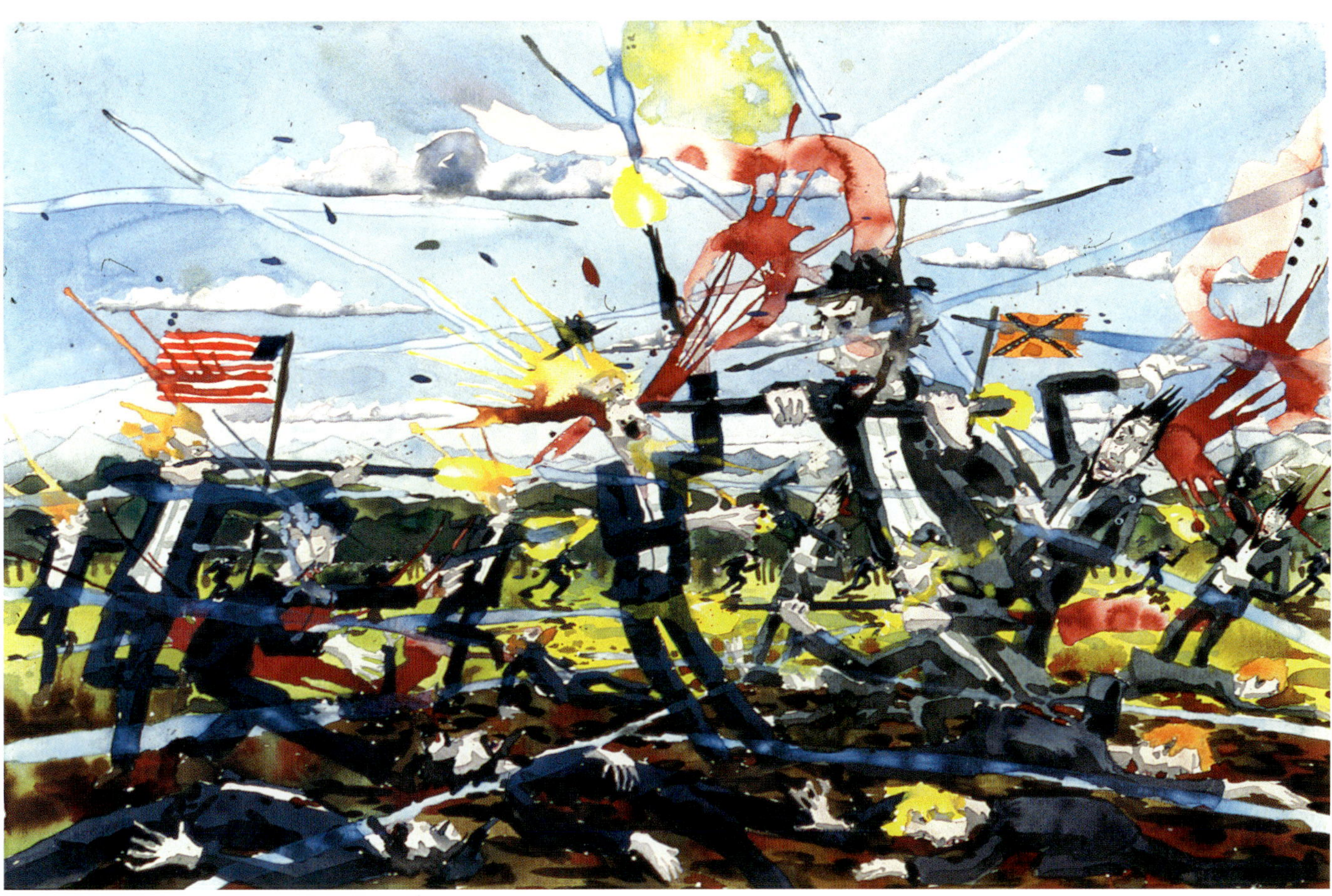

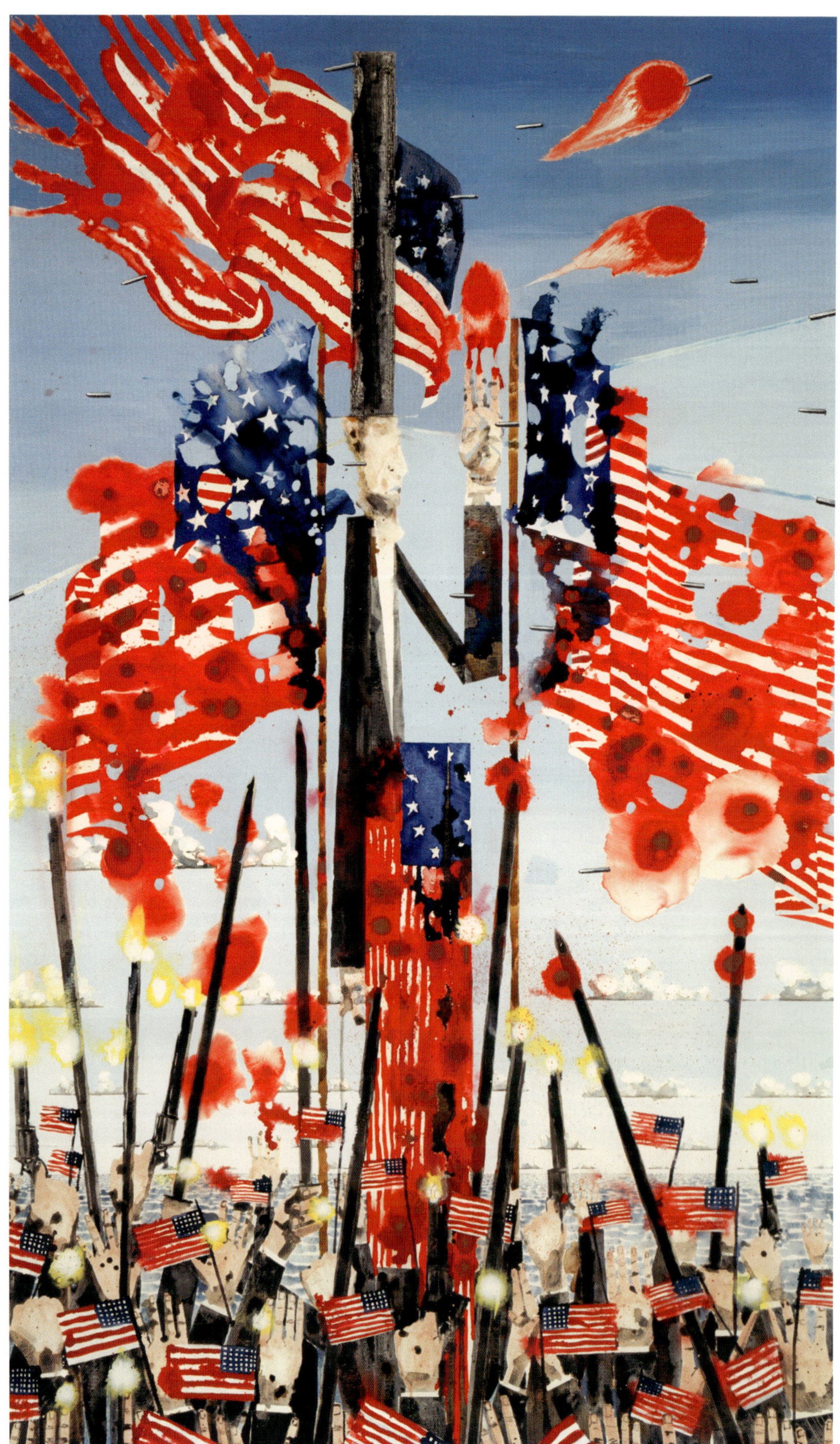

21
BARNABY FURNAS
Second Inaugural, 2003
Urethane on linen
71⅞ x 42 inches
Collection Pam and Bob Goergen

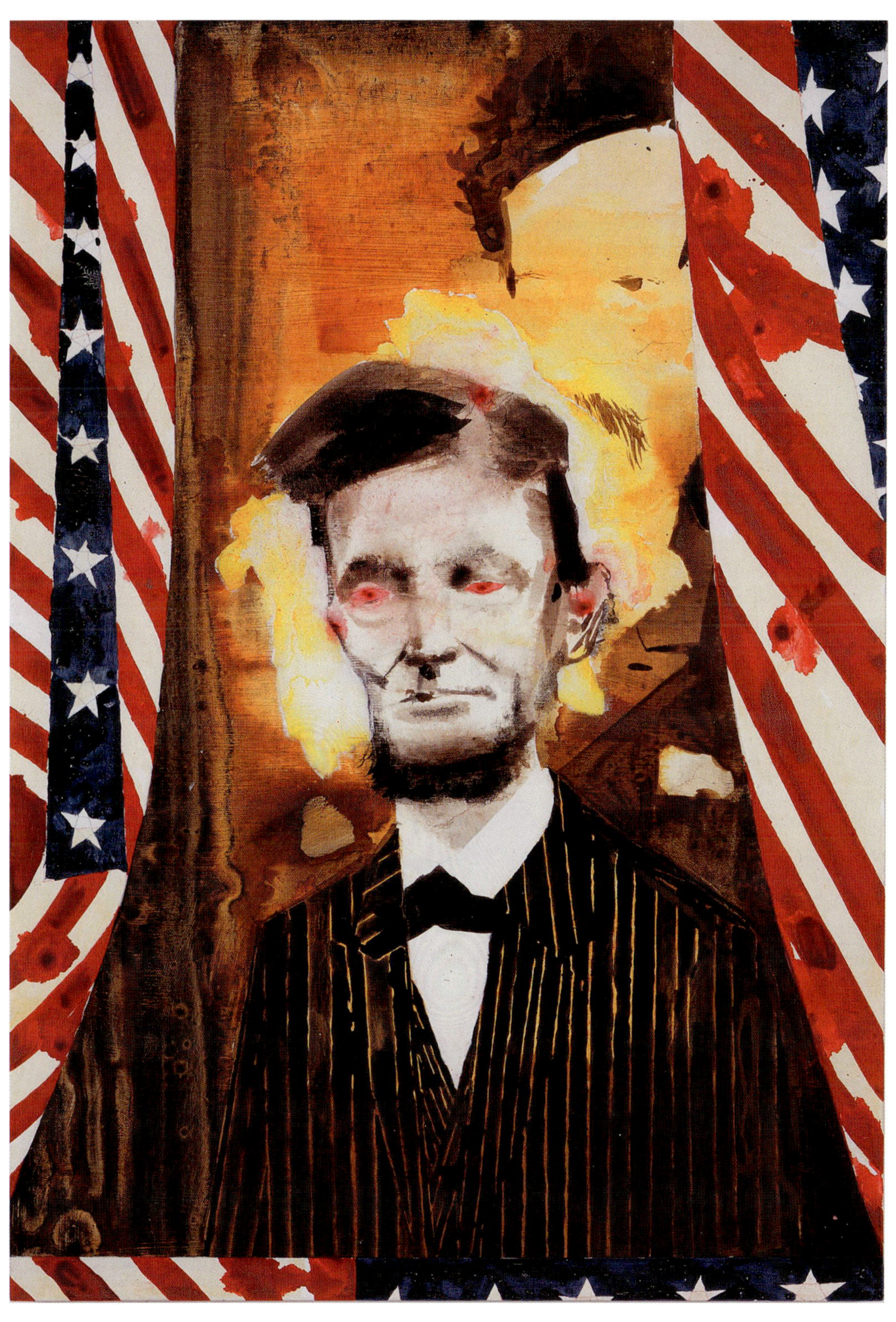

22
BARNABY FURNAS
Assassination (Abraham Lincoln), 2007
Ink and urethane on linen
30 x 20 inches
Private Collection, New York

Deborah Grant

n *Where Good Darkies Go* (2006), a group of forty-four paintings in acrylic on birch panels,[1] Deborah Grant has reproduced, reconfigured, and reimagined the people, animals, and trappings of domestic life created by Bill Traylor, a well-known self-taught artist from Alabama. Traylor, who lived from 1856 to 1949, was born a slave and lived most of his life on a plantation. He started drawing and painting at age 83, and developed a rich vocabulary of silhouette figures that seem to exist in a gravity-free world of magic and folklore. Critic Greg Tate has noted that Grant's appropriation of Traylor's work resembles the strategies of artists like Richard Prince and Sherrie Levine, who reproduce work by other artists or images from advertising to comment on originality, media and consumer culture, and the nature of reality itself.[2] However, Tate argues, Grant—who has borrowed images from Pablo Picasso, Cy Twombly, and Jean-Michel Basquiat—distinguishes herself from other appropriation artists by treating her imagery not as highly theoretical illustrations of Marxist or Baudrillardian concepts, but as powerful signs and clues from other worlds and fields of learning. In this respect, Tate says, Grant (who also creates her own original drawings) continues the legacy of another pioneering African-American painter, Jean-Michel Basquiat (1960–1988), whose paintings layer telling fragments from art, music, history, and popular culture.

Grant refers to her general working method as "random select."[3] She chooses images by artists that interest her because of their "social, political, religious, or humorous content," then commits herself to studying the work and teasing out all its facets of meaning, which she subsequently employs to reshape the original imagery. Grant compares this process to the sampling and hyperlinking techniques of rap MCs and Wikipedia encyclopedists, who expand messages by embedding them with references. She recalls first seeing Traylor's work at the Visionary Museum of self-taught artists in Baltimore as a student looking for alternatives to the current top 100 list of established artists. Traylor's precise lines and "direct mark" impressed her, and she views her reinterpretations of them as a process of "finding my own voice in the context of another artist's work." Her exploration of an artist working outside the canon of art history, she suggests, is similar to Picasso's search for a "raw base" in African and Oceanic forms in works like his famous antiwar painting *Guernica* of 1937 (which Grant reworked in an image anagrammatically entitled *A Gin Cure*). Even though she breaks down Traylor's wild images of life, love, magic, and tragedy into the cool grid beloved of Conceptual artists, Grant knows that they have the power to strip away history and art-world artifice. Like a sampled old-school hook in a hip-hop hit, the exhibition's selection of sixteen panels from *Where Good Darkies Go* sparks thrilling thoughts of a lost visionary and other worlds, times, and places.

1. *The Old, Weird America* features a selection of 16 panels (see pls. 23–28).

2. Greg Tate, "Come Join the Hieroglyphic Zombie Parade," in *Deborah Grant: By the Skin of Our Teeth*, exh. broch. (Dallas: Dunn and Brown Contemporary, 2007), n.p.

3. This and all subsequent quotes by the artist are from a telephone interview with the author, November 13, 2007.

23
DEBORAH GRANT
Where Good Darkies Go (detail), 2006
Acrylic on birch panel
44 panels, 24 x 18 inches each
Courtesy the artist and
Dunn and Brown Contemporary, Dallas

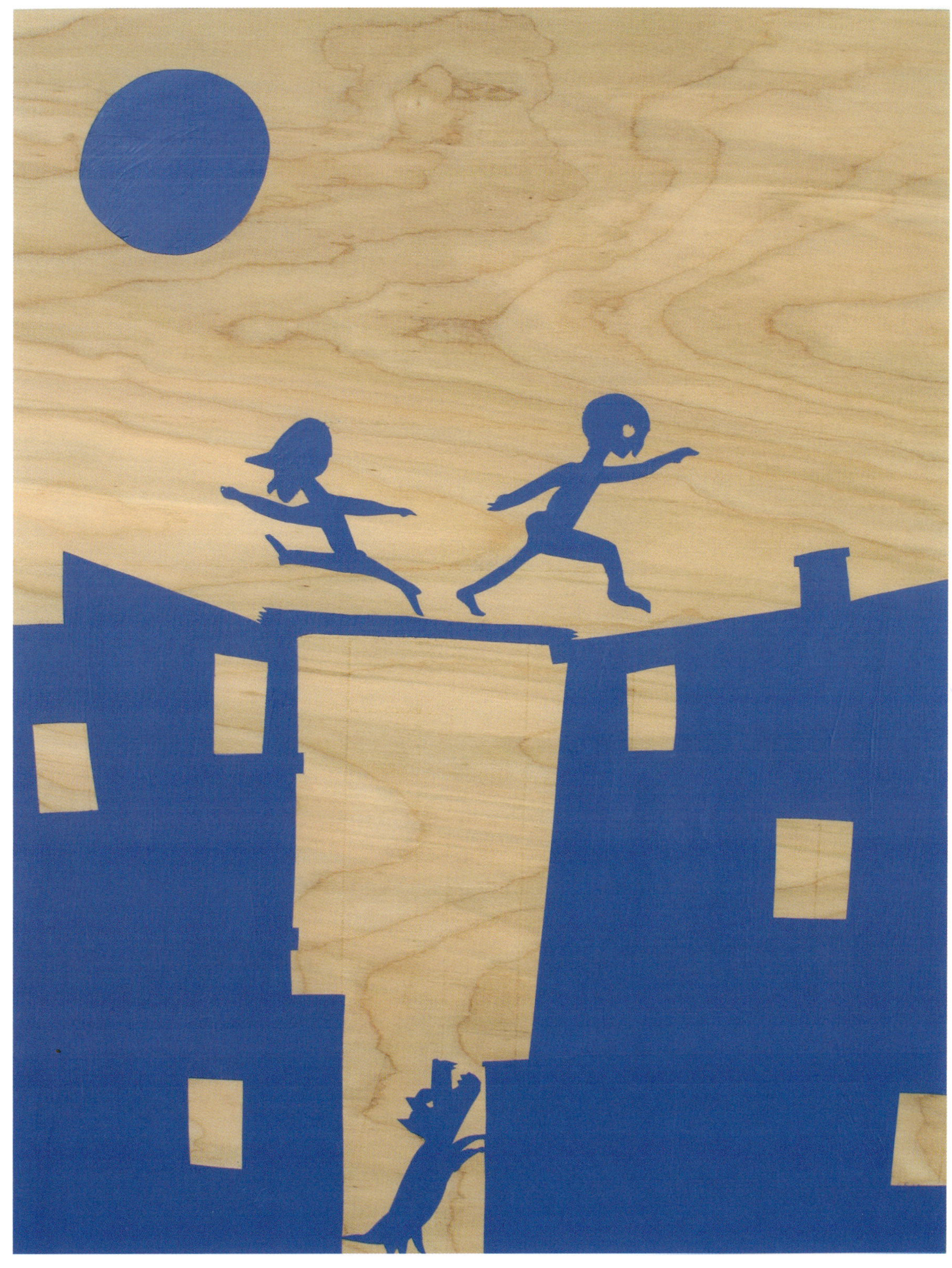

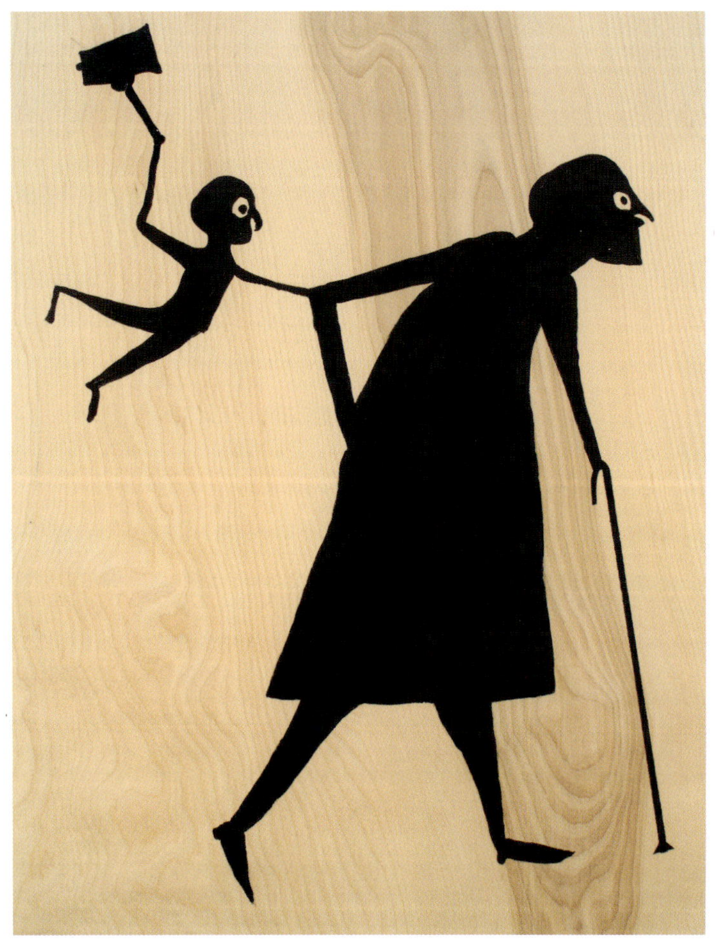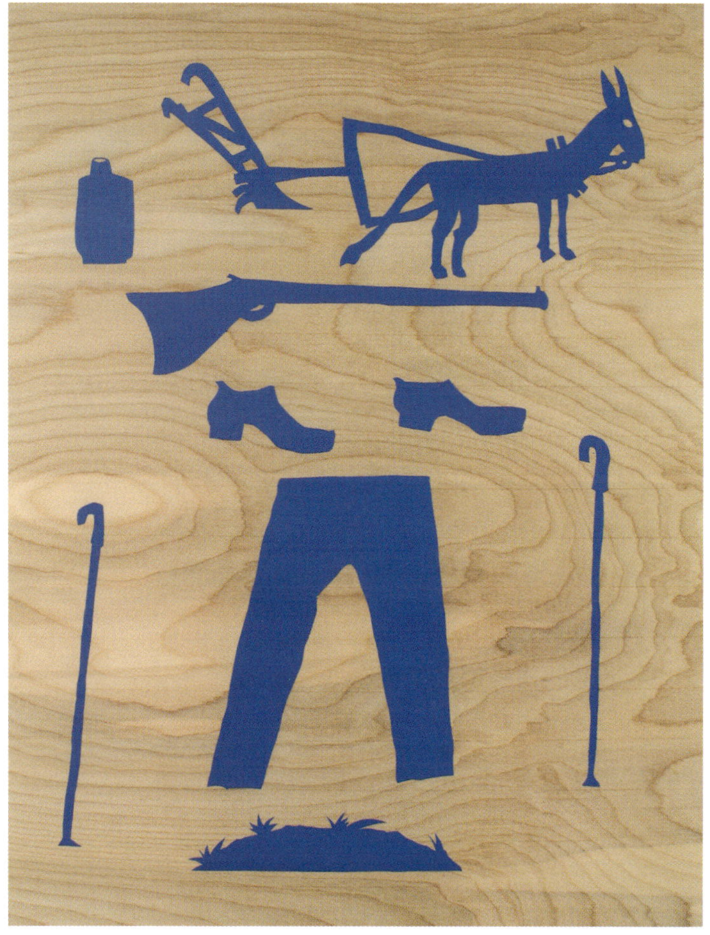

24–27
DEBORAH GRANT
Where Good Darkies Go (details), 2006
Acrylic on birch panel
44 panels, 24 x 18 inches each
Courtesy the artist and Dunn and Brown Contemporary, Dallas

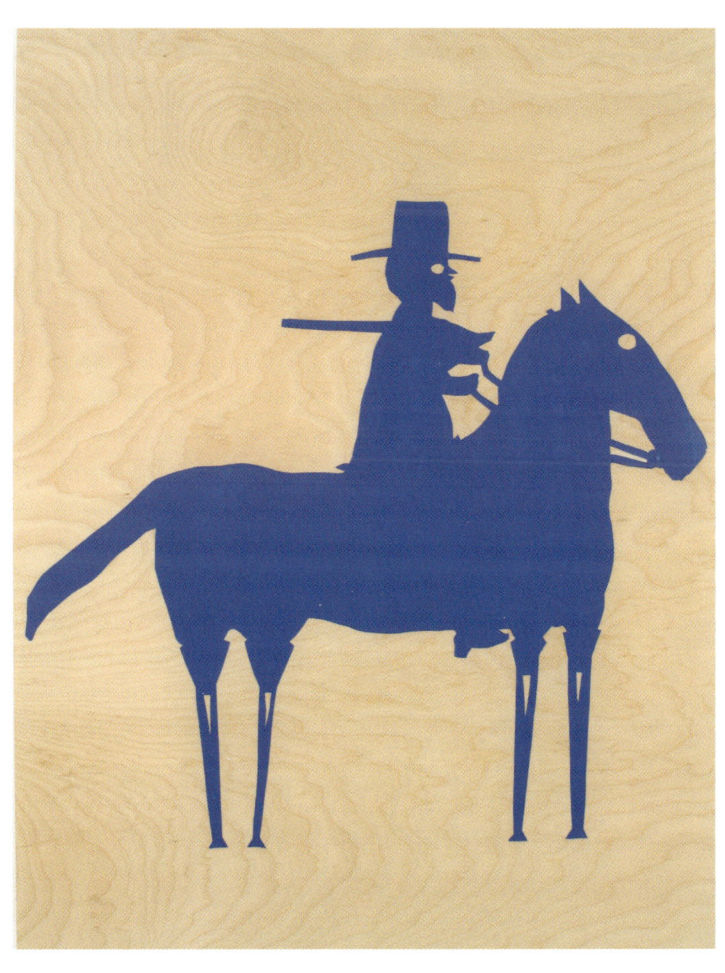 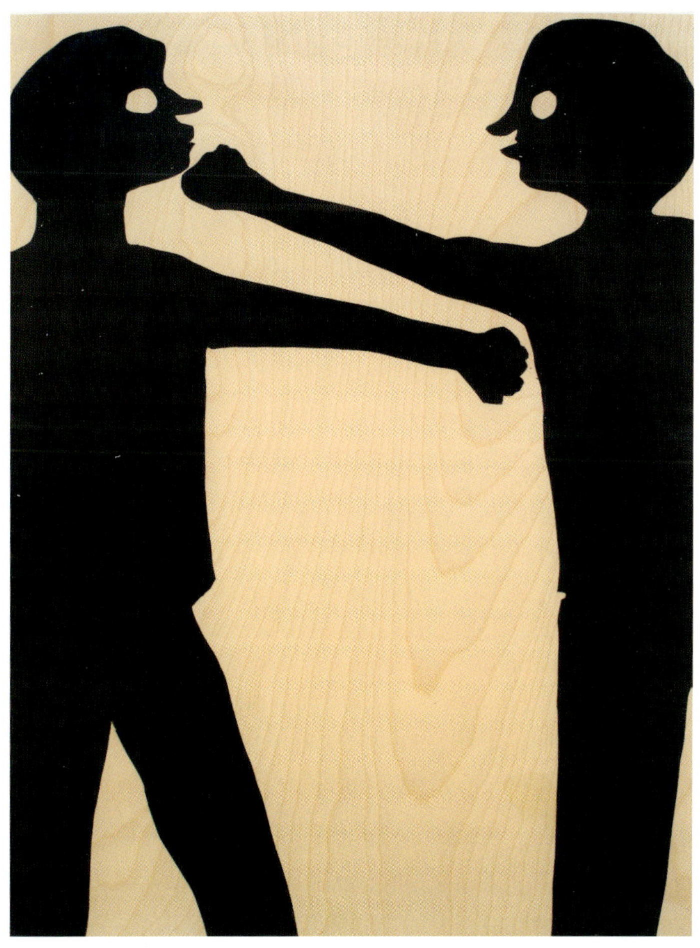

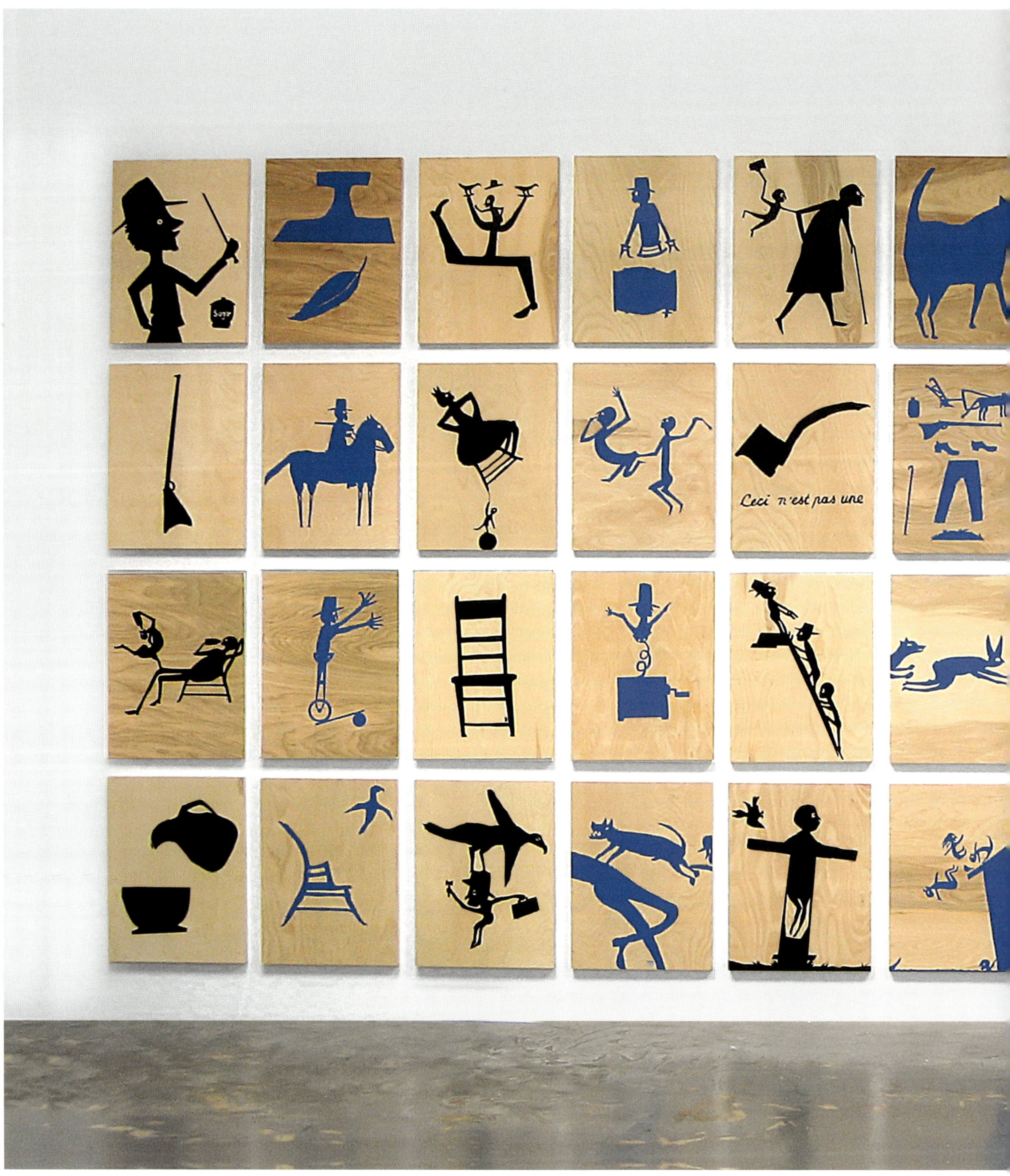

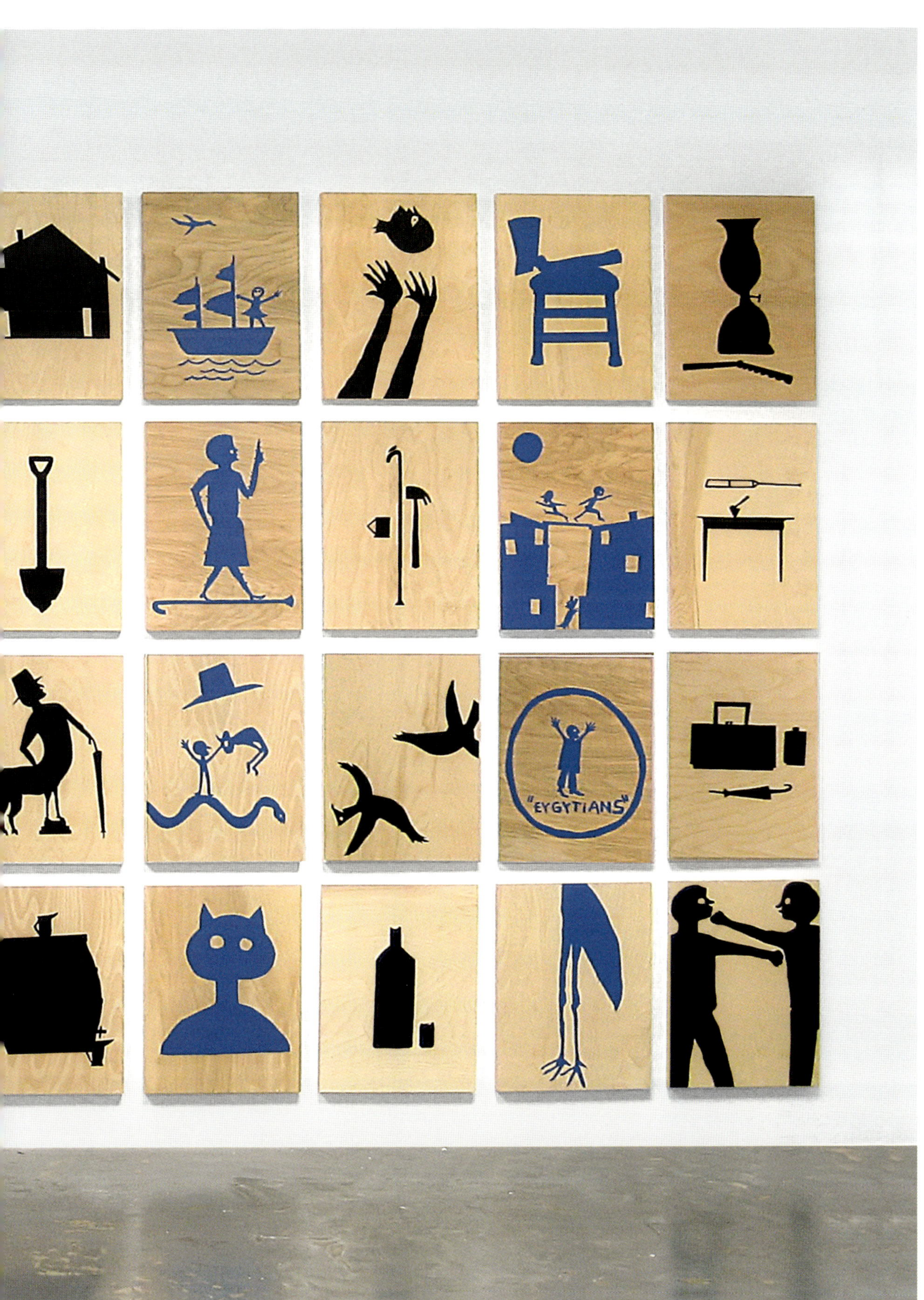

28
DEBORAH GRANT
Where Good Darkies Go, 2006
Acrylic on birch panel
44 panels, 24 x 18 inches each
(16 panels in exhibition, numbered top
to bottom, left to right: 1, 2, 5, 6, 7, 9, 13,
14, 15, 20, 23, 27, 34, 35, 36, 38)
Courtesy the artist and
Dunn and Brown Contemporary, Dallas

Matthew Day Jackson

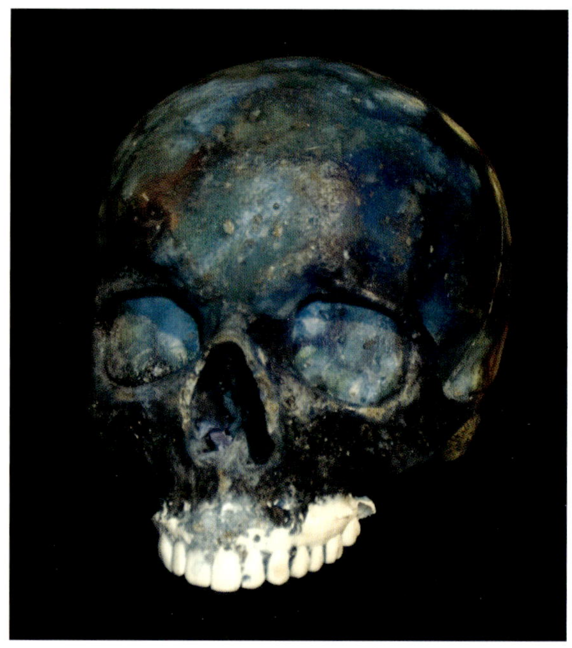

Matthew Day Jackson moves through America's various histories—social, aesthetic, and geologic—like a prospector. Surveying the country's thick forests of imagery and material culture, he collects ideas and ingredients for sculptures and two-dimensional works that serve as highly personal yet incisive interpretive guides. Among his projects are a Viking ship with a hull made from his discarded sculptures and a sail sewn from his old heavy metal T-shirts (symbolizing a burial vessel for his old ways of making art); a portrait of Eleanor Roosevelt (1884–1962) made from yarn, stained wood, feathers, and tooled leather (celebrating the First Lady's soul and ideals); and a Conestoga wagon made from recycled industrial ply-wood (suggesting an alternative means of navigating a world of dwindling resources).[1] Jackson's work, which emphasizes common and found objects such as maga-zine and poster images, tree branches, and hobby store bric-a-brac, is inspired by the revolutionary ex-ample of the Russian Constructivists, who rejected traditional art materials in favor of nonprecious indus-trial products they believed would be the building blocks of a new communist society. "Using common objects means they're everybody's, and everybody can interpret them—not just specialists," Jackson states. "There's something hopeful and regenerative about this, and I'd even like people to forget this is art."[2]

For *The Old, Weird America*, Jackson is creating a new work entitled *The Garden of Earthly Delights (Spiritual America)* (2008) after a three-panel painting (c. 1505–1510) by Hieronymus Bosch (c. 1450–1516) showing fantastical visions of the Garden of Eden, the evolution of sin, and Hell, and after a recent exhibi-tion featuring contemporary Americana by artist Richard Prince. Among the two- and three-dimen-sional objects, which he often modifies with drawing or collage, Jackson is considering for the wall-scaling, multipart work are reproductions of unspoiled Ameri-can landscapes by painter Albert Bierstadt (1830–1902); posters advertising the movie *Evil Dead* (1981); photo-graphs of astronauts, the wreckage of New York's

World Trade Center, and Tommy Smith and John Carlos's black power protest at the 1968 Olympics; and a charred map of the United States. Ambitious in scale and allegorical impact, the disparate parts of *The Garden of Earthly Delights (Spiritual America)*, Jackson says, "fight against the mythology of linearity" in cultural interpretation. Instead, he describes it as an open-ended "webwork" of information and a mirror for society. It contains images of fear and conflict, and "zombie narratives" of individuals "not recognizing alternatives or options," he acknowledges. But the work also suggests transformation and regeneration. "Cycles of destruction seem built into the idea of America, but perhaps an apocalypse might be some-thing like a pause, or a comma, before a new, less fractured and fractious world begins."

1. Chrissie Iles and Philippe Vergne, *Whitney Biennial 2006: Day for Night*, exh. cat. (New York: Whitney Museum of American Art, 2006), 258.

2. This and all subsequent quotes from the artist are from a tele-phone interview with the author, December 7, 2007.

27–30
MATTHEW DAY JACKSON
Garden of Earthly Delights (Spiritual America) (details), 2008
Posters, needlepoint, glass and steel vitrine, wool, paint,
C-print, fake taxidermy, wood, blower scoop
180 x 180 x 60 inches (approximately)
Courtesy the artist

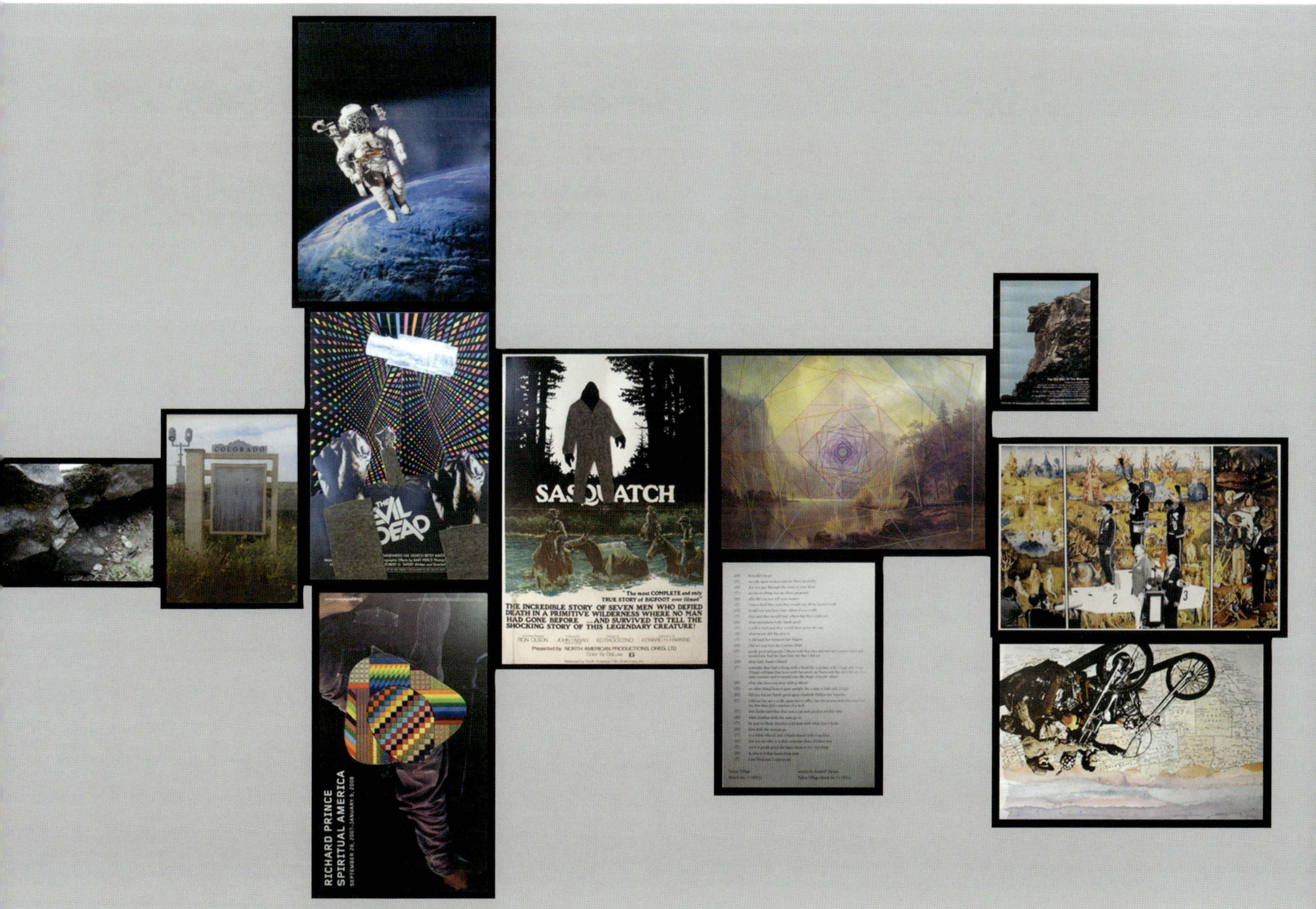

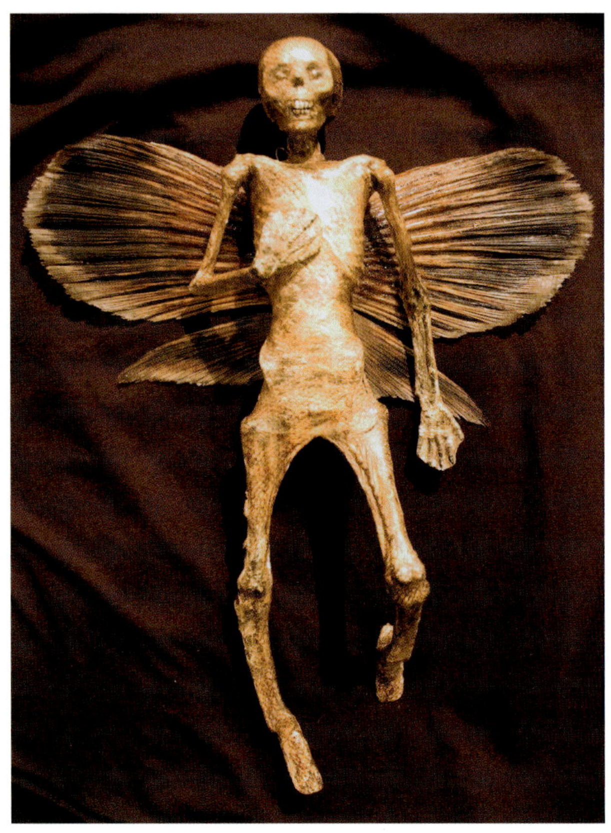

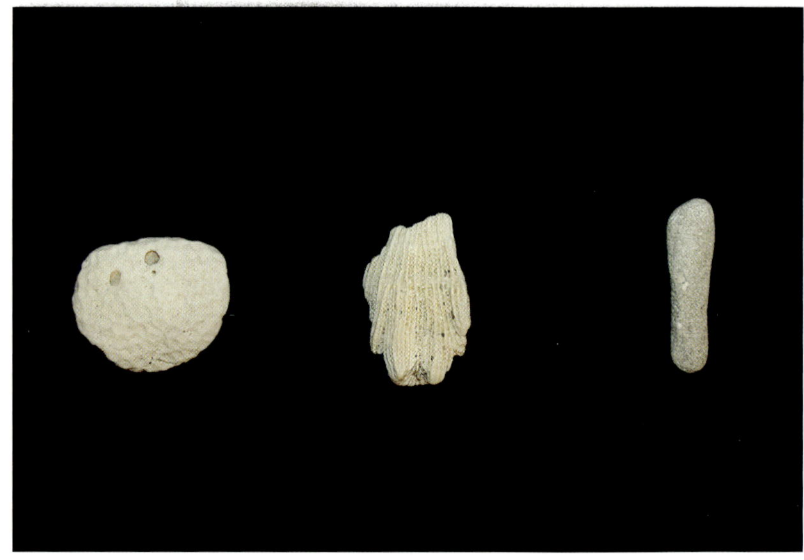

31–36
MATTHEW DAY JACKSON
Garden of Earthly Delights (Spiritual America) (details), 2008
Posters, needlepoint, glass and steel vitrine, wool, paint,
C-print, fake taxidermy, wood, blower scoop
180 x 180 x 60 inches (approximately)
Courtesy the artist

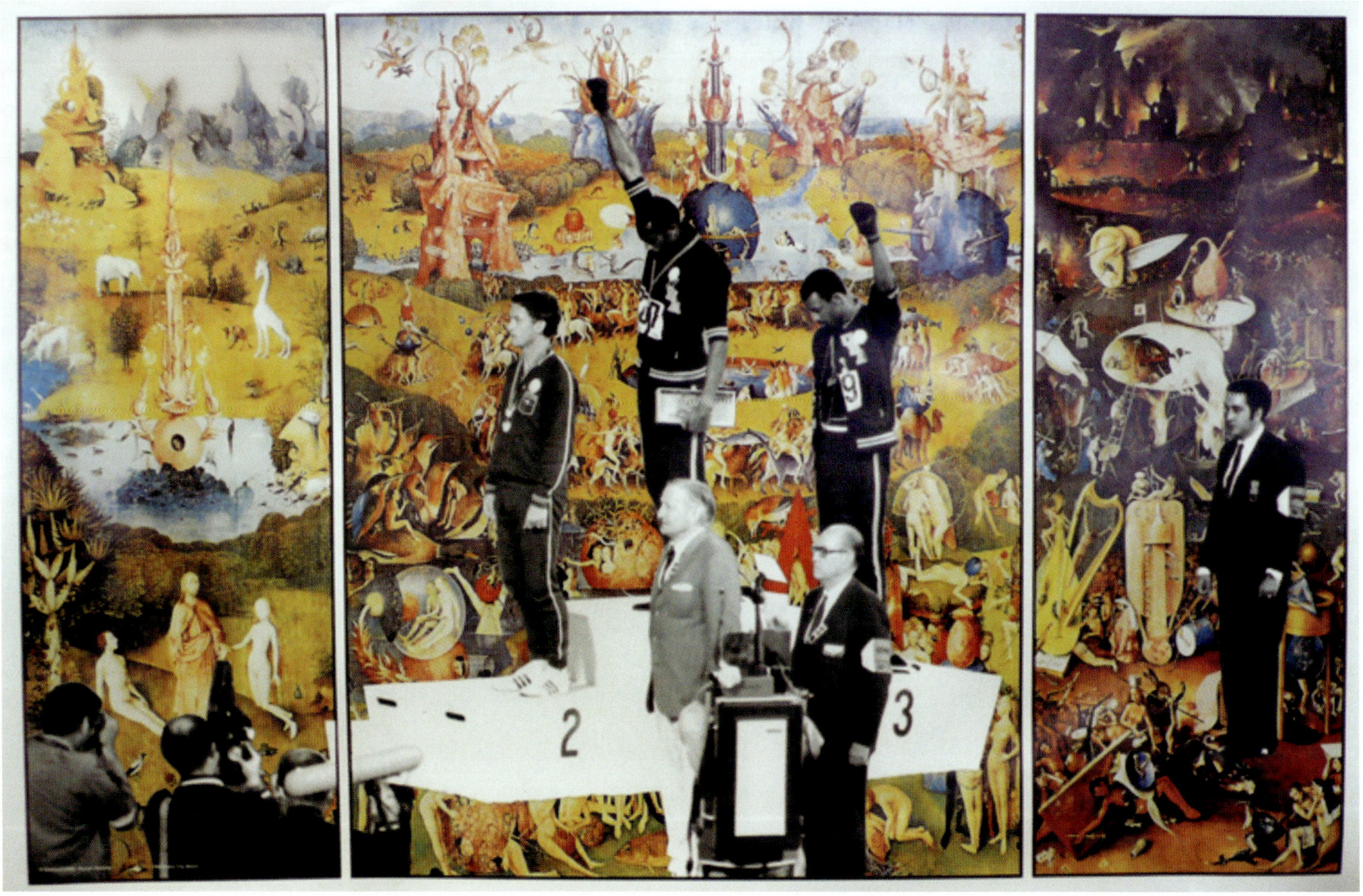

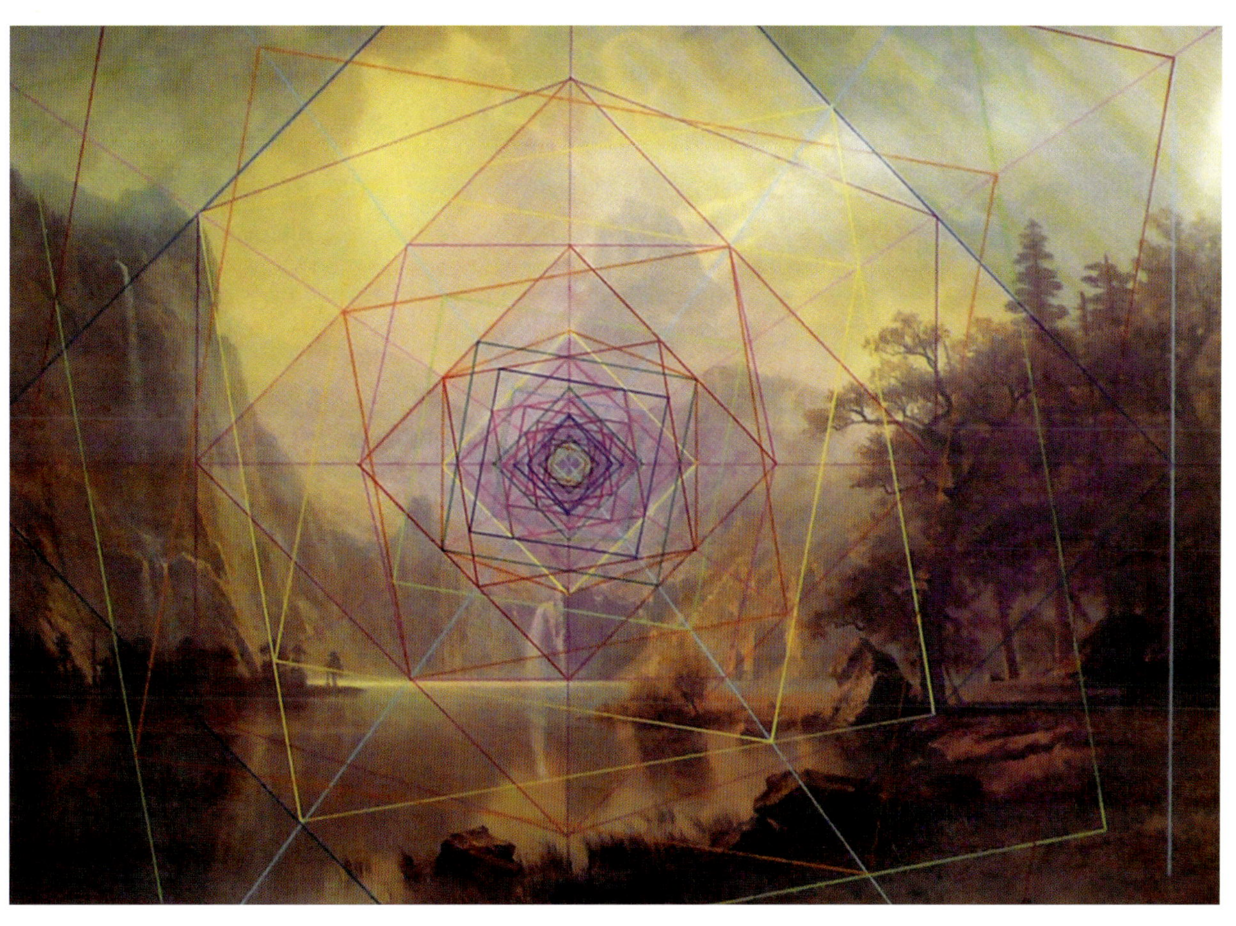

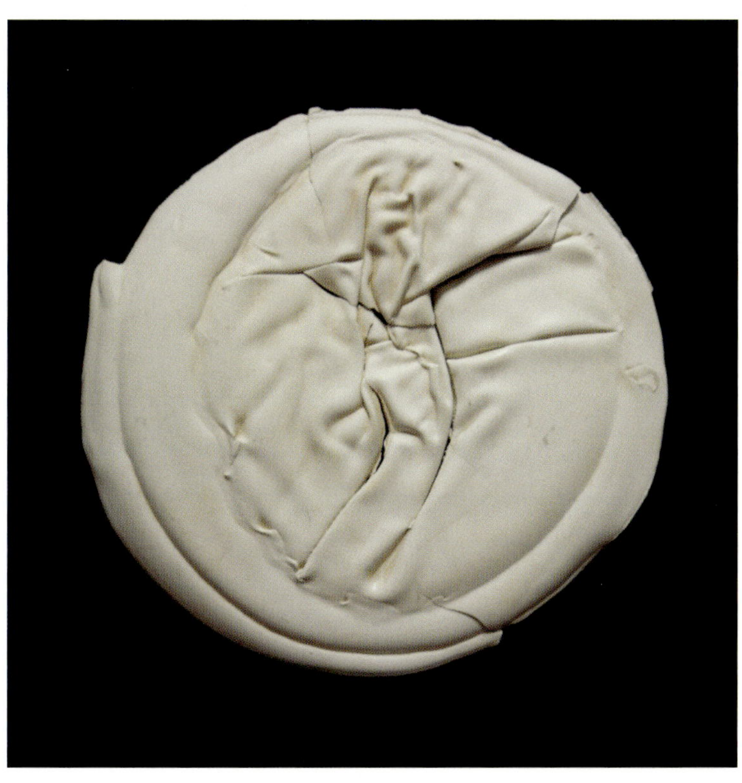

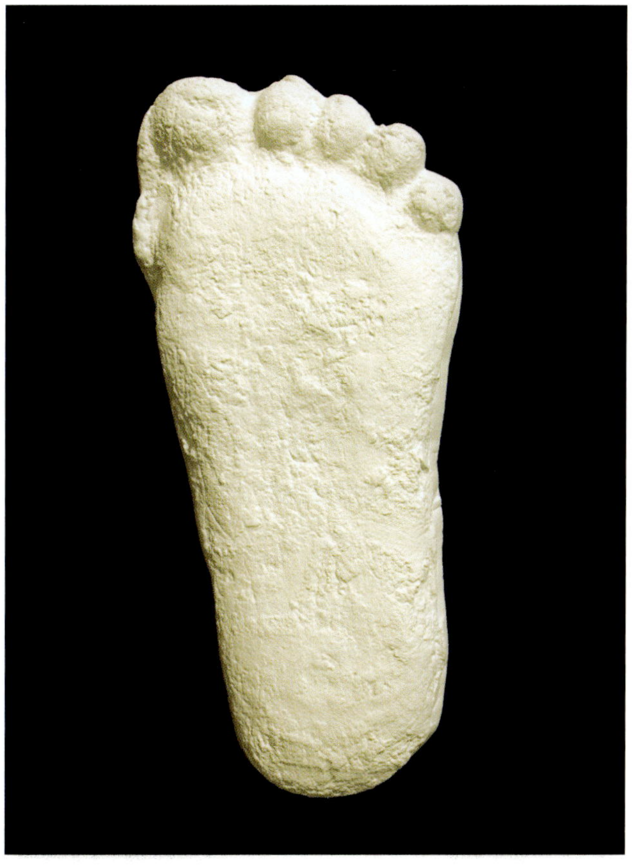

Brad Kahlhamer

Brad Kahlhamer paints and draws Ur-American scenes—fantastical spaces populated by head-butting bison, screaming eagles, Indians, cowboys, and sexy "urban prairie girls." Describing his work in the context of this exhibition, Kahlhamer, an artist of Native descent, says he depicts "the Eldest Weird America—the America before the word *America*."[1] His images incorporate a dazzling array of realistic styles, from loose, washy watercolor sketches, to alternately scratchy and fluid line drawings, to lovingly modeled Marvel comics-style grotesqueries. This virtuoso technique is the result of a lifetime of practice. "When I was about four, I just started lying on my stomach and drawing," Kahlhamer says, and so complete was his mastery of the languages of American illustration that he landed a position as an art director for Topps chewing gum's trading cards. At Topps, Kahlhamer rubbed elbows with legendary cartoonists such as Art Spiegelman, Drew Friedman, Mark Newgarden, and Kaz. Like these masters, Kahlhamer combines images and texts, but his words—sometimes scrawled, sometimes calligraphic—have less in common with the driving narratives of comics than with the fractured stories of song lyrics, which he regularly writes and performs with his alt-country band. The works are peppered with non-sequitur textual clues: "Grassland Creature," "Lakota Thrifty Mart," "Lt. Col. George Arnold Custer, 7th Cavalry Commander."

Kahlhamer's iconography is connected to his own story. He was born in Arizona and adopted and reared by a white German-American family in Wisconsin. Kahlhamer thinks of his work as a "third place" separate from the "first place" of his conventional American upbringing with his adoptive parents, and the "second place" of his Native heritage.[2] At once epic and playfully ironic, his work is an attempt to reconcile two worlds: the mainstream, familiar America he grew up in, and his lost origins, which he has explored through countless road trips to reservations and meetings with Native communities. Works on paper in watercolor and ink like *Desert Forest City* (2006), *Waqui Totem USA* (2006), and *Indian Summer USA* (2006) synthesize America-Indian, post-European contact, and popular-culture motifs in swirling compositions that morph between the loosely and tightly rendered, straightforward and caricatured. Grand processionals of skulls and Native men and women, with the occasional self-portrait, iconic animal, or rifle-toting babe thrown in for good measure, suggest an irreverent Pantheon of earliest America. Concerned with the "social landscape" as well as cycles of destruction and regeneration (witness the bloody aerial battle of eagles in *Desert Forest City*), he depicts the richness, romance, and tragedy as well as the pervasive kitschification of Native cultures with absurdist equanimity. He also makes small, Kachina-style dolls from scrap wood, cloth, and occasionally his own hair, which serve as personal talismans. Blending wood and other materials he finds near his studio in New York's Bowery with aspects of Native and avant-garde art, these hundreds of figurines, Kahlhamer says, represent "a gathering of my tribe." At the heart of his project is an investigation of what he calls "cultural DNA." Unafraid of contradictions or stereotypes, Kahlhamer draws on his own experiences, imagination, and fearless sense of humor to unravel a complex personal and national legacy that began long before that fateful day the first conquistador or pilgrim set foot on these shores.

1. This and all subsequent uncited quotes by the artist are from a telephone interview with the author, November 2, 2007.

2. Jeffrey Deitch, "Brad Kahlhamer's Friendly Frontier," in *Brad Kahlhamer* (Milan: Edizioni Charta, 2007), 8.

37 *(page 85)*
BRAD KAHLHAMER
Waqui Totem USA, 2006
Watercolor and ink on paper
82 x 62 inches
Collection Nerman Museum of Contemporary Art, Johnson County Community College, gift of Marti and Tony Oppenheimer and the Oppenheimer Brothers Foundation
Photograph: E.G. Schempf

38–50 *(pages 86 and 87)*
BRAD KAHLHAMER
Dolls, 1984–2004
Mixed media figurines
Approximately 12 x 4 x 2 inches each
Courtesy the artist

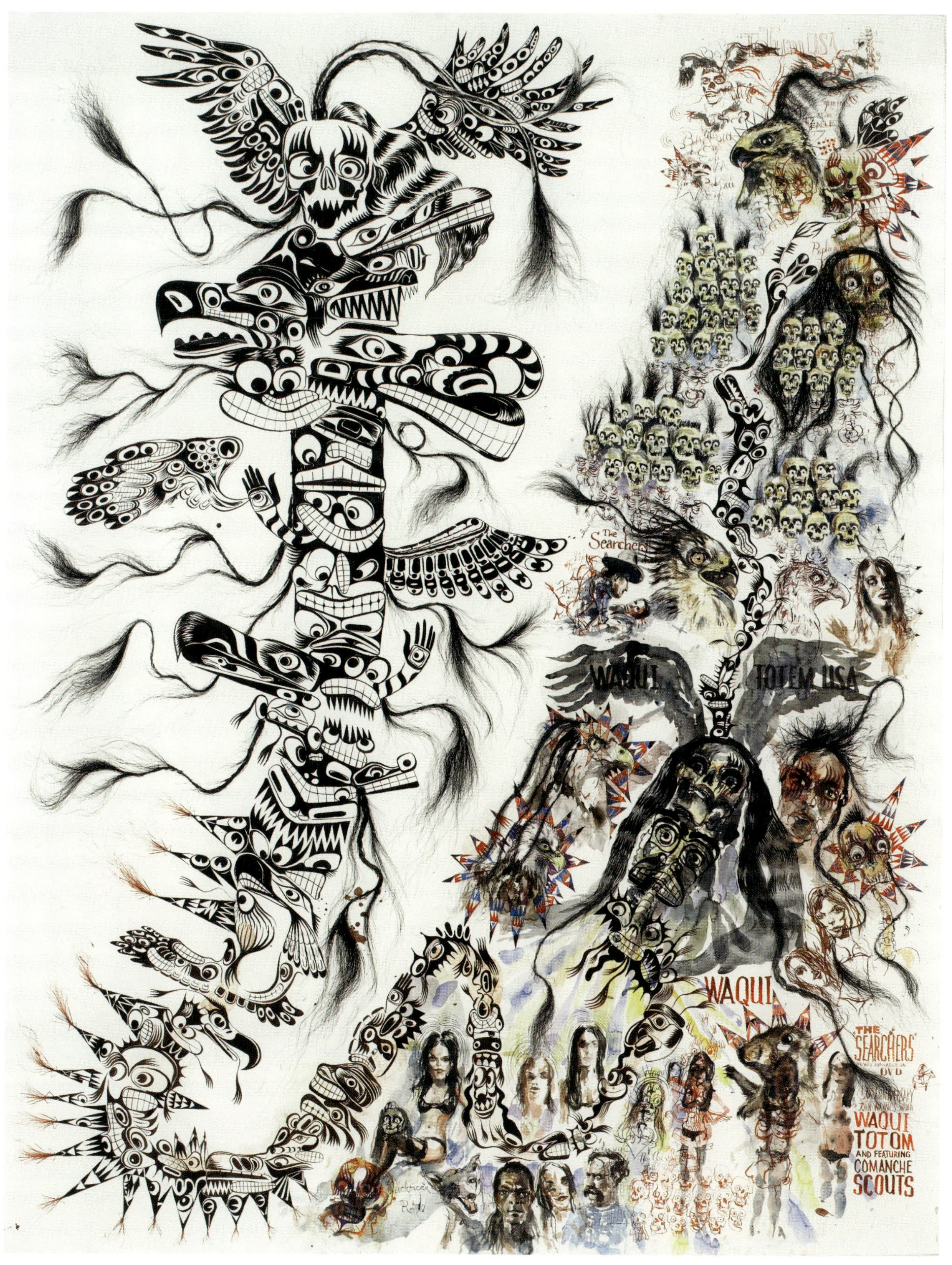
TOTEM USA
The Searchers
WAQUI
TOTEM USA
WAQUI
THE SEARCHERS
WAQUI
TOTOM
AND FEATURING
COMANCHE
SCOUTS

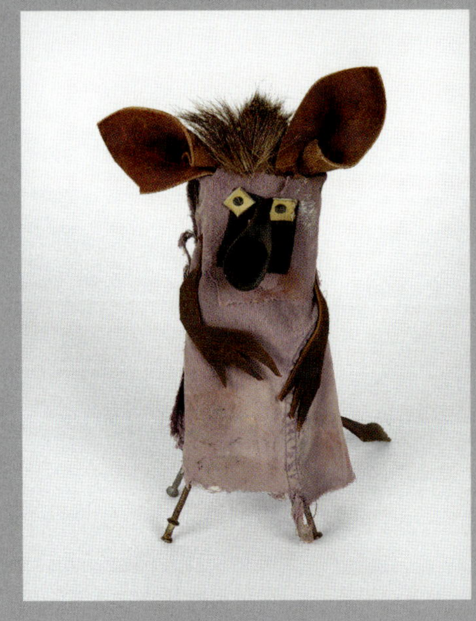
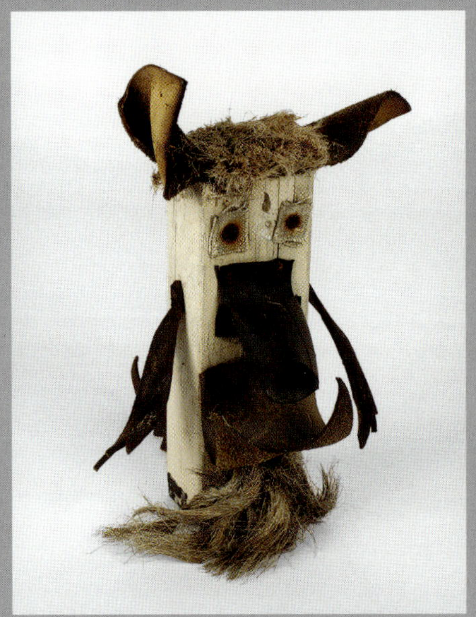
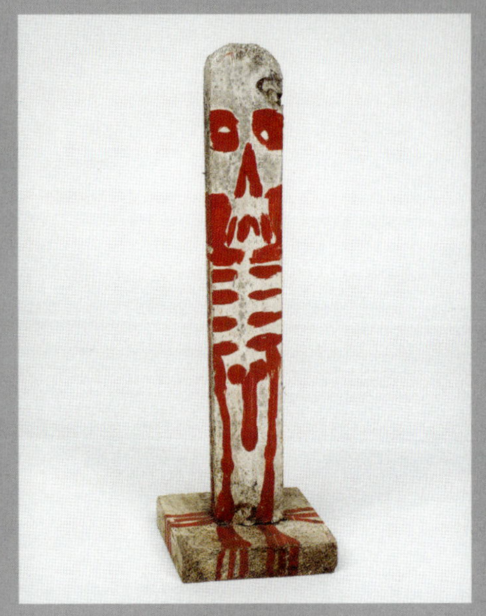
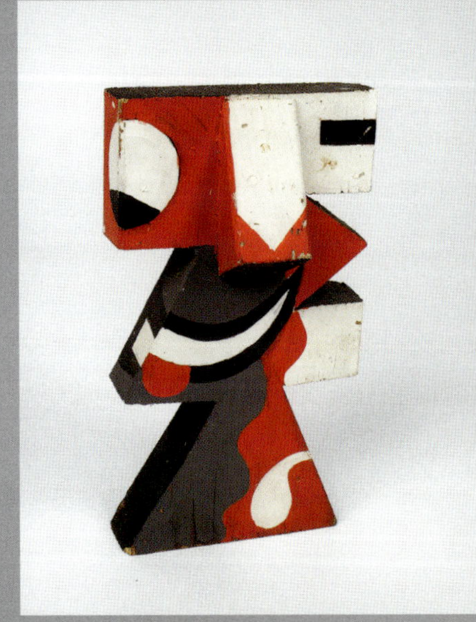
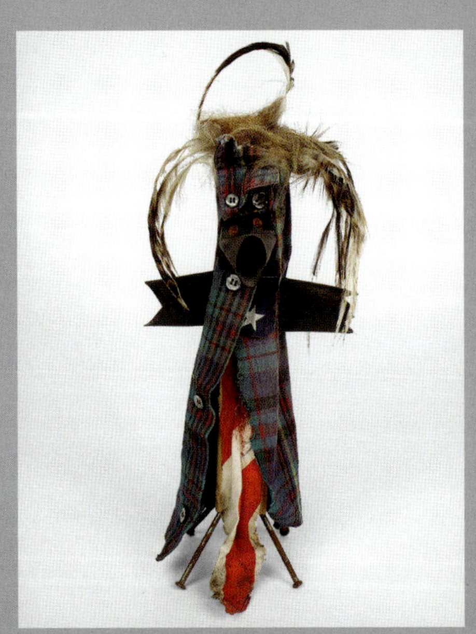
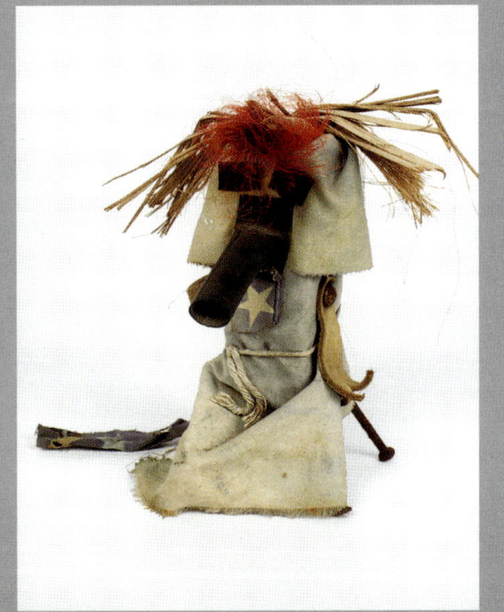
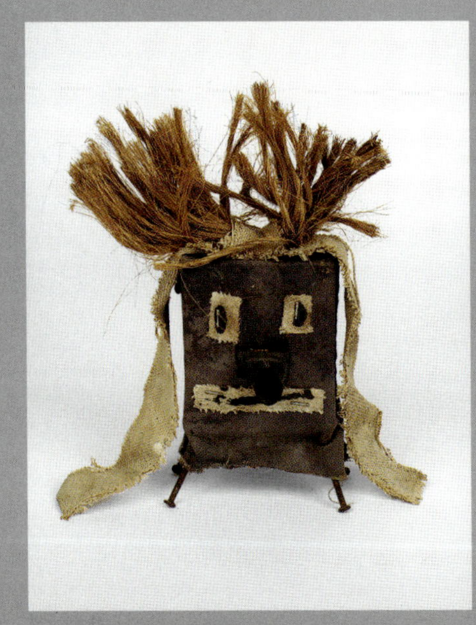
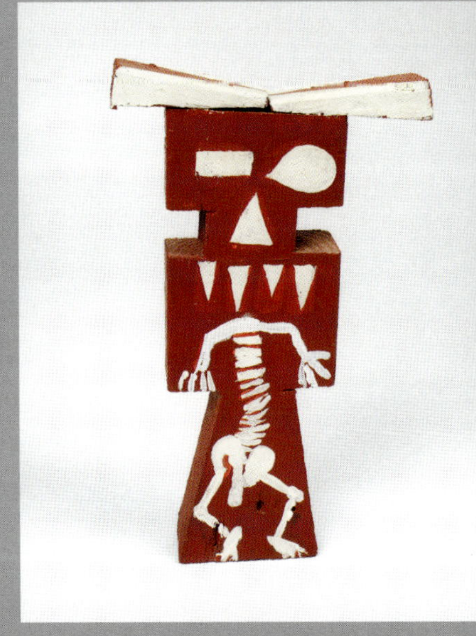
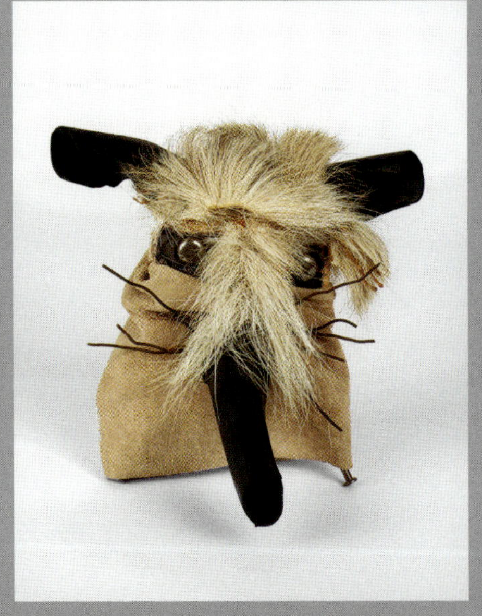

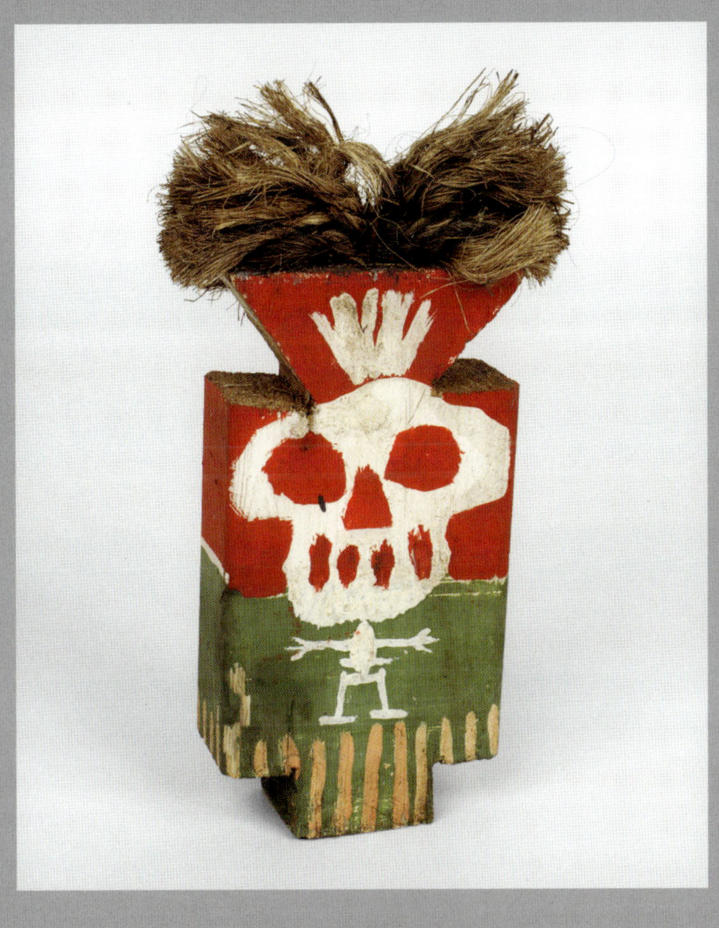

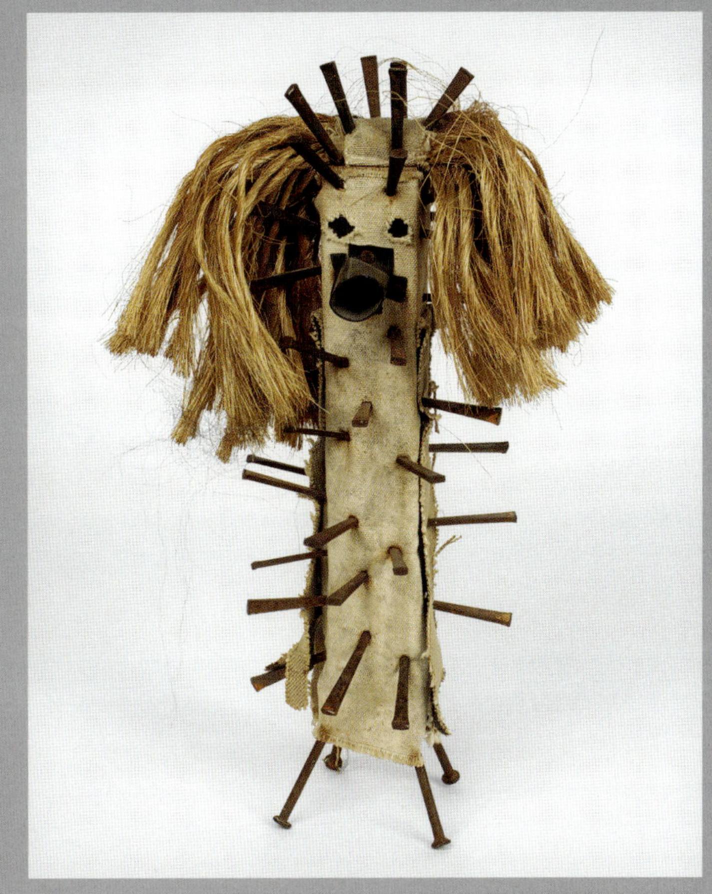

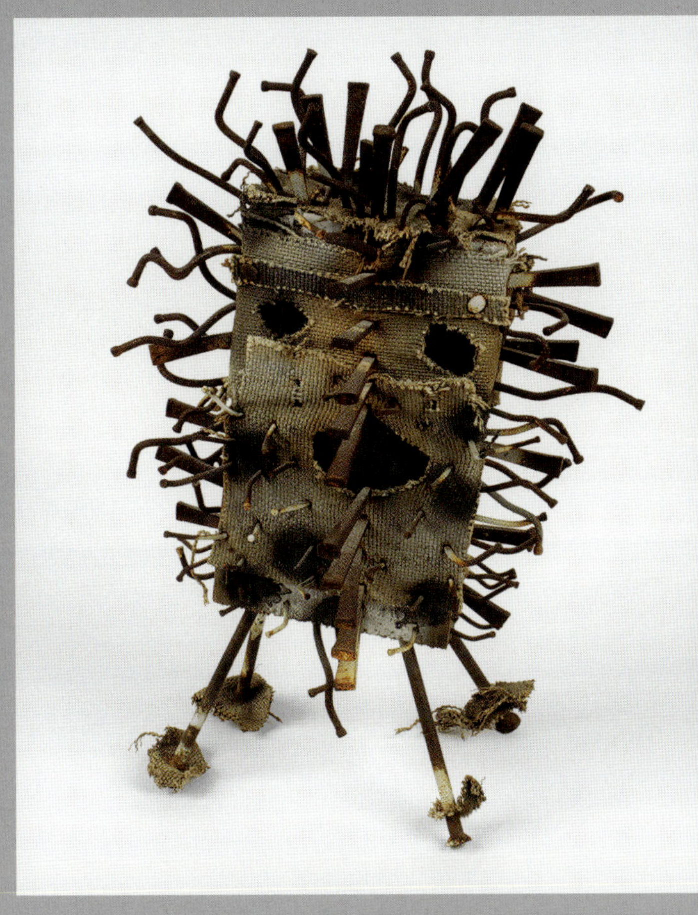

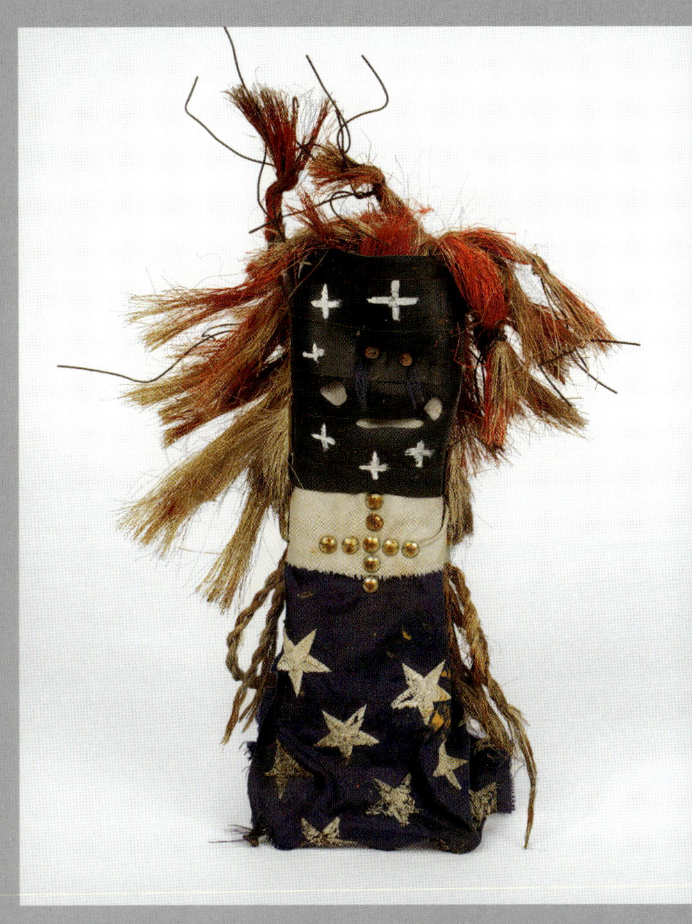

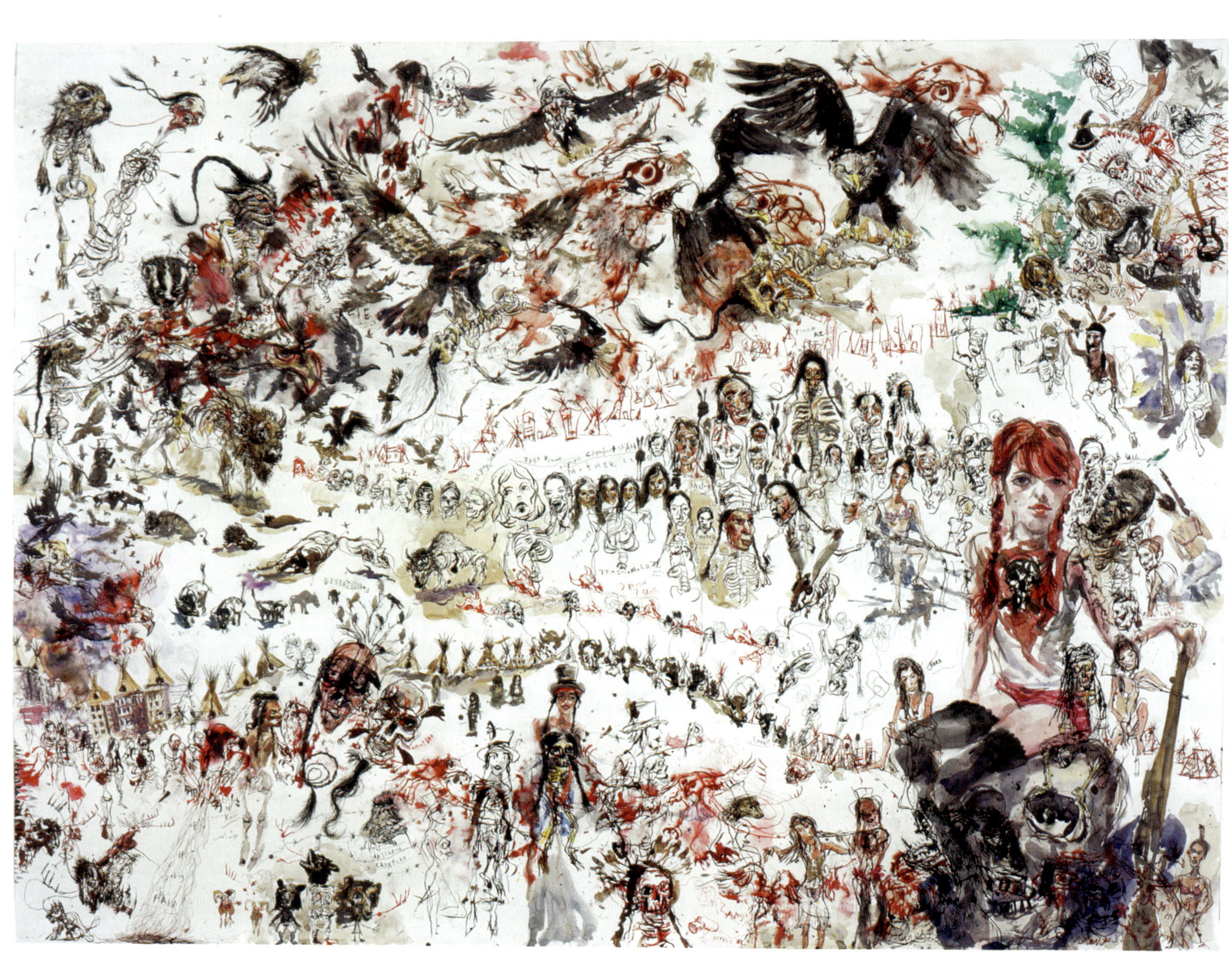

51
BRAD KAHLHAMER
Desert Forest City, 2004
Ink and watercolor
62 x 82 inches
Collection Stefan Simchowitz

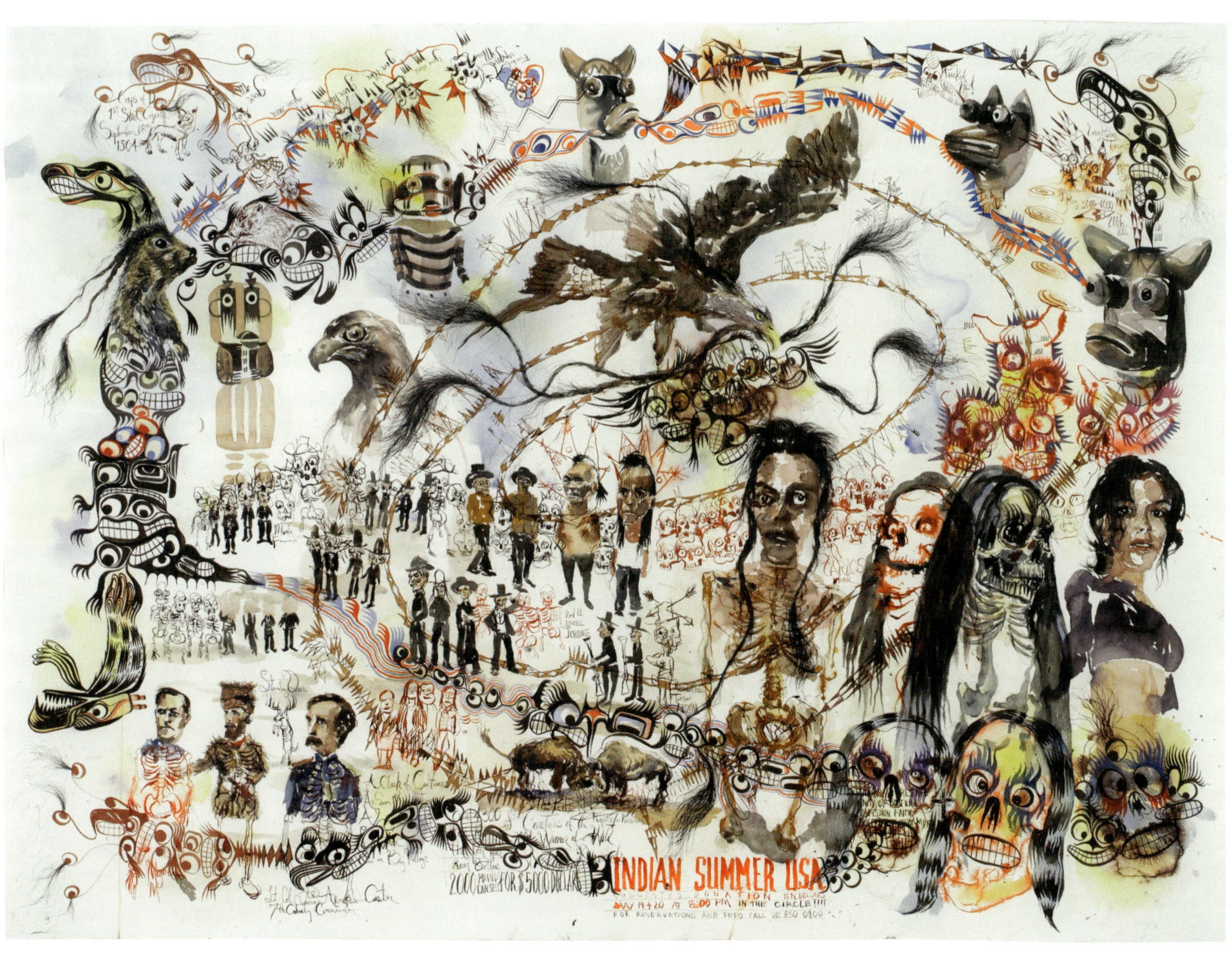

52
BRAD KAHLHAMER
Indian Summer USA, 2006
Watercolor and ink on paper
45 x 60 inches
Collection Neils Kantor

Margaret Kilgallen

Margaret Kilgallen made paintings, drawings, and mixed-media installations, conjuring up a timeless, folkloric America. Using the warm colors and bold designs of Mexican and Indian storefront sign painting, and the flat, contour-line figurative style of Depression-era cartooning, she created an animated, authentic world of tough broads, hobos, and hand-lettered messages. Kilgallen, who died of breast cancer in 2001 a the age of thirty-three, was a member of San Francisco's "Mission School," which includes Chris Johansen, Phil Frost, and her husband, Barry McGee. The group moves fluidly between graffiti and gallery projects, and draws on the street, especially the low-income, melting pot Mission District, for ideas and materials. Kilgallen rejected the notion of the work of art as a precious object and often painted and drew on scrap cardboard and wood. She also occasionally incorporated found signs and appealingly weathered objects, such as used bars of soap, in her multipart works. Intrepid and expressive women, particularly those who reflected her own interests in music and surfing, like old-time banjo player Matokie Slaughter and pioneering Olympic swimmer Fanny Durack, were of special interest to Kilgallen. Her work is filled with female images, often depicted fighting, smoking, and riding waves, as well as female names, rendered in a dazzling array of ornate antique American typefaces, which she studied as a book conservator at the San Francisco Public Library. Above all, however, Kilgallen was interested in the handmade, which she viewed as evidence of hard work, unfiltered expression, and noncommercial ingenuity:

I'm definitely interested in the past, and in a past that maybe I idealize as a time when things were well-made, and when maybe you couldn't go to Home Depot to find what you needed but you had to make it on your own. And the thing is, often people refer to that as the past, and I don't really think of it as the past because people still do that all the time today. It's just often in the city when there's so many things to look at and so many things going on—you don't see those things. But I see those things. On any day in the Mission in San Francisco, you can see a hand-painted sign that is kind of funky, and maybe that person, if they had money, would prefer to have had a neon sign. But I don't prefer that. I think it's beautiful, what they did and that they did it themselves. That's what I find beautiful.[1]

Her multi-panel works perpetually shift perspectives between individual portraits and landscapes, as well as between representation and text, as Kilgallen envisions an exuberantly hodgepodge world populated by all manner of self-styled and self-reliant individuals.

Kilgallen's contribution to *The Old, Weird America,* an installation combining works on panel and wall paintings of 2001 entitled *Main Drag,* depicts a charmingly desolate Anytown, USA. Shops and motels advertise their existence with slyly laconic signs, and obsolete or subcultural slang words hover over the work as signs of transient times and characters. The inhabitants of this deadbeat streetscape—hard-bitten dames, bedraggled surfers, and all manner of lowdown folks—are at once caricatures and noble figures. The down-and-out, Kilgallen seems to say in this antiheroic, ironically celebratory panorama, may be a drag, but it is one of the main sources of the American character.

1. "Influences, Train Marking, & Graffiti," interview, *Art:21—Art in the Twenty-first Century,* PBS series (2001): episode "Place," available at http://www.pbs.org/art21/artists/kilgallen/clip1.html, accessed January 6, 2008.

53
MARGARET KILGALLEN
Main Drag (installation view), 2001
Mixed media installation
Dimensions variable
Courtesy the Estate of Margaret Kilgallen

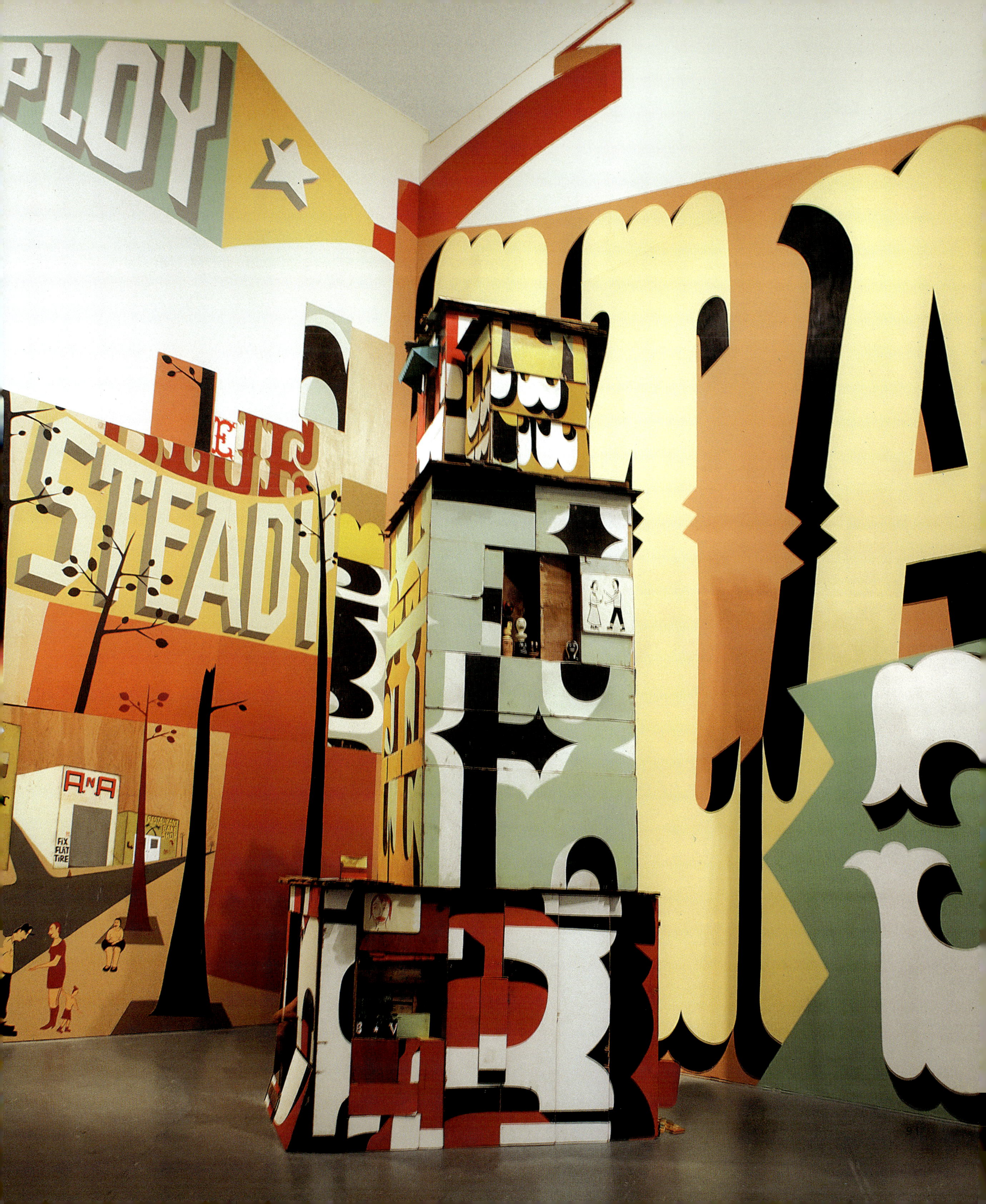

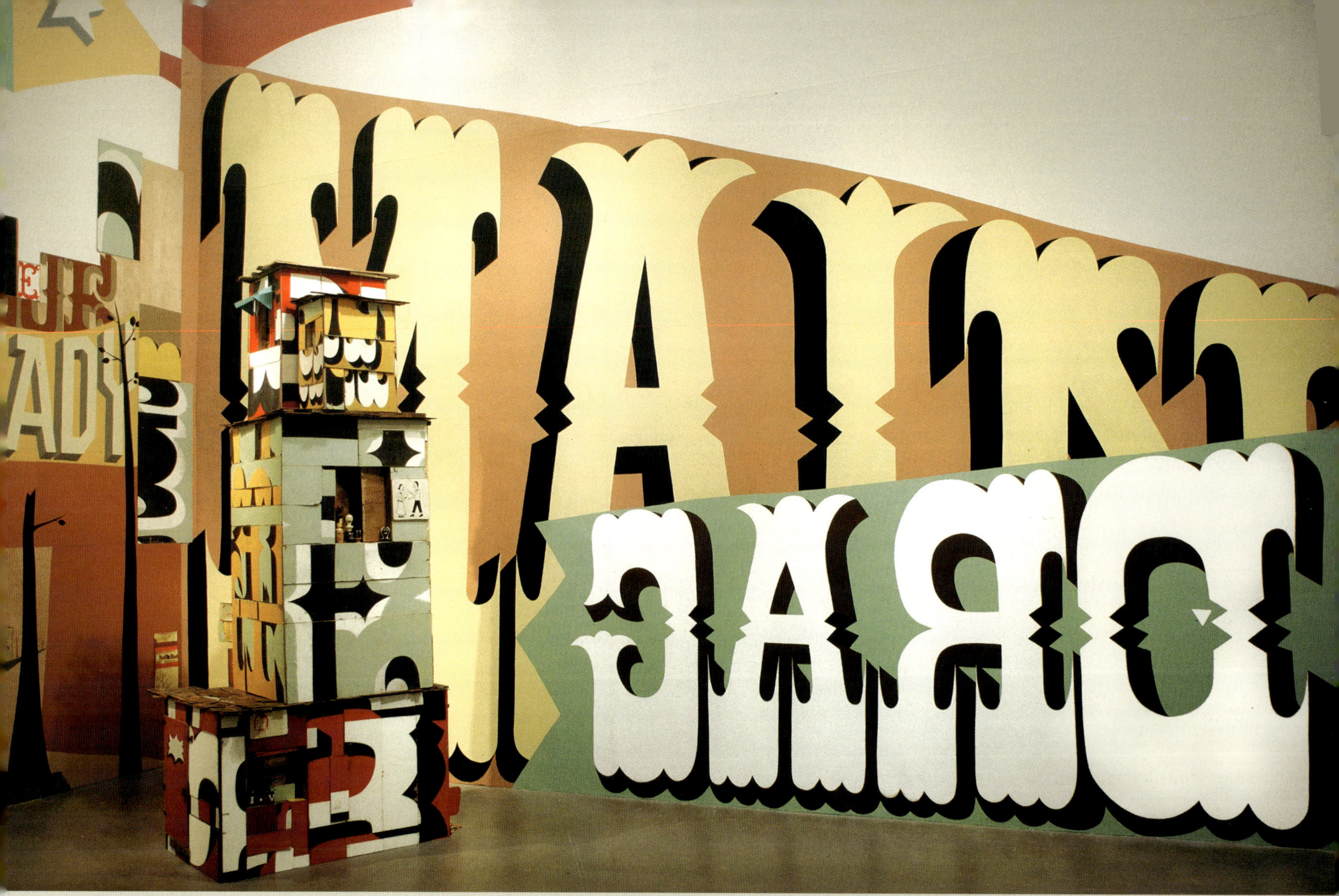

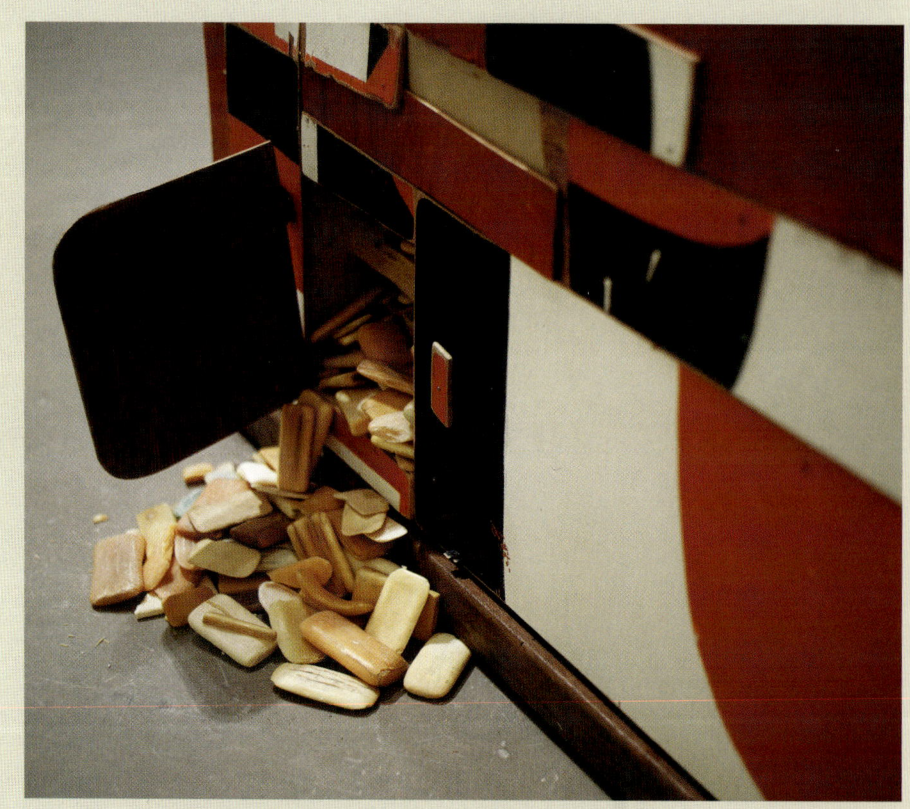

54–57
MARGARET KILGALLEN
Main Drag (installation view and details), 2001
Mixed media installation
Dimensions variable
Courtesy the Estate of Margaret Kilgallen

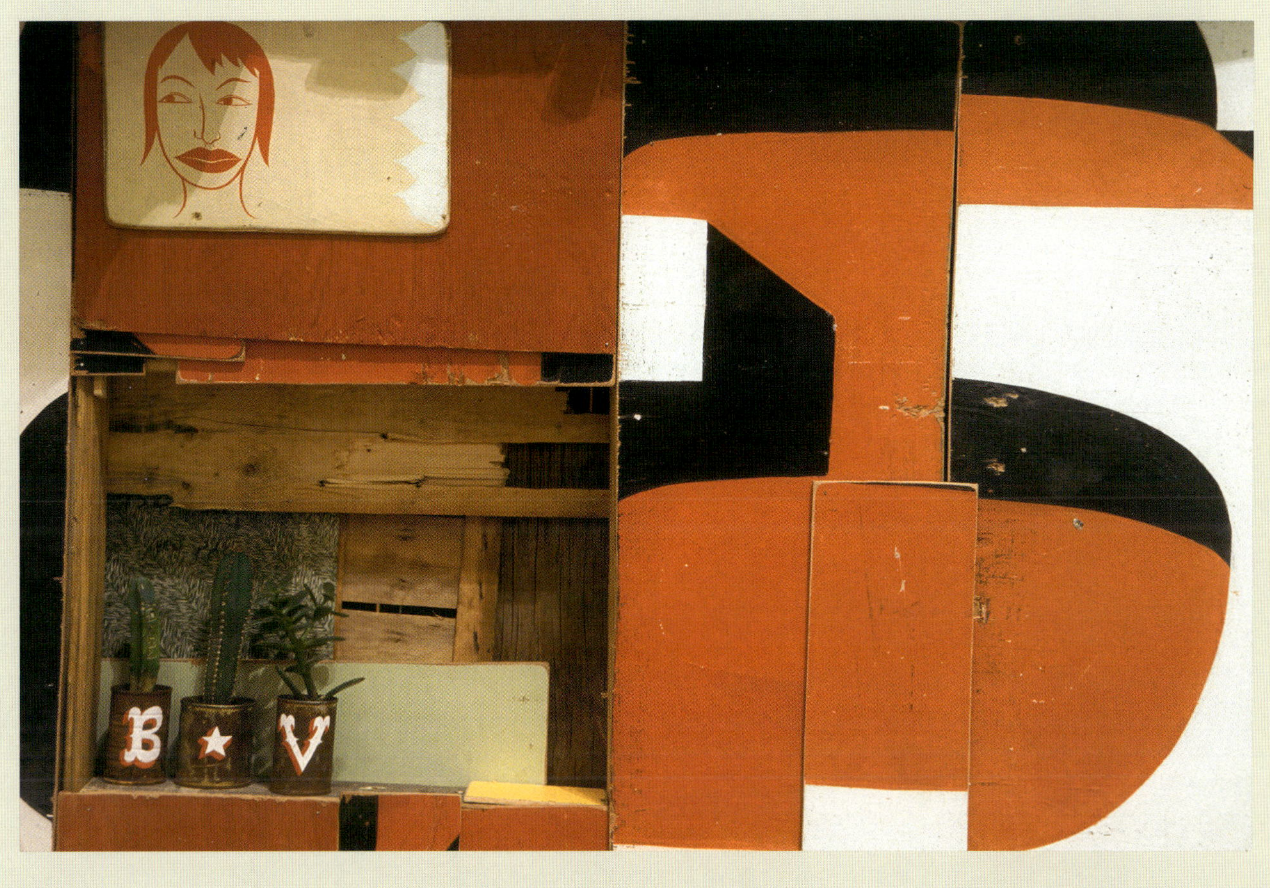

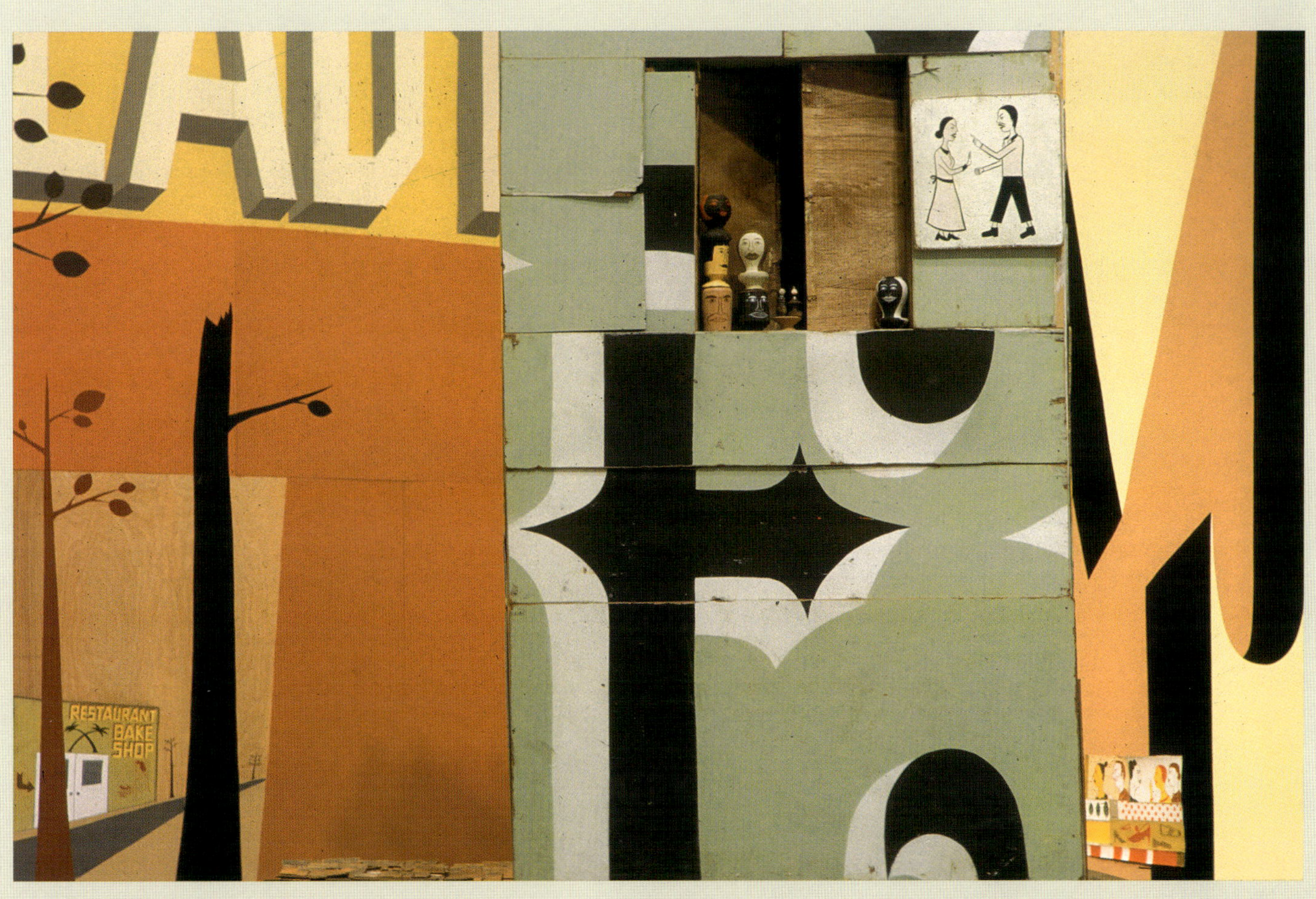

RESTAURANT
BAKE
SHOP

McDermott & McGough

From 1980 to 1995, David McDermott and Peter McGough, partners in art and life, lived in the past. Dressing, living, and working as artists and gentlemen-about-town from the early twentieth century, they wore top hats and paper collars, drove a Model T Ford, and lived in a townhouse in New York's East Village that was illuminated only by candlelight. This was not playacting, says McGough: "This was an experiment in time. We were trying to build a bubble environment and a fantasy we could live in."[1] McDermott & McGough, as the duo is known, are fascinated by "what's beyond what we know" and a strong connection to the past provides them keys to unravel life's mysteries. Their paintings, sculptures, photographs, and installations (all of which have two dates, one for the subject and one for the actual year the work was completed) are attempts at time travel and—to the best of the artists' ability—at bringing to life intellectual and emotional history. Paraphrasing Mary Baker Eddy (1821–1910), founder of Christian Science, McGough says, "Time is a mortal thought . . . and man made it up!" For the artists, "every year, hour, and minute exists at the same time," and just as works of art can be transporting, so too can be the practice of inhabiting different centuries and their mindsets. Religion, medicine, advertising, fashion, and above all gay culture—an often hidden history—are special interests for the team, who are no longer a couple but continue their artistic collaboration, with McDermott based in Ireland in an intact nineteenth-century farmhouse, and McGough in New York in a 1930s Moderne skyscraper.

The painting *In Praise of Shame, 1915* (2000), whose style McGough describes as "Robert Ryman meets late Francis Picabia," consists of six small, circular portraits of early twentieth-century dandies set against concentric rings of color on a textured white background. It takes its title from an eponymous poem by Lord Alfred Douglas (1870–1945). Linking love and shame, this verse was cited as evidence at the sensational 1895 trial of writer Oscar Wilde (1854–1900), Douglas's lover, and the work's peephole-style vignettes hint at the titillation aroused by Wilde's spirited defense of homosexuality. *Divine Fury, 1932* (2002) includes five male portraits and a "Cubist time tunnel" consisting of two male figures in a square made of alternating red and yellow bands, all superimposed on a larger portrait taken from an ad featuring the impossibly handsome Arrow collar man by famed illustrator J. C. Leyendecker. The work, with its sequentially lettered male faces, McGough states, was inspired by hand-colored picture postcards and the old gay boast to have "slept with a man who slept with Oscar Wilde." *Sacred Love, 1960* (2006) is a painted wood sculpture of a gray-suited man towering over a tiny tract home mounted on a pedestal emblazoned with the work's title. According to McGough, the work addresses the sprawling suburban neighborhoods of mid-century America, like the ones he and McDermott grew up in, and the lives of closeted gay men in them. A toppled, cracked vase enclosed in a glass vitrine like an ancient Greek relic, *San Francisco Earthquake Box, 1906* (1988) was inspired by a small piece of melted glass labeled "From the San Francisco Earthquake 1906" that McDermott's grandmother kept as a souvenir. After the devastation of the AIDS epidemic, it is hard not to read this shattered piece of flower-painted ceramic as a memorial to the victims in San Francisco's gay community and the vitality they brought to that Victorian city.

1. This and all subsequent quotes by Peter McGough are from a telephone interview with the author, November 21, 2007.

57
McDERMOTT & McGOUGH
Divine Fury, 1932, 2002
Oil on linen
60 x 48 inches
Courtesy the artists

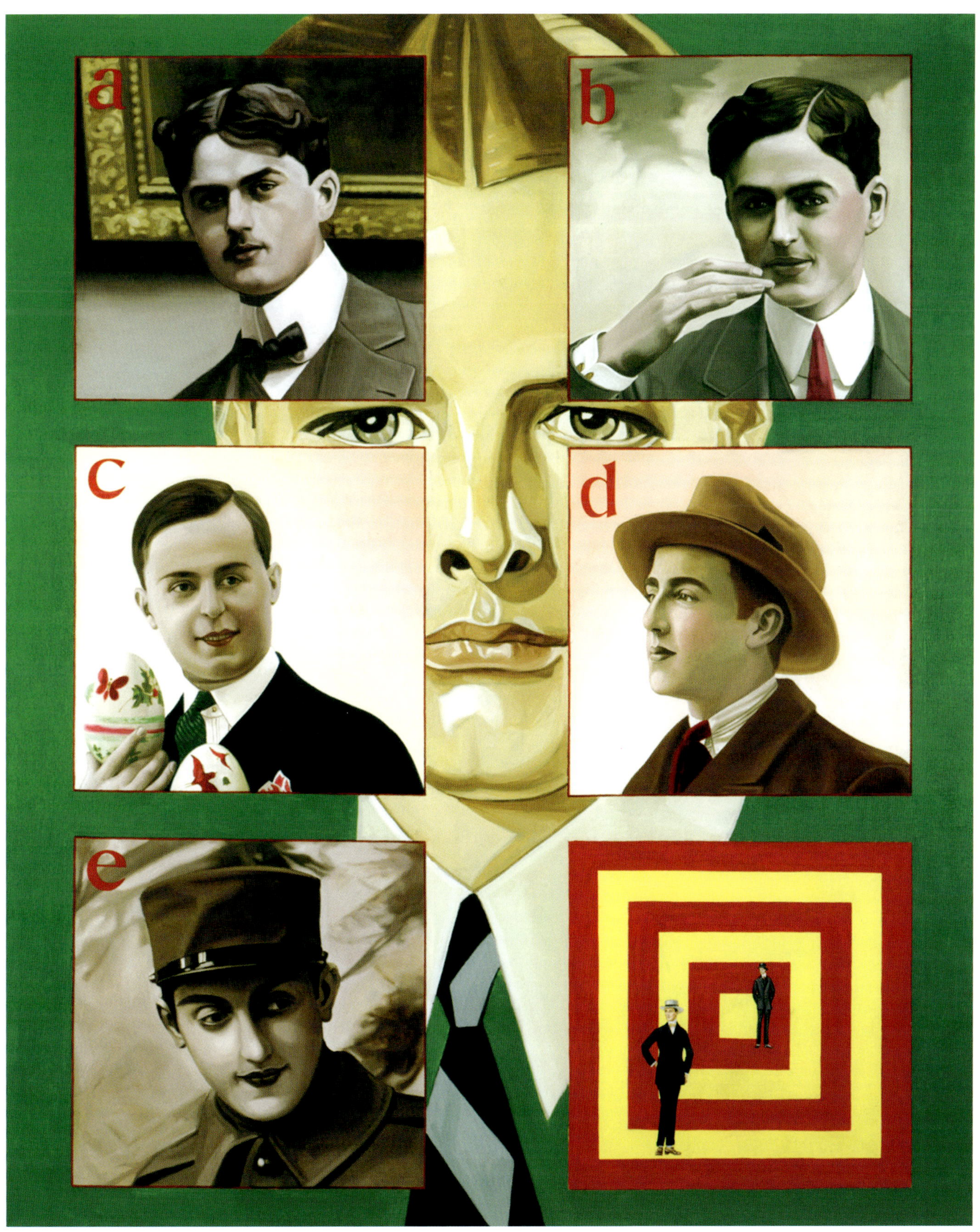
a
b
c
d
e

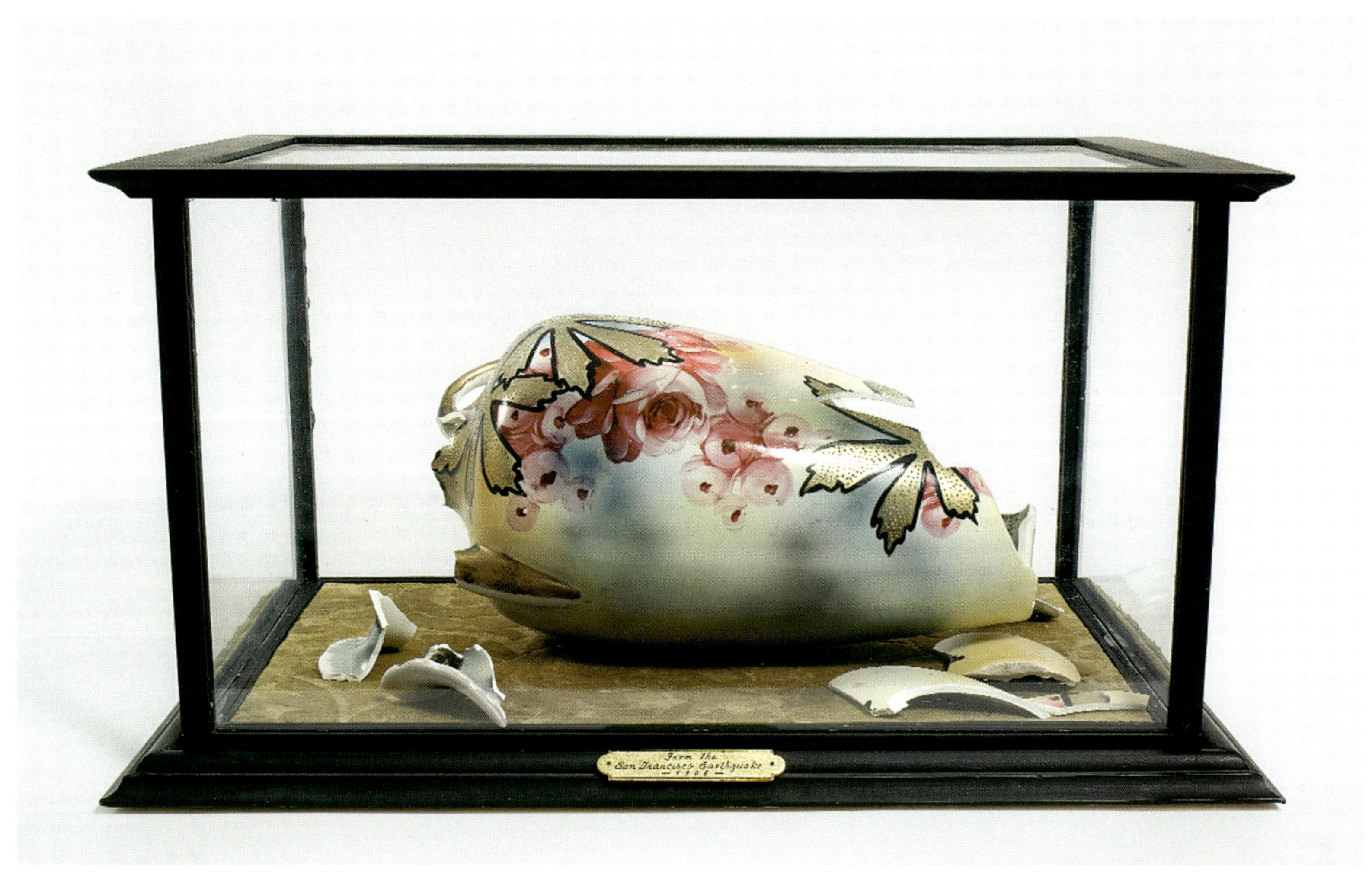

58

McDERMOTT & McGOUGH
San Francisco Earthquake Box 1906, 1988
Ceramic, glass, velvet, wood, and wooden plaque
12½ x 18¾ x 10¼ inches
Nicholas Robinson Collection

59

McDERMOTT & McGOUGH
In Praise of Shame 1915, 2000
Oil on linen
40 x 30 inches
Collection the artists

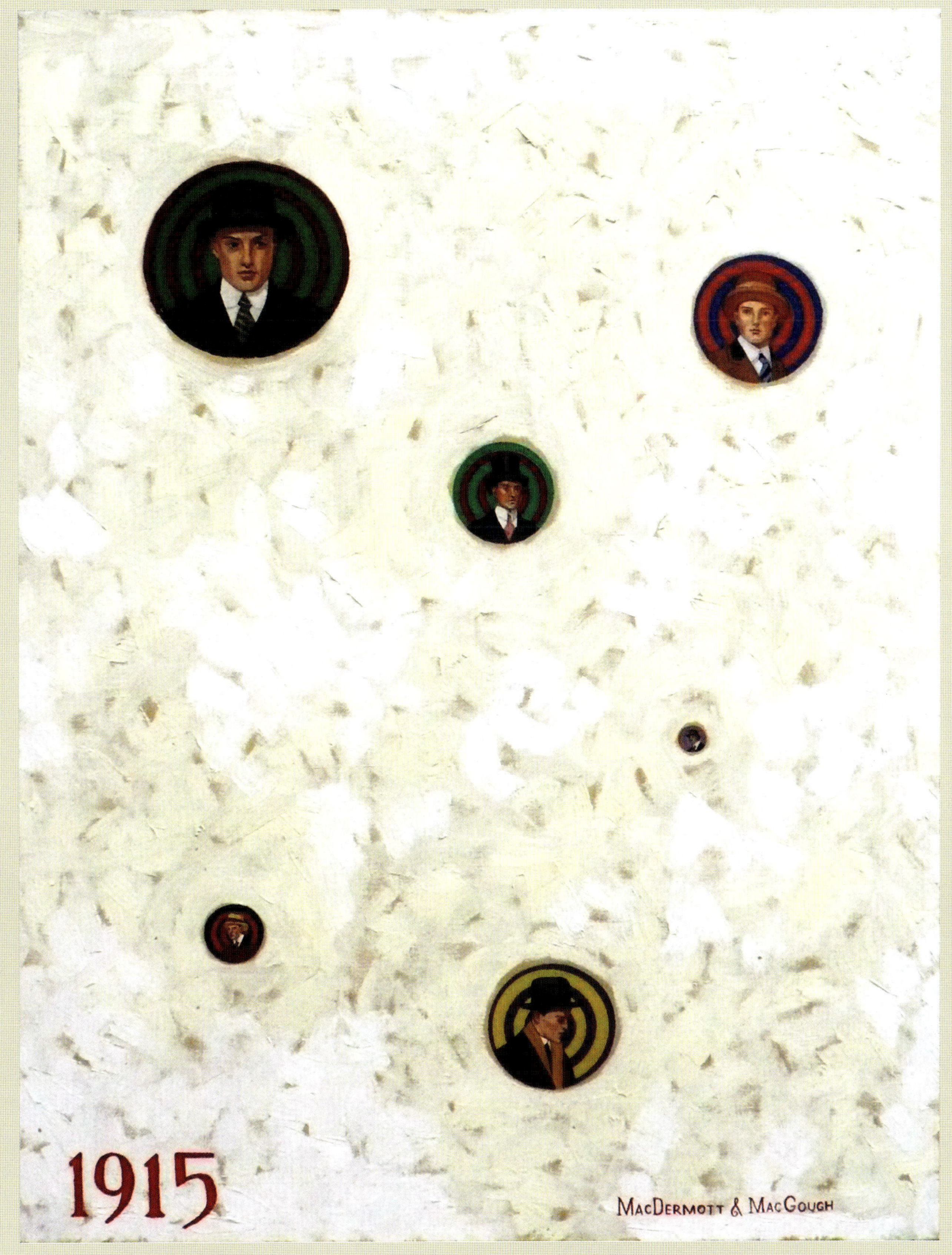

1915
MacDermott & MacGough

60
McDERMOTT & McGOUGH
Sacred Love and Pain, 1960, 2006
Oil on wood
48 x 12 x 16 inches
Courtesy the artists and Cheim & Read, New York

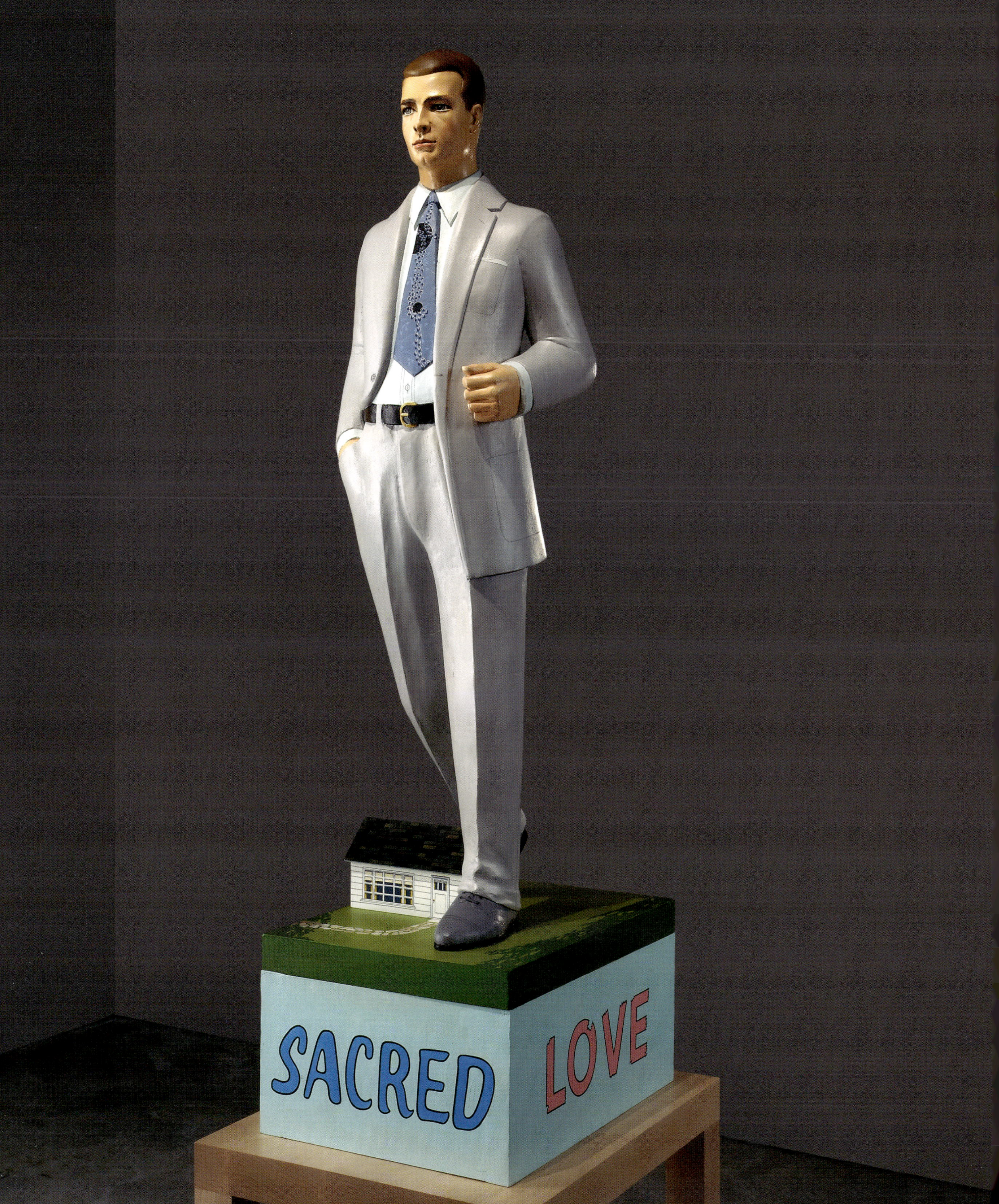

SACRED
LOVE

Aaron Morse

One of Aaron Morse's strongest child-hood memories is of camping under a tree on an open plain in Utah during a violent thunderstorm. He remembers being impressed by the terrific power of the storm and by the realization that nature was completely indifferent to his existence. As an artist exploring aspects of social history, he now draws inspiration from authors and filmmakers who have depicted the human struggle against those impersonal forces of nature. In this exhibition, Morse's four paintings grapple with ideas of the sublime in the early American landscape. Two works, *Magua (#2)* (2004) and *Deerslayer (#2)* (2006), were inspired by James Fenimore Cooper's novel *The Deerslayer* (1841), which chronicles the adventures of Natty Bumppo, an eighteenth-century guide and frontiersman who moves between the worlds of Natives and European settlers in what is now New York State. To make his Magua images, which are named after a villainous Huron Indian character in Cooper's *The Last of the Mohicans* (1826), Morse scanned, and then digitally collaged and distorted images from a variety of sources, including a condensed, comic book-style version of *The Deerslayer* published by *Classics Illustrated* (fig. 50). "Even though they were written while the country was still in formation, Cooper's novels are already nostalgic for the unspoiled frontier before westward expansion," Morse says. "There is a continual recycling of the myth of virgin wilderness in our culture; I wanted to exaggerate this by starting with a version of the novel that was itself an imaginary distortion."[1] The individual images— scenes of hunting, fighting, and canoeing— are arranged as sequential panels in the painting, creating an action-packed effect that Morse likens to a movie trailer: "I wanted an all-at-once picture that combined close-ups, landscape, and action with narrative and emotional content, abstraction and stylization." Both because it is less often depicted in films and because of its epic struggles, the early American period described in *The Deerslayer* and also depicted in Currier and Ives prints and Herman Melville's novels is a fresh source of inspiration for Morse—one that feels alive and exciting in the urbanized, industrialized twenty-first century.

More contemporary visions of the American wilderness by writers like Cormac McCarthy inspired the 2006 paintings *The Good Hunt* and *The Good Hunt (#2)*. Both depict hunters standing in front of huge hauls of prey: bear, moose, elk, mountain lions, and dozens of other animals. One hunter, hefting a mountain lion and wearing a bowler hat, is clearly white; the other, standing with his long rifle next to a crouching woman, Morse says, is "ethnically indeterminate," and based on a publicity still of the British-born actor Daniel Day-Lewis in the role of Hawkeye in the 1992 film *The Last of the Mohicans*. Morse, who admires McCarthy's violent 1985 novel *Blood Meridian* about a scalp-hunting gang on the Texas-Mexico border, used combinations of washy opaque and translucent surfaces (incorporating glittering glass beads in the painting titled *The Good Hunt*) to create scenes of conscienceless slaughter that echo the amoral universe and stylized storytelling of McCarthy's novel. In an age of global warming and mass extinctions, these works with their dispassionate sangfroid serve as memento mori for a vanishing natural abundance, as well as attempts to envision the legacy of destruction on which the country was settled.

1. This and all subsequent quotes by the artist are from telephone interviews with the author, February 2 and November 7, 2007.

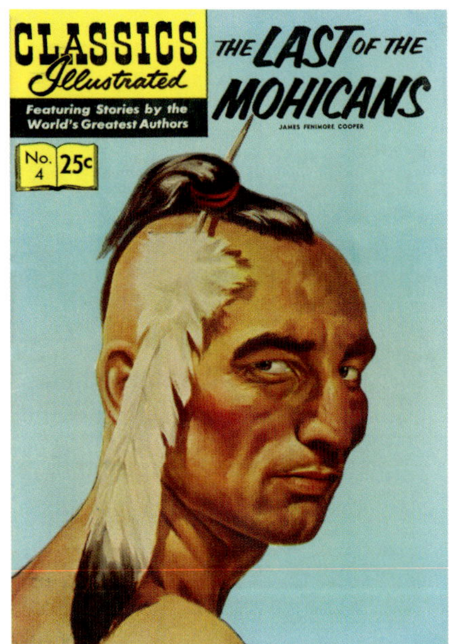

Fig. 50
Comic book cover,
The Last of the Mohicans,
Classics Illustrated #4, 1946.
© Gibertton Company, Inc.

61
AARON MORSE
The Good Hunt (#2), 2006
Acrylic, watercolor, pencil on paper
90 x 22 inches
Courtesy the artist, ACME., Los Angeles,
and Guild and Greyshkul, New York

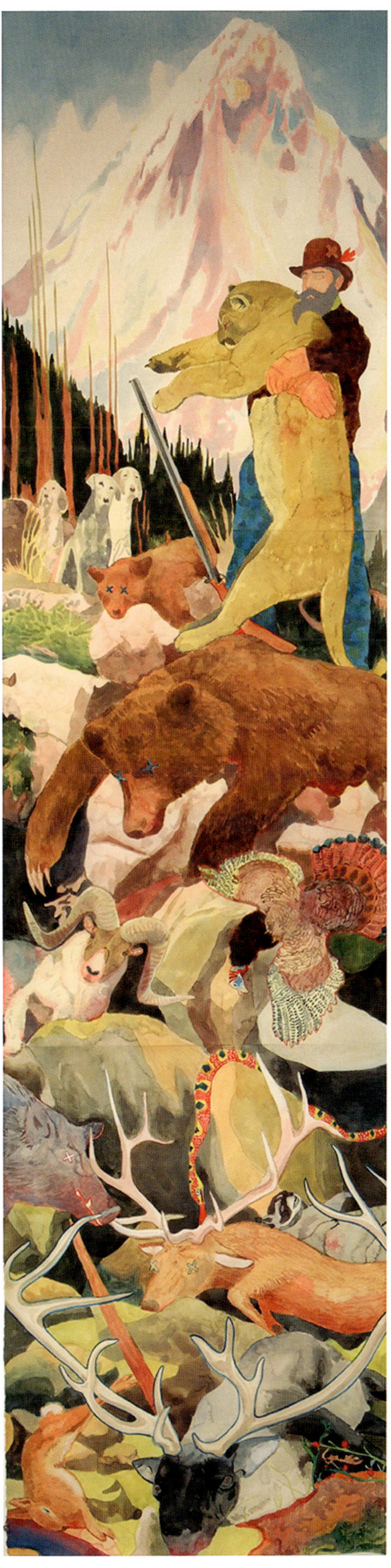

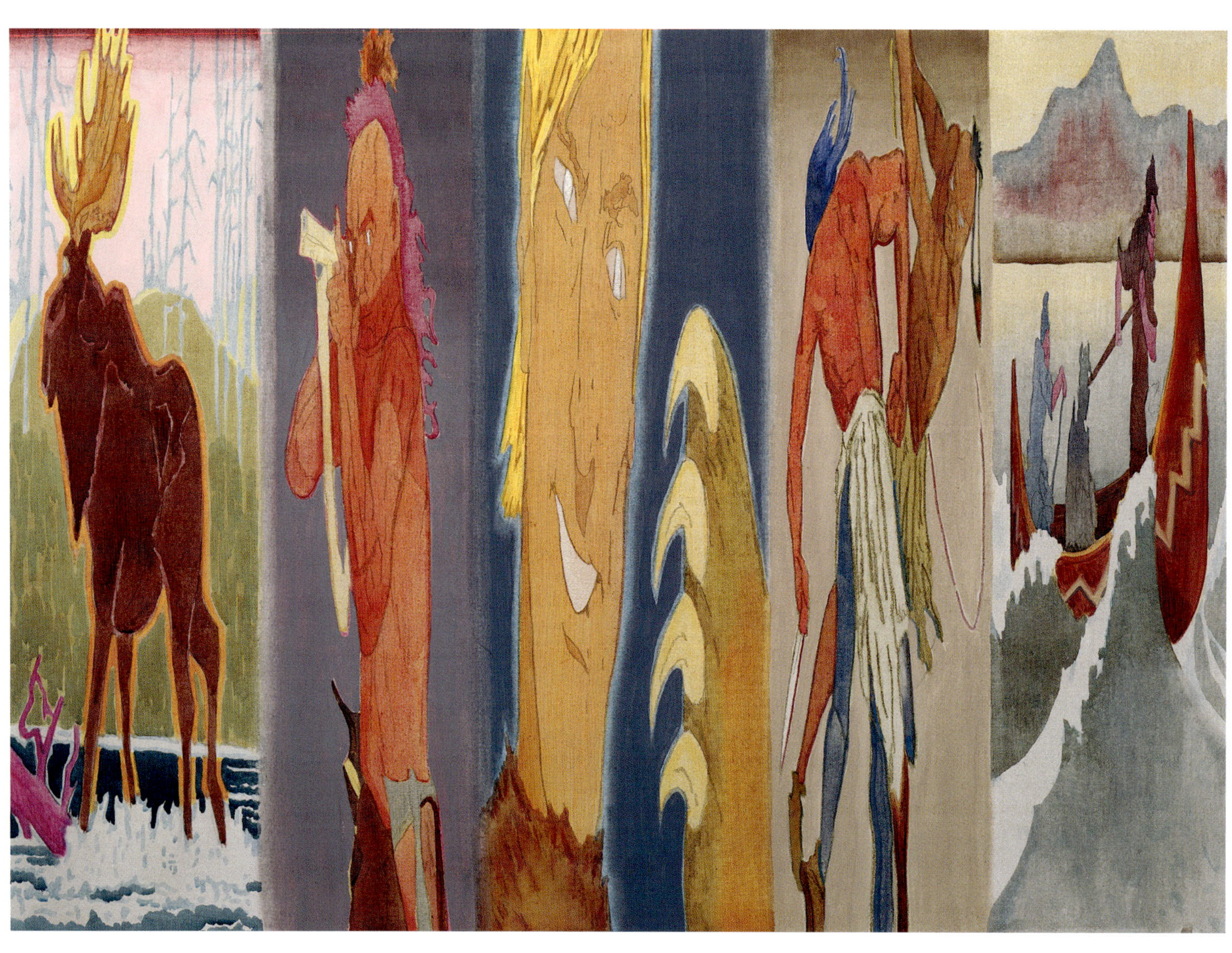

59
AARON MORSE
Magua (#2), 2004
Acrylic on linen
36 x 48 inches
Collection Lance and Jennifer Volland

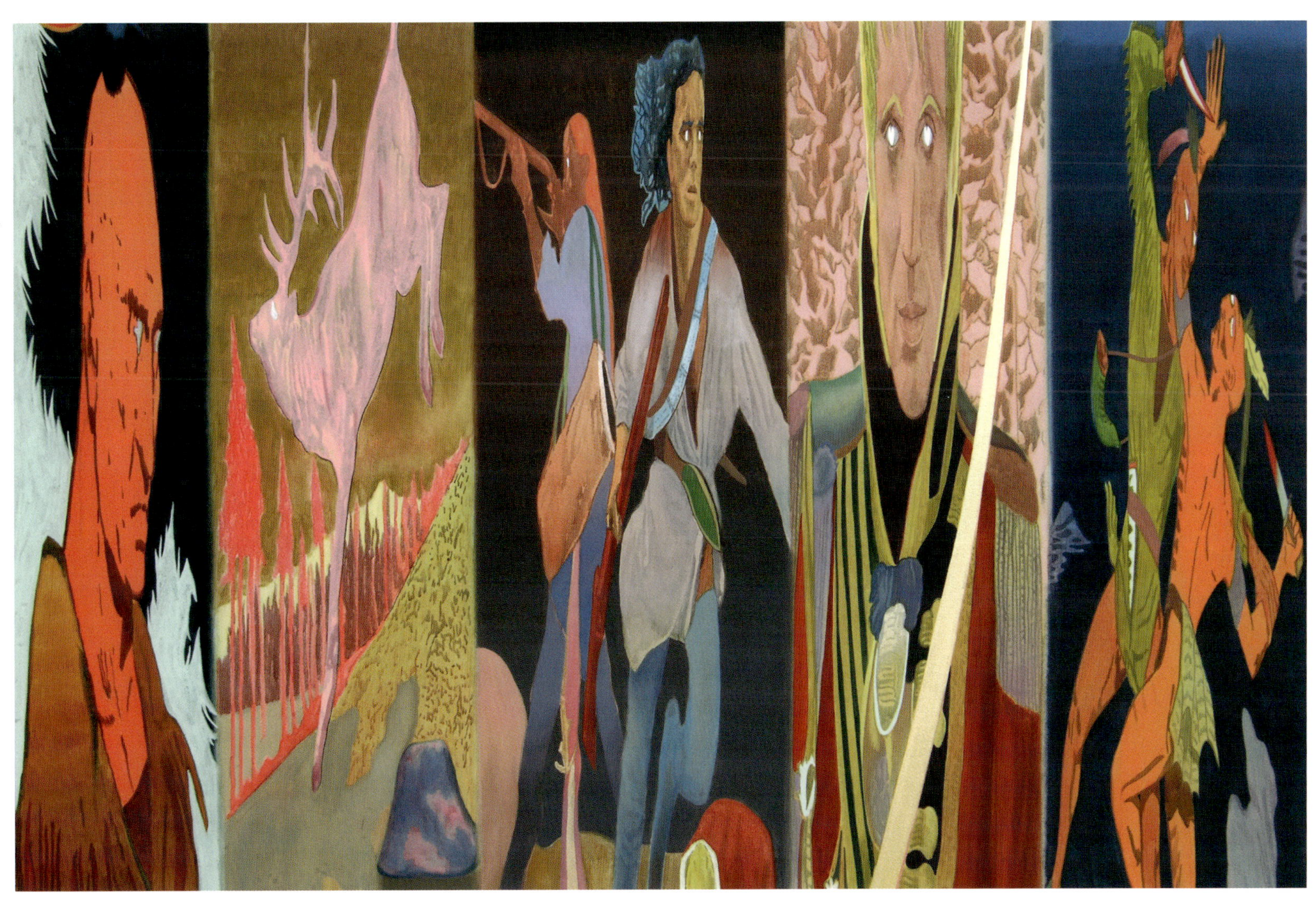

60

AARON MORSE
Deerslayer (#2), 2006
Acrylic, oil on canvas
60 x 88 inches
Courtesy the artist, ACME., Los Angeles,
and Guild and Greyshkul, New York

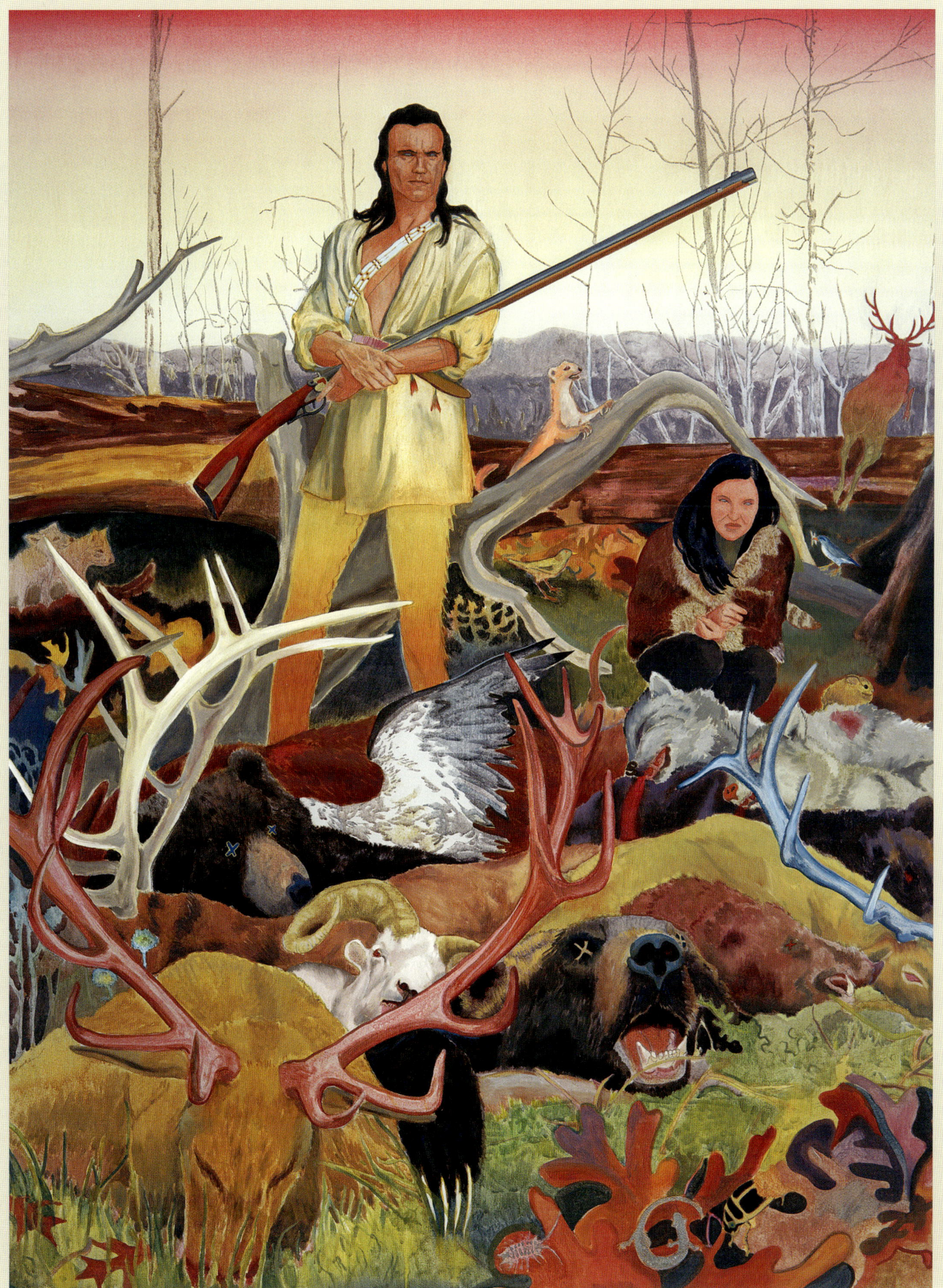

Cynthia Norton

Ninnie Nuevo, Ninnie Naive, Ninnie Nonesuch, Ninnie Nova, Ninnie Nouveau, Ninnie Nu Ninnie. These are some of the aliases of Louisville-based sculptor and performance artist Cynthia Norton. Part riverboat chanteuse and part basement scientist, Norton, a.k.a. Ninnie, classifies herself as a practitioner of the "womanly arts," by which she means generally any homespun, ingenious, jury-rigged, or intuitive act of creativity—whether in domestic or artistic spheres.[1] She builds stringed instruments out of tennis rackets, constructs Rube Goldbergesque performing sculptures, and sings in a distinctive off-key style. Norton's projects are diverse and freewheeling, but saturated with meaning and precedent. Although she has deep roots in the "hillbilly, Appalachian, and bluegrass" places of Kentucky, she does not exist exclusively in one time. "I'm interested in novelty and nostalgia," Norton says. "I like to find uncanny stories from the past and use them to describe something new." For example, backed by a swampy, rattletrap band on a 1995 CD entitled *Cotton Candy Country*, she updated country and folk classics to chronicle events from her childhood in Athens (pronounced Ay-thens), Kentucky. Her adaptation of "Pretty Polly," a ballad of a woman murdered by her fiancé, was inspired by seeing a television news story about the brother of a childhood friend who was discovered by the police holding his baby and chant-

ing, "I didn't mean to do it," after having killed his wife. Norton substituted the name of this acquaintance, Gary, for the song's traditional villain, Willie, and added the refrain: "I didn't mean to do it, Polly/ Was all that he could moan...."[2]

For *The Old, Weird America*, Norton contributes two kinetic sculptures: *Fountain (emotion)* (2002) and *Dancing Squared* (2004). *Fountain (emotion)*, a working moonshine still made of, among other common household objects, a magazine rack, is a backwoods nod to Marcel Duchamp, who notoriously renamed a urinal *Fountain* and displayed it as sculpture in 1917. Through acts like this, which many regard as the first gestures of Conceptual art, Duchamp introduced the concept of the readymade, or a found object not normally considered to be art. Norton, who regards history and music as readymades, thinks of moonshiners as ancestors of contemporary performance artists: "they do something for society, but they're outside of what society allows." *Fountain (emotion)*, which quietly distills real liquor in the gallery, is her subversive homage to those who have sought to lubricate our thinking, through both art and something harder.

Similarly, her kinetic sculpture *Dancing Squared*, a large-scale whirligig consisting of four spinning square-dance dresses mounted at the corners of a rotating square armature, is also about intoxication—this time spiritual. "*Dancing Squared* is about how we organize ourselves spiritually," Norton says. "Square dancing is very mathematical and patterned, and it's about connecting and disconnecting with partners." She was inspired by the spontaneous, ecstatic dances of Shaker and Quaker congregations—which many, including artist Dan Graham in his book and video projects *Rock My Religion*, see as a spark for the manic energy of rock 'n' roll. Other cosmological and religious designs also shaped the work. Its square form came from ancient astrological charts, and its movement came from rotating Buddhist prayer wheels. As the electric motors hidden within each of the red dresses start their crinolines whirling, and the entire sculpture starts spinning in sympathy with their centrifugal forces, *Dancing Squared* exuberantly synthesizes the dialectic between puritanical perfectionism and wild abandon that fuels metaphysical America.

62 *(page 107)*
CYNTHIA NORTON
Fountain (emotion), 2002
Mixed media, copper coil, pressure cooker, bucket, magazine rack, wood
44 x 50 x 32 inches
Courtesy the artist

63–64
(below and pages 108–109)
CYNTHIA NORTON
Dancing Squared, 2004
Aluminum, hardware, electric motors, dresses, wire
90 x 180 x 180 inches
Collection Laura Lee Brown and Steve Wilson, Louisville, Kentucky

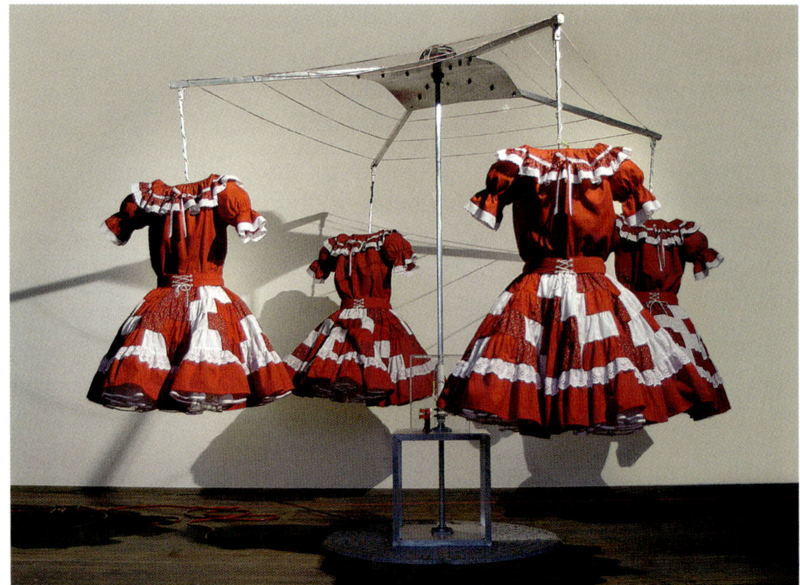

1. All quotes by the artist are from a telephone interview with the author, November 1, 2007.

2. Greil Marcus, *The Old, Weird America* (New York: Picador, 1997), 178–79.

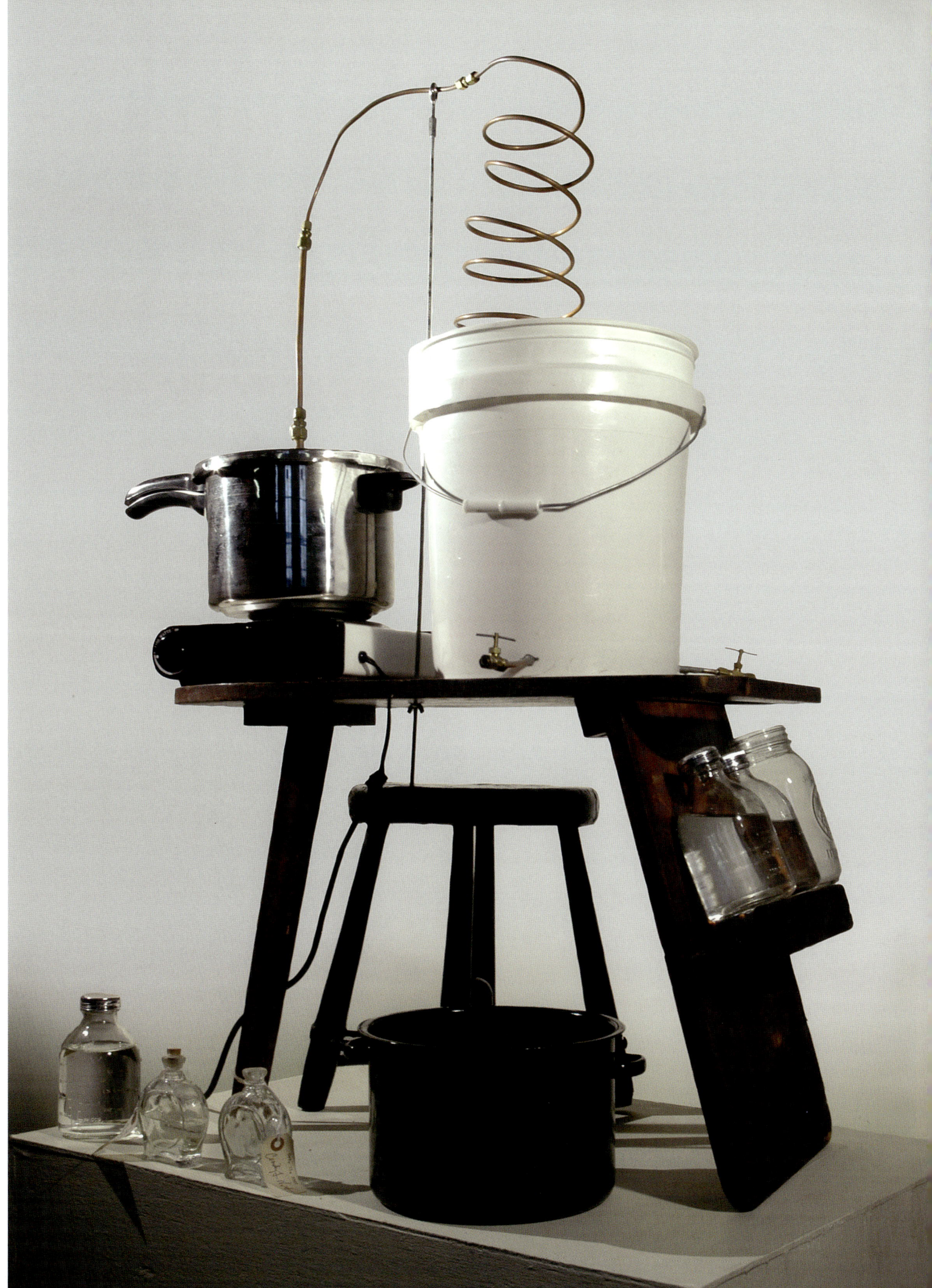

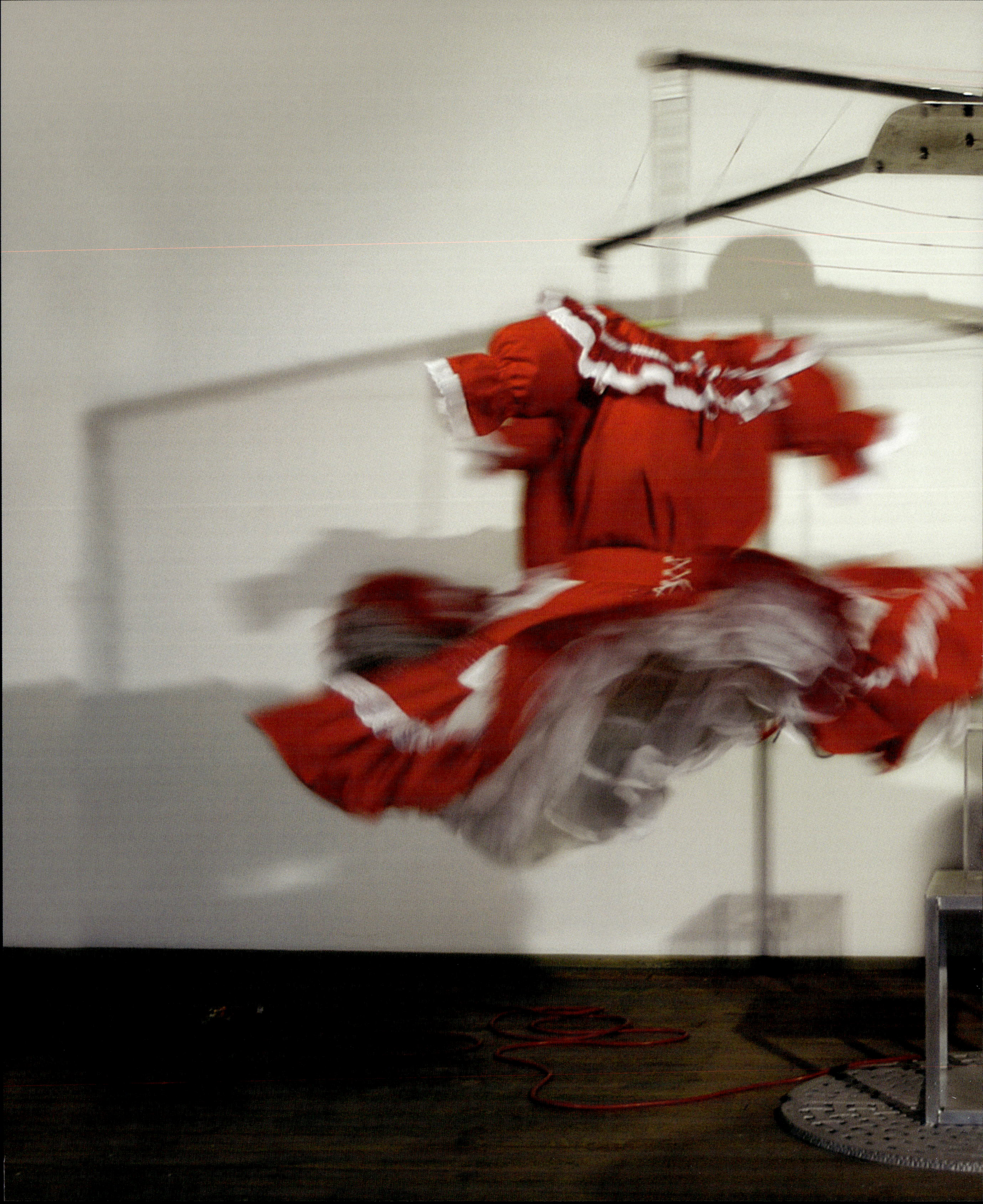

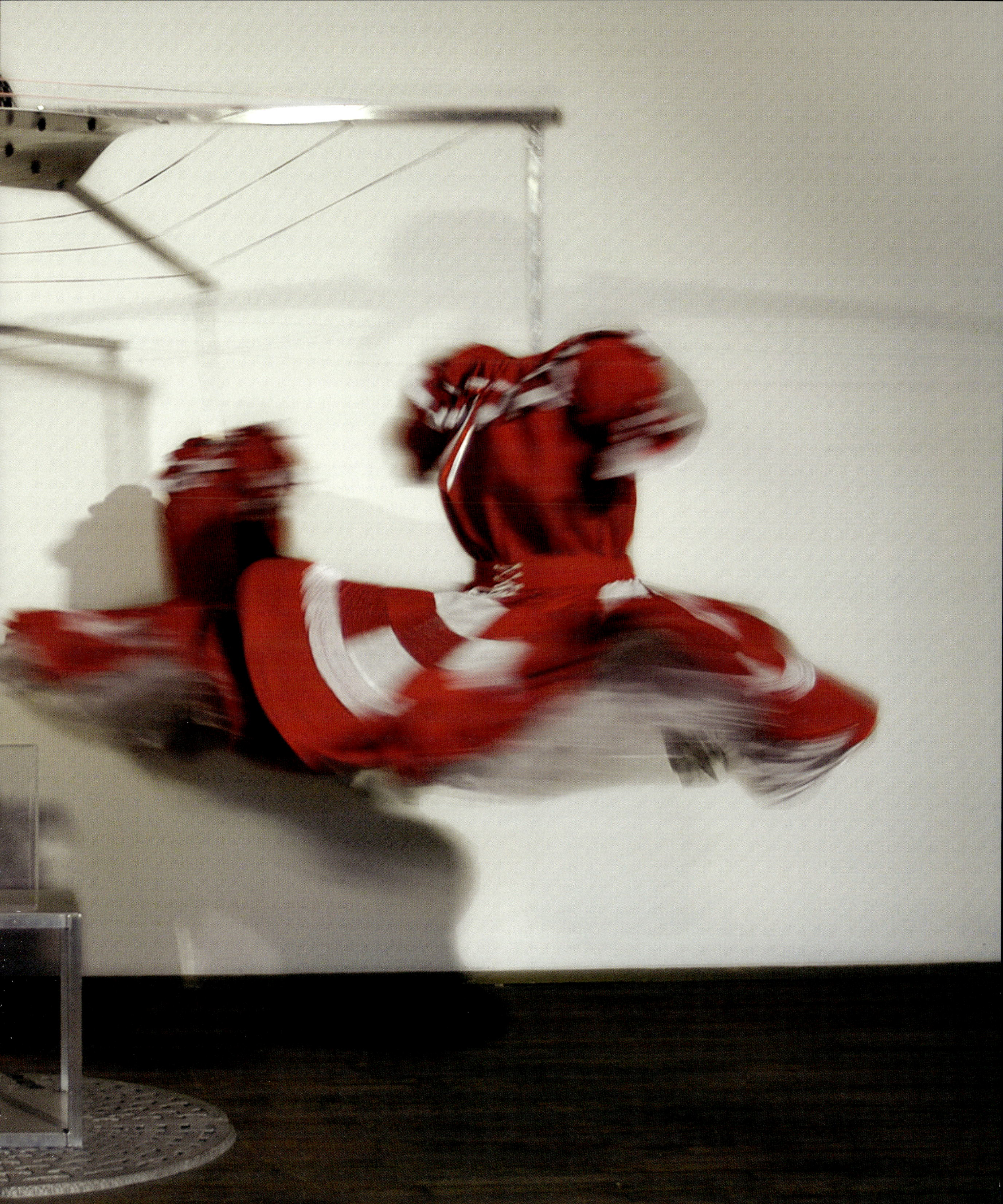

Greta Pratt

*P*hotographer Greta Pratt documents the ways that Americans remember the past. For years, she stalked places and events like parades, pageants, Civil War battlefields, and Mt. Rushmore, collecting images of what she calls "vernacular history"—how people retell the foundational stories of their towns, regions, and countries. In 2005, Pratt collected these photographs in a book entitled *Using History*, which juxtaposes shots of Native powwow dancers and tourists posing with cigar store Indians; Juneteenth Day reenactors and black waiters parking their cars as they arrive to work at Confederate Balls (fig. 51); and staged Wild West shootouts and bumper stickers of Osama Bin Laden with crosshairs on his forehead. Sure, America had some problems with indigenous populations, slavery, and frontier justice, these playful, often downright funny scenes remind us, but that's all in the past, and now we all get along. This is the dominant belief that binds the culture, Pratt says, but she also understands that history is usually written by the winners and can be reinterpreted to justify the present. Working in post-9/11 America, when the flag and other important national characters and symbols seem especially charged, she views her work as "a quest to understand how I, and we, remember history, and to address how what we commemorate about the past reflects the culture of today."[1] Like the many spectators captured in her images, Pratt is enthralled by attempts to bring history to life, and her work attempts to expose the ways that present concerns shape historical understanding.

On several of her photographic road trips, Pratt encountered an Abraham Lincoln impersonator, Gerald Bestrom, who travels the country in a mobile home painted to look like a log cabin (see fig. 5). Through Bestrom, she was introduced to the Society of Lincoln Presenters, an organization of men (and women, who channel Mary Todd Lincoln) whose motto is "Would I might rouse the Lincoln in you all." Her work *19 Lincolns* (2005), composed of eighteen portraits of nineteen of these presenters at a 2000 meeting of the society in Hodgenville, Kentucky, was a result of these introductions. Presenters, Pratt discovered, are generally drawn to Lincoln's high moral character. They respect the fact that he rose from humble origins through hard work, as well as the fact that he was not especially handsome or popular in his own time. Revisionist historians have recently posited new theories about Lincoln's sexuality, health, and dark *Weltanschauung*, but the presenters celebrate his life as an exemplar of American goodness above all. Collaborating with these top-hatted and bewhiskered performers on their portraits, Pratt came to view them as "a metaphor for the country—a group held together by a particular understanding of history." Like them, she sees her artistic role as an extension of the idealized figure of "the engaged American citizen who tries to say things that are important and have people understand them."

1. This and all subsequent quotes by the artist are from a telephone interview with the author, November 15, 2007.

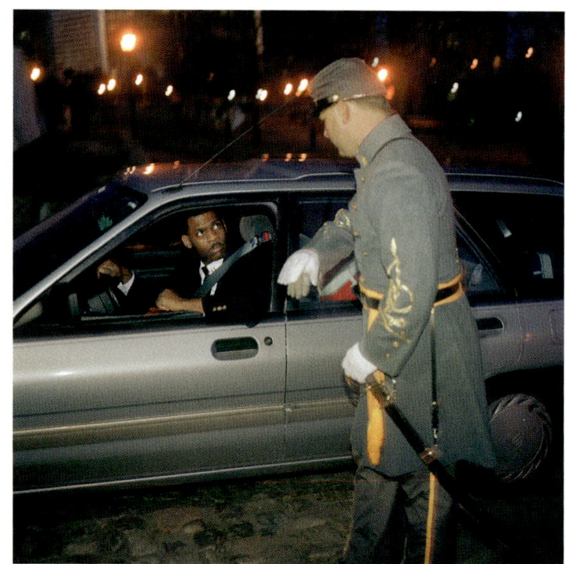

Fig. 51
Greta Pratt, *Waiter Arriving for a Confederate Ball, Richmond, Virginia*, 1996
Lambda print
30 x 30 inches
Courtesy the artist

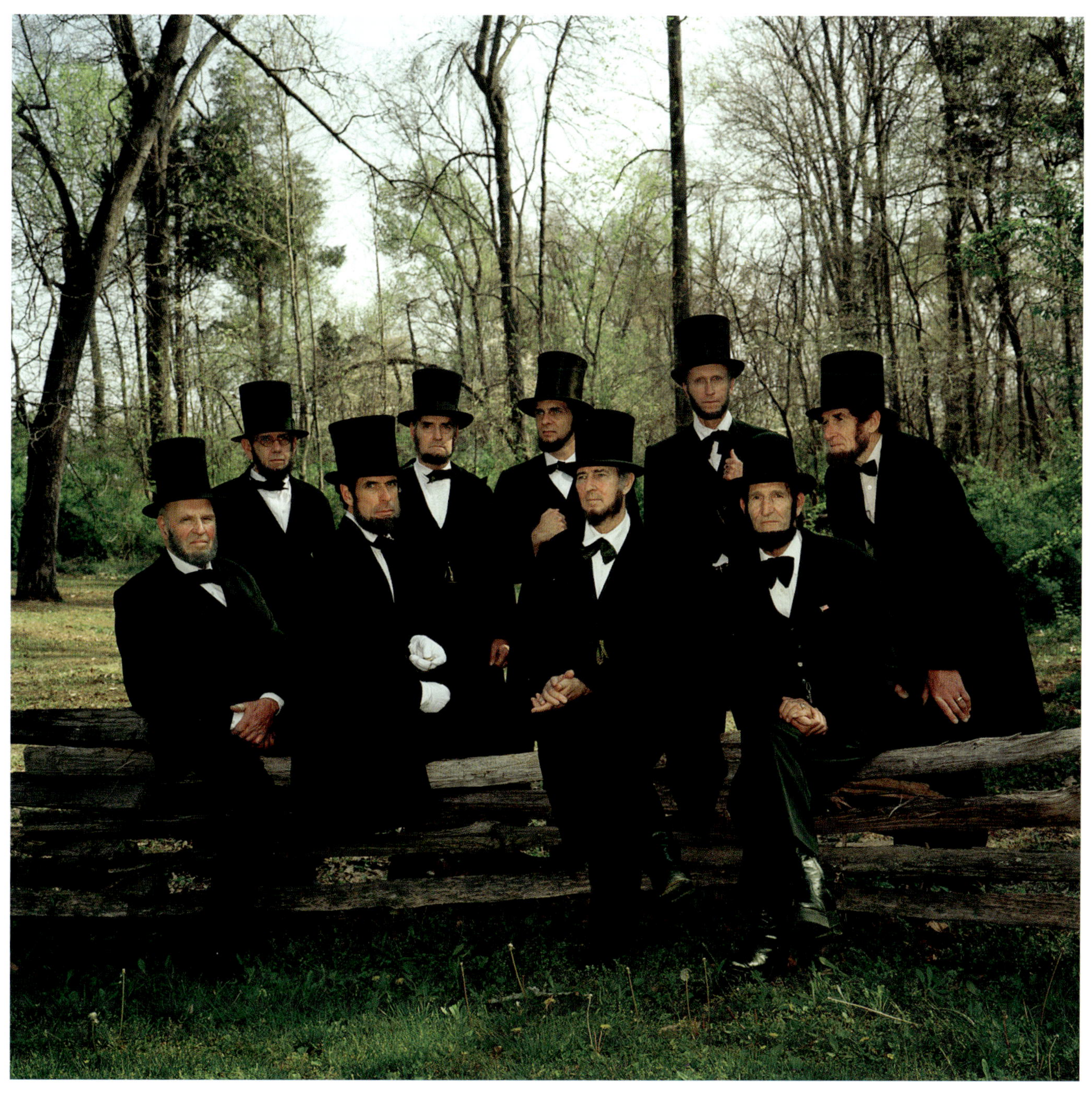

65
GRETA PRATT
Nine Lincolns, 2000
Lambda print
30 x 30 inches
Courtesy the artist

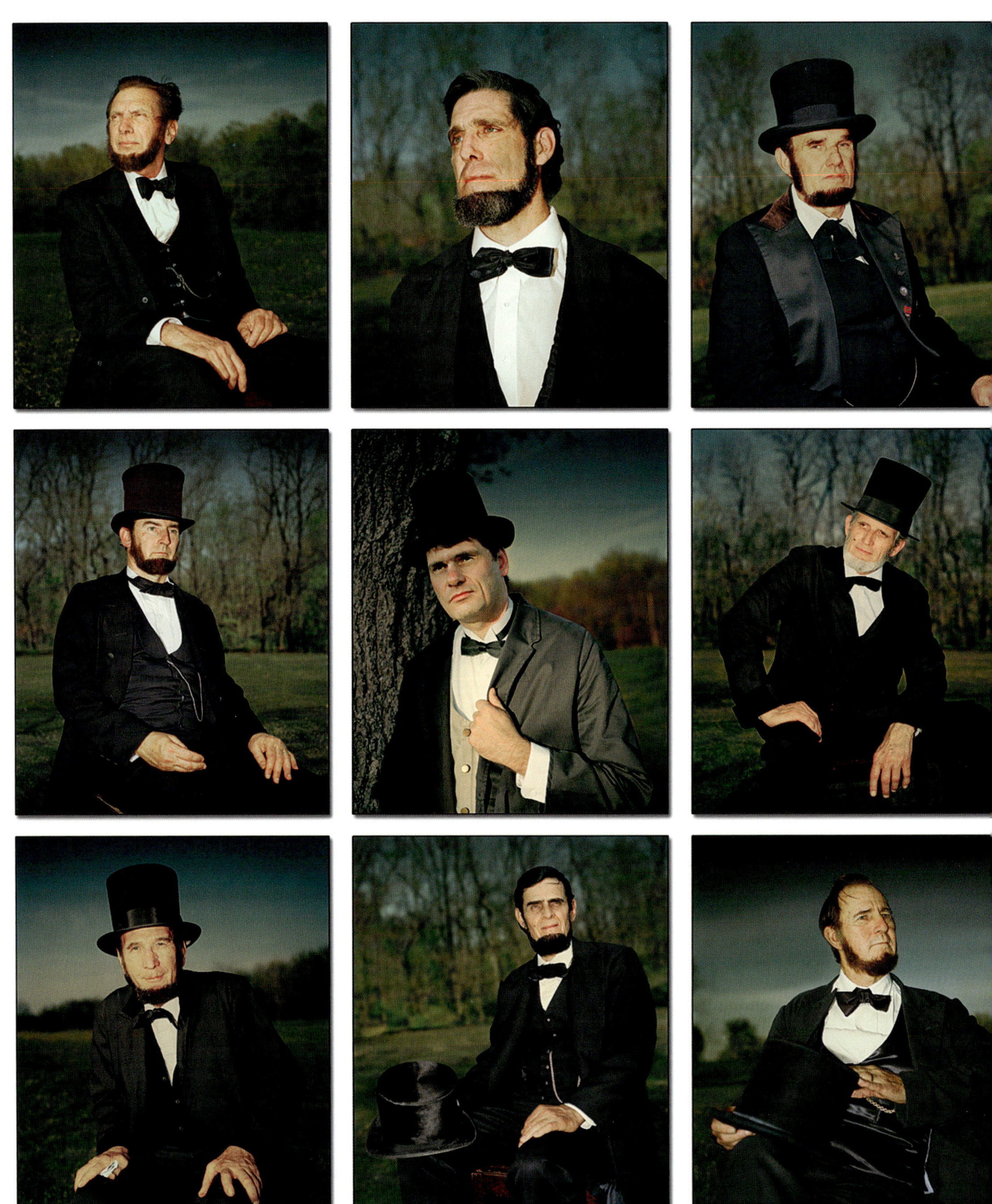

66
GRETA PRATT
Nineteen Lincolns, 2005
18 archival inkjet prints
28 x 24 inches each
Courtesy the artist

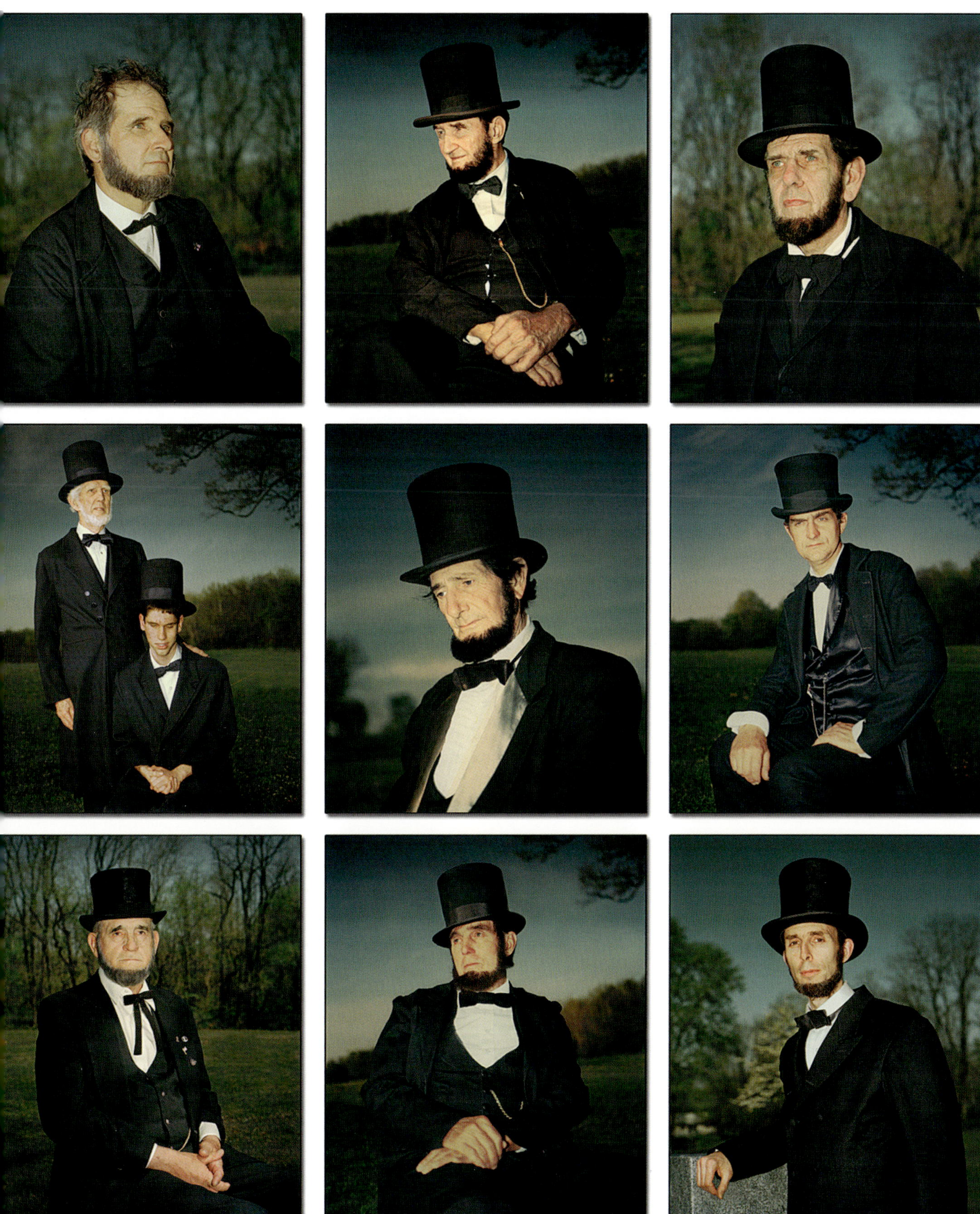

David Rathman

avid Rathman began his career publishing comic books, zines, and artist's books in the early 1980s, and his current paintings and drawings continue to combine words and pictures and to tell stories. He carries with him notebooks in which he records his inspirations, including newsstand headlines, overheard conversations, and song lyrics. In the studio, he matches these street-level haikus to images also culled from life and popular culture, sometime using them as titles and sometimes including them as handwritten captions in the work itself. The eight small drawings in ink on paper in *The Old, Weird America* are spare, archetypal vignettes from the Wild West, each labeled with a scrawled phrase. The words "My Vices Were Magnificent" hover above an outlaw about to be hanged; "Hell You Ain't Dead. Just Shut Up a Little" is the caption above a gunman kneeling to help a fallen friend; and "It's Funny to Start Thinking About Women" annotates the image of a cowpoke sitting by a campfire. To make these works, Rathman spent hours carefully freeze-framing VHS tapes of Western movies so he could take Polaroids of iconic or beautifully composed scenes. He then distilled the photographic images by removing the background clutter and occasionally combined elements from different snapshots to create spare vignettes of the Wild West. Rathman's riflemen, sheriffs, and bandits, he says, reflect his genuine love of spaghetti westerns—especially those starring Clint Eastwood—the Italian films that gave the romance of the West a modernist twist in the 1960s and 1970s.

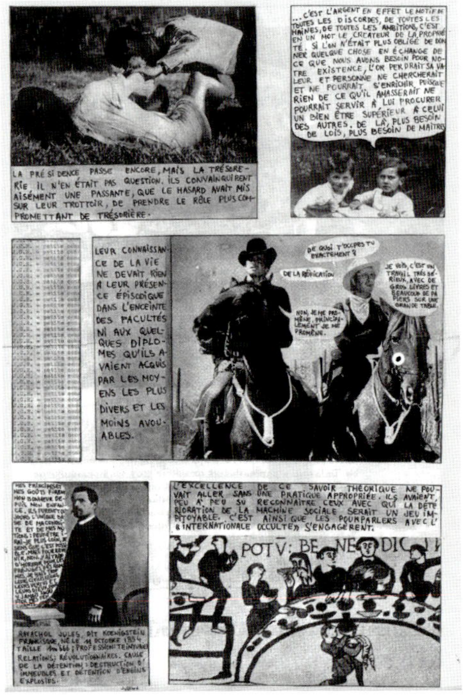

Rathman's cowboy remixes may have an early ancestor in the work of French artist André Bertrand, who, in 1966, recaptioned a Western comic book so that its two horsemen discussed the Marxist-inspired theory of the Situationist International movement (fig. 52); aligned with the May 1968 uprisings in France, the Situationists attempted to counter the alienation and consumerism of contemporary society by disrupting the flow of everyday life through *détournement*, a subversive appropriation of existing works of art, and *dérive*, an antiauthoritarian "drift" through urban life. In Bertrand's hand-lettered text bubbles, the dialogue unfolds: "What's your scene, man?" "Reification." "I guess that means pretty hard work with big books and piles of paper on a big table?" "No, I drift. Mostly, I just drift." And Rathman doesn't deny a rough-hewn existentialism in his work. His taut, condensed form of storytelling has something in common with painter Edward Hopper's bleak scenes of Americans lost in thought, as well as with the hard-boiled lyrics of country music by George Jones, Johnny Cash, and Willie Nelson, which Rathman shunned for rock 'n' roll while growing up in Montana, but learned to admire while working on the series. "I've always felt like I'm dropping down in the middle of a story. I'm fascinated by the pivotal instant right before or after something momentous happens," Rathman says.[1] Because images of cowboys are so ingrained in the American psyche as clichéd symbols of taciturn tough guys, it's shocking to see them expressing vulnerable or questioning thoughts. Rathman, a former high school wrestler, is interested in "a certain kind of aggressiveness as well as a certain kind of melancholy" that he associates with American masculinity. By creating images of archetypal American characters that include clues to their own mythological deconstruction, Rathman makes gently humorous and satiric symbols appropriate for a time in which the paths of romance and reality in the United States seem radically divergent.

Fig. 52
André Bertrand, *Le Retour de la Colonne Durutti* **(*The Return of the Durutti Column*)** (detail), 1966
Four-page comic book

1. This and all subsequent quotes by the artist are from a telephone interview with the author, November 19, 2007.

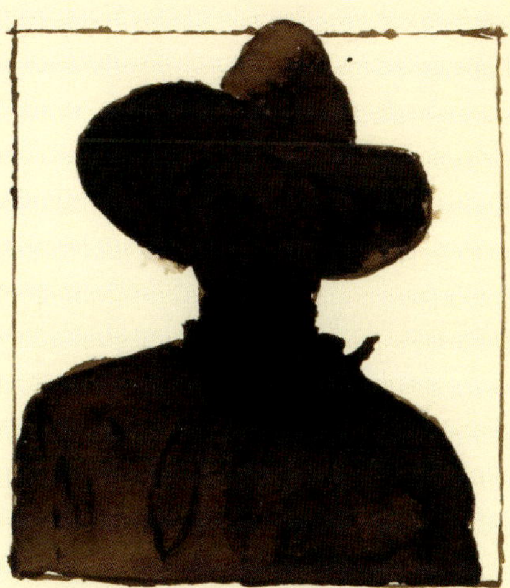

67
DAVID RATHMAN
Wanted [Baby-Red], 2001
Ink on paper
12 x 11 inches
Collection Lio Malca, New York

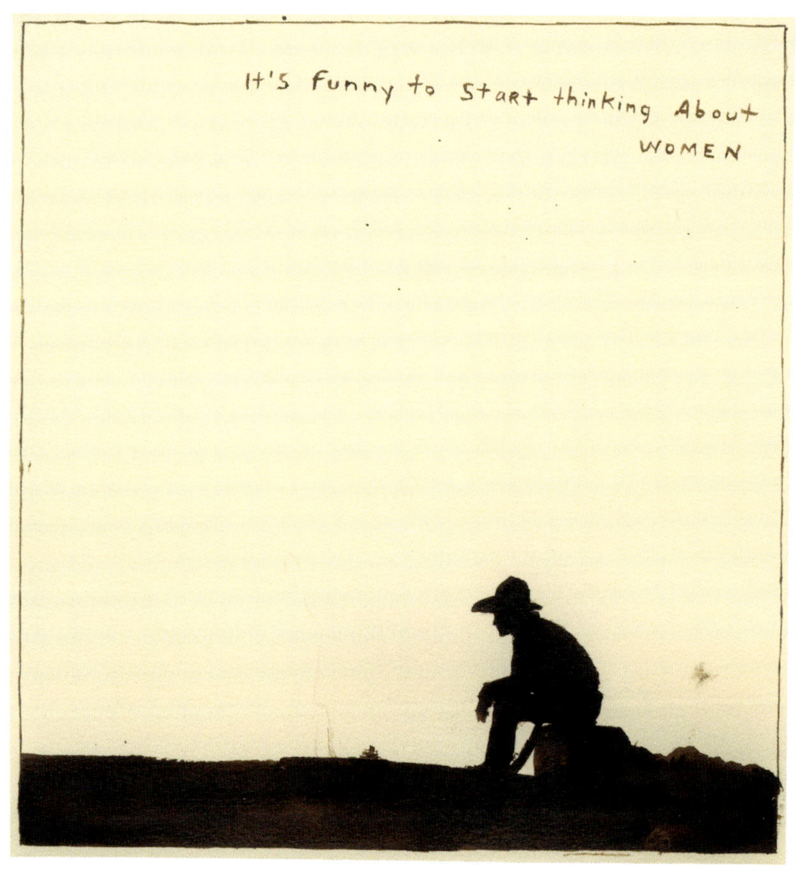

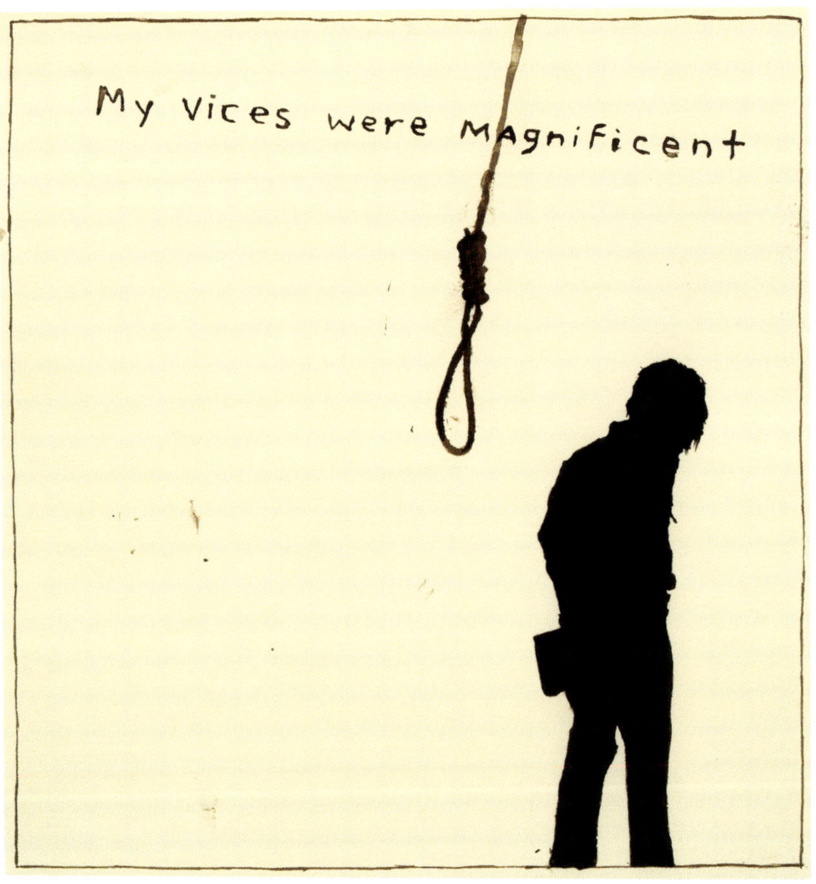

68
DAVID RATHMAN
It's Funny to Start Thinking About Women, 2001
Ink on paper
12 x 11 inches
Collection Lio Malca, New York

69
DAVID RATHMAN
My Vices Were Magnificent, 2001
Ink on paper
12 x 11 inches
Collection Lio Malca, New York

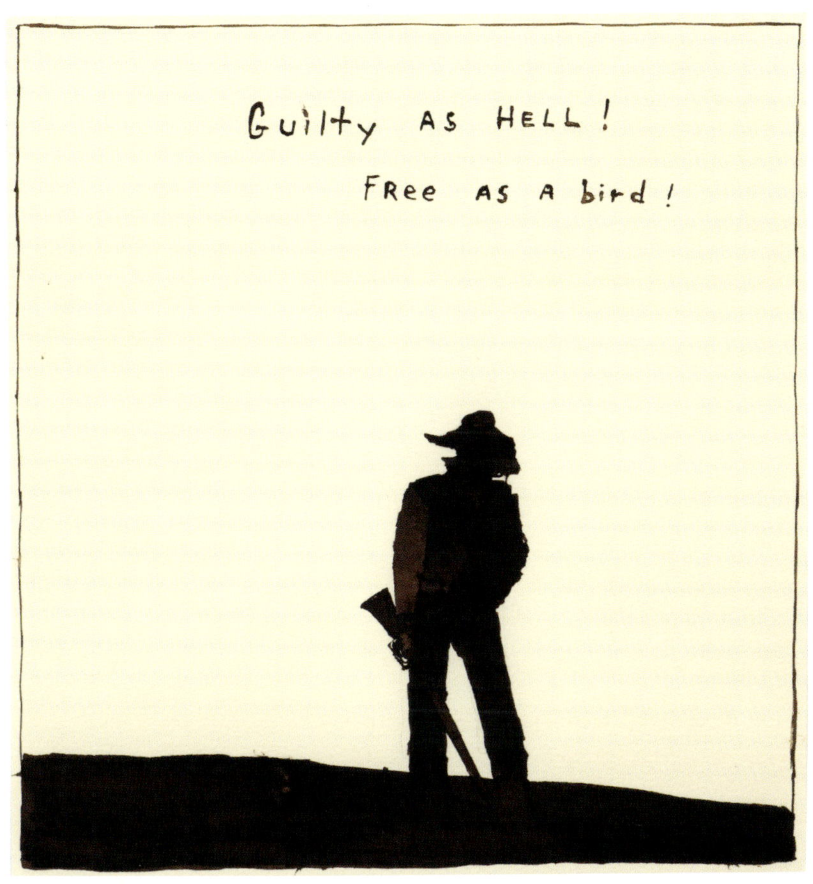

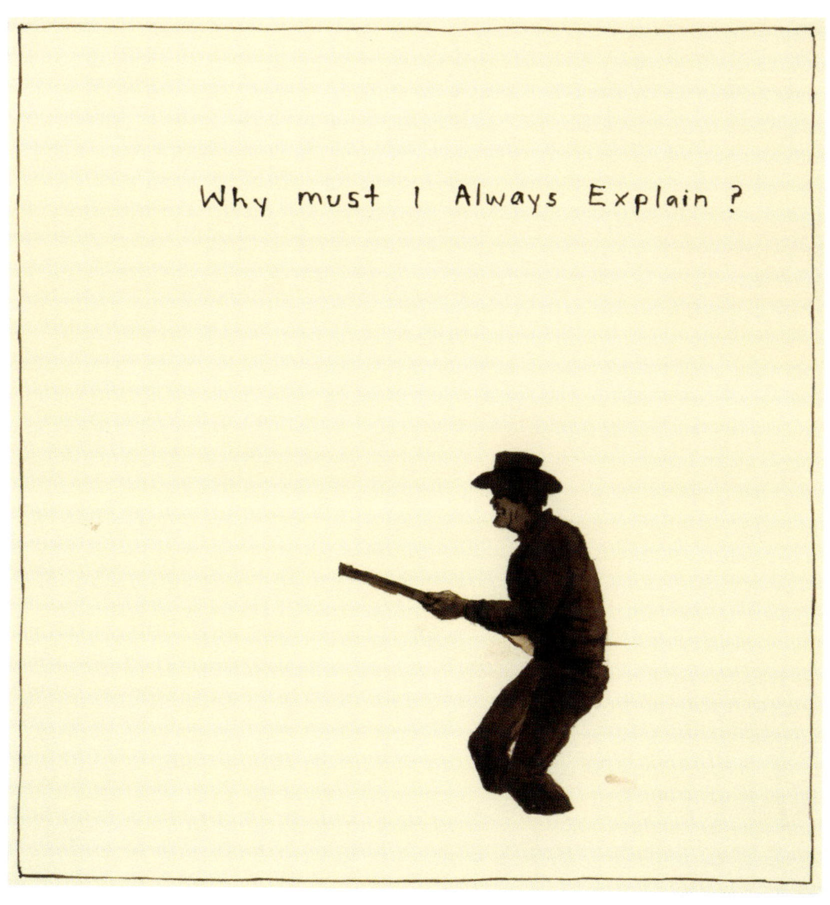

70
DAVID RATHMAN
Guilty As Hell! Free As a Bird!, 2001
Ink on paper
12 x 11 inches
Collection Lio Malca, New York

71
DAVID RATHMAN
Why Must I Always Explain?, 2001
Ink on paper
12 x 11 inches
Collection Lio Malca, New York

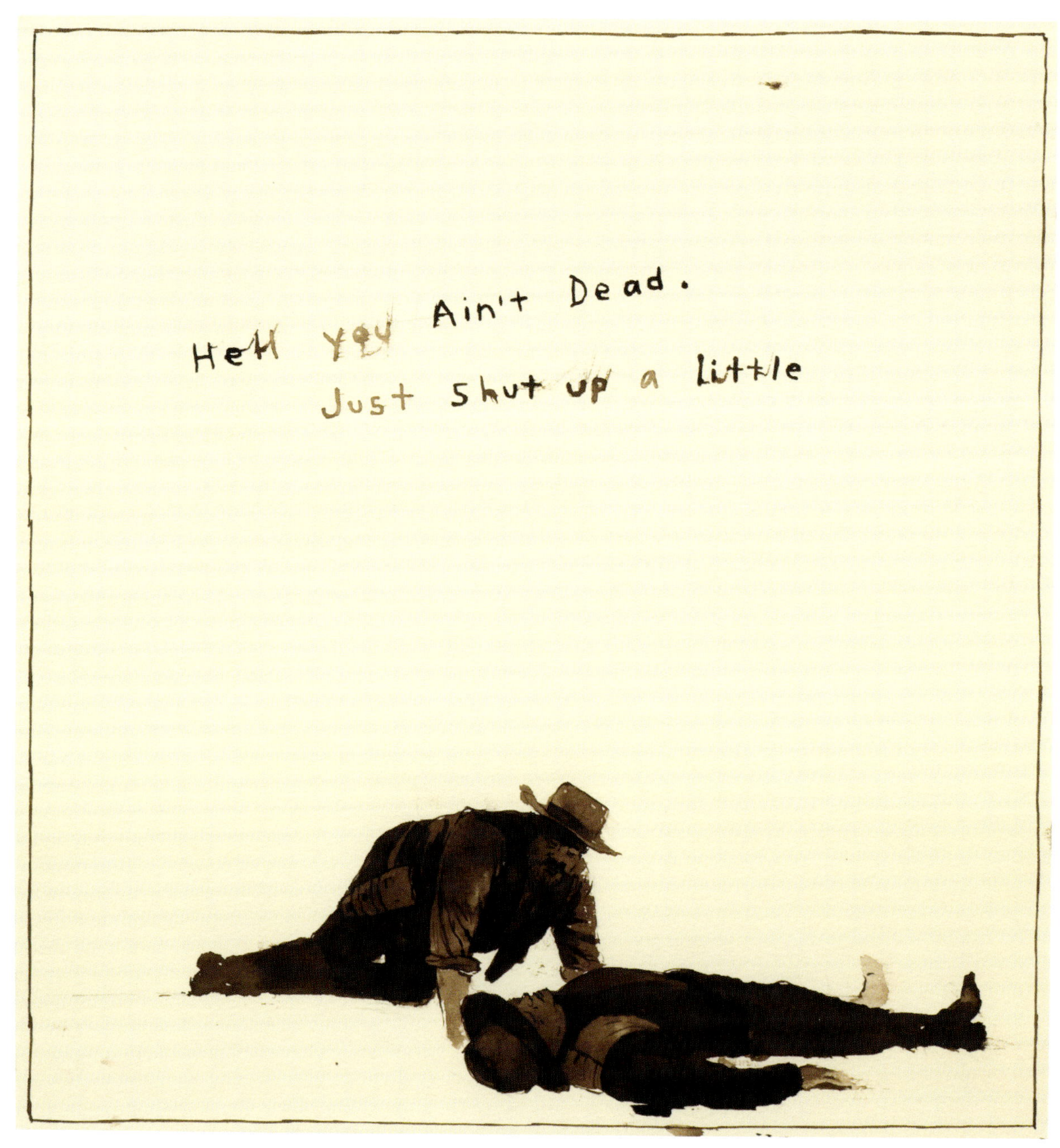

72
DAVID RATHMAN
Hell You Ain't Dead. Just Shut Up a Little, 2001
Ink on paper
12 x 11 inches
Collection Lio Malca, New York

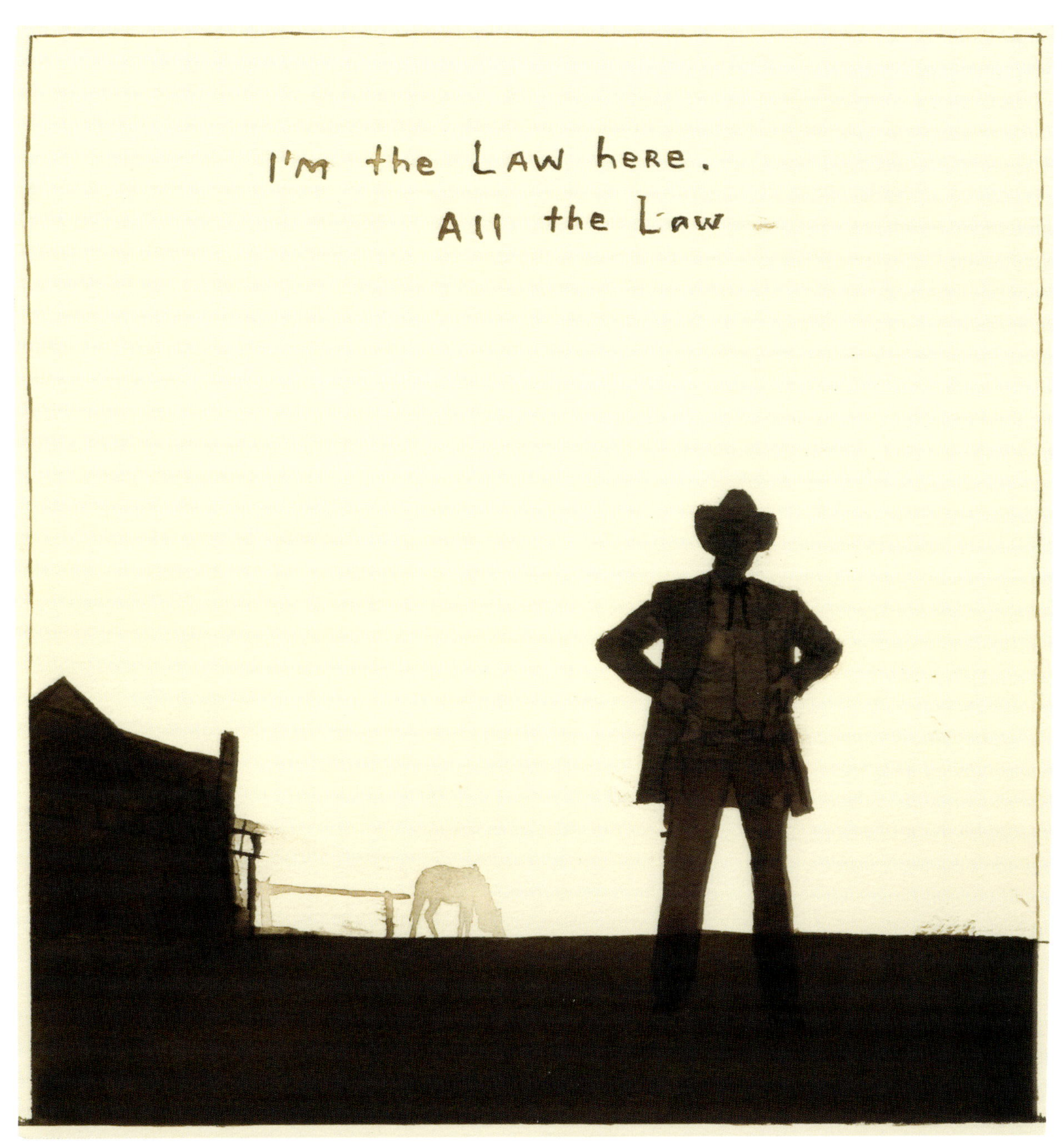

73
DAVID RATHMAN
I'm the Law Here. All the Law, 2001
Ink on paper
12 x 11 inches
Collection Lio Malca, New York

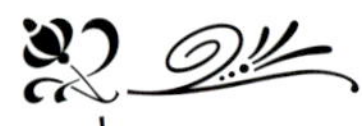

Dario Robleto

Hair braids made from a stretched and curled tape recording of poet Sylvia Plath. Shrapnel from various wars. Paper pulp made from soldiers' letters home. Hand-ground vinyl from 45 rpm "dance craze" records. Human bones. These are only a few of the unusual materials San Antonio artist Dario Robleto includes in his intricately researched, fabricated, and titled sculptures and two-dimensional works. Likening his practice to alchemy, Robleto uses his own unique blend of mystery, reverence, and humor to transmute precious and ordinary materials into works of art that grapple with—as well as actually embody—histories of love, loss, and redemption. Robleto, who says he was drawn to art because of its capacity to express morals and ethics, employs charged objects because they allow him to "operate close to life."[1] As in the Catholic's fascination with saints' relics and slivers of the True Cross, the homeopath's belief that trace amounts of diseases have healing powers, and his own passion for DJ-ing and sampling song hooks, Robleto knows that small fragments of certain substances can have powerful effects—in the case of his work, they can "tweak the ways people look at things" by lending them auras of authenticity. He also knows that his choices of materials have the power to evoke what he calls "historical empathy," an awareness of lessons learned within the shared continuum of human experience.

Since 9/11 Robleto has dedicated himself to "a sustained meditation" on violence, mourning, and militarism in American culture. Several of his works in *The Old, Weird America* are part of the artist's Chrysanthemum Anthems series, inspired by the wars in the Middle East and reflecting a commitment to using art to illuminate the destructive forces at loose in the world. *The Pause Became Permanence* (2005) is a glass-topped pedestal containing black-framed plaques bearing newspaper stories on the last three surviving Civil War widows, the only remaining one of whom, Alberta Martin, died in 2004. Decorated with melted shrapnel, hair lockets made by war widows, paper flowers containing pulp made from letters written by soldiers serving overseas, and lockets made from audio recordings of Civil War veterans, the framed articles—each relating the tale of an unconventional May-September marriage—commemorate the end of a living link to that crucial and bloody period in American history. *Your Lullaby Will Find a Home in My Head* (2005)

is inspired by the many forms of mourning handiwork common among war widows. It features a hair braid made from a tape recording of the bleak poem "November Graveyard" by Sylvia Plath (1932–1963), material from a mourning dress, and objects made from actual wartime bullets, letters, and human bone, all set in a nineteenth-century mourning frame, which Robleto enigmatically describes as coming "from another's loss" in the work's characteristically extensive and detailed medium line. Other works use the material form of the music album to look at origin stories in American culture. *Shaker Apothecary* (2007) takes the form of a Shaker medicine cabinet and includes, along with real healing herbs like angelica root, devil's shoestring root, and butcher's broom, carefully scraped and ground vinyl from popular dance-craze hits from the 1950s and 1960s, including "The Watusi," "The Mashed Potato," and "The Funky Chicken." As artist Dan Graham and others have pointed out, the Shakers, known for their freeform, ecstatic dancing, may be the original rock 'n' rollers. *Lamb of Man/Atom and Eve/ Americana Materia Medica* (2006), a large three-part panel, tells the stories of American spirituality, science, and medicine through a series of imaginary album covers. Made from cut paper in the styles of vintage vinyl art, the invented LPs "A Sound Odyssey in Faithology: Would You Follow the Heart of a Poet?"; "Vibrations in Physics Today: Working on a Love Freed from Knowing Its Own Decay…"; and "Negro Prison Songs: Shout the Words As If They'll Save You" exuberantly emblematize the conflicting currents of faith and empiricism running through American culture.

1. All quotes by the artist are from an interview with the author, November 28, 2007.

74
DARIO ROBLETO
Your Lullaby Will Find a Home in My Head, 2005
Hair braids made from a stretched and curled audio tape recording of Sylvia Plath reciting "November Graveyard," homemade paper (pulp made from soldiers' letters to mothers and daughters from various wars, ink retrieved from letters, sepia), excavated and melted bullet lead, carved ribcage bone and ivory, mourning dress fabric and thread, silk, mourning frame from another's loss, walnut, glass
26 x 3½ x 30 inches
Collection Carlos Bacino, Houston

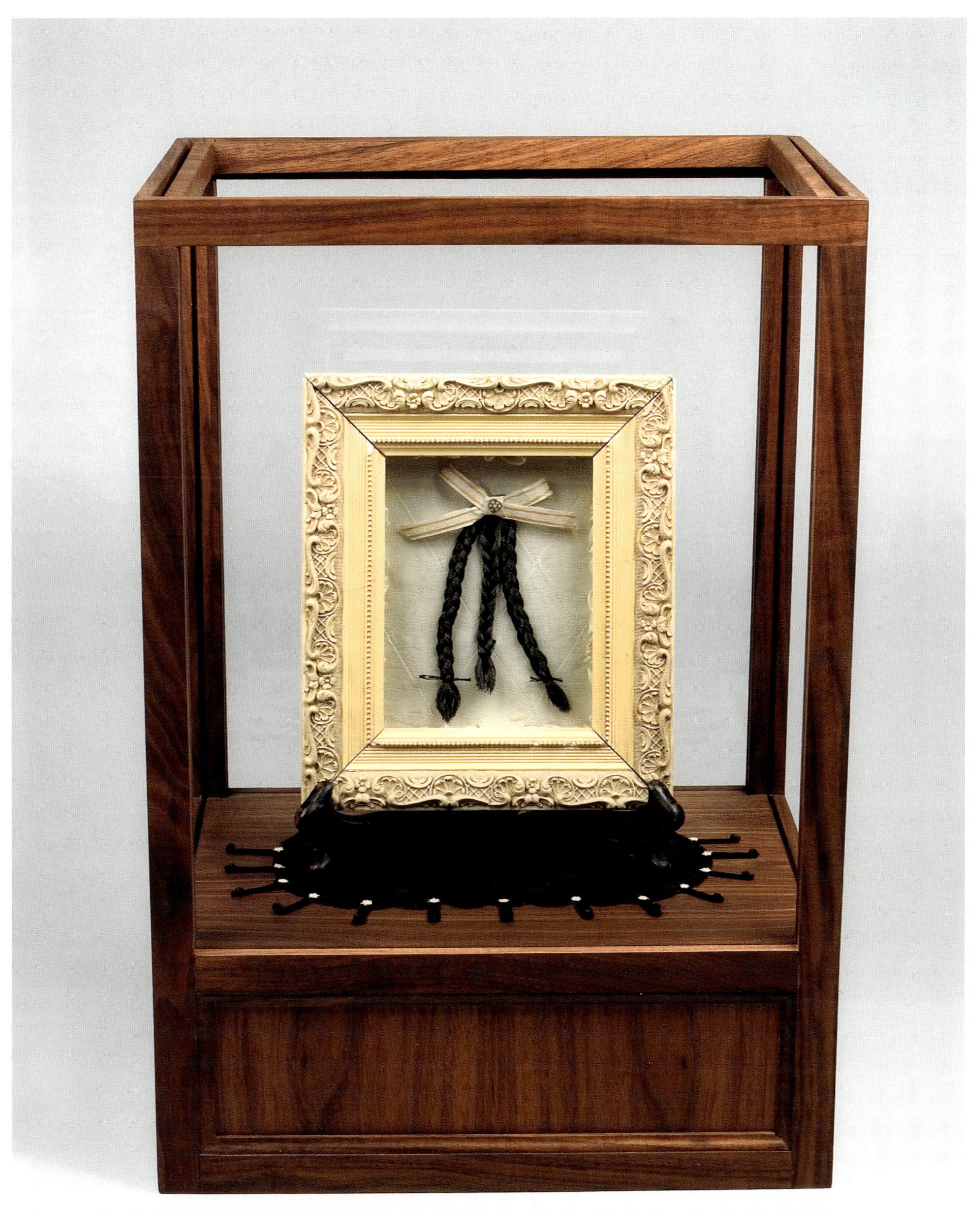

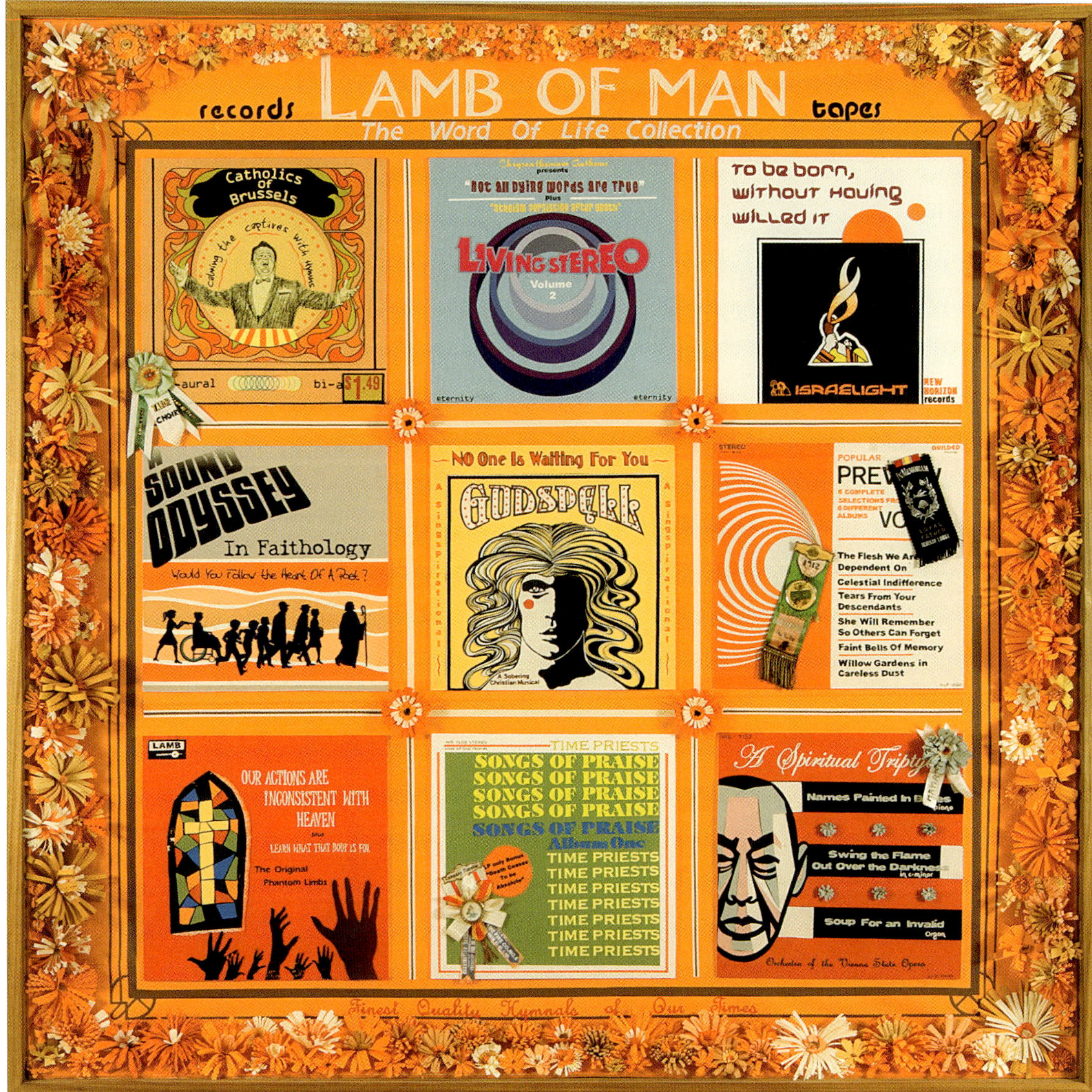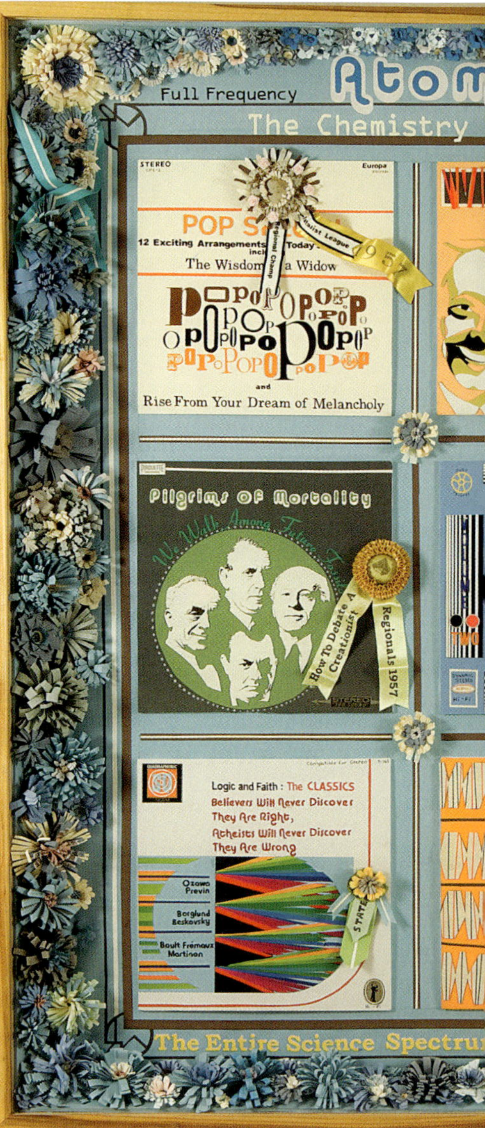

75

DARIO ROBLETO

Lamb of Man/Atom and Eve/Americana Materia Medica, 2006–2007

Colored paper, cardboard, ribbon, foamcore, glue, willow

Three panels, 60 x 48 x 180 inches overall

Courtesy the artist and D'Amelio Terras, New York

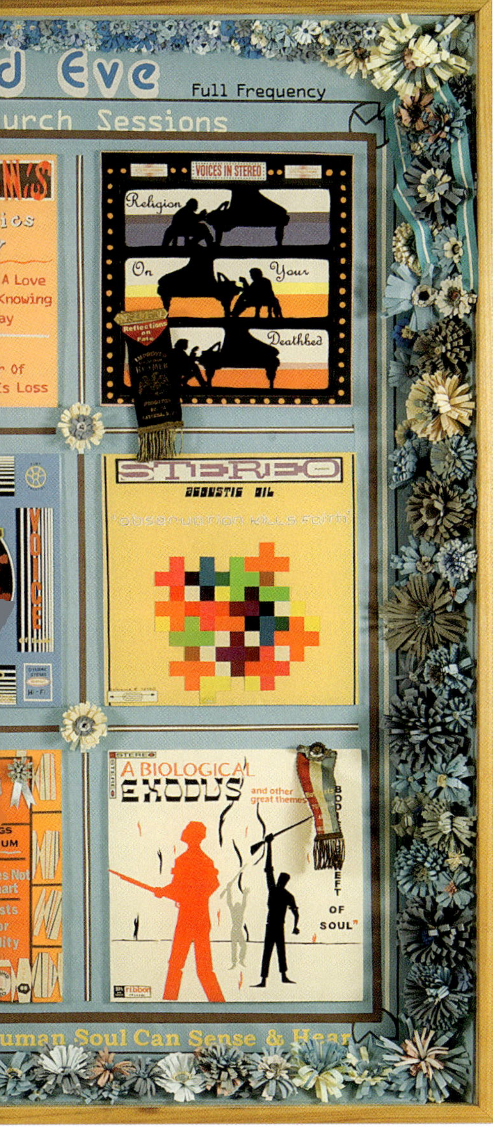
d Eve
Full Frequency
urch Sessions
VOICES IN STEREO
Religion
On   Your
Deathbed
STEREO
ACOUSTIC OIL
A BIOLOGICAL
EXODUS
and other great themes
EFT OF SOUL
uman Soul Can Sense & Hear

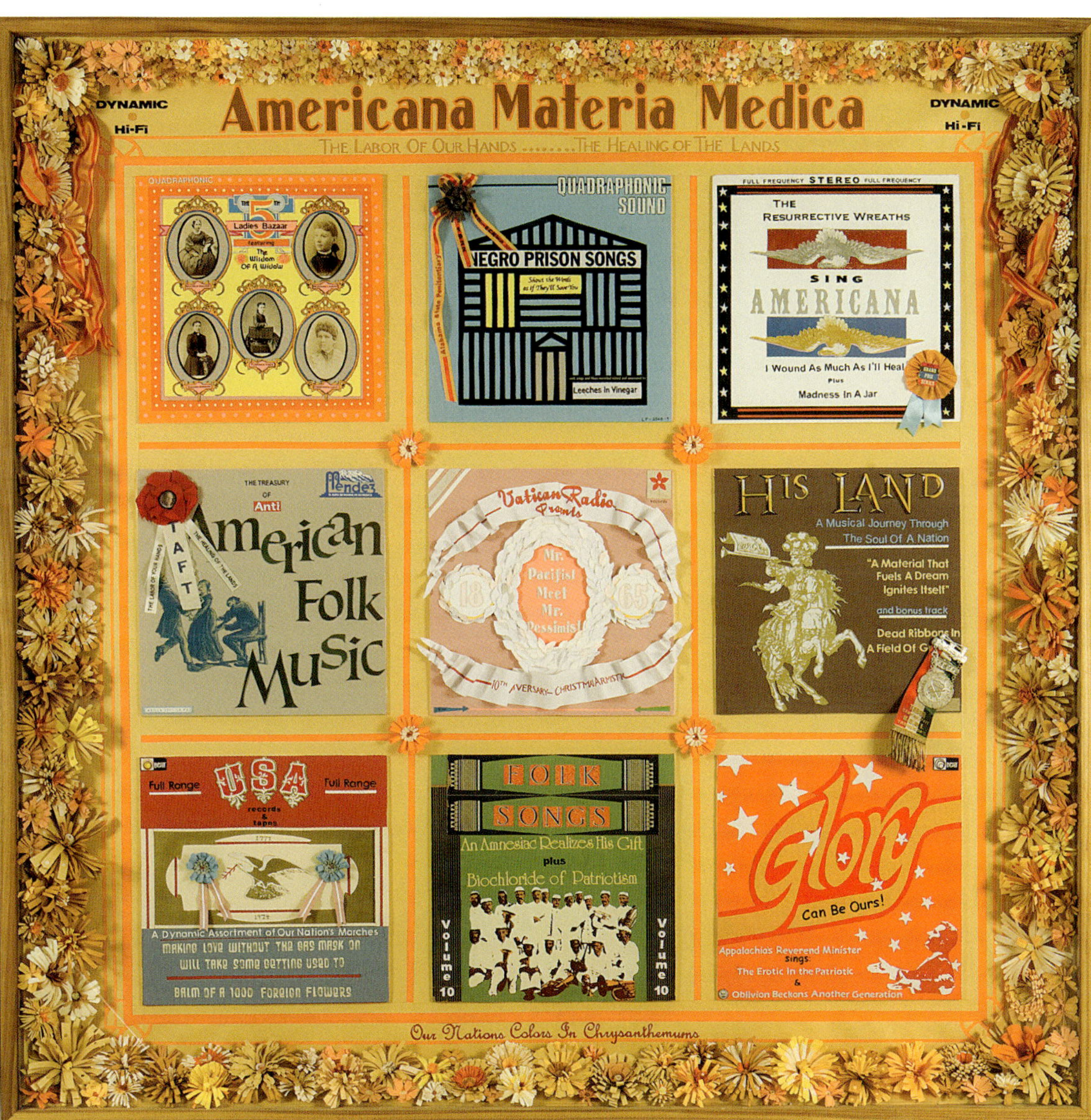
DYNAMIC
Hi-Fi
Americana Materia Medica
DYNAMIC
Hi-Fi
THE LABOR OF OUR HANDS........THE HEALING OF THE LANDS
Ladies Bazaar
featuring
The Wisdom Of A Widow
QUADRAPHONIC
SOUND
NEGRO PRISON SONGS
Leeches in Vinegar
FULL FREQUENCY STEREO FULL FREQUENCY
THE
RESURRECTIVE WREATHS
SING
AMERICANA
I Wound As Much As I'll Heal
Plus
Madness In A Jar
THE TREASURY OF
Anti
Mendez
American Folk Music
AFT
Vatican Radio presents
Mr. Pacifist Meet Mr. Pessimist
18   65
10TH ANIVERSARY - CHRISTMAS & EASTER
HIS LAND
A Musical Journey Through
The Soul Of A Nation
"A Material That
Fuels A Dream
Ignites Itself!"
and bonus track
Dead Ribbons In
A Field Of G
USA
records & tapes
Full Range   Full Range
A Dynamic Assortment of Our Nation's Marches
MAKING LOVE WITHOUT THE GAS MASK ON
WILL TAKE SOME GETTING USED TO
BALM OF A 1000 FOREIGN FLOWERS
FOLK SONGS
An Amnesiac Realizes His Gift
plus
Biochloride of Patriotism
Volume 10   Volume 10
Glory
Can Be Ours!
Appalachia's Reverend Minister
sings
The Erotic in the Patriotic
&
Oblivion Beckons Another Generation
Our Nations Colors In Chrysanthemums

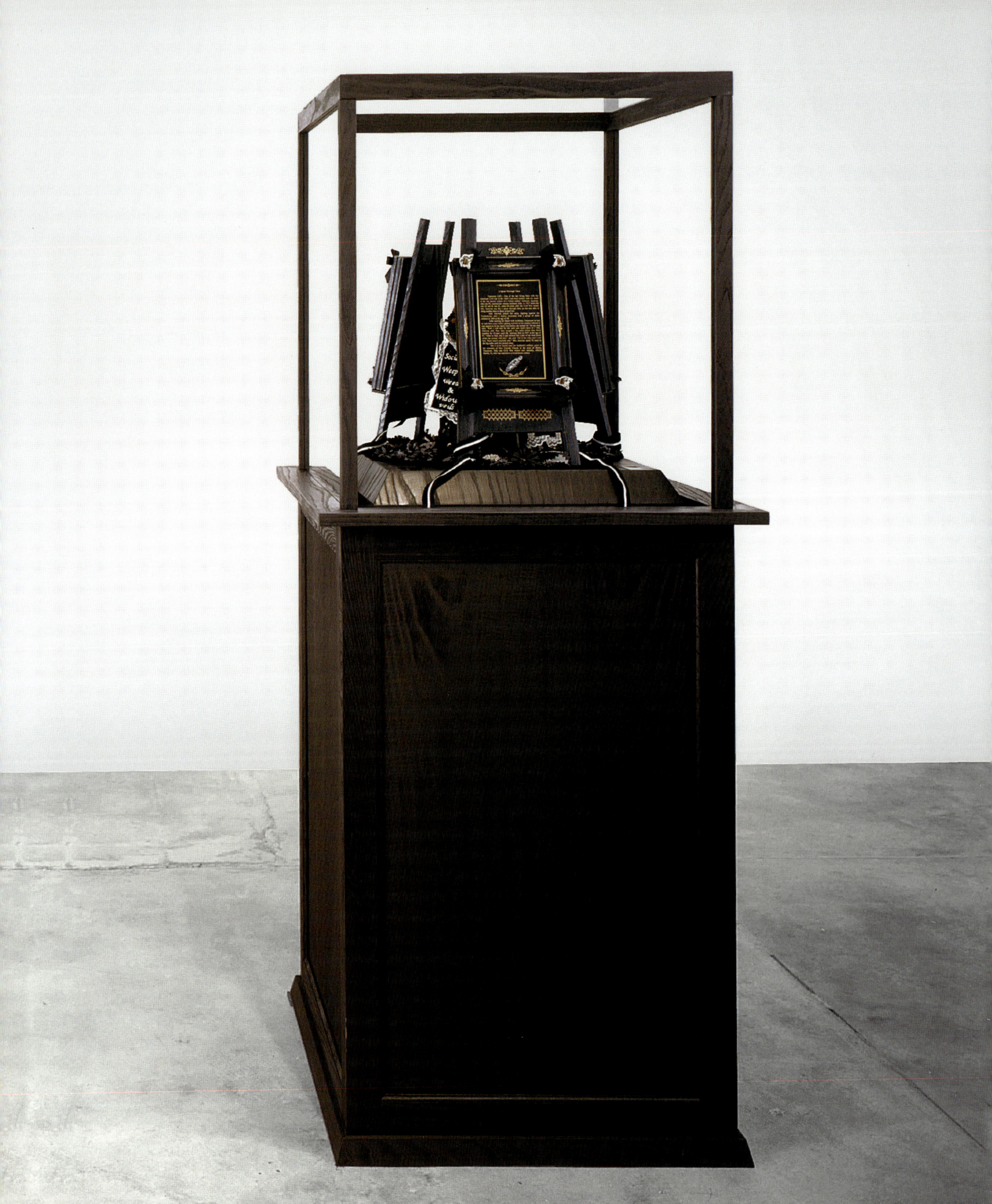
Soci
Weep
weed
&
Widow
veils

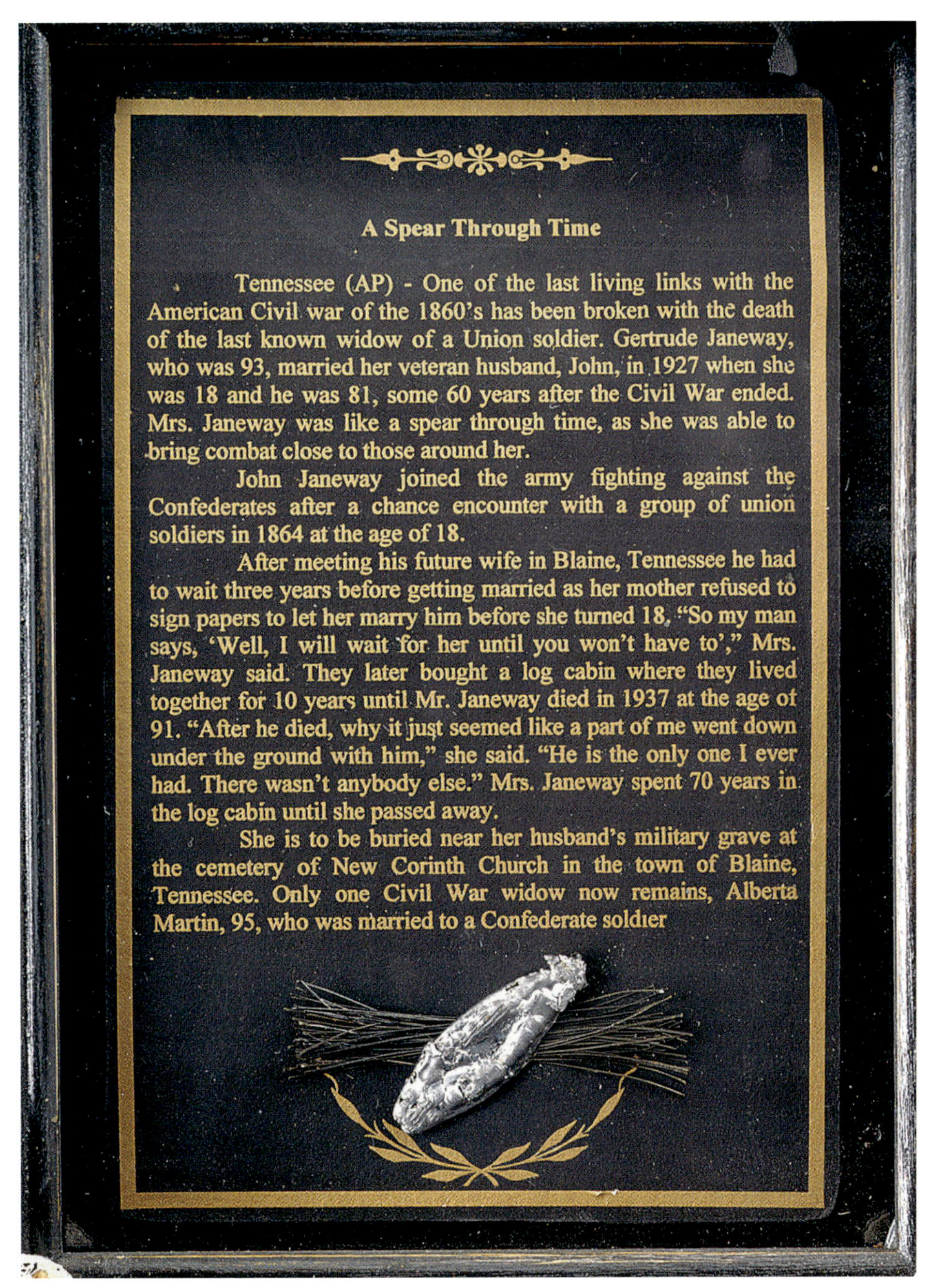

76–77

DARIO ROBLETO

The Pause Became Permanence (installation view and detail), 2005–2006
Ink-dyed willow and ash, hair lockets made of stretched and curled audio tape
recordings of the last known Confederate and Union Civil War soldier's voices,
excavated and melted shrapnel from various wars, hair flowers braided by war
widow's mourning dresses, colored paper, silk, ribbon, milk paint, glass, typeset
69 x 26 x 26 inches
San Antonio Museum of Art, purchased with funds provided by an anonymous
donor in honor of Nancy Brown Negley

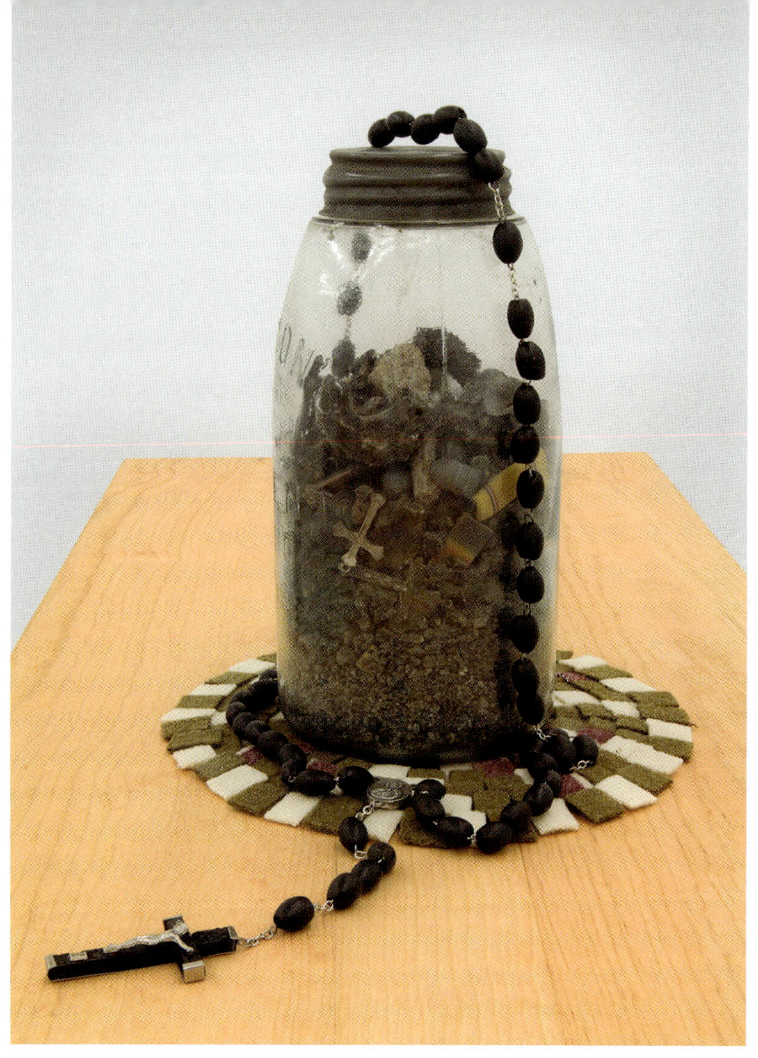

78
DARIO ROBLETO
A Rosary for Rhythm, 2007
Melted and carved vinyl records of Jerry Lee Lewis's and
Little Richard's "Whole Lotta Shakin' Goin' On," ground
hip bone dust, cast pewter, metal chain
9 ½ x 4 ½ x 4 ½ inches
Courtesy the artist and D'Amelio Terras, New York

and

Salvation Cocktails, 2007
Veteran's old mason jar, soldiers' rosaries and crucifixes excavated from various battlefields, ground fulgurites (glass
produced by lightning strikes when heat from blast melts
surrounding sand), ground trinitite (glass produced during
the first atomic test explosion when heat from blast melted
surrounding sand), military buttons and medals, excavated
fired bullets, spent shell casings and shrapnel from various
wars, military blanket wool from various wars
9½ x 4½ x 4½ inches
Courtesy the artist and D'Amelio Terras, New York

79–80 (right and page 127)
DARIO ROBLETO
Shaker Apothecary (with *A Rosary for Rhythm* and
Salvation Cocktails), 2007
Pine, hand-ground vinyl 45 rpm dance-craze records,
various medicinal botanicals, carved bone calcium, typeset
40 x 160 x 15 inches
Courtesy the artist and D'Amelio Terras, New York

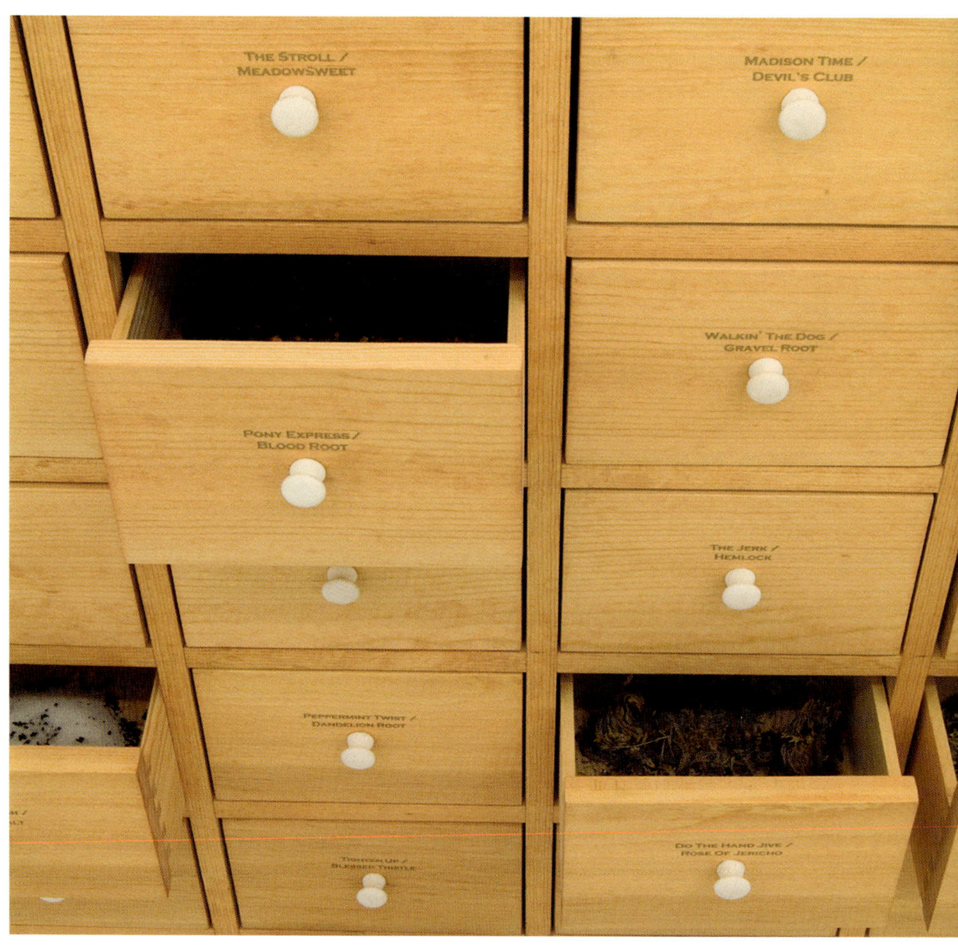

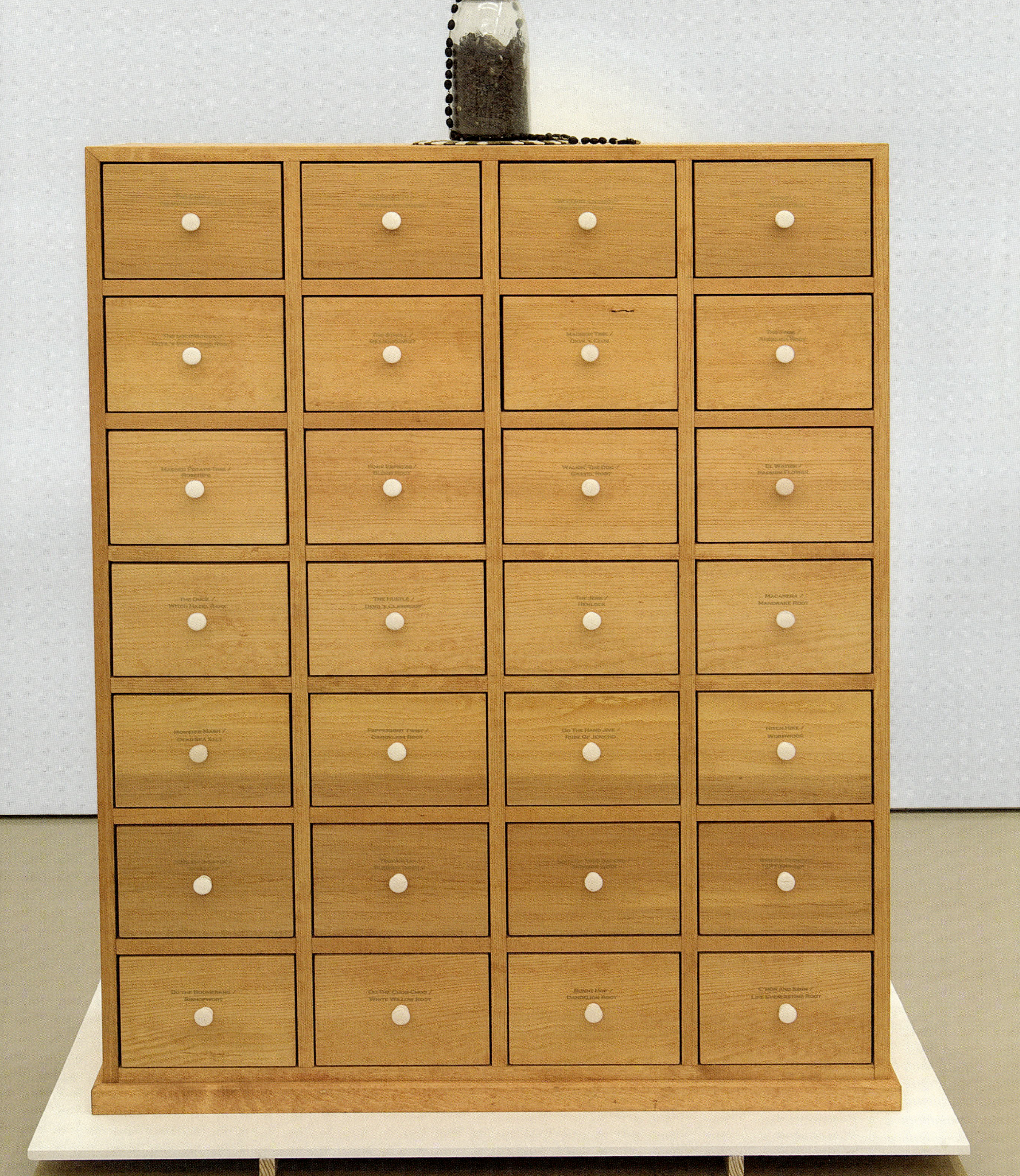

THE LOCOMOTION / DEVIL'S SHOESTRING ROOT
THE STROLL / BLACK COHOSH
MADISON TIME / DEVIL'S CLUB
THE STRUT / ANGELICA ROOT
MASHED POTATO TIME / ROSE HIPS
PONY EXPRESS / BLOOD ROOT
WALKIN' THE DOG / GRAVEL ROOT
EL WATUSI / PASSION FLOWER
THE DUCK / WITCH HAZEL BARK
THE HUSTLE / DEVIL'S CLAW ROOT
THE JERK / HEMLOCK
MACARENA / MANDRAKE ROOT
MONSTER MASH / DEAD SEA SALT
PEPPERMINT TWIST / DANDELION ROOT
DO THE HAND JIVE / ROSE OF JERICHO
HITCH HIKE / WORMWOOD
TIGHTEN UP / BLESSED THISTLE
DO THE BOOMERANG / BISHOPWORT
DO THE CHOO-CHOO / WHITE WILLOW ROOT
BUNNY HOP / DANDELION ROOT
C'MON AND STIR / LIFE EVERLASTING ROOT

Allison Smith

*I*n her sculptures, installations, and interdisciplinary projects incorporating performance, Allison Smith looks for the revolutionary in the traditional. Often describing herself as "a Conceptual artist whose subject is making things," Smith draws on early American craft techniques and the more recent practice of historical reenactment as a means of illuminating social history—the ways ordinary people think and interact.[1] An openly gay artist of Confederate ancestry reared near important Civil War battlefields in Manassas, Virginia, Smith looks to the past—to the ways earlier generations expressed themselves in what they made and how they lived—for information on how to live in a time of war, and how to navigate the slipperiness of gender and identity as well as the artificial divide between art and craft. Working against the prevailing disdain of the folkish, the handmade, and the communal in contemporary art, Smith seeks out craft forms that are embedded with historical and political meaning, and uses them to explore contemporary concerns and

conflicts. In 2005, she organized a large-scale public art event on Governor's Island in New York Harbor entitled *The Muster*. Dressed in a nonpartisan Civil War uniform of her own design, she enlisted an army of over 125 artist and activist participants—all of whom wore symbolic costumes and camped in agitprop-style installations— to respond to her question "What Are You Fighting For?" Emphasizing "proclamation over protest" and eliciting responses ranging from the earnest to the absurd, *The Muster* employed a long-established American form of direct, democratic civic organization used during the Revolutionary and Civil Wars. This present-day muster both provided a legitimizing context for contemporary activism and historicized its presence in art.

For *The Old, Weird America*, Smith has contributed seven life-size dolls made in her own image from traditional nineteenth-century materials: ceramic, linen, cotton, and wool. The dolls are dressed in the flamboyant uniforms of Civil War Zouaves, volunteer soldiers who fought on both Union and Confederate sides. The Zouaves modeled their bright red-and-blue uniforms on French colonial troops, who had themselves adopted the native dress of the *Zouaoua* tribe from Algeria and Morocco.[1] Many Zouaves, Smith noted, were former fire fighters from New York City, wore large handlebar moustaches, tasseled fezzes and turbans, and cultivated a daring, acrobatic combat style. They also included a number of Vivandières, or female aides who assisted in parades, ammunition carrying, and ministering to the dead and wounded. Smith was interested in the Zouaves for a variety of reasons. She saw something "queer" in their unconventional appearance, gender roles, and fighting techniques. She also started working on the dolls in a ceramics studio in France during the height of French protests against the American war in Iraq and came to see the Zouaves against the backdrop of that conflict: "I like the particular brew of references brought together by Zouaves, whose uniforms suggest the red/blue state metaphor, and a union of binary opposites in general. I find them utterly confounding."[2] Arranged in compositions inspired by photographs of Civil War soldiers, living and dead, Smith's dolls are emblems of the complexities of her own interests and experiences.

81
ALLISON SMITH
Marie Tepe, "French Mary," Vivandière of the 114th Pennsylvania Volunteer Infantry, Collis's Zouaves, 2005
Slip cast ceramic, linen, wool, cotton, leather, hemp fibers, brass, glass
72 x 24 x 10 inches
Courtesy the artist

82 *(page 129)*
ALLISON SMITH
Victory Hall (installation view, Bellwether Gallery, New York), 2005
Photograph courtesy Bellwether Gallery

1. Allison Smith, unpublished notes emailed to the author, February 6, 2008.

2. Ibid.

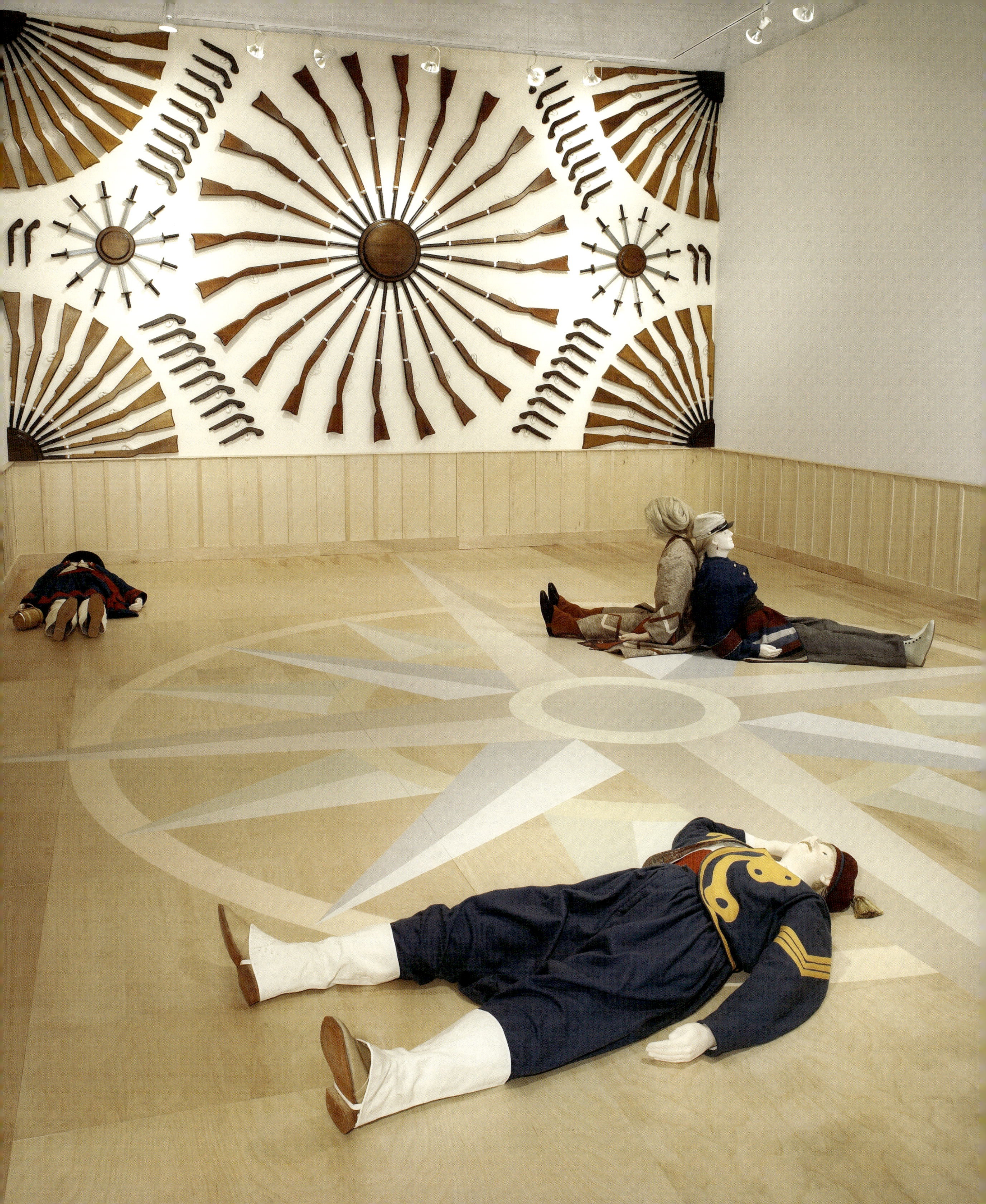

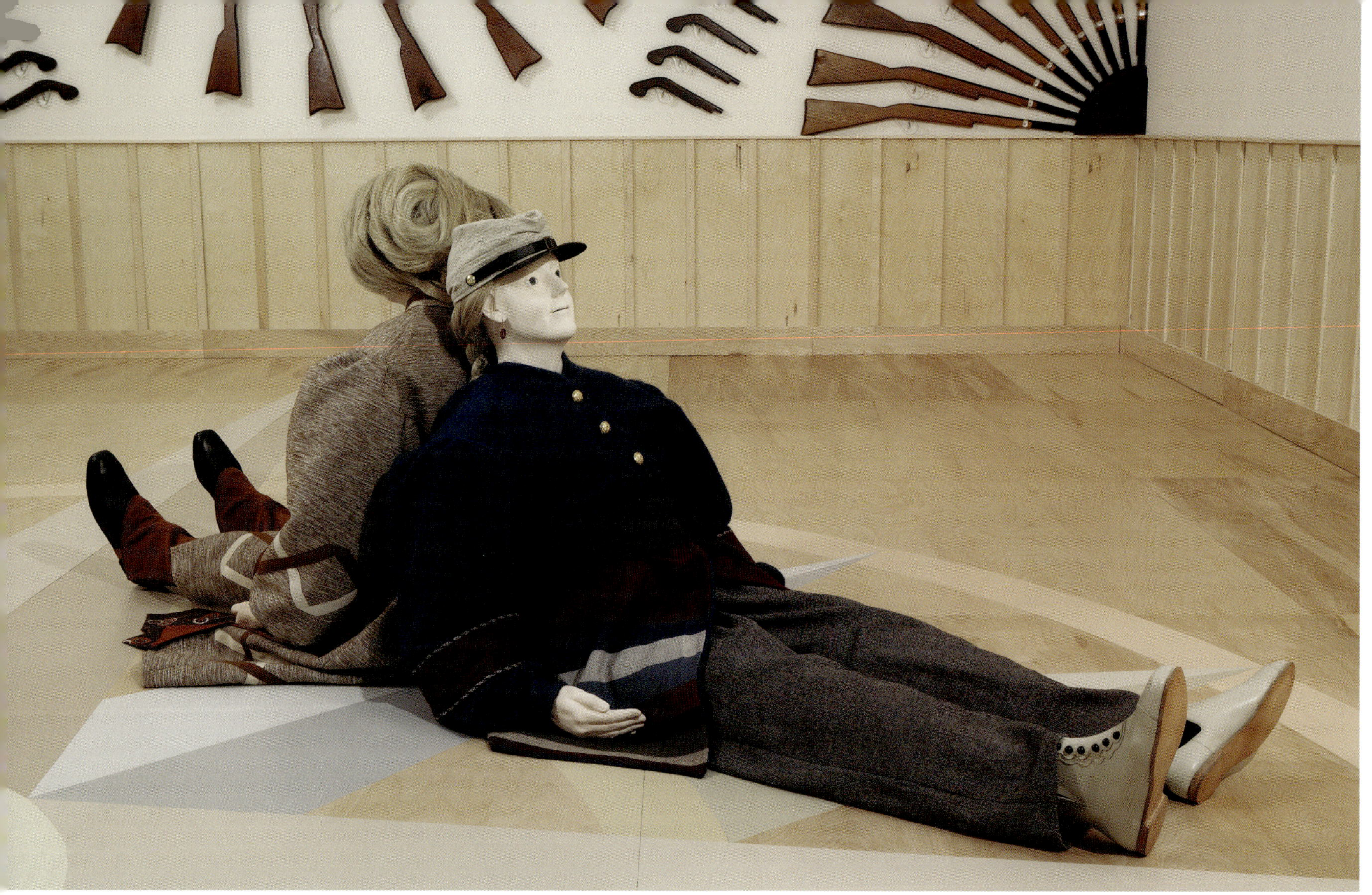

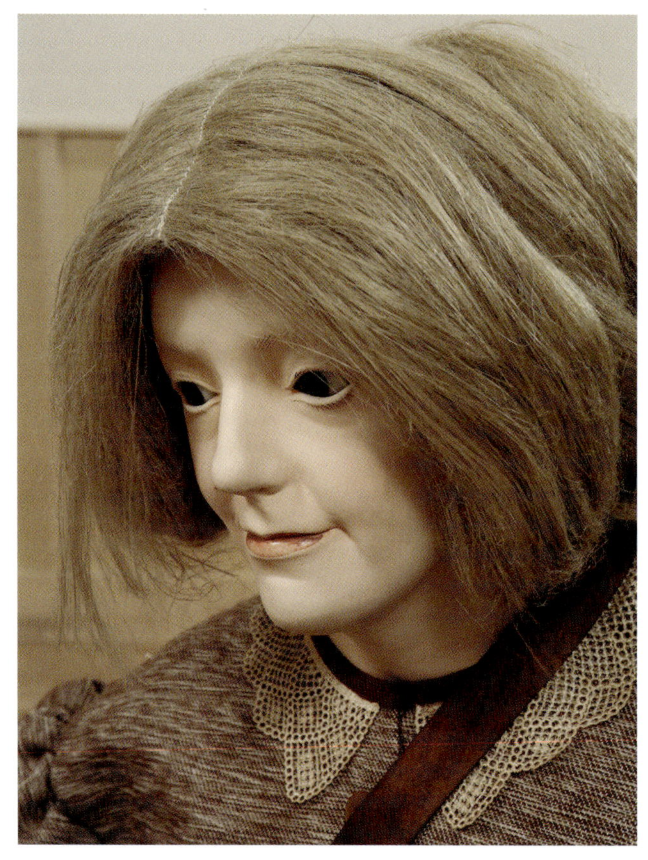

83
ALLISON SMITH
Dr. Mary Edwards Walker (with *Eliza Wilson of the 5th Wisconsin Volunteer Infantry* [back]), both 2005
Slip cast ceramic, linen, wool, cotton, leather, hemp fibers, brass, glass
72 x 24 x 10 inches
Courtesy the artist

84
ALLISON SMITH
Eliza Wilson of the 5th Wisconsin Volunteer Infantry (detail), 2005
Slip cast ceramic, linen, wool, cotton, leather, hemp fibers, brass, glass
72 x 24 x 10 inches
Courtesy the artist

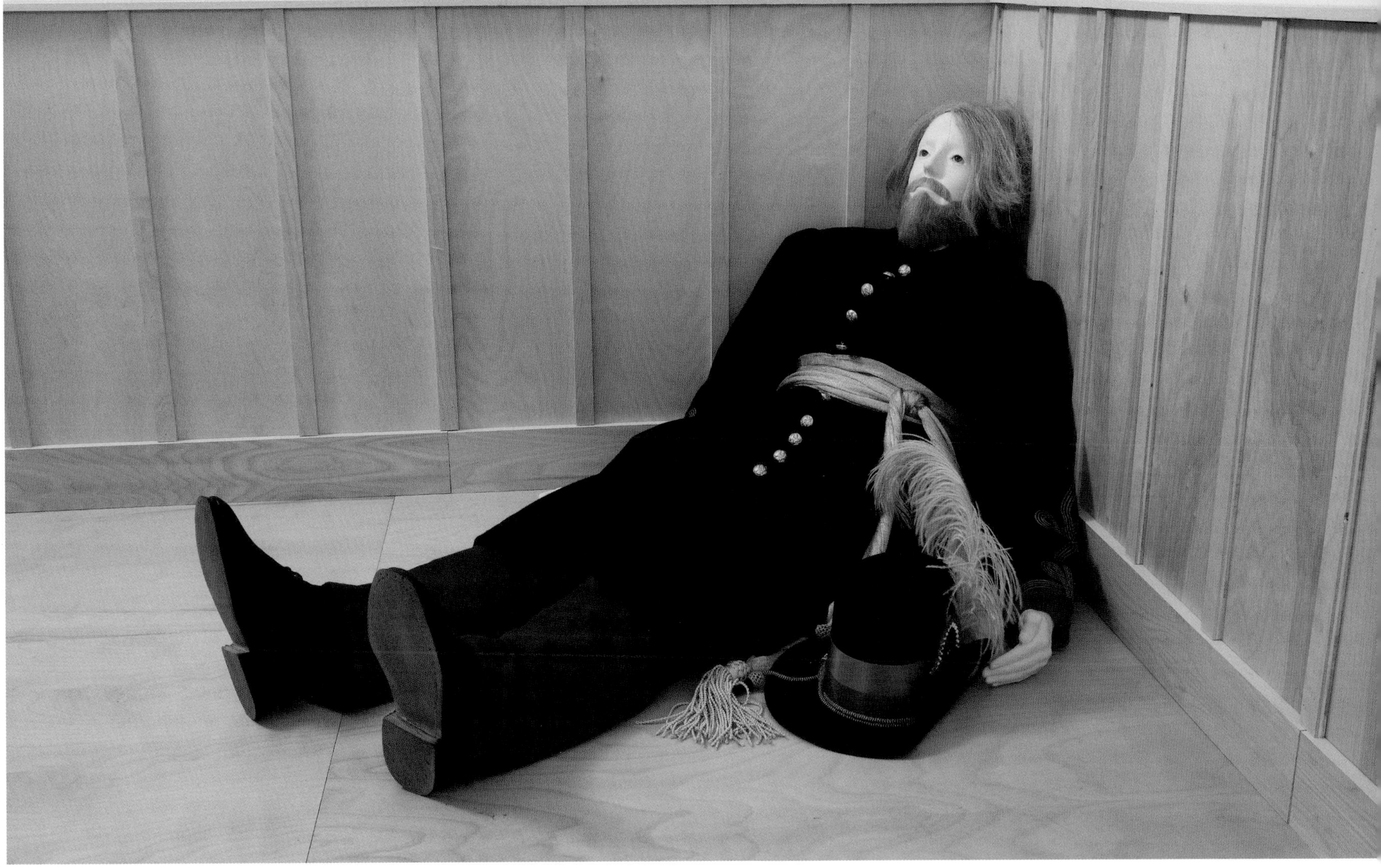

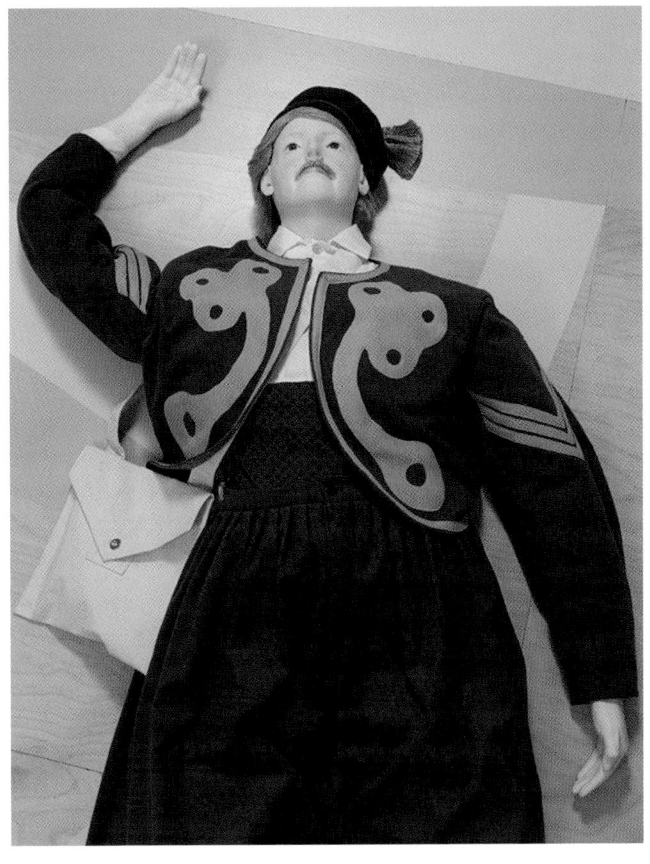

85
ALLISON SMITH
Officer of the 5th New York Volunteer Infantry, Duryée's Zouaves, 2005
Slip cast ceramic, linen, wool, cotton, leather, hemp fibers, brass, glass
72 x 24 x 10 inches
Courtesy the artist

86
ALLISON SMITH
Soldier of the 146th New York Zouaves Volunteer Infantry, 2005
Slip cast ceramic, linen, wool, cotton, leather, hemp fibers, brass, glass
72 x 24 x 10 inches
Courtesy the artist

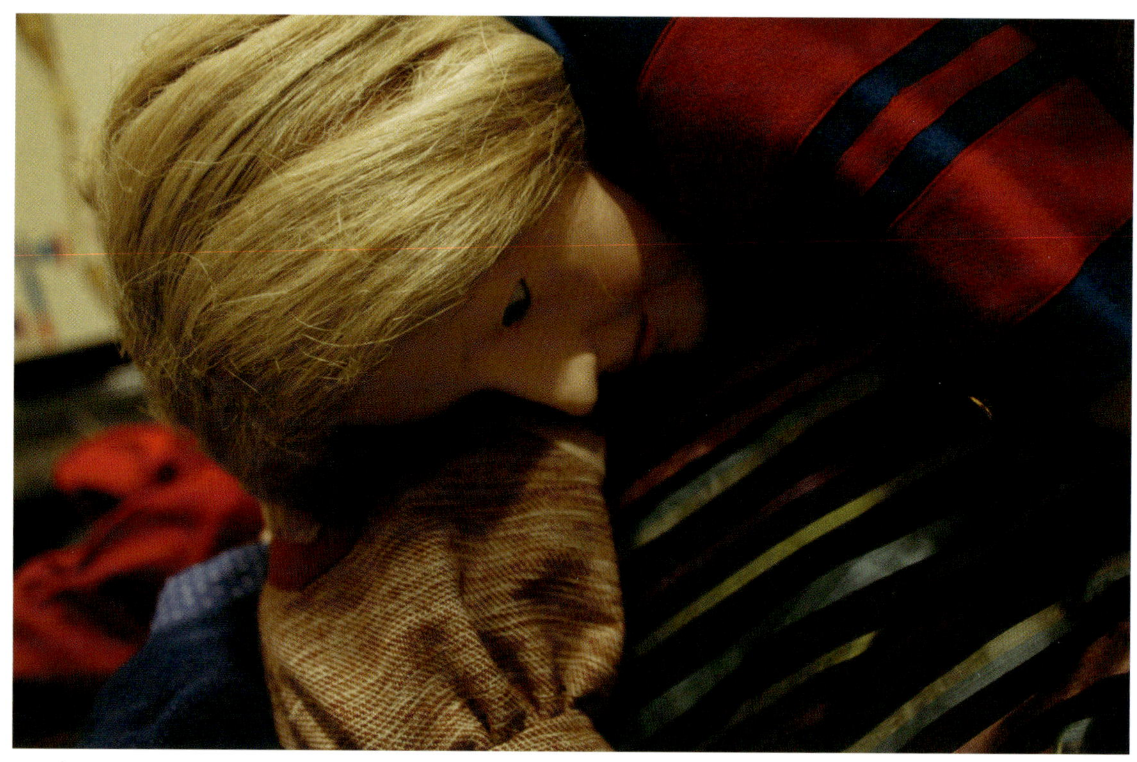

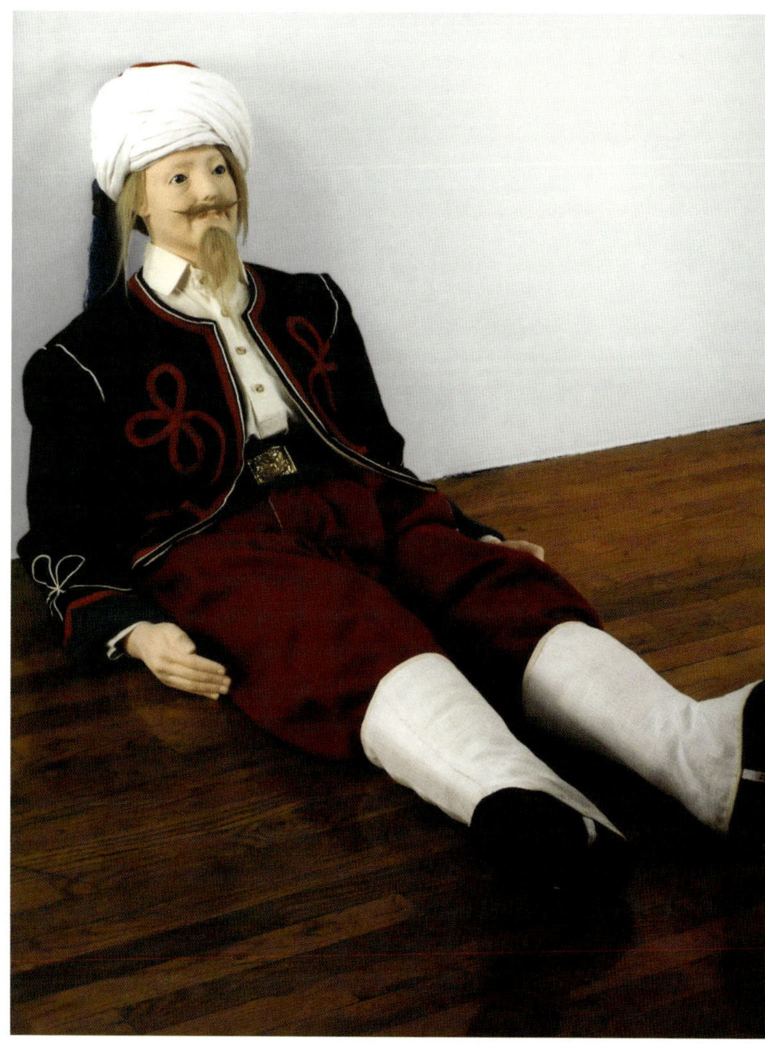

87 and 89 *(top and page 133)*
ALLISON SMITH
Pile (detail and installation view), 2007
Photograph courtesy Bertha & Karl Leubsdorf Art Gallery,
Hunter College, New York

88 *(left)*
ALLISON SMITH
Soldier of the 114th Pennsylvania Infantry, Collis's Zouaves, 2005
Slip cast ceramic, linen, wool, cotton, leather, hemp fibers, brass, glass
72 x 24 x 10 inches
Courtesy the artist

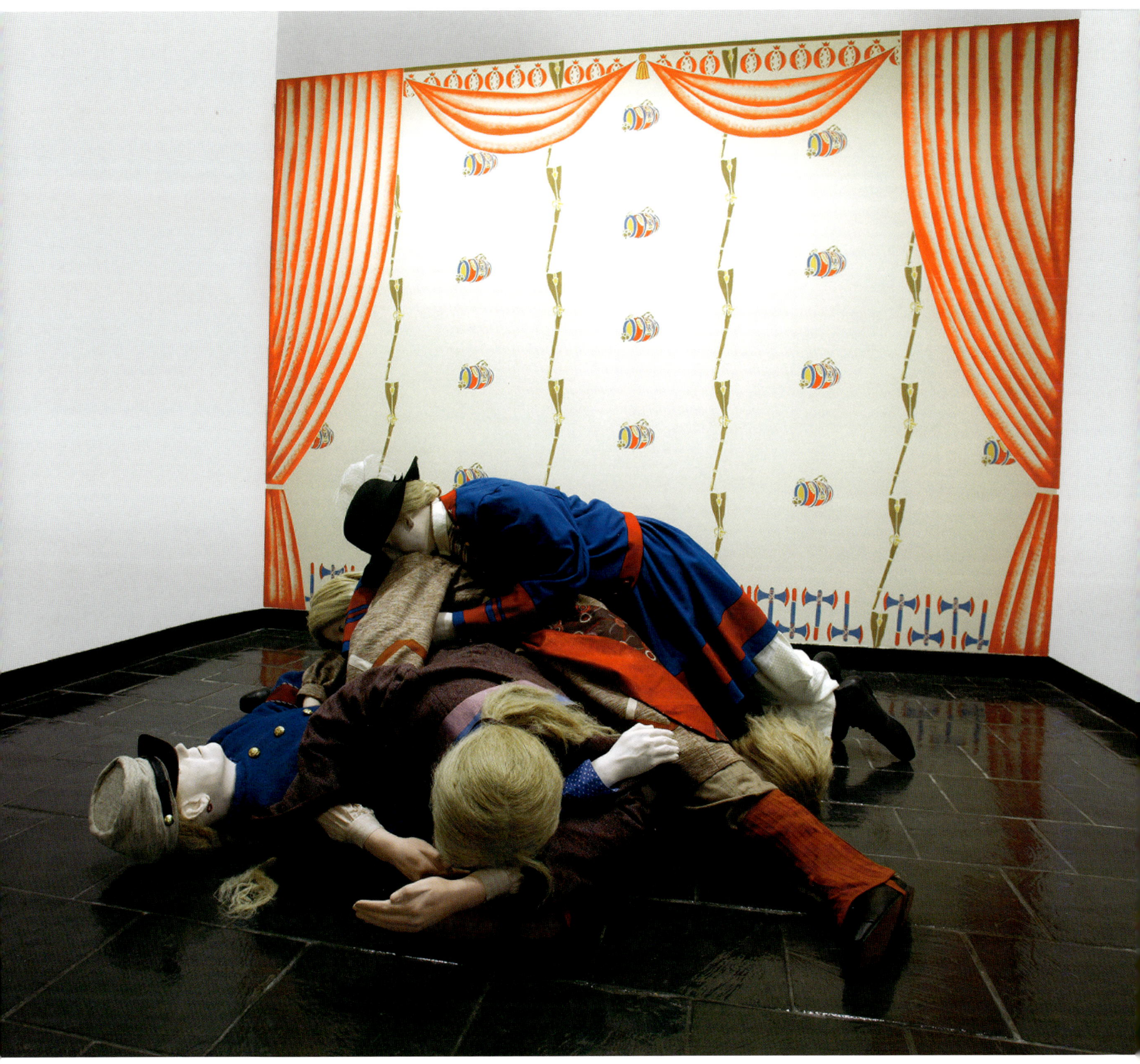

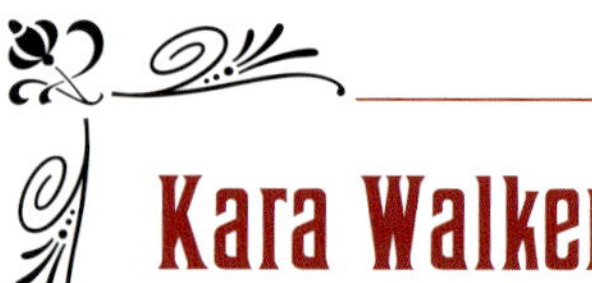

Kara Walker

Kara Walker has earned international notoriety by taking the genteel medium of cut-paper silhouettes out of art history's parlor room and into the wrestling ring of contemporary racial, sexual, and power politics. Whether deploying her silhouettes on walls in large-scale tableaux or animating them as Balinese-style shadow puppets in videos, Walker is a satirist of the most daring type. Her work is filled with outrageous stereotypes, perversions, and violence as well as pitiless humor. Walker's deft scissoring yields images of an absurdly tragicomic antebellum South filled with pickaninnies, crackers, coprophilia, bestiality, lynchings, and rapes that leave few sensibilities unoffended. Her fifteen-minute, fifty-seven second DVD *8 Possible Beginnings: Or, the Creation of African-America, a Moving Picture by Kara E. Walker* (2005) uses silhouette puppets and snippets of historical photographs and engravings to envision and play out a cracked origin myth for black America. Consisting of surreal vignettes accompanied by subtitles, sound effects, and cheerful slave-era ditties, the work begins with "uppity niggers" being thrown over the side of a slave ship. The floating survivors are eaten by a giant black woman who emerges from an island and then are defecated onto the New World. A muscular male slave has sex with, and is impregnated, by a scrawny plantation master, eventually giving birth to a mutant cotton boll. Br'er Fox and Br'er Rabbit lynch slaves, while a white boy gambols under the hanging tree. And a slave girl is pursued by a menacing white man in a scene with a voiceover by Walker's daughter that includes the chilling phrase "I wish I were white."

Filled with black protagonists, black silhouettes, and black humor, Walker's work has been controversial, early on provoking the anger of an older generation of African-American artists who viewed the work as complicit with white racism. Walker, however, views the very act of representing African Americans—positively or negatively—as fraught, saying, "Every image produced of 'us' is mediated—filtered through the grounds of years of misrepresentation, bitterness and suspicion."[1] Her discovery of the silhouette medium, she says, provided a way to navigate the minefield of racial representation:

> I had a catharsis looking at early American varieties of silhouette cuttings. . . . What I recognized, besides narrative and historicity and racism, was this very physical displacement: the paradox of removing a form from a blank surface that in turn creates a black hole. I was struck by the irony of so many of my concerns being addressed: blank/black, hole/whole, shadow/substance, etc.[2]

Walker defends her scathing images drawn from the toxic yet mesmerizing racist obsessions perpetually simmering beneath the surface of American society, stating simply, "I want people to respond and to be aware that if a goody-two-shoes like me can have all this going on in her head, then nobody's safe."[3] Her work updates the *Verfremdungseffekt*, or alienation effect, of German playwright Bertolt Brecht's epic theater for contemporary America by depicting a world of white fear and domination, and black anger and self-hatred where none of the inhabitants manifests the slightest awareness of the ways racism infects and debases their world.

1. Ariella Budick, "Review: Kara Walker at the Whitney Museum," *Newsday*, October 14, 2007, available at http://www.newsday.com/entertainment/arts/nyffart5408506oct14,0,4005884.story, accessed December 6, 2007.

2. Hilton Als, "The Shadow Act," *The New Yorker* 83, no. 30 (October 8, 2007): 75.

3. Burdick.

90–94 *(pages 135–137)*
KARA WALKER
Video stills from *8 Possible Beginnings or: The Creation of African-America, a Moving Picture by Kara E. Walker*, 2005
DVD video, running time: 15:57 minutes (with sound)
Courtesy the artist and Sikkema Jenkins & Co., New York

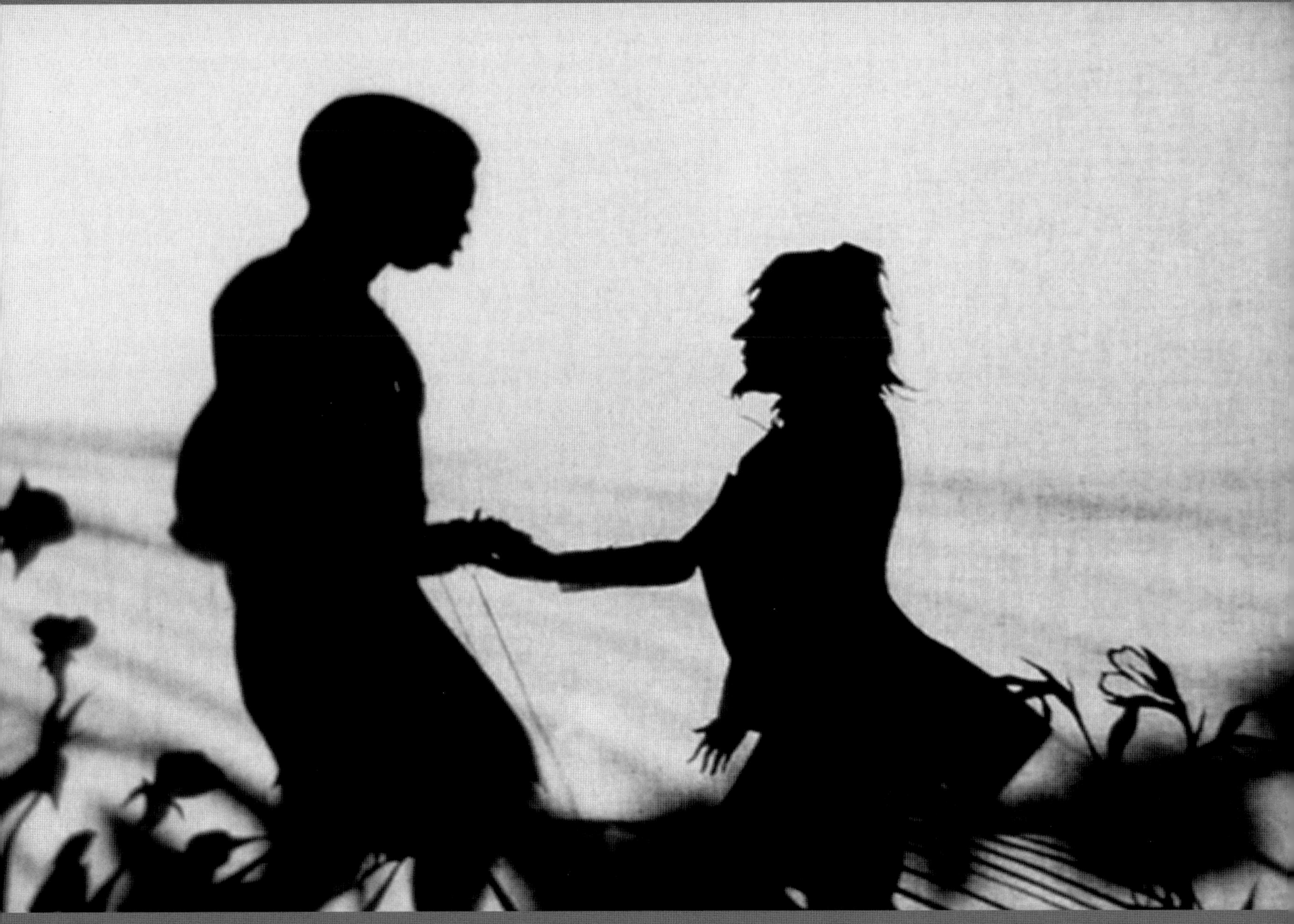

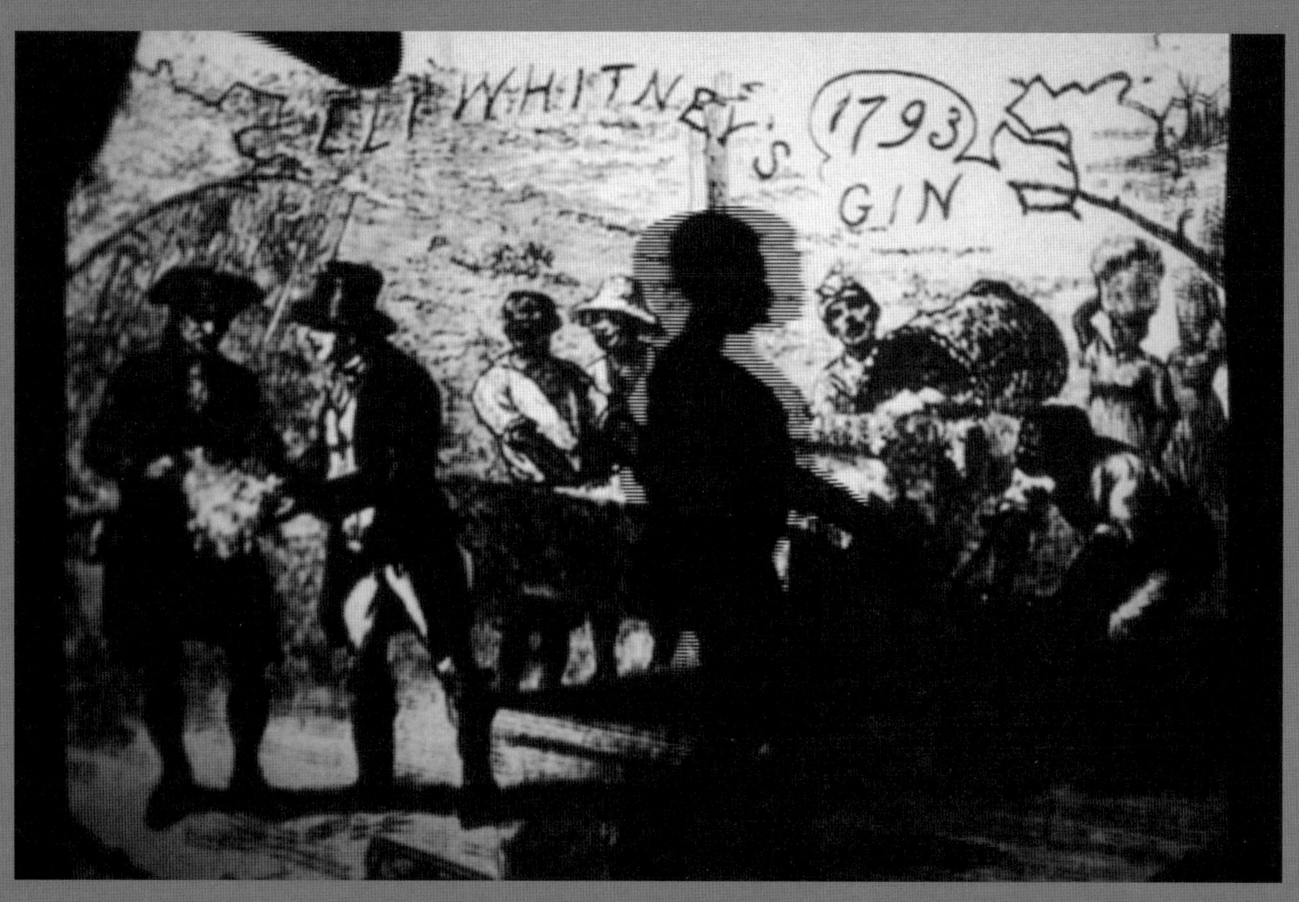
ELI WHITNEY'S
1793
GIN

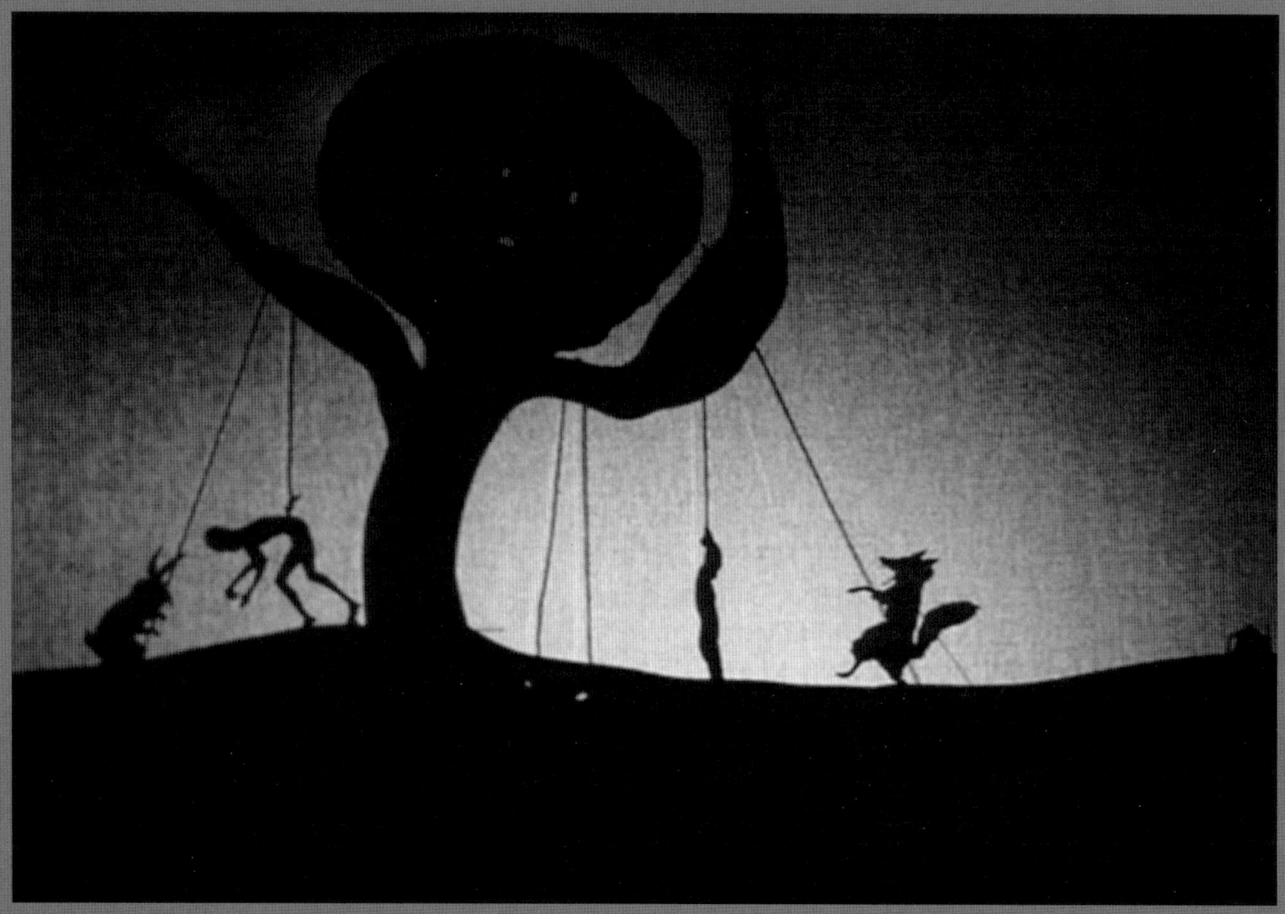

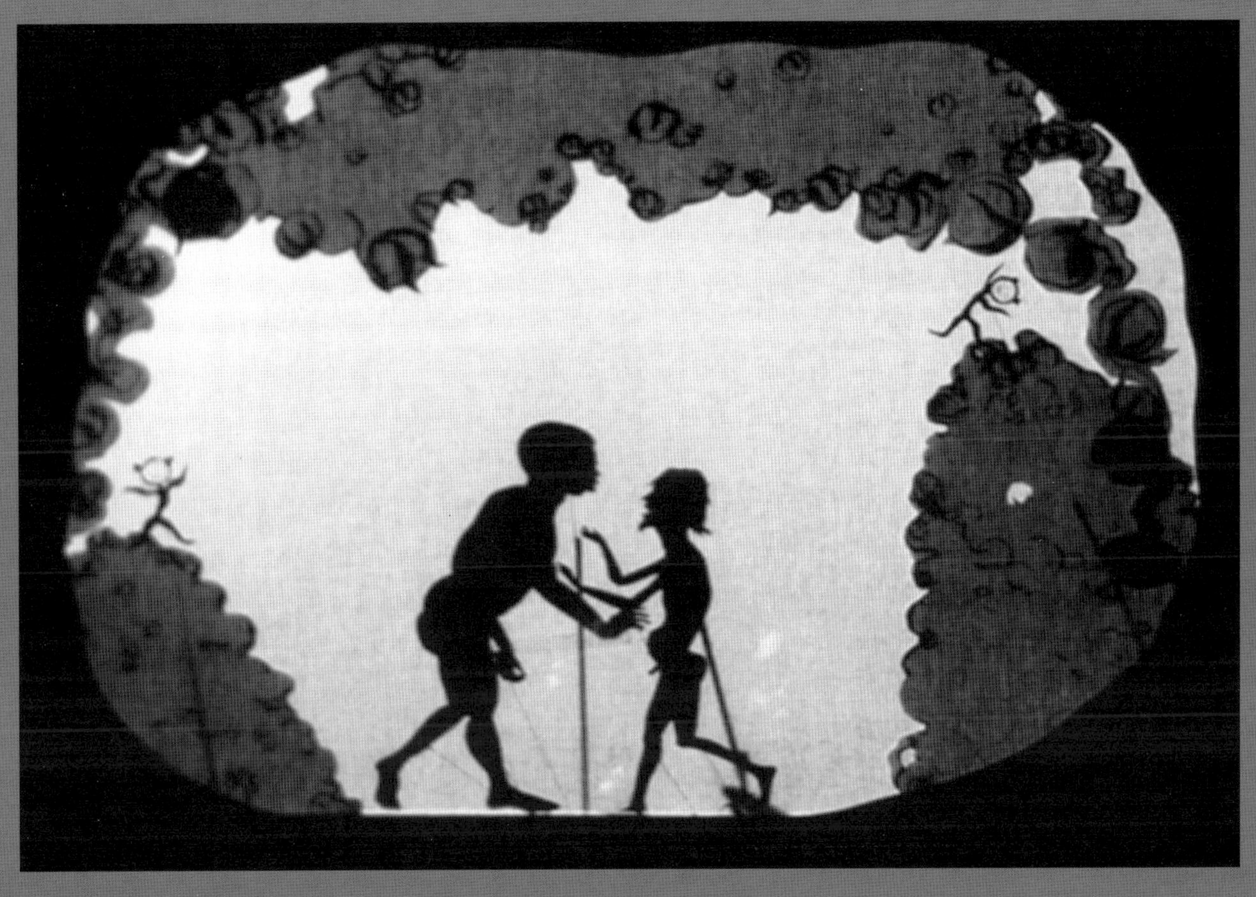

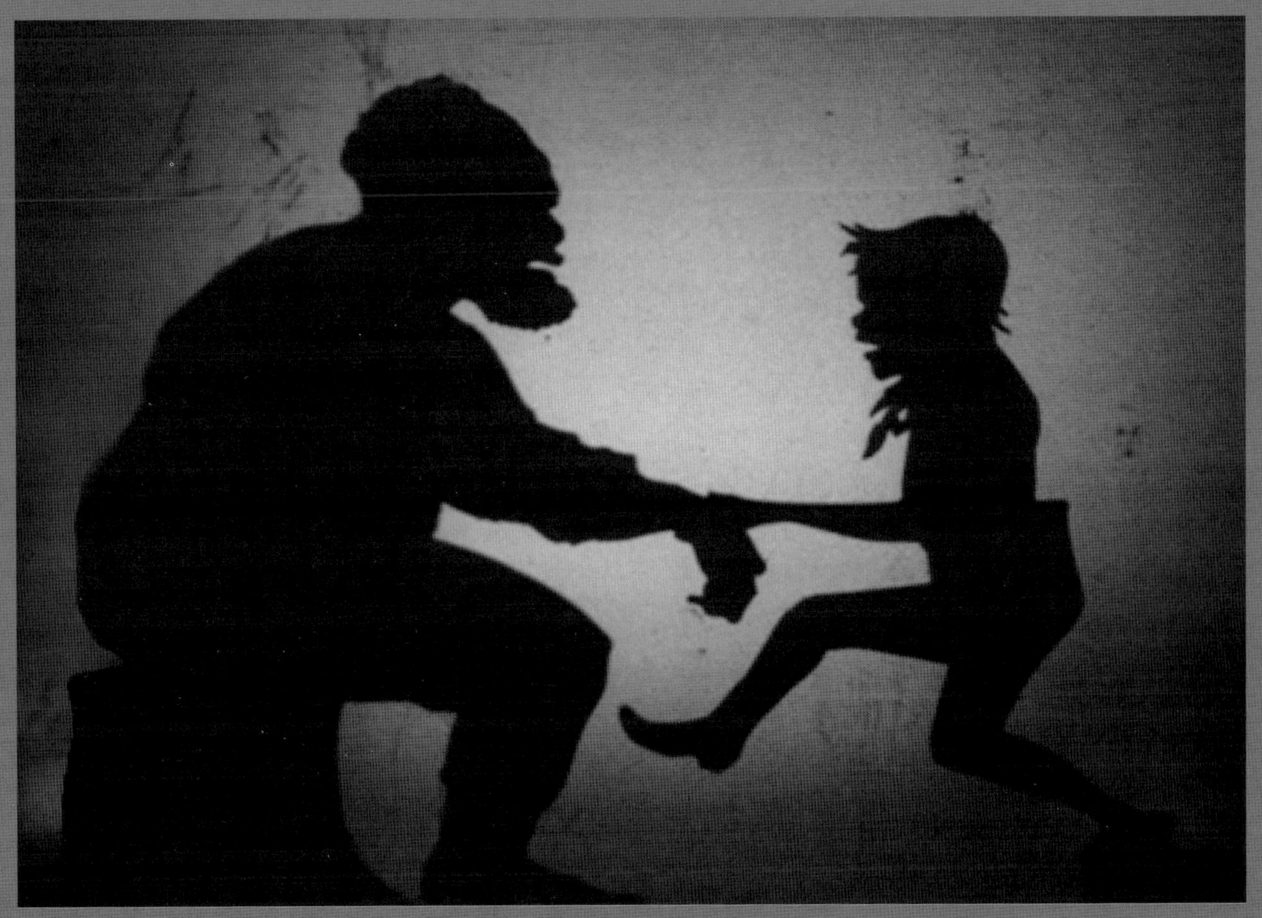

Charlie White

Charlie White's color photograph *1957* (2006), showing teenagers lounging on a car, is a perfect period piece. Every detail of this picture—from the bobby socks and saddle shoes to the greaser haircuts to the vintage Buick—jibes with images from the popular imagination of young people in America around the time of its title year. And it should. *1957* is a painstakingly composed and constructed photograph that borrows elements from iconic images to define its specified time. Working with cast actors and prop houses, White staged a scene that incorporates features from Joseph Sterling's *The Age of Adolescence (guys leaning out of car)* (1961, fig. 53), a documentary photograph that captures the antics of a group of adolescent boys, and Norman Rockwell's *The Problem We All Live With* (1964), his *Look* magazine illustration depicting an African-American schoolgirl, Ruby Bridges, marching into a segregated New Orleans school. The scene, which White intended to read as a frieze, begins on the left with a close quotation of Rockwell: a black girl in yellow, schoolbook tucked under her arm, strides out of the frame. In the center of the composition, two boys, arms and torsos hanging from the car's windows, ape poses from Sterling's photograph. However, the work's even, non-atmospheric lighting, along with a host of invented elements, cuts through the sentimental or historical patina that we tend to lay over representations of this period. In White's image, the no-goodnik girl on the trunk, the white-haired official character who sits in the passenger seat of another parked car, and the hands-on-hips silhouette of a woman in the background, along with the apprehensive backward glance of the girl exiting at the right edge of the frame, give the work a tense edge of volatility and surveillance that seems more appropriate to post-9/11 than mid-twentieth-century America. White clearly understands that 1957, the year of Sputnik, the Little Rock Nine's forceful integration of an Arkansas high school, and the legendary, tail-finned Chevy Bel Air, was a pivotal moment in American culture. "The year was a powder keg waiting to explode," he says. "With the Cold War escalating, the birth of a highly entitled youth culture, the introduction of rock and roll, and the National Guard escorting black teenagers into white high schools, the latent threat of violence in that period was a harbinger of today's fractious, individualized society. I wanted to overlay this historical complexity onto the types of images we generally look at with a whitewashed, ahistorical nostalgia—as a sort of reminder, perhaps, of the American reflex to cleanse political realities from our collective memory of the past."[1]

1957 is part of a series of similarly fabricated and provocative portraits, entitled Everything Is American, that includes images inspired by mythological, Freudian, and social archetypes as well as real events, including the 1969 Manson Family murder trials, the 1978 Jonestown Massacre, and gymnast Kerri Strug's dramatic injury at the 1996 Olympics. Rife with art-historical quotations and psychosexual overtones, the series, White says, allegorizes a wide range of power struggles in American culture—"the disempowered, those reaching for power, those about to lose power." The series' title, he says, aims to be critical but leaves interpretation up to the viewer. As in *1957*, the series' images leave much unsaid, preferring instead to create subtly tweaked parallel realities, where seemingly familiar images pulse with undercurrents of discord, fear, and madness. Whether or not you believe what White suggests—that the images in Everything Is American represent the global, toxic runoff of the country's contemporary culture of inauthenticity and exploitation—it is clear that *1957* powerfully encapsulates many aspects of the American mythological, the American artificial, and the American uncanny.

Fig. 53
Joseph Sterling, *The Age of Adolescence (guys leaning out of car)*, 1961
Gelatin silver print
11 x 14 inches
Courtesy Stephen Daiter Gallery, Chicago

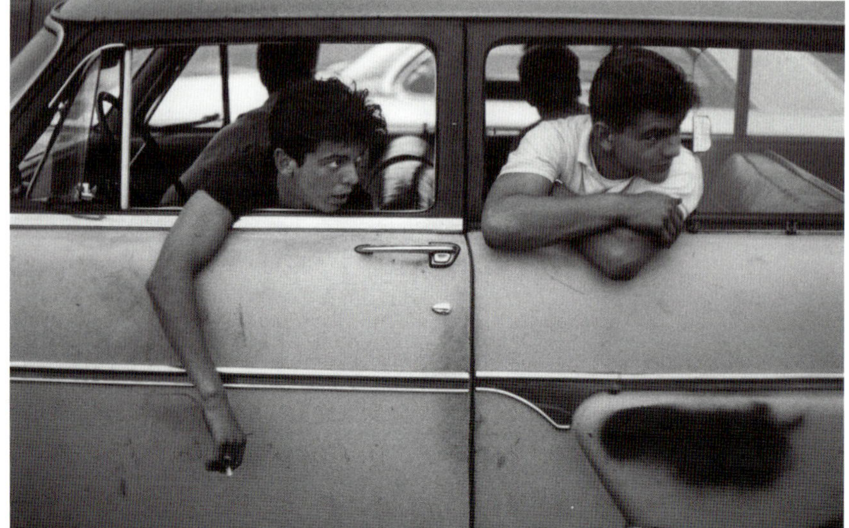

1. This and other quotes by the artist are from a telephone interview with the author, November 29, 2007.

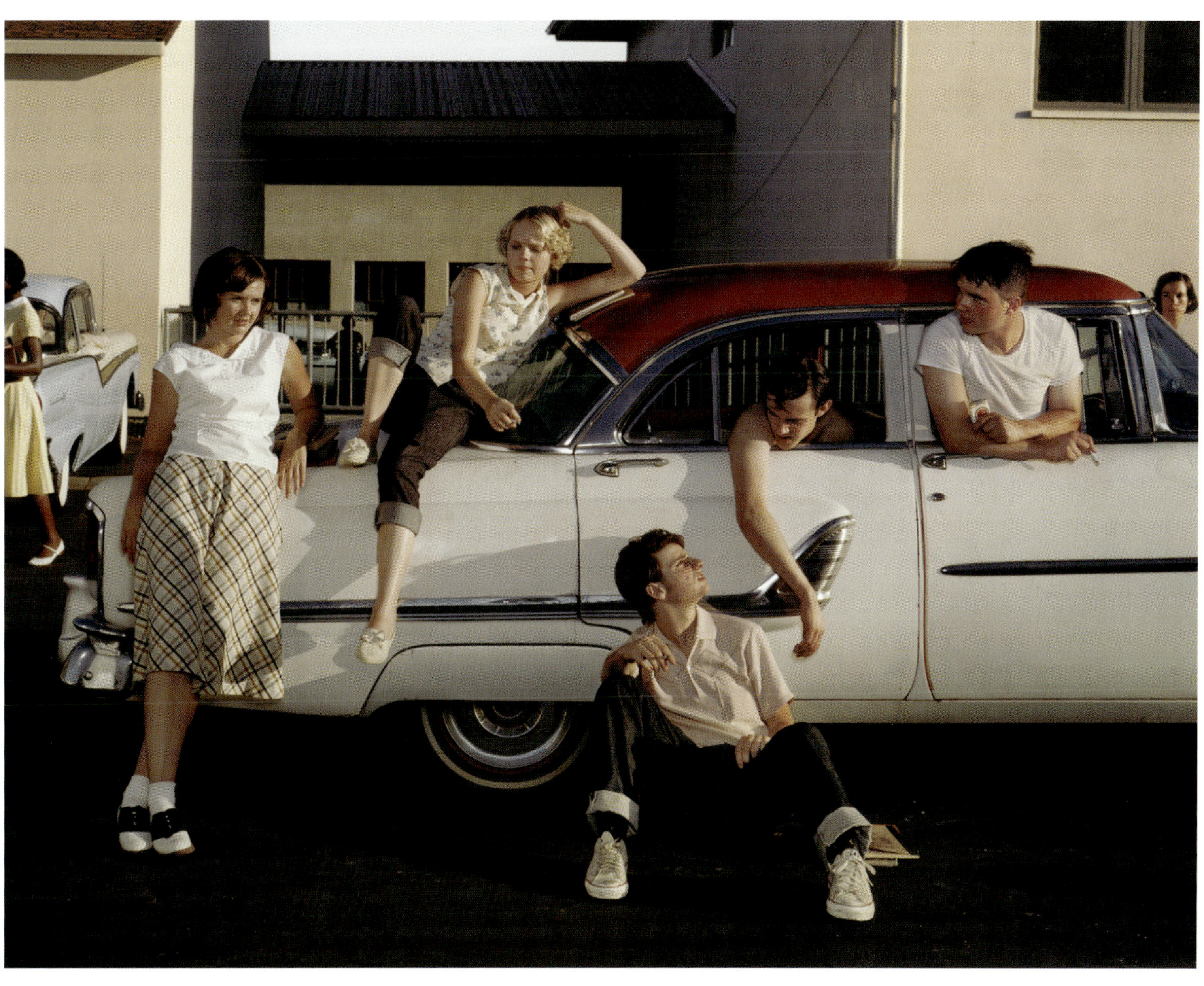

95
CHARLIE WHITE
1957, 2006
C-print
44¾ x 56 inches
Courtesy Wohnmaschine, Berlin

CATALOGUE OF THE EXHIBITION

Dimensions are listed height preceding width preceding depth.

ERIC BELTZ
Breath of Satan, 2007
Graphite on Bristol board
23 x 17 inches
Collection Chris DeBolt, Los Angeles

Fuck You Tree, 2007
Graphite on Bristol board
40 x 30 inches
Collection Chris DeBolt, Los Angeles

Good Luck Assholes, 2007
Graphite on Bristol board
28 x 22 inches
Collection Jeffrey and Elana Rose, Los Angeles

JEREMY BLAKE
Winchester, 2002
DVD: color, sound, 18 minutes (continuous loop)
Courtesy Kinz, Tillou + Feigen, New York

The All-American Boy, 2004
Oil on canvas
12 x 10 inches
Private Collection

Big Pink, 2004
Oil on canvas
12 x 14 inches
Private Collection

SAM DURANT
*Pilgrims and Indians, Planting and Reaping,
Learning and Teaching*, 2006
Mixed media, motorized platform
Courtesy the artist and Blum & Poe, Los Angeles

BARNABY FURNAS
Untitled Battlescene, 1999
Watercolor on paper
6 1/4 x 8 1/2 inches
Collection Fern and Lenard Tessler, New York

Cemetery Ridge, April 24, 2001, 2001
Watercolor on paper
25 x 37 inches
Collection Greg S. Feldman, New York

Flys on Shit, May 18, 2001, 2001
Watercolor on paper
13 1/2 x 17 1/4 inches
Collection Suzanne Feldman

Untitled Battlescene, October 17, 2001, 2001
Watercolor on paper
12 5/8 x 19 inches
Collection the artist

Untitled, July 16, 2001, 2001
Watercolor on paper
12 x 18 inches
Collection Jennifer Tytel

Frontal Assault III, 2002
Watercolor on paper
18 x 24 inches
Collection Sherri Grace

Second Inaugural, 2003
Urethane on linen
71 7/8 x 42 inches
Collection Pam and Bob Goergen

John Brown, 2005
Urethane and dye on linen
72 x 60 inches
Private Collection, New York

Assassination (Abraham Lincoln), 2007
Ink and urethane on linen
30 x 20 inches
Private Collection, New York

DEBORAH GRANT
Where Good Darkies Go, 2006
Acrylic on birch panel
44 panels (16 in exhibition), 24 x 18 inches each
Courtesy the artist and Dunn and Brown
Contemporary, Dallas

MATTHEW DAY JACKSON
Garden of Earthly Delights (Spiritual America), 2008
Posters, needlepoint, glass and steel vitrine, wool,
paint, C-print, fake taxidermy, wood, blower scoop
180 x 180 x 60 inches (approximately)
Courtesy the artist

BRAD KAHLHAMER
Dolls, 1984–2004
Mixed media figurines
Approximately 12 x 4 x 2 inches each
Courtesy the artist

Desert Forest City, 2004
Ink and watercolor
62 x 82 inches
Collection Stefan Simchowitz

Indian Summer USA, 2006
Watercolor and ink on paper
45 x 60 inches
Collection Neils Kantor

Waqui Totem USA, 2006
Watercolor and ink on paper
82 x 62 inches
Collection Nerman Museum of Contemporary Art,
Johnson County Community College, gift of Marti
and Tony Oppenheimer and the Oppenheimer
Brothers Foundation

MARGARET KILGALLEN
Main Drag, 2001
Mixed media installation
Dimensions variable
Courtesy the Estate of Margaret Kilgallen

McDERMOTT & McGOUGH
San Francisco Earthquake Box 1906, 1988
Ceramic, glass, velvet, wood, and wooden plaque
12 1/2 x 18 3/4 x 10 1/4 inches
Nicholas Robinson Collection

In Praise of Shame, 1915, 2000
Oil on linen
40 x 30 inches
Collection the artists

Divine Fury, 1932, 2002
Oil on linen
60 x 48 inches
Courtesy the artists

Sacred Love and Pain, 1960, 2006
Oil on wood
48 x 12 x 16 inches
Courtesy the artists and Cheim & Read, New York

AARON MORSE
Magua (#2), 2004
Acrylic on linen
36 x 48 inches
Collection Lance and Jennifer Volland

Deerslayer (#2), 2006
Acrylic, oil on canvas
60 x 88 inches
Courtesy the artist, ACME., Los Angeles
and Guild and Greyshkul, New York

The Good Hunt, 2006
Acrylic, glass beads on canvas
64 x 43 inches
Collection Paul Rickert, San Francisco

The Good Hunt (#2), 2006
Acrylic, watercolor, pencil on paper
90 x 22 inches
Courtesy the artist, ACME., Los Angeles,
and Guild and Greyshkul, New York

CYNTHIA NORTON
Fountain (emotion), 2002
Mixed media, copper coil, pressure cooker, bucket, magazine rack, wood
44 x 50 x 32 inches
Courtesy the artist

Dancing Squared, 2004
Aluminum, hardware, electric motors, dresses, wire
90 x 180 x 180 inches
Collection Laura Lee Brown and Steve Wilson, Louisville, Kentucky

GRETA PRATT
Nineteen Lincolns, 2005
18 archival inkjet prints
28 x 24 inches each
Courtesy the artist

Nine Lincolns, 2000
Lambda print
30 x 30 inches
Courtesy the artist

DAVID RATHMAN
Guilty As Hell! Free As a Bird!, 2001
Ink on paper
12 x 11 inches

Hell You Ain't Dead. Just Shut Up a Little, 2001
Ink on paper
12 x 11 inches

I'm the Law Here. All the Law, 2001
Ink on paper
12 x 11 inches

It's Funny to Start Thinking About Women, 2001
Ink on paper
12 x 11 inches

The Leaves Are Slowly Falling From the Family Tree, 2001
Ink on paper
12 x 11 inches

My Vices Were Magnificent, 2001
Ink on paper
12 x 11 inches

Wanted [Baby-Red], 2001
Ink on paper
12 x 11 inches

Why Must I Always Explain?, 2001
Ink on paper
12 x 11 inches

All Collection Lio Malca, New York

DARIO ROBLETO
Your Lullaby Will Find a Home in My Head, 2005
Hair braids made from a stretched and curled audio tape recording of Sylvia Plath reciting "November Graveyard," homemade paper (pulp made from soldiers' letters to mothers and daughters from various wars, ink retrieved from letters, sepia), excavated and melted bullet lead, carved ribcage bone and ivory, mourning dress fabric and thread, silk, mourning frame from another's loss, walnut, glass
26 x 3½ x 30 inches
Collection Carlos Bacino, Houston

The Pause Became Permanence , 2005–2006
Ink-dyed willow and ash, hair lockets made of stretched and curled audio tape recordings of the last known Confederate and Union Civil War soldier's voices, excavated and melted shrapnel from various wars, hair flowers braided by war widow's mourning dresses, colored paper, silk, ribbon, milk paint, glass, typeset
69 x 26 x 26 inches
San Antonio Museum of Art, purchased with funds provided by an anonymous donor in honor of Nancy Brown Negley

Lamb of Man/Atom and Eve/
Americana Materia Medica, 2006–2007
Colored paper, cardboard, ribbon, foamcore, glue, willow
Three panels, 60 x 48 x 180 inches overall
Courtesy the artist and D'Amelio Terras, New York

A Rosary for Rhythm, 2007
Melted and carved vinyl records of Jerry Lee Lewis' and Little Richard's "Whole Lotta Shakin' Goin' On," ground hip bone dust, cast pewter, metal chain
9½ x 4½ x 4½ inches
Courtesy the artist and D'Amelio Terras, New York

Salvation Cocktails, 2007
Veteran's old mason jar, soldiers' rosaries and crucifixes excavated from various battlefields, ground fulgurites (glass produced by lightning strikes when heat from blast melts surrounding sand), ground trinitite (glass produced during the first atomic test explosion when heat from blast melted surrounding sand), military buttons and medals, excavated fired bullets, spent shell casings and shrapnel from various wars, military blanket wool from various wars
9½ x 4½ x 4½ inches
Courtesy the artist and D'Amelio Terras, New York

Shaker Apothecary , 2007
Pine, hand-ground vinyl 45 rpm dance-craze records, various medicinal botanicals, carved bone calcium, typeset
40 x 160 x 15 inches
Courtesy the artist and D'Amelio Terras, New York

ALLISON SMITH
Dr. Mary Edwards Walker, 2005
Slip cast ceramic, linen, wool, cotton, leather, hemp fibers, brass, glass
72 x 24 x 10 inches

Eliza Wilson of the 5th Wisconsin Volunteer Infantry, 2005
Slip cast ceramic, linen, wool, cotton, leather, hemp fibers, brass, glass
72 x 24 x 10 inches

Lizzie Clawson Jones, 2005
Slip cast ceramic, linen, wool, cotton, leather, hemp fibers, brass, glass
72 x 24 x 10 inches

Marie Tepe, "French Mary," Vivandière of the 114th Pennsylvania Volunteer Infantry, Collis's Zouaves, 2005
Slip cast ceramic, linen, wool, cotton, leather, hemp fibers, brass, glass
72 x 24 x 10 inches

Officer of the 5th New York Volunteer Infantry, Duryée's Zouaves, 2005
Slip cast ceramic, linen, wool, cotton, leather, hemp fibers, brass, glass
72 x 24 x 10 inches

Soldier of the 114th Pennsylvania Infantry, Collis's Zouaves, 2005
Slip cast ceramic, linen, wool, cotton, leather, hemp fibers, brass, glass
72 x 24 x 10 inches

Soldier of the 146th New York Zouaves Volunteer Infantry, 2005
Slip cast ceramic, linen, wool, cotton, leather, hemp fibers, brass, glass
72 x 24 x 10 inches

All courtesy the artist

KARA WALKER
8 Possible Beginnings or: The Creation of African-America, a Moving Picture by Kara E. Walker, 2005
DVD video, running time: 15:57 minutes (with sound)
Courtesy the artist and Sikkema Jenkins & Co., New York

CHARLIE WHITE
1957, 2006
C-print
44¾ x 56 inches
Courtesy Wohnmaschine, Berlin

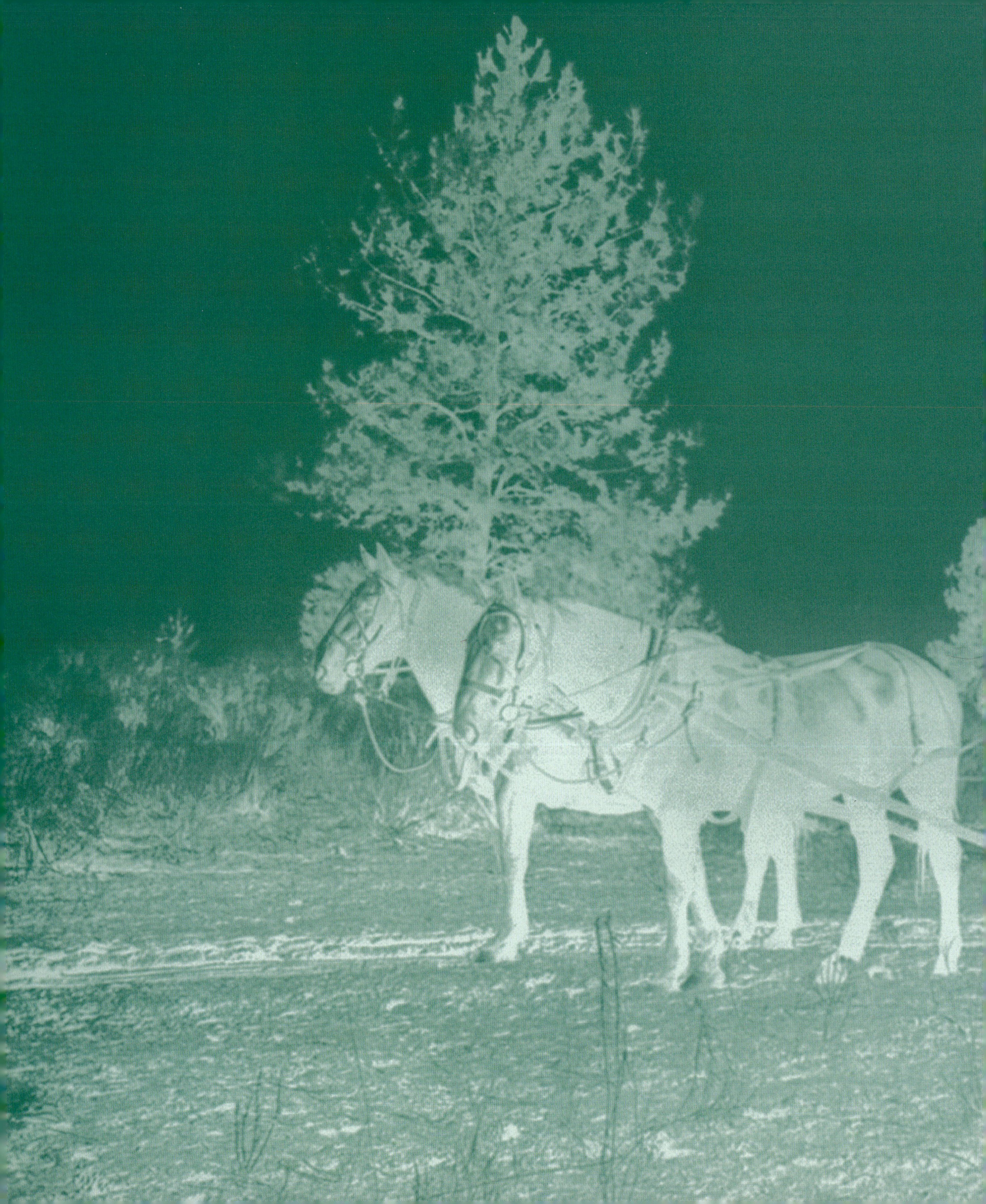

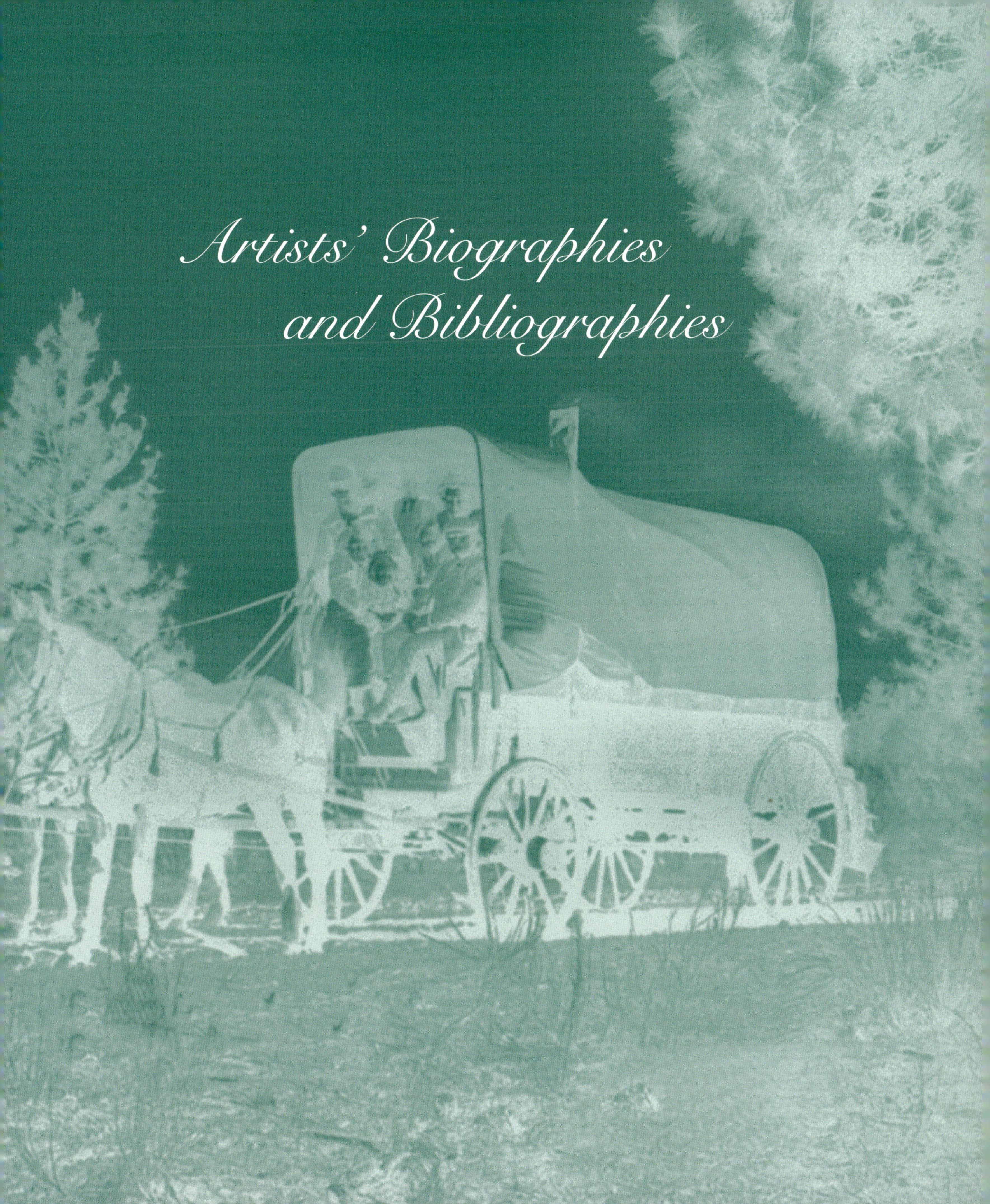
Artists' Biographies
and Bibliographies

ERIC BELTZ

Born 1975, Orange, California

2000, BFA, California State University, Fullerton

2004, MFA, University of California, Santa Barbara

Lives and works in Santa Barbara, California

Selected One-Person Exhibitions

2007
HISTROY!, Acuna-Hansen Gallery, Los Angeles.

2005
Hypnobotany: Visions of a Field Naturalist, Santa Barbara Contemporary Arts Forum, California.

Selected Group Exhibitions

2007
Promised Land, Morgan Lehman Gallery, New York.

Harry Smith Anthology Remixed, Alt.Gallery, London, England.

2006
Flaunt Junc Gallery, Los Angeles.

Draw, Paper, Scissors, Domestic Setting, Los Angeles.

Selected Bibliography

Ollman, Leah. "Sending Clear And Subversive Messages." *Los Angeles Times*, November 16, 2007, p. E22.

Ollman, Leah. "What This Group Can Do With Paper." *Los Angeles Times*, June 2, 2006, p. E19.

Schwendener, Martha. "Art In Review: Promised Land." *New York Times*, July 20, 2007, p. B25.

Woodard, Josef. "The Secret Psychedelic Life of Plants." *Santa Barbara News-Press*, May 20-26, 2005, Scene section, p. 15.

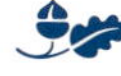

JEREMY BLAKE

Born 1971, Fort Sill, Oklahoma

1993, BFA, The School of the Art Institute of Chicago, Illinois

1995, MFA, California Institute of the Arts, Valencia

Died 2007, New York

Selected One-Person Exhibitions

2008
Wild Choir: Cinematic Portraits by Jeremy Blake, Corcoran Gallery of Art, Washington.

2006
Jeremy Blake, Honor Fraser Inc., Venice, California.

2005
Sodium Fox, Feigen Contemporary, New York.

2003
Jeremy Blake; Winchester. Museo Nacional Centro de Arte Reina Sofia, Madrid.

The 59th Minute: Video Art on the Times Square Astrovision, sponsored by Creative Time, Panasonic, and American Museum of the Moving Image, New York.

2002
Cerca Series: Jeremy Blake, Museum of Contemporary Art San Diego, California.

Jeremy Blake: All Mod Cons, Blaffer Gallery, University of Houston, Texas.

2001
Chemical Sundown, Dot, London.

The Forty Million Dollar Beatnik, Works on Paper, Inc., Los Angeles.

2000
Jeremy Blake: Bungalow 8, Contemporary Arts Center, Cincinnati.

Selected Group Exhibitions

2006
The Searchers, White Box, New York.

2005
Extreme Abstraction, Albright-Knox Art Gallery, New York.

2004
Whitney Biennial, Whitney Museum of American Art, New York.

2001
010101: Art in Technological Times, San Francisco Museum of Modern Art, California.

BitStreams, Whitney Museum of American Art, New York.

2000
Whitney Biennial, Whitney Museum of American Art, New York.

Selected Bibliography

Leffingwell, Edward. "Jeremy Blake at Feigen Contemporary." *Art in America* 92, no. 2 (February 2004):119.

Levin Dan. "After Death, Unfinished Artwork Gets a Life." *The New York Times*, November 29, 2007, p. E1.

MacSweeney, Eve. "Strange Days" *Vogue* (October 2003): 284.

Richards, Chris. "Music to the Eye: Jeremy Blake's 'Moving Paintings' Are a Brilliant Coda to a Life That Ended on a Sad Note." *The Washington Post*, November 8, 2007, p. C1.

SAM DURANT

Born 1961, Seattle, Washington

1986, BFA, Massachusetts College of Art, Boston

1991, MFA, California Institute of the Arts, Valencia

Lives and works in Los Angeles

Selected One-Person Exhibitions

2007
Scenes from the Pilgrim Story: Myths, Massacres and Monuments, Blum & Poe, Los Angeles.

Scenes from the Pilgrim Story: Natural History, Catriona Jeffries Gallery, Vancouver.

Echoplex Joseph Beuys Ideas/Crash, Fat, Felt, Amerika, Politics, Recovery, Monument, Paula Cooper Gallery, New York.

2006
Scenes from the Pilgrim Story: Goodbye Merry Mountt, Galleria Emi Fontana, Milan.

Scenes from the Pilgrim Story: Myth, Massacres and Monuments, Massachusetts College of Art, Boston.

2005
Proposal for White and Indian Dead Monuments Transposition, Washington D.C, Paula Cooper Gallery, New York.

2004
12 Signs: transposed and illuminated (with various indexes), S.M.A.K. Ghent, Belgium.

We Are All Outlaws in the Eyes of Amerika, Galleria Emi Fontana, Milan.

Edward Said, The Suburban, Oak Park, Illinois.

2003
We Are the People, Project Row House, Houston.

Sam Durant, Kunstverein Düsseldorf, Germany.

2002
Sam Durant, Museum of Contemporary Art, Los Angeles.

2001
Southern Tree, Tree of Knowledge, Dead Tree (part one), Galleria Emi Fontana, Milan.

2000
Proposal for Monument in Friendship Park, Jacksonville, FLA., Blum & Poe, Santa Monica, California.

1999
Into the Black, Kapinos, Berlin.

Selected Group Exhibitions

2007
Black Panther, Rank and File, Southeastern Center for Contemporary Art, Winston-Salem, North Carolina.

Been Up So Long It Looks Like Down To Me, Presentation House Gallery, Vancouver.

Panic Room: Works from The Dakis Joannou Collection, Deste Foundation, Athens.

Summer of Love: Art of the Psychedelic Era, Tate Liverpool, England.

2006
Black Panther, Rank and File, Yerba Buena Center for the Arts, San Francisco.

Monuments for the USA, White Columns, New York.

2005
Touch of Evil, Estacion Tijuana, Mexico.

Getting Emotional, Institute of Contemporary Art, Boston.

2004
100 Artists See God, iCI (Independent Curators International), New York.

Baja to Vancouver: The West Coast and Contemporary Art, CCA Wattis Institute for Contemporary Arts, California Institute of the Arts, San Francisco; Museum of Contemporary Art San Diego; Seattle Art Museum; Vancouver Art Gallery.

Whitney Biennial, Whitney Museum of American Art, New York.

2003
Dreams and Conflicts: The Viewer's Dictatorship: Delays and Revolutions, Biennale di Venezia, Venice.

Somewhere Better Than This Place: Alternative Social Experience in the Spaces of Contemporary Art, The Contemporary Arts Center, Cincinnati.

2002
The Lunatics Have Taken Over the Asylum, Works on Paper, Inc., Los Angeles.

Air Guitar: Art Reconsidering Rock Music, Milton Keynes Gallery, England.

1999
What Your Children Should Know About Conceptualism, NAK Neuer Aachener Kunstverein, Aachen, Germany.

Other Narratives, Contemporary Arts Museum Houston.

1998
L.A. or Lilliput?, Long Beach Museum of Art, California.

1997
Scene of the Crime, Hammer Museum, University of California, Los Angeles.

Selected Bibliography

Ketchum-Heap of Birds, Shanna. "On Legitimizing the Body Politic: America's Founding Myth Reconsidered." *Sam Durant: Scenes from the Pilgrim Story: Myths, Massacres and Monuments*. Exh. cat. Boston: Massachusetts College of Art, 2007 (12-25).

Leclere, Mary. "The Time of the Now." *Sam Durant: 12 Signs, Transposed and Illuminated (with various indexes)*. Exh. cat. Ghent, Belgium: S.M.A.K., 2004 (50–62).

Meyer, James. "Impure Thoughts: The Art of Sam Durant." *Artforum* 38, no.8 (April 2000): 112–117.

BARNABY FURNAS

Born 1973, Philadelphia, Pennsylvania

1995, BFA, School of Visual Arts, New York

2000, MFA, Columbia University, New York

Lives and works in New York

Selected One-Person Exhibitions
2007
Focus: Barnaby Furnas, The Modern Art Museum of Fort Worth, Texas.

Stuart Shave/Modern Art Inc., London.

2006
Marianne Boesky Gallery, New York.

Anthony Meier Fine Art, San Francisco.

2005
Baltic Centre for Contemporary Art, Gateshead, England.

Lever House, New York.

2004
Modern Art Inc., London.

2001, 2002, 2003
Marianne Boesky Gallery, New York.

Selected Group Exhibitions

2007
True Romance: Allegories of Love from the Renaissance to the Present, Kunsthalle Wien, Vienna.

The Fractured Figure, Deste Foundation, Athens.

Dream and Trauma: Works from the Dakis Joannou Collection, Athens, Kunsthalle Wien and Museum Moderner Kunst Stiftung Ludwig Wein, Vienna.

Art in America: Now, Museum of Contemporary Art, Shanghai.

Between Two Deaths, Zentrum für Kunst und Medientechnologie, Karlsruhe, Germany.

2006
USA Today, The Royal Academy of Arts (in collaboration with the Saatchi Gallery), London.

Imagination Becomes Reality, Part IV: Borrowed Images, Sammlung Goetz, Munich.

2005
PILLish: Harsh Realities and Gorgeous Destinations, Museum of Contemporary Art Denver, Colorado.

2004
Whitney Biennial, Whitney Museum of American Art, New York.

2003
War (What Is It Good For?), Museum of Contemporary Art, Chicago.

Funny Papers: Cartoons and Contemporary Drawing, Daniel Weinberg Gallery, Los Angeles.

2002
Officina Americana, Galleria d'Arte Moderna, Bologna, Italy.

The Fourth Annual Altoids Curiously Strong Collection, L.A.C.E., Los Angeles.

Selected Bibliography

Karnes, Andrea. "*Focus: Barnaby Furnas.*" Exh. broch. Fort Worth, Texas: The Modern Art Museum of Fort Worth, 2007.

Kastner, Jeffrey. "Art In Review." *The New York Times*, October 13, 2006, p. E36.

Momin, Shamin. "Interview." *Barnaby Furnas.* Exh. cat. Gatesheard, England: Baltic Center for Contemporary Art, 2005.

Trachtman, Paul. "Back to the Figure." *Smithsonian* (October 2007): 106–107.

☛ DEBORAH GRANT

Born 1968, Toronto, Canada

1996, BFA, Columbia College, Chicago

1996, Skowhegan School of Painting and Sculpture, Maine

1999, MFA, Tyler School of Art, Pennsylvania

Lives and works in New York

Selected One-Person Exhibitions

2007
Getting Blood Out of Bed Sheets, Steve Turner Contemporary, Los Angeles.

By the Skin of Our Teeth, Dunn and Brown Contemporary, Dallas.

2006
a gin cure, Roebling Hall, New York.

2004
Like a Witch's Teat, SATELLITE Manhattan, New York.

2002
Random Select Drawings and Paintings by Deborah Grant, The Scene Gallery, New York.

Selected Group Exhibitions

2007
Arte Povera Now and Then, Esso Gallery and Books, New York.

Intelligent Design, Momenta Art, Brooklyn.

*M*A*S*H**, Amory Group Exhibition, New York.

Emergency Room Show, P.S.1 Contemporary Art Center, MOMA, Long Island City, New York.

2005
Relics and Remnants, Jamaica Center for the Arts, New York.

Propeller, Steve Turner Gallery, Beverly Hills, California.

Greater New York, P.S.1 Contemporary Art Center, MOMA, New York.

Out Door Façade; The Check Is In the Mail, Triple Candie, New York.

2004

Notorious Improprieties, Samson Projects, Boston.

Seeds and Roots, The Studio Museum in Harlem, New York.

2003

Hands On Hands Down, The Studio Museum in Harlem, New York.

Comic Release: Negotiating Identity for a New Generation, Carnegie Mellon's Regina Gouger Miller Gallery, Pittsburgh, Pennsylvania.

2002

AIM 22 Show, Bronx Museum, New York.

2001

Rumors of War, Triple Candie, New York.

Freestyle, The Studio Museum in Harlem, New York.

Selected Bibliography

Boucher, Brain. "Deborah Grant at Roebling Hall." *Art In America*, 92, no. 2 (October 2006): 190–191.

Mitchell, Charles Dee. "Deborah Grant at Dunn and Brown Contemporary." *The Dallas Morning News*, April 18, 2007.

Myers, Holly. "Deborah Grant engages Picasso on His own Terms at Steve Turner Contemporary." *Los Angeles Times*, February 2, 2007.

Smith, Roberta. "A Gin Cure." *The New York Times*, May 26, 2006.

MATTHEW DAY JACKSON

Born 1974, Panorama City, California

2001, MFA, Mason Gross School of the Arts, Rutgers University, New Jersey

1997, BFA, University of Washington, Seattle

Lives and works in Brooklyn

Selected One-Person Exhibitions

2007

Diptych, Mario Diacono at Ars Libri Ltd., Boston.

The Lower 48, Perry Rubenstein Gallery, New York.

Workspace: Matthew Day Jackson, Blanton Museum of Art, Austin.

2006

Paradise Now! (Limbo), Cubitt Artists Space, London.

Paradise Now! Portland Institute of Contemporary Art, Portland, Oregon.

Oracle (Days of Future Passed) Mario Diacono at Ars Libri, Boston

2005

Matthew Day Jackson, Perry Rubenstein Gallery, New York.

2004

By No Means Necessary, The Locker Plant, Chinati Foundation, Marfa, Texas.

Selected Group Exhibitions

2007

Americans in New York, Galerie Michael Rein, Paris.

In the Line of Time and the Plane of Now, Wallspace Gallery, New York.

Uncertain States of America – American Art in the 3rd Millennium, Herning Kunstmuseum, Denmark.

2006

USA Today, Royal Academy of Art, London.

The Searchers, White Box, New York.

Whitney Biennial, Whitney Museum of American Art, New York.

Selected Bibliography

Arning, Bill, "Matthew Day Jackson." *Modern Painters* 19, no. 8 (October 2007): 58–60.

Jones, Kristin M., "Matthew Day Jackson." *Frieze* 97 (March 2006): 167.

Morton, Tom, "Matthew Day Jackson and America's art of stone." *TANK magazine* 4, no. 8 (2005): 84.

Smith, Roberta. "Spotting an Aesthetic Dispute and Embracing All Sides." *The New York Times*, December 17, 2005, p. B13.

BRAD KAHLHAMER

Born 1956, Tucson, Arizona

1982, BFA, University of Wisconsin-Fond du Lac

Lives and works in New York

Selected One-Person Exhibitions

2006
Brad Kahlhamer & Aaron Spangler, Kantor/Feuer Gallery, Los Angeles.

Girls & Skulls, Deitch Projects, New York.

2005
Let's Walk West, Bakalar Gallery, Massachusetts College of Art, Boston.

2003
Apache Junction USA, Modern Art, Inc., London.

2001
Brad Kahlhamer, Galleria Francesca Kaufmann, Milan.

2000
Brad Kahlhamer: Almost American, Madison Art Center
(now Madison Museum of Contemporary Art), Wisconsin.

1999
Friendly Frontier, Deitch Projects, New York.

Selected Group Exhibitions

2006
Radar, Denver Art Museum, Colorado.

2005
Monuments for the USA, White Columns, New York.

2004
Lewis and Clark Territory: Contemporary Artists Revisit Place, Race and Memory, Tacoma Art Museum, Washington.

Monument to Now, Deste Foundation Center for Contemporary Art, Athens.

2003
Supernova, San Francisco Museum of Modern Art.

2000
Greater New York: New Art in New York Now, P.S.1 Contemporary Art Center, MOMA, Long Island City, New York.

Selected Bibliography

Cash, Stephanie. "The Hills are Alive." *Art in America* 56, no. 2 (February 2007): 56–65.

Grabner, Michelle. "Brad Kahlhamer." *New Art Examiner* 28, nos. 8–9 (May–June 2001): 95–96.

Sussman Susser, Deborah. "Brad Kahlhamer at the Museum of Contemporary Art." *Art in America* 93, no. 3 (March 2005): 145–146.

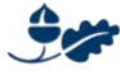

MARGARET L. KILGALLEN

Born 1967, Washington D.C.

1989, BFA, Colorado College, Colorado Springs

2001, MFA, Stanford University, Palo Alto, California

Died 2001, San Francisco

Selected One Person Exhibitions

2005
In the Sweet Bye & Bye, REDCAT, Los Angeles.

2000
Hammer Projects: Margaret Kilgallen, Hammer Museum, University of California, Los Angeles.

1999
To Friend and Foe, Deitch Projects, New York.

1998
Sincere Sin, John Berggruen Gallery, San Francisco.

1997
Three Sheets to The Wind, The Drawing Center, New York.

Selected Group Exhibitions

2004

Beautiful Losers, Contemporary Arts Center, Cincinnati; Yerba Buena Center for the Arts, San Francisco; Orange County Museum of Art, Newport Beach.

2002

Whitney Biennial, Whitney Museum of American Art, New York.

Made in California, Los Angeles County Museum of Art.

1999

Half Past, The Institute of Contemporary Art, Boston.

Off the Hook, The Luggage Store Gallery, San Francisco.

Bay Area Now, Yerba Buena Center for the Arts, San Francisco.

Selected Bibliography

Berry, C. "Like a Folk Tale." *Print* 57, no.1 (2003):102–107,112,120.

Dambrot, S. N. "Barry McGee and Margaret Kilgallen at the UCLA Hammer Museum." *Artweek* 31, no. 4 (April 2000): 27–28.

Paterson, C. "Margaret Kilgallen." *Flash Art* 38 (October 2005): 126–127.

Porges, M. "Margaret Kilgallen." *Artforum* 36, no. 9 (May 1997): 113–14.

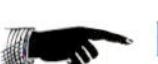

McDERMOTT & McGOUGH

David Walter McDermott

Born 1952, Hollywood, California

1970, BFA, University of Syracuse, New York

Lives and works in Ireland

Peter Thomas McGough

Born 1958, Syracuse, New York

1976, University of Syracuse, New York

1978, The Fashion Institute of Technology, New York

Lives and works in New York

Selected One-Person Exhibitions

2006

A True Story Based on Lies, Cheim & Read, New York.

2000

Hitler & Homosexuals: The Lust That Comes from Nothing, Akureyri Art Museum, Iceland.

1997

Messers MacDermott & MacGough, Paintings: Photographs and Time Experiment 1950, Provincial Museum of Modern Art, Ostende, Belgium.

1996

1936, Galleria Gian Ferrari, Charta, Italy.

1993

Galleria Gian Enzo Sperone, Rome, Italy.

1989

Robert Miller Gallery, New York.

Selected Group Exhibitions

2000

Aftökur & ùtrymingar, Akureyri Art Museum, Iceland.

2001

Between Earth and Heaven—New Classical Movements in the Art of Today, Provincial Museum of Modern Art, Ostende, Belgium.

2000

Protest & Survive, The White Chapel Gallery, London. .

1995, 1991, & 1987

Whitney Biennial, Whitney Museum of American Art, New York.

Selected Bibliography

Breidenbach, Tom. "McDermott & McGough." *Artforum* 41, no. 8 (April 2006): 244.

Grundberg, Andy. "Archaic Manner With Modern Overtones." *The New York Times*, November 30, 1990.

Levi Strauss, David. "McDermott & McGough: Fraenkel Gallery." *Artforum* 19, no. 2 (October 1990): 176–177.

Nickas, Bob. "McDermott & McGough Talk to Bob Nickas." *Artforum* 41, no. 7 (March 2003): 90–91, 267.

Ratcliff, Carter. "Modern Life." *Artforum* 24, no. 9 (May 1986): 12.

AARON MORSE

Born 1974, Tucson, Arizona

1996, BFA, The University of Arizona, Tucson

1998, MFA, The University of Cincinnati

Lives and works in Los Angeles

Selected One-Person Exhibitions

2008
Timeline, Hammer Museum, University of California, Los Angeles.

2007
The City on a Hill, ACME., Los Angeles.

2006
The War Is Over, Guild and Greyshkul, New York

2005
Aaron Morse, ACME., Los Angeles.

2003
Origins, ACME., Los Angeles.

Selected Group Exhibitions

2007
Oppenheimer Collection, Nerman Museum of Contemporary Art, Johnson City Community College, Overland Park, Kansas.

Fata Morgana, Galerie Schmidt Maczollek, Germany.

2006
Twice Drawn, The Frances Young Tang Teaching Museum and Art Gallery at Skidmore College, Saratoga Springs, New York.

2005
Liquid Los Angeles: Currents of Contemporary Watercolor Painting, Pasadena Museum of California Art.

2004
Matrix 213: Some Forgotten Place. Berkeley Art Museum and Pacific Film Archive, University of California, Berkeley.

2003
International Paper, Hammer Museum, University of California, Los Angeles.

Selected Bibliography

Morse, Aaron. "Self-portrait." *tema celeste* 96 (Summer 2003): 80–81.

Pagel, David. "The Past's View of the Past Made New: Aaron Morse at ACME."

Los Angeles Times, October 24, 2003, p. E28.

Wood, Eve. "Aaron Morse." *Art Papers* 29, no. 4 (July–August 2005): 55.

Zuckerman Jacobson, Heidi. *Matrix 213: Some Forgotten Place.* Exh. broch. Berkeley, California: Berkeley Art Museum and Pacific Film Archive, 2004.

CYNTHIA NORTON

Born 1970, Miami, Florida

1992, BFA, University of Kentucky, Lexington

1995, MFA, The School of the Art Institute of Chicago

2004, MA, University of Louisville, Kentucky

Lives and works in Louisville, Kentucky

Selected One-Person Exhibitions

2007
Life Cycle, Swanson Reed Contemporary, Louisville.

2004
Dancing Squared, Swanson Reed Contemporary, Louisville.

1994
Bun In the Oven, The School of the Art Institute of Chicago.

1992
Tart Art, Kaufman Beauty School, Lexington, Kentucky.

Cicatrix, Barnhart Gallery, Lexington, Kentucky.

Selected Group Exhibitions

2006
Maiza Hixson, Sarah Lyon, Cynthia Norton, Galerie Steineck, Vienna.

2005
Nowhere, Galerie Eugen Lendl, Graz, Austria.

Homegrown Southeast, Southeastern Center for Contemporary Art, Winston-Salem, North Carolina.

1998
Eleven, Eleven, Artemisia Gallery, Chicago.

1995
Rolywholyover, Nexus Foundation, Philadelphia.

1993
Opening Pandora's Box, Gallery 2, The Art Institute of Chicago.

Selected Performance

2006
Containment, The Present Tense, Performance Festival, Boston.

Selected Bibliography

Gardner, Ann Marie, and Jordan, Jay. "Nowhere." *Pitch Magazine* 1 (Spring 2006): 13–16.

Marcus, Greil. *The Old, Weird America*. New York: Picador, 1997 (178–179).

Snyder, Mark. "The Present Tense @ Midway Studios." *Big Red and Shiny* (2006), http://www.bigredandshiny.com/cgi-bin/ retrieve.pl?issue=issue44§ion=review&article=THE_PRESENT_ TENSE_3151716 (accessed November 2, 2007).

Vowell, Sara. "Ninnie/Cotton Candy Country." *Art Papers* 19, no. 7 (July–August 1995): 78–80.

GRETA PRATT

Born 1955, Minneapolis, Minnesota

1984, BFA, University of Minnesota, Minneapolis

2005, MFA, State University of New York, New Paltz

Lives and works in New Jersey and Virginia

Selected One-Person Exhibitions

2008
Greta Pratt: American Identity, Gordon Art Galleries, Old Dominion University, Virginia.

2007
Greta Pratt: Nineteen Lincolns, Atlanta Contemporary Art Center, Georgia.

Greta Pratt: The Lincoln Impersonators, Bernard Toale Gallery, 2007, Boston.

2006
Greta Pratt: Using History, Museum of Contemporary Photography, Columbia College Chicago.

2005
Greta Pratt: Using History, Gallery 13, Minneapolis.

2000
In Search for the Corn Queen, O. K. Harris Works of Art, New York.

Selected Group Exhibitions

2007
Mr. President, University at Albany Gallery, New York.

The American Experience, Smithsonian American Art Museum, Washington.

2006
Ahistoric Occasion: Artists Making History, Massachusetts Museum of Contemporary Art, North Adams.

2005
8 x 10, Candace Perich Gallery, New York.

Nineteen Lincolns, Samuel L. Dorsky Museum, New York.

2001
ExtraOrdinary: American Place in Recent Photography, Madison Art Center (now Madison Museum of Contemporary Art), Wisconsin.

Selected Bibliography

Marling, Karal Ann. "Touring History With Greta Pratt: We Have Seen The Past, America—And It Is Now!" *Using History*. Göttingen, Germany: Steidl, 2005 (n.p.).

Mitchell, John E. "Shooting Lincoln Again." *North Adams Transcript*, July 13, 2006.

Speigleman, Arthur. "Photographer Snaps America's Past In Today's Scenes." *Reuters*, June 27, 2006.

Strickland, Rennard. "Public History, Vernacular Storytelling, And The Search For Self: Observations On Identity and the Spirit of Place In the American Experience." *Using History*. Göttingen, Germany: Steidl, 2005 (n.p.).

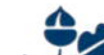 DAVID RATHMAN

Born 1958, Choteau, Montana

Lives and works in Minneapolis, Minnesota

Selected One-Person Exhibitions

2006
*Somebody's Got to Go***,** Clementine Gallery, New York.

2005
Swole Plumb to a Strut, Mary Goldman Gallery, Los Angeles.

2004
I Threw Away the Rose, Clementine Gallery, New York.

2001
To Hell With Them Small Towns, Clementine Gallery, New York.

2000
Facts and Figures, Franklin Art Works, Minneapolis.

1996
Paintings and Prints, Montgomery Glasoe, Minneapolis.

Selected Group Exhibitions

2003
Today's Man, John Connelly Presents, New York.

2002
Dialogues: Amy Cutler/David Rathman, Walker Art Center, Minneapolis.

The Good, the Bad, and the Ugly, Galerie Weiland, Berlin.

2001
Works on Paper, Finesilver Gallery, San Antonio.

New Work: MCAD/McKnight Artists, Minneapolis College of Art and Design, Minnesota.

Selected Bibliography

Wood, Eve. "David Rathman at Mary Goldman Gallery." *Artillery* (November–December 2007).

Fallon, Michael. "David Rathman at Weinstein Gallery." *Art Papers* 31, no. 3 (May–June 2007): 65.

Valdez, Sarah. "David Rathman at Clementine." *Art in America* 89, no. 12 (December 2001): 120–121

Trainor, James. "David Rathman at Clementine." *Tema Celeste* 13, no. 88 (November–December 2001).

DARIO ROBLETO

Born 1972, San Antonio, Texas

1993, The University of Texas at San Antonio, Texas

1996, Yale University Summer School of Music and Art, Connecticut

1996, The University of Texas at El Paso, Texas

1997, BFA, The University of Texas at San Antonio, Texas

Lives and works in San Antonio, Texas

Selected One-Person Exhibitions

2008
Alloy of Love, Frye Art Museum, Seattle.

2006
Chrysanthemum Anthems, Weatherspoon Art Museum, University of North Carolina, Greensboro.

2004
Diary of a Resurrectionist, Galerie Praz-Delavallade, Paris.

2003
Cerca Series: Dario Robleto; Surgeon, Scalpel and Soul, Museum of Contemporary Art San Diego.

2001
I Thought I Knew Negation Until You Said Goodbye, Contemporary Arts Museum Houston.

2000
The Polar Soul, ArtPace, San Antonio, Texas.

Selected Group Exhibitions

2007
6th Bienal do Mercosul, Porto Alegre, Brazil.

2006
Ahistoric Occasion: Artists Making History, Massachusetts Museum of Contemporary Art, North Adams.

The Gospel of Lead: Dario Robleto and Jeremy Blake, Arthouse, Austin, Texas.

2004
Whitney Biennial, Whitney Museum of American Art, New York.

Gene(sis): Contemporary Art Explores Human Genomics, Henry Art Gallery, University of Washington, Seattle.

Rock My World: Recent Art and the Memory of Rock 'n' Roll, Wattis Institute for Contemporary Arts, California College of the Arts, San Francisco.

2001
One Planet Under a Groove: Hip Hop and Contemporary Art, The Bronx Museum of the Arts, New York.

Selected Bibliography

Baum, Kelly, "Sincerely" *Artlies* (Winter 2007): 36–41.

Craig, Gerry. "Dario Robleto: The Phantasm of Matter." *Sculpture* 26, no. 2 (March 2007): 40–41.

Duncan, Michael. "Remixing the Past." *Art in America*, 95, no. 10 (November 2007): 202–205.

Holley, Joe. "Conceptual Artist As Mad Scientist." *The New York Times*, April 13, p. AR33.

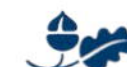

ALLISON SMITH

Born 1972, Manassas, Virginia

1995, BA, Eugene Lang College, New York

1995, BFA, Parsons School of Design, New York

1999, MFA, Yale University School of Art, New Haven

2000, Whitney Museum Independent Study Program, New York

Lives and works in New York

Selected One-Person Exhibitions, Performances, and Public Art Events

2007
Allison Smith: Notion Nanny, Berkeley Art Museum and Pacific Film Archive, University of California, Berkeley.

2006
New Works 06.3, Artpace, San Antonio, Texas.

Notion Nanny, Qube gallery, Shropshire, England.

2005
Victory Hall, Bellwether, New York.

The Muster, a project of the Public Art Fund, Governors Island, New York.

Armory at the Bellwether, The Armory Show: International Fair of New Art, Bellwether, New York.

2002
Stilleven, evenStill, Bellwether, Brooklyn.

Selected Group Exhibitions

2008

On Procession, Indianapolis Museum of Art, Indiana.

Inner & Outer Space, Mattress Factory, Pittsburgh

2007

Grow Your Own, Palais de Tokyo, Paris.

2006

Ahistoric Occasion: On the Uses of History, Massachusetts Museum of Contemporary Art, North Adams.

2005

You are Here, Ballroom Marfa, Texas.

Greater New York 2005, P.S.1 Contemporary Art Center, MOMA, Long Island City, New York

Selected Bibliography

Carrington, Sarah, and Allison Smith. "Notion Nanny: Tinker, Tailor, Merchant and Maker." *Knitknit* 6 (2006): 20–21.

Eccles, Tom, Allison Smith, James Trainor, and Anne Wehr. *Allison Smith: The Muster: What Are You Fighting For?*, New York: Public Art Fund, 2007.

Hull, Timothy Marvel. "Entrenched with Allison Smith." *Swingset 8* (2007): cover, 32–36.

Wolf, Matt, and Allison Smith. "Reenacting Stonewall, Jackson That Is." *Journal of Aesthetics & Protest* 1, no. 4 (2005): 222–233.

KARA WALKER

Born 1969, Stockton, California

1991, BFA., Atlanta College of Art, Georgia

1994, MFA., Rhode Island School of Design, Providence

Lives and works in New York

Selected One-Person Exhibitions

2007–2008
Kara Walker: My Complement, My Enemy, My Oppressor, My Love, Walker Art Center, Minneapolis.

2007
Kara Walker: Harper's Pictorial History of the Civil War (Annotated), Addison Gallery of American Art, Andover, Massachusetts.

2006
Kara Walker, Sikkema Jenkins & Co., New York.

Kara Walker at the Met: After the Deluge, The Metropolitan Museum of Art, New York.

2005
Song of the South, REDCAT, Los Angeles.

2002
Kara Walker, Slavery!, Slavery!, 25th International Biennial of Sao Paolo, Brazil.

2001
The Emancipation Approximation, The Tel Aviv Museum of Art, Israel.

1997
Presenting Negro Scenes Drawn Upon My Passage Through the South and Reconfigured for the Benefit of Enlightened Audiences Wherever Such May Be Found, By Myself, Missus K.E.B. Walker, Colored, Renaissance Society, University of Chicago.

Selected Group Exhibitions

2006
Black Alphabet: Contexts of Contemporary African American Art, Zacheta National Gallery of Art, Warsaw, Poland.

2005
Drawing from The Modern, 1975–2005, Museum of Modern Art, New York.

Getting Emotional, Institute of Contemporary Art, Boston.

2003
Comic Release: Negotiating Identity for a New Generation, Carnegie Mellon University, Pittsburgh.

Black President: The Art and Legacy of Fela Anikulapo-Kuti, The New Museum, New York.

2002
Moving Pictures, Solomon R. Guggenheim Museum, New York.

1998

Secret Victorians, Contemporary Artists and a 19th-Century Vision, Hayward Gallery, London.

Selected Bibliography

Belcove, Julie. "History Girl." *W Magazine* (March 2007): 406–412.

Cotter, Holland. "A Nightmare View of Antebellum Life That Sets Off Sparks." *The New York Times*, May 9, 2003, p. E36.

Richard, Frances. "Kara Walker at Walker Art Center." *Artforum* 88, no. 4 (January 2007): 97.

Yablonsky, Linda. "Kara Walker." *Art & Auction* 30, no. 6 (February 2001): 46–52.

 CHARLIE WHITE

Born 1972, Philadelphia, Pennsylvania

1994, Summer Program, Yale, New Haven

1995, BFA, School of Visual Arts, New York

1998, MFA, Art Center College of Design, Pasadena, California

Lives and works in Los Angeles

Selected One-Person Exhibitions

2006

Everything Is American, Brändström & Stene, Stockholm.

2000

And Jeopardize The Integrity Of The Hull, Andrea Rosen Gallery, New York.

2001

Understanding Joshua, Andrea Rosen Gallery, New York.

1999

In A Matter Of Days, Andrea Rosen Gallery, New York.

Selected Group Exhibitions

2007

Sympathy For The Devil: Art and Rock and Roll Since 1967, Museum of Contemporary Art, Chicago

Art In America: Now, Shanghai Museum of Contemporary Art, China.

Six, Art Center College of Design, Pasadena.

Between The Two Deaths, Zentrum für Kunst und Medientechnologie, Karlsruhe, Germany.

Rock And Roll, Norrköpings Konstmuseum Kristinaplatsen, Sweden.

2004

I Feel Mysterious, Palm Beach Institute of Contemporary Art, Florida.

Sex and Flowers, Studio Technica, Oslo, Norway.

Beginning Here: 101 Ways, School of Visual Arts, New York.

Dreamweavers, Yancey Richardson Gallery, New York.

Otherwise: Phantastic Art, Oberösterreichisches Landesmuseum, Linz, Austria.

2000

My Reality: Contemporary Art and the Culture of Japanese Animation, Norton Museum of Art, Palm Beach.

Octopus 2003: More Than Real Live, Gertrude Contemporary Art Spaces, Melbourne, Australia.

Strange Worlds, The Bertha and Karl Leubsdorf Art Gallery at Hunter College, New York.

2002

2002 California Biennial, Orange County Museum of Art, Newport Beach.

Selected Bibliography

Dery, Mark. "L.A. Creep Show." *Art + Text* 74 (August–October 2001): 48–55.

Hoffman, Jens. "Understanding Charlie." *Hot Rod* 17 (2002).

Kastner, Jeffrey. "Charlie White." *Artforum* 44, no. 7 (March 2006): 290.

Shreve, Jenn. "The Wizard of ID." *Wired* 54, no. 4 (February 2004): 124–129.

CATALOGUE

Editors: Polly Koch and Heather Brand

Publication Coordinators: Toby Kamps and Justine Waitkus

Design: Don Quaintance, Public Address Design, Houston

Design/Production Assistant: Elizabeth Frizzell, Public Address Design

Typography: Composed in Caslon 540 and Adobe Caslon (text),
and Blackoak, Copperplate, Snell Roundhand, Teniers, and
William Page 506 (display)

Printing: Earthcolor, Houston

Binding: Universal Bookbindery, San Antonio

A NOTE ON THE TYPOGRAPHY
The typography in this book is derived from various letterforms and wood
types used from the late eighteenth to early twentieth century. The text
face, Caslon 540, is based on William Caslon's first English oldstyle typeface
of 1725. Snell Roundhand, designed by Matthew Carter, is taken from the
script letterforms of late-eighteenth-century English writing master Charles
Snell. Blackoak was designed by Joy Redick based on wood type examples
in the collection of the Smithsonian Institution. Teniers and William Page
506, both designed by Jordan Davies, are authentic reproductions of wood
type letterpress specimens from ca. 1885. Copperplate Gothic, "the banker's
typeface," was designed by American designer Frederic W. Goudy in 1905.